TOEFL Junior
全真模考题
强化训练

Answer Book

韩国多乐园TOEFL Junior研发中心 编著

浙江教育出版社·杭州

音频

图书在版编目(CIP)数据

TOEFL Junior全真模考题强化训练 / 韩国多乐园
TOEFL Junior研发中心编著. -- 杭州 ：浙江教育出版社，
2024.1
　ISBN 978-7-5722-7183-0

　Ⅰ．①T… Ⅱ．①韩… Ⅲ．①TOEFL－习题集 Ⅳ.
①H310.41-44

　中国国家版本馆CIP数据核字(2024)第012992号

版权登记号　图字：11—2023—447

Perfect TOEFL Junior Practice Test Book 1 + 1 MP3 CD
Perfect TOEFL Junior Practice Test Book 2 + 1 MP3 CD
Perfect TOEFL Junior Practice Test Book 3 + 1 MP3 CD
Copyright © 2024, Darakwon, Inc.
All rights reserved.
Chinese language translation rights © 2024
by Zhejiang Education Publishing House
Chinese language translation rights arranged with Darakwon Press

TOEFL Junior全真模考题强化训练
TOEFL JUNIOR QUAN ZHEN MOKAOTI QIANGHUA XUNLIAN
韩国多乐园TOEFL Junior研发中心　编著

责任编辑　赵清刚
美术编辑　韩　波
责任校对　马立改
责任印务　时小娟
封面设计　李　倩
版式设计　李　倩
出版发行　浙江教育出版社
　　　　　地址：杭州市天目山路40号
　　　　　邮编：310013
　　　　　电话：（0571）85170300 - 80928
　　　　　邮箱：dywh@xdf.cn
印　　刷　三河市良远印务有限公司
开　　本　880mm×1230mm　1/16
成品尺寸　210mm×275mm
印　　张　30
字　　数　538 000
版　　次　2024年1月第1版
印　　次　2024年1月第1次印刷
标准书号　ISBN 978-7-5722-7183-0
定　　价　75.00元（全两册）

Table of Contents

Answers, Scripts, and Explanations

Practice Test 1

Answers

Listening Comprehension

1.~5. BAACD	6.~10. BCDDA	11.~15. DCAAC	16.~20. BDCDA
21.~25. BABAC	26.~30. CDBBA	31.~35. DBBCC	36.~40. BBCBD
41.~42. CB			

Language Form and Meaning

1.~5. BDABB	6.~10. ACBDB	11.~15. ACBDD	16.~20. ACBBD
21.~25. BABDD	26.~30. ADBAA	31.~35. CDBDA	36.~40. ADACD
41.~42. BA			

Reading Comprehension

1.~5. CCABC	6.~10. BABBA	11.~15. BDBCC	16.~20. ABBBD
21.~25. CBAAB	26.~30. DACCB	31.~35. DBABB	36.~40. BCDDB
41.~42. BC			

Scripts

1.

Girl:	Bill, are you going to the soccer game this evening?
Boy:	I wish I could, but my parents want me to go home immediately after school.
Girl:	How come? Are you in some kind of trouble?
Boy:	No, it's not that. Today's my sister's birthday, so we're going out to eat at her favorite restaurant. I'll have to take a pass on the game.

2.

Woman:	Jimmy, I'm a little worried about your grade this semester. You started out with an A, but you almost failed the last test.
Boy:	I'm sorry, Mrs. Wingo. Is it possible for me to do an extra report for bonus points?
Woman:	I don't normally allow that, but I'll make an exception in your case. Here's what I want you to do.

3.

Girl:	Can you believe how hard it's raining today?
Boy:	I know. And it's supposed to keep raining all weekend.
Girl:	Oh, no. That's terrible. I was planning to go cycling with some of my friends tomorrow morning.
Boy:	You'd better cancel those plans. The weather forecast is calling for thundershowers.
Girl:	That's too bad. I guess I'll have to go cycling next week.

4.

Boy: Jenny, I've been looking all over for you. Do you happen to know Brian's phone number?

Girl: Sure. It's 953-1202. What do you need to talk to him about?

Boy: He's one of my partners on that group project in Mr. Jacobs' class. I need to talk to him about it immediately. Thanks for the number. I'll talk to you later.

5.

Boy: Mr. Williamson, I don't understand why I got a bad grade on this essay. I thought that I did a pretty decent job on it.

Man: Well, your paper had several spelling mistakes. And your grammar wasn't good either.

Boy: Are grammar and spelling that important?

Man: Of course they're important. You need to do both well to write an A paper.

6.

Boy: I tried to finish all of the math problems, but I couldn't. I can't figure out how to solve number three.

Girl: Math problems ... ? Oh my goodness. I totally forgot about our homework.

Boy: Class starts in ten minutes. You have time to do it.

Girl: You're right. Thanks for reminding me. I've got to get going.

7.

Girl: How did you do on the pop test we had in Mr. Norton's class?

Boy: Pretty well. I answered nine out of the ten questions correctly. How'd you do on it?

Girl: I made a couple of silly mistakes, so I only got an eight out of ten.

Boy: At least it's not worth too many points. It won't affect your grade that much.

8.

Woman: Attention, everyone. There is a severe winter storm that is approaching rapidly. According to the weather forecast, it's going to drop at least ten centimeters of snow in the next two hours. I've decided to cancel classes for the rest of the day. All students and teachers need to leave school and return to their homes immediately.

9.

Woman: Our next guest is Dr. Walt Campbell. He's an expert on French history. He's going to talk to us about Napoleon this evening. In case you don't know, Napoleon ruled over France in the early 1800s. His armies conquered virtually the entire European mainland. He was finally defeated at the Battle of Waterloo in 1815. That battle marked the end of Napoleon's rule.

10.–13.

Boy: Ms. Martin, do you have a couple of minutes to speak with me? It's kind of important.

Woman: Sure, David. What's going on?

Boy: I need to talk about the report that we're supposed to hand in tomorrow. Um ... is it possible for me to get an extension on it?

Woman: Why do you need an extension? Every other student in the class is going to turn his or her report in on time.

Boy: Well, I haven't had enough time to do the report. Coach Grubbs has kept the soccer team practicing late after school every day this week. So by the time I get home, I'm totally worn out. I just haven't

	had enough energy to write the paper.
Woman:	David, I think you need to get your priorities straight.
Boy:	What do you mean?
Woman:	I mean that you're supposed to be focusing on learning at school rather than athletics. The soccer team is of lesser importance.
Boy:	But ...
Woman:	Look. I know how important soccer is to you. But your classes are more important. So I'm going to have to reject your request. You need to get that report to me by tomorrow.
Boy:	Yes, ma'am. But I don't know how good it's going to be.
Woman:	Do your best. Why don't you go to the library now and start doing some research? You've got an hour before you have to go to your next class. Use this time wisely. You can start gathering all of the information you need right now.
Boy:	All right. Thanks.

14.–17.

Girl:	Hey, John. Did you happen to go to the game yesterday?
Boy:	I sure did. Congratulations on winning. I was impressed with how well everyone on the team played.
Girl:	Yeah, Angie did a great job, didn't she?
Boy:	She's an outstanding goalkeeper. She made a couple of impressive saves. But you had a good game, too.
Girl:	Uh, I guess I played all right.
Boy:	All right? What are you talking about? You scored two goals. And you had some great passes as well.
Girl:	Oh, thanks. I guess I did play pretty well, didn't I?
Boy:	That's one way of putting it. So ... when is your next game going to be? Do you have a game this Friday or Saturday?
Girl:	No, we don't play any more games this week. However, we have two games next week. The first is on Tuesday night, and the second is on Thursday night. Do you think you can make it to one?
Boy:	I'll do my best to go to both. I can definitely attend the Tuesday game, but I'm not sure about the soccer game on Thursday.
Girl:	Awesome. Now that we're winning some games, we hope that more fans will start coming. We could use some big crowds. We play much better when we've got lots of people cheering for us.
Boy:	Yeah, that makes sense. I'll tell some of my friends and get them to go along with me. I'm sure that they'll love to see your team play.

18.–22.

Girl:	George, what did Mr. Stevenson want to talk to you about after class today?
Boy:	Oh, uh, he just told me about a science fair that's going to be held next month.
Girl:	A science fair? That's peculiar. I didn't think that the school was having one this year.
Boy:	You're right. We're not.
Girl:	Then what science fair was he talking about?
Boy:	It's a special event sponsored by the city. A bunch of students from all of the schools in the city are going to compete in it. Mr. Stevenson thinks that I ought to enter the contest. So that's why he told me about it.
Girl:	Really? I wonder why he told you and not the rest of the students. Are you some kind of scientific genius or something?
Boy:	Uh, I don't know about that. But I enjoy spending lots of time in the school's science lab. Mr. Stevenson and I have been doing some research in chemistry during my free time. So he wants me to do something related to that research for the science fair.

Girl:	Wow. I never knew that about you. I always wondered where you went after school. I thought you were playing sports.
Boy:	No, I don't really enjoy sports. I don't have that much athletic ability.
Girl:	Yeah, neither do I. So, uh, can you tell me about the experiments you're doing? I actually kind of enjoy science myself.
Boy:	It's a little hard to explain. Instead, why don't you visit the science lab after school today? I can show you what I am working on.
Girl:	That sounds great. I'll see you at the lab then.

23.–26.

Boy:	Mary, a few of us are going to the shopping mall to hang out after school. Do you want to go? We're all planning to take the bus together around three thirty.
Girl:	Sorry, Joe. I'd really love to spend time with everyone today, but I can't. I have something else to do after school.
Boy:	Do you mind if I ask what you're doing?
Girl:	Not at all. I'm going to go to the airport.
Boy:	The airport? Are you taking a trip somewhere?
Girl:	No, I'm not going anywhere. But my sister Andrea is flying home this evening. She has been in Italy for the last six months.
Boy:	Isn't she a college student? What was she doing in Italy?
Girl:	She was in Italy as an exchange student. She was studying at a university in Florence. Her major is art history, so she wanted to study in Italy to get the chance to see all of the great medieval and Renaissance art that's in the country.
Boy:	Wow. That sounds pretty cool. Did she have a good time?
Girl:	I think so. I didn't actually talk to her that much while she was gone. Calling Italy is a little too expensive for me. And my sister rarely checks her email even when she's at home. So I only chatted with her a couple of times. But it seems like she enjoyed herself. She sounded rather happy in the few emails that I received from her. She sent some pictures, too. She looked good in them. I can't wait to see all of the pictures that she took.
Boy:	That's great. I'd love to be an exchange student someday. Well, anyway, I've got to get going. Have fun meeting your sister.
Girl:	Thanks. I will. And please tell everyone why I can't meet them today. I promise to be there next time.

27.–29.

Woman Teacher:	Of all the species of squirrels that exist, probably the most interesting one is the flying squirrel. It doesn't really fly though. After all, the squirrel doesn't have wings, and it can't take off from the ground either. Instead of flying, it glides.
Boy:	How is it able to do that?
Woman:	Its body has a special membrane that stretches between its legs and feet. This membrane is found on both sides of its body. It's made of skin and fur and is very flexible. Normally, the membrane is tucked along the sides of its body. Take a look at the picture on page 156 in your books ... See it? That ridge-like fold of fur along its side is the membrane.
	So, um, what does the squirrel do with that membrane ... ? Let me tell you. First, in order to take to the air, the flying squirrel needs to be high above the ground. It typically jumps from tall trees. When it leaps into the air, it stretches its legs. This causes the membrane to unfold and to become taut. I guess it's sort of like a, uh, like a parachute at that point. This membrane catches the air and allows the squirrel to glide. In some cases, it can even act like a wing and enable the squirrel to gain a small amount of altitude. Yes, Gina?

Girl: How far can one of these squirrels glide?

Woman: Hmm ... In general, they make relatively short glides of around five to thirty meters. However, the longest glide ever observed by a person was nearly ninety meters. Why don't we take a look at a video, and then you can see the flying squirrel in action?

30.–33.

Woman Teacher: Two of the oldest civilizations in human history are Egypt and Mesopotamia. We talked about both of them during the past two days, right? As I hope you all remember, they were fairly different societies. But I want to talk today about how they had some similarities. For one, they both built rather large structures. Now, when I mention Egypt, what do you usually think about ... ? Yeah, that's right. Pyramids. The Egyptians built pyramids all over the place. Many of them are still standing. Okay ... But when I mention Mesopotamia, what kinds of buildings do you think about ... ? No one ... ? Yeah, that's what I thought. Well, the Mesopotamians built ziggurats. That's Z-I-G-G-U-R-A-T-S. There's a picture of them on page 218 in your books. Take a look ...

Here's a picture of a pyramid ... As you can see, the main differences between the two are their shapes and sizes. Notice that the Egyptian pyramid is more triangular in shape. Also, the pyramid is smooth sided, and its sides are rather steep. But look at the ziggurat here. You can see that it has a stepped appearance. By "stepped," I mean that the ziggurat looks like it has different levels, doesn't it? It looks sort of like a lot of different-sized boxes stacked on top of one another. The biggest box is on the bottom, and the boxes get smaller as you go higher. Oh, and notice that the ziggurat has a set of stairs leading to the top. The pyramid lacks this. Why did ziggurats have stairs ... ? Each had a temple at the top. So the Mesopotamians climbed the stairs to reach the temple.

This brings me to another key difference. Ziggurats were places of worship. They were used by priests to pray to the various Mesopotamian gods. But the pyramids were tombs for the pharaohs. Uh, they were the kings of ancient Egypt. Many pharaohs built pyramids to be their tombs when they died. The largest one took nearly twenty years to build. How did the Egyptians and Mesopotamians build these huge structures ... ? That's a good question. No one is sure, but people have some theories. Let me tell you about a few of them right now.

34.–38.

Male Teacher: One of the most beautiful creatures in the forest is the deer. It lives pretty much everywhere in the world except for Australia and Antarctica. There are many species of deer. However, the one I want to talk about is the white-tailed deer. It mostly lives in North America. I'm sure that many of you have seen this deer before. I actually saw a couple of them near the road as I drove to school this morning. Anyway, the first thing I should mention is that we have different names for male and female deer. The male is usually called a buck. Some people call it a stag or a hart though. That's H-A-R-T, not H-E-A-R-T. The female deer, on the other hand, is called a doe. And a baby deer is a fawn.

There are several differences between stags and does. A stag is bigger than a doe. A stag weighs 100 kilograms on average. However, some of them can grow to be much larger than that. As for females, they average around seventy kilograms in weight. Another big difference between the two is antlers. Antlers are the long, sharp, pointed bony protrusions on a deer's head. They begin as two short, stubby knobs. As they grow, they can form several branches that have many points. But only stags have antlers. Does don't have them. Oh, here's something you might not know: Antlers fall off every year. Stags lose their antlers during the winter, and then new ones grow during the spring and summer.

Deer are mammals, so that means the mothers give birth to live animals. A doe has between one and three fawns when it gives birth. The fawns have white spots when they're born. For the first six weeks of their lives, they drink their mother's milk. Remember, uh, that's another characteristic of mammals.

But fawns don't exclusively drink milk. They can walk pretty much as soon as they're born. So they can forage for grass and other food right away.

39.–42.

Woman Teacher: One of my favorite American writers is Edgar Allan Poe. I'm sure that all of you have heard about him. Can any of you tell me something about him? Tony?

Boy: I believe he lived during the nineteenth century. And I remember that he had a bunch of problems. I mean, uh, I think he suffered from depression or something.

Woman: That's a good start. Thanks, Tony. He's correct, class. Poe was born in 1809 and died in 1849. His short life was quite sad. His parents died before he turned three, so he lived with a foster family. Poe dealt with a number of issues during his life. He had gambling and drinking problems. He suffered from depression. His life was definitely not a happy one.

Many people believe that Poe's dark life heavily influenced his writing. So let's talk about Poe's literature. He made a number of contributions to the world of literature. Jessica, do you happen to know any of them?

Girl: He wrote that poem called *The Raven*. I really like it a lot. It's kind of creepy, but that seems characteristic of Poe's writing. He wrote several works of horror as well, didn't he?

Woman: You are correct. As for *The Raven*, we're going to read that as soon as we finish talking about Poe's life, so hold on for a moment concerning it. Also, you're right about Poe's works of horror. He is said to have invented that genre as well as the modern detective story. He also wrote some early science fiction and is considered one of the founders of the modern short story. That's a pretty impressive résumé, isn't it?

Poe is most famous, however, for his horror stories. The most well known are *The Fall of the House of Usher*, *The Masque of the Red Death*, and *The Pit and the Pendulum*. Each story deals with death in very gruesome ways. We're going to read one of those stories. We're also going to read *The Murders in the Rue Morgue*, which is the first modern detective tale. You're going to love it. But, for the time being, let's look at some of Poe's poetry.

Explanations

Listening Comprehension

1. B；本题考查固定搭配。take a pass on sth. 意为"决定不参加某个活动或不接受某个机会"，所以男生的意思是他不会参加今晚的足球比赛。

2. A；本题为推断题。老师对男生说她有些担心他的成绩，再结合后面老师提到男生原本成绩是 A，现在却差点不及格，可以推断出她很担心男生的成绩。

3. A；本题为细节题。女生对男生说："I was planning to go cycling with some of my friends tomorrow morning."，由此可知，周末她本来是要和朋友一起骑车。

4. C；本题为推断题。男生提到他需要 Brian 的电话号码的原因是他需要 talk to him about it immediately。鉴于女生已经提供了 Brian 的电话号码，由此推断男生接下来应该会给 Brian 打电话。

5. D；本题为目的题。男生在对话开始就说："I don't understand why I got a bad grade on this essay."，由此可知，他并不理解自己为什么会得到这样的分数。

6. B；本题为推断题。男生提醒女生他们还有数学作业，而女生表示她完全忘记了这件事。男生接着说还有十分钟就要上课了，女生之后表示"I've got to get going."，由此推断，她接下来很可能要去做数学作业。

7. C；本题为主旨题。在整个对话中，男生和女生讨论了随堂测试以及他们的分数。

8. D；本题为目的题。校长首先提到 severe winter storm 很快就会到来，然后提到她将取消当天接下来的所有课程。所以提及 winter storm 的原因是解释为什么要取消当天的课程。

9. D；本题为推断题。首先提到 Dr. Walt Campbell 是法国历史的专家且他将讲述关于曾经统治法国的拿破仑，由此可以推断，Dr. Campbell 十分了解拿破仑。

10. A；本题为主旨题。在对话一开始，男生就说道："I need to talk about the report that we're supposed to hand in tomorrow."，接着男生提到了他希望延迟报告提交的时间，这也是整个对话的主要内容。故本题答案为 A。

11. D；本题为细节题。男生首先说道："Well, I haven't had enough time to do the report."，之后男生接着解释了原因：本周每天的足球训练都到很晚，回家之后就累瘫了。

12. C；本题为推断题。男生提及足球队时说道："Coach Grubbs has kept the soccer team practicing late after school every day this week."，由此可以推断，男生暗示足球队占用了他很多的时间。

13. A；本题为细节题。根据老师对男生的建议"Why don't you go to the library now and start doing some research?"可知，答案选 A。

14. A；本题为主旨题。对话的大部分内容都在说女生的足球队，他们还谈论了足球队的上一场比赛和一些之后的比赛，故本题答案选 A。

15. C；本题为细节题。根据原文"However, we have two games next week. The first is on Tuesday night, and the second is on Thursday night."可知，下一场比赛在下周二。故本题答案为 C。

16. B；本题为推断题。女生询问男生是否去看了她的上一场比赛，以及是否会去她接下来的两场比赛。接着她说道："Now that we're winning some games, we hope that more fans will start coming. We could use some big crowds. We play much better when we've got lots of people cheering for us."。所以她暗示的是对于前来观看比赛的观众数量较少的不满。

17. D；本题为目的题。根据原文"I'll tell some of my friends and get them to go along with me. I'm sure that they'll love to see your team play."可知，男生将邀请朋友和他一起去观看女生的比赛。

18. C；本题考查词汇。peculiar 意为"不寻常的；特别的"，所以女生说这句话的意思是她对于男生提及 science fair 感到疑惑。

19. D；本题为目的题。在对话一开始女生问男生和老师的谈话内容，他回答说是关于科学展览一事。所以男生提及 science fair 是因为这是和老师谈话的内容，故选 D。

20. A；本题为细节题。根据原文"Mr. Stevenson and I have been doing some research in chemistry during my free time."可知，答案选 A。

21. B；本题为细节题。根据原文"Mr. Stevenson and I have been doing some research in chemistry during my free time."可知，答案选 B。

22. A；本题为推断题。通过对话可知，老师告知了男生科学展览一事以及男生正在和老师一起进行化学研究，结合这两点可以推断，男生将参加科学展览。

23. B；本题为主旨题。对话主要围绕女生在意大利学习的姐姐展开，由此可知答案选 B。

24. A；本题为细节题。根据女生提到她姐姐时说的"She was in Italy as an exchange student. She was studying at a university in Florence."可知，本题答案为 A。

25. C；本题为推断题。对话中提到女生将要去机场接她的姐姐，她还对男生说："I can't wait to see all of the pictures that she took."，由此可以推断，女生很期待见到她的姐姐，故答案选 C。

26. C；本题为推断题。女生说放学后有事，对于男生的询问她回答说："I'm going to go to the airport."，之后又提到她的姐姐要从意大利回来，故答案选 C。

27. D；本题为主旨题。讲话的内容主要围绕着飞鼠如何在空中滑翔，由此可知答案选 D。

28. B；本题为细节题。根据原文"This membrane catches the air and allows the squirrel to glide."可知，这层膜的作用是帮助飞鼠在空中滑翔，故答案选 B。

29. B；本题为推断题。根据原文 "Why don't we take a look at a video, and then you can see the flying squirrel in action?" 可以推断，接下来老师将播放关于飞鼠的视频，故答案选 B。

30. A；本题为主旨题。根据原文 As you can see, the main differences between the two... 以及 "This brings me to another key difference." 可知，讲座主要围绕着金字塔和塔庙两者的区别展开，故答案选 A。

31. D；本题为推断题。根据原文 "Now, when I mention Egypt, what do you usually think about...? Yeah, that's right. Pyramids. The Egyptians built pyramids all over the place. Many of them are still standing. Okay...But when I mention Mesopotamia, what kinds of buildings do you think about...? No one...? Yeah, that's what I thought. Well, the Mesopotamians built ziggurats." 可知，老师通过提问表明人们对美索不达米亚以及塔庙的了解远远少于对埃及和金字塔的了解，故答案选 D。

32. B；本题为细节题。根据原文对金字塔的描述 "Also, the pyramid is smooth sided, and its sides are rather steep. But look at the ziggurat here. You can see that it has a stepped appearance." 可知，本题答案为 B。

33. B；本题为目的题。根据老师对法老的描述 "But the pyramids were tombs for the pharaohs. Uh, they were the kings of ancient Egypt. Many pharaohs built pyramids to be their tombs when they died." 可知，她提及法老是为了指出他们修建了金字塔，故答案选 B。

34. C；本题为主旨题。根据讲座最开始提到的 "There are many species of deer. However, the one I want to talk about is the white-tailed deer." 可知，本题答案选 C。

35. C；本题为推断题。根据原文 "I'm sure that many of you have seen this deer before. I actually saw a couple of them near the road as I drove to school this morning." 可以推断，他居住的地区有很多鹿，故答案选 C。

36. B；本题为推断题。通过强调拼写单词，老师暗示一些学生会把这个单词拼错，故答案选 B。

37. B；本题为细节题。根据原文 "But only stags have antlers. Does don't have them... Antlers fall off every year. Stags lose their antlers during winter, and then new ones grow during the spring and summer."，可以排除选项 A，选项 C 和 D 未提及，故答案选 B。

38. C；本题为细节题。根据原文关于小鹿的描述 "The fawns have white spots when they're born." 可知，本题答案选 C。

39. B；本题为主旨题。讨论主要围绕 Edgar Allan Poe 的文学作品展开，故答案选 B。

40. D；本题为细节题。根据原文 "His parents died before he turned three, so he lived with a foster family." 可排除选项 A 和 C。选项 B 有一定的迷惑性，题目问的是 Edgar Allan Poe 小时候发生的事情，depression 并没有明确说是小时候的事，故排除，因此答案选 D。

41. C；本题为目的题。根据原文 "We're also going to read *The Murders in the Rue Morgue*, which is the first modern detective tale." 可知，老师提及这本书的目的是接下来将阅读该书，故答案选 C。

42. B；本题为推断题。原文最后提到 "But, for the time being, let's look at some of Poe's poetry."，由此可知，接下来将阅读一些 Edgar Allan Poe 的诗歌，故答案选 B。

Language Form and Meaning

1. B；本题考查时态。根据时间 today 可知这里指的是女生的现状，所以需要使用现在进行时 "be+*v.*-ing" 的形式。

2. D；本题为词义辨析题。固定搭配 assign homework 意为 "布置作业"，reserve 意为 "预约"，approve 意为 "批准"，request 意为 "要求"，故答案选 D。

3. A；本题考查宾语从句。根据题意可知，这里问的应该是 "你需要做什么？"，故答案选 A。

4. B；本题考查单词形式。本空前有不定冠词 a，所以答案应该是一个单数名词。再根据题意推断此处应该选意为 "回复" 的名词，故答案选 B。respond 为动词，意为 "回答"；responsive 为形容词，意为 "积极反应的；热情的"；responder 为名词，意为 "应答者"。

5. B；本题考查非限定性定语从句。这里的先行词为 community center，故关系代词使用 which；同时句意为 "坐落于……"，固定搭配为 be located，故答案选 B。

6. A；本题考查句间关系。前面提到了一些中心将举行的活动，之后又提到了中心还将赞助一场足球比赛和棒球比赛，根据句意可知此处应该选 A。those 指代前面提到的 "art, music, and language classes"。

7. C；本题为词义辨析题。demand 意为"要求"；approve 意为"批准"；invite 意为"邀请"；consider 意为"考虑"。根据题意可知，本题选 C。

8. B；本题考查比较级。本句是之前和过去的对比，意为"今年的活动将比过去的那些活动好得多"，故答案选 B。

9. D；本题考查固定搭配。be proud to do sth. 为固定搭配，意为"做某事很骄傲"，故本题答案选 D。

10. B；本题考查固定搭配。experience doing sth. 意为"做某事的经验"，在本题中意为"运营城市的经验"，故答案选 B。

11. A；本题为词义辨析题。appropriate 意为"合适的"；approximate 意为"大概的"；approachable 意为"平易近人的"；approving 意为"赞许的"。故本题选 A。

12. C；本题考查固定搭配。be on your best behavior 意为"举止得当"，故本题选 C。

13. B；本题考查固定搭配。apologize for sth. 意为"为某事道歉"，本题的意思是"为我的行为道歉"，故答案选 B。

14. D；本题为词义辨析题。cheat on 意为"作弊；欺骗"，故本题选 D，意思是"在考试中作弊"。

15. D；本题为词义辨析题。excuse 为名词，需要使用形容词修饰，故形容词 acceptable "可接受的"为答案；accept 为动词，acceptance 为名词，accepting 为动名词。

16. A；本题考查句子结构。the moment I arrived home 的意思是 as soon as I arrived home，符合题意，故答案选 A。

17. C；本题为词义辨析题。immediately 意为"立即"；apparently 意为"明显地"；decisively 意为"果断地"；dramatically 意为"剧烈地"。根据句意可知，答案选 C。

18. B；本题为词义辨析题。justification 意为"辩解；正当理由"；consideration 意为"体贴；斟酌"；ramification 意为"分支"；criticism 意为"批判；意见"。根据句意可知，答案选 B。

19. B；本题考查宾语从句。根据句意可知，本空应该填"无论什么惩罚"，故答案选 B。

20. D；本题考查固定搭配。as...as possible 意为"尽可能……"，故本题答案选 D。

21. B；本题考查修饰词。句中 over 为形容词，需要使用副词修饰且为副词在前，故本题答案选 B。

22. A；本题考查固定搭配。the next chapter in my life 为固定搭配，意为"我人生中的下一个篇章"，故本题答案选 A。

23. B；本题为词义辨析题。apply for 意为"申请"；depart for 意为"动身前往"；register for 意为"注册；报名参加"；enroll for 意为"报名参加"。故本题答案选 B。

24. D；本题考查动词形式。going to be doing sth. 意为"将要做某事"，故本题答案为 D。

25. D；本题考查被动语态。Nathaniel 以及他的家人是被邀请去作者家中，所以 invite 应该使用被动语态，故答案选 D。

26. A；本题为词义辨析题。attend 意为"出席"；graduate 意为"毕业"；resist 意为"抗拒"；request 意为"要求"。故本题答案选 A。

27. D；本题考查修饰词。Located 在题中为过去分词作状语，修饰 the Palace，故本题答案为 D。

28. B；本题考查定语从句。which 指代 2000 rooms，故答案选 B。

29. A；本题考查时间状语。during 意为"在……期间"，故本题答案选 A。

30. A；本题考查最高级。one of + 最高级，意为"最……的之一"，prominent 的最高级为 most prominent，故本题答案选 A。

31. C；本题考查固定搭配。Following the events of 意为 after the events of，故本题答案为 C。

32. D；本题为词义辨析题。design 意为"设计"；construct 意为"建造"；rehabilitate 意为"恢复"；transform 意为"转化"。故本题答案为 D。

33. B；本题考查动词形式。这句话指的是现在，所以需要使用一般现在时。而 Versailles 是单数名词，因此动词需要使用第三人称单数形式，故本题答案为 B。

34. D；本题为词义辨析题。permanently 意为"永久地"；consistently 意为"一贯地"；continually 意为"不断地"；annually 意为"每年地"。故本题答案为 D。

35. A；本题考查比较级。形容词比较级 + than 意为"比……更"，所以本题应该选 harsh 的比较级 harsher 作为答案，故本题选 A。

36. A；本题为词义辨析题。ensure 意为"确保"；promise 意为"承诺"；recall 意为"回想起"；trust 意为"信任"。故本题答案为 A。

37. D；本题考查 may 的用法。may 一般情况下作为情态动词，意为"可能，也许"，在这里的意思是"可以，能够"，故本题答案选 D。

38. A；本题考查固定搭配。on the top of 意为"在……之上"，故本题答案为 A。

39. C；本题考查被动语态。egg 和 protect 为被动关系，所以 protect 应该使用被动语态，同时本句描述的是一般情况，故应该使用一般现在时，答案选 C。

40. D；本题为词义辨析题。basic 意为"基本的"；significant 意为"重要的"；partial 意为"偏袒的"；vital 意为"至关重要的"。it is important / vital that 为固定搭配，意为"……是很重要的"，故本题选 D。

41. B；本题考查固定搭配。protect A from B 意为"保护 A 免受 B 的伤害"，同时应该使用被动语态，因为 eggs 是被保护的，故本题答案选 B。

42. A；本题为词义辨析题。entire 为形容词，前面的 this 说明后面修饰的是一个单数的名词，故答案选 A。

Reading Comprehension

1. C；本题为词义辨析题。objective 意为"目标"，skill 意为"技能"，experience 意为"经验"，goal 意为"目标"，achievement 意为"成就"，故本题答案选 C。

2. C；本题为细节题。原文提到 winning the county essay-writing contest (Julie Johnston)，可知答案选 C。

3. A；本题为推断题。根据原文"Furthermore, our athletic teams all had winning records, and the girls' volleyball team, led by Coach Alice Stevens, managed to come in second place in the entire state."可知答案选 A。其他选项均未提及。

4. B；本题为细节题。根据原文"All students have to read at least five books and write short reports on them during the summer."可知，答案选 B。

5. C；本题为指代题。them 在这里指代的是前面的 five books，故本题答案选 C。

6. B；本题为词义辨析题。feel free to swing by 意为"欢迎过来看看"，因此本题答案选 B。

7. A；本题为主旨题。这篇文章重点描述了学校数学队参加比赛并获得了第三名的好成绩。因此，本题答案选 A。

8. B；本题为目的题。这篇文章描述了学校数学队的表现，同时也提到了其他一些学校的表现。因此，文章目的主要是描述比赛结果，故答案选 B。

9. B；本题为细节题。文章中提到了比赛时间、比赛地点、参赛队伍以及比赛结果，但是并未提及颁发了什么奖项，故答案选 B。

10. A；本题为词义辨析题。数学队的成绩从去年的 0 分提升到今年的 85 分，可推测 dramatic 意为"巨大的；显著的"，故本题答案选 A。sincere 意为"真诚的"，indescribable 意为"难以形容的"，unexpected 意为"意料之外的"。

11. B；本题为细节题。根据原文"Overall, Molly Reed led the team by scoring an incredible twenty-five points. That made her the leading scorer in the entire tournament."可知，Molly Reed 是整个比赛中得分最高的选手，故答案选 B。其他选项原文均未提及。

12. D；本题为细节题。Mrs. Gibbons 提道"They took on teams that had twice as many students, but they still managed to capture third place."，由此可知，有一些队伍的人数是本校数学队的两倍，故选项 D 符合原文。选项 A 与原文"I'm so proud of this group."矛盾，选项 B 和 C 原文均未提及。

13. B；本题为主旨题。本文介绍了一些不同队伍的选拔信息，包括教练信息、选拔时间以及注意事项。故本题选 B。

14. C；本题为细节题。根据表格中的 Tryout Time 一栏可知，Boys' Soccer 将在 March 8–9 举行，故本题选 C。

15. C；本题为目的题。根据原文 "However, according to state rules, girls may participate on the boys' soccer team. All interested girls should speak with Coach McCloud prior to tryouts." 可知，女生可以加入男生足球队，而女生们在参加选拔之前需要和 Coach McCloud 谈一谈，故本题选 C。

16. A；本题为推断题。根据原文 "The coaches have all agreed that any student may participate on two athletic teams so long as one is the track team." 可知，教练们互相沟通并达成了一致，故本题选 A。

17. B；本题为细节题。根据原文 "Finally, all students must submit an injury release form to the coach of the team they want to play on. No students will be permitted to try out until it has been turned in." 可知，学生们在参加选拔前必须提交 injury release form，否则不能参加选拔，故答案选 B。

18. B；本题为指代题。原文中 it 是 turn in 的内容，根据原文可知，应该指的就是 an injury release form，故本题选 B。

19. B；本题为主旨题。这篇文章主要讲述的是 Sir Francis Drake 一生中的冒险经历，故本题选 B。

20. D；本题为词义辨析题。revere 意为"尊敬，崇敬"，fear 意为"害怕；畏惧"，fame 意为"使闻名"，notice 意为"注意"，regard 意为"被认为是；尊敬"，故答案选 D。考生还可以通过上下文推断出单词意思，yet 表示转折，yet 后面说 Sir Francis Drake 在其他国家被认为是海盗，说明 yet 前面说的是"海盗"的反面意思，由此也可以推测出本题答案。

21. C；本题为目的题。根据原文 "Their soldiers, called conquistadors, effectively defeated the Aztec and Inca empires." 可知，作者提到 conquistadors 是为了说明他们打败了 Aztec 和 Inca 这两个帝国，故答案选 C。

22. B；本题为细节题。根据原文 "On account of their strength in the New World, the Spanish acquired a great amount of treasure. Thus there were constantly ships filled with treasure sailing across the Atlantic Ocean to Spain. Many sailors from other countries tried to capture these ships." 可知，船员们想抢占西班牙船只的原因是上面有大量的财宝，故本题答案选 B。

23. A；本题为细节题。根据原文 "In September 1580, one of Drake's ships and fifty-six men reached home after having circumnavigated the world." 可知，Sir Francis Drake 在 1580 年环游世界之后回到了家乡，circumnavigated 意为"环绕航行"，故本题答案选 A。

24. A；本题为细节题。原文提到了 Sir Francis Drake 出生和去世的时间，他常常对抗的国家的船员以及人们对他的评价，但没有提到他的船的名字，故本题选 A。

25. B；本题为推断题。根据原文 "Three years later, King Phillip II of Spain sent an enormous fleet, called the *Spanish Armada*, to defeat England. Drake was made second in command of the English fleet that emerged victorious against the Spanish." 中的 emerged victorious against the Spanish 可知，英国舰队战胜了西班牙舰队，故本题选 B。

26. D；本题为词义辨析题。run out 意为"用完；耗尽"，change 意为"改变"，escape 意为"逃脱"，remove 意为"移开；废除"，end 意为"结束，终止"，故本题答案选 D。

27. A；本题为主旨题。文章主要描述了地震和海啸产生的原因，故答案选 A。

28. C；本题为细节题。根据原文 "However, tsunamis are the direct result of earthquakes and cannot happen without them." 可知，海啸是地震的直接结果，而且没有地震就不会发生海啸，故本题答案选 C。in tandem with 意为"与……协同"。

29. C；本题为指代题。It 在这里指代是前一句中的 crust，故本题答案为 C。

30. B；本题为词义辨析题。adjoin 意为"毗邻"，approach 意为"靠近，临近"，border 意为"接壤，毗邻"，reside 意为"居住，定居"，appear 意为"出现，呈现"，故本题答案为 B。

31. D；本题为细节题。根据原文 "Instead, it is comprised of a number of plates. There are a few enormous plates and many smaller ones." 可知，答案选 D。

32. B；本题为词义辨析题。perceive 意为"注意到，察觉到"，comprehend 意为"理解"，detect 意为"发现，察觉"，locate 意为"定位"，prevent 意为"阻止"，故本题答案为 B。

33. A；本题为细节题。文章第三段提到了大部分地震的严重程度、造成的损害以及人员伤亡，但是没有提及严重的地震发生的频率，故本题答案为 A。

34. B；本题为推断题。根据原文"A large tsunami—one more than ten meters in height—can travel far inland. As it does that, it can flood the land, destroy human settlements, and kill large numbers of people."可推断，答案选 B。

35. B；本题为主旨题。本篇文章主要讲的是意外情况下产生的发明和发现，故本题选 B。

36. B；本题为词义辨析题。arduous 意为"艰辛的，困难的"，detailed 意为"详细的"，tough 意为"艰苦的，艰难的"，specific 意为"明确的，具体的"，constant 意为"连续发生的"，故本题答案选 B。

37. C；本题为词义辨析题。replete with 意为"充满"，aware of 意为"意识到"，inspired by 意为"受……启发"，full of 意为"充满"，concerned about 意为"关心，担忧"，故本题答案选 C。

38. D；本题为词义辨析题。endeavor 意为"努力"，research 意为"研究"，dream 意为"梦想"，request 意为"请求，要求"，attempt 意为"努力，尝试"，故本题答案为 D。

39. D；本题为细节题。根据原文"Instead, he had invented Teflon, which is today most commonly used to make nonstick pots and pans."可知，Teflon 现在被用于制作不粘锅，故本题答案选 D。

40. B；本题为细节题。根据原文"John Pemberton was a pharmacist in Atlanta, Georgia. He was attempting to create a tonic that people could use whenever they had headaches. While he was not successful in that endeavor, he managed to invent Coca-Cola, the world-famous carbonated soft drink."可知，John Pemberton 是发明可口可乐的人，故本题答案选 B。

41. B；本题为修辞题。最后一段的第一句"Scientists have also made crucial discoveries by accident when they were conducting experiments."为该段主旨句，之后使用了 Alexander Fleming 的例子支持这个主旨句，故本题答案选 B。

42. C；本题为推断题。原文提到 penicillin 在过去几十年里救了数百万人的生命，由此可推断作者认为这是一个"十分宝贵"的医疗用品，故本题答案选 C。

Answers

Listening Comprehension

1.~5. CAADB	6.~10. CCABD	11.~15. BACBA	16.~20. DCCAB
21.~25. BCCBB	26.~30. ABCAA	31.~35. DBBAB	36.~40. DDCAC
41.~42. AB			

Language Form and Meaning

1.~5. DBCAC	6.~10. ACBCB	11.~15. CAACD	16.~20. ADBAC
21.~25. DACBA	26.~30. CBDAC	31.~35. ADBBD	36.~40. ACADB
41.~42. DA			

Reading Comprehension

1.~5. ABBDB	6.~10. CDBCA	11.~15. CBCBD	16.~20. BCADB
21.~25. BBDAC	26.~30. CBDBC	31.~35. DBACC	36.~40. BADCB
41.~42. CC			

Scripts

1.

Boy:	You don't look happy, Claire. What's the matter?
Girl:	I left my new smartphone on the bus today. My parents are going to be upset when they find out what I did.
Boy:	Didn't they just give you that phone three days ago?
Girl:	Yeah. That's why they're not going to be pleased when I talk to them.

2.

Man:	Congratulations, Tina. You got the highest grade in the class on your report.
Girl:	Thank you, sir. I worked hard on it.
Man:	It definitely showed. You have a knack for writing. Have you considered writing for the school paper?
Girl:	I've never really thought about it. I suppose it could be fun. Maybe I'll talk to the person in charge of it and get some more information.

3.

Girl:	Someone said your bike got stolen from the bicycle rack outside this morning.
Boy:	That's right. When I checked on my bike at lunch, it was gone.
Girl:	Did you remember to lock it up?
Boy:	I did. Someone cut the chain on the lock. The school needs to put an end to these thefts. Mine is the

third bike that has been stolen in the past month.

4.

Woman: Bill, I understand you saw some students bullying Tim during lunchtime.

Boy: Um ... I guess so. But I'm not exactly sure who they were.

Woman: You don't have to be afraid to give me their names. Bullying is something we need to stop. But we can't do that unless students have the courage to point out who the bullies are.

Boy: Yes, you're right.

5.

Boy: Oh, no. I left my homework at home. What am I going to tell Ms. Winkler?

Girl: You can't give her that excuse. You already used it once this week.

Boy: But this time I'm telling the truth.

Girl: You shouldn't have lied to her the first time. Now she's going to accuse you of not doing your homework when you actually did it.

6.

Girl 1: Are you going to take part in the spelling bee?

Girl 2: Yes, I am. I signed up for it after third period ended. How about you?

Girl 1: I'm not that good at spelling. I don't want to embarrass myself in front of everyone.

Girl 2: Go ahead and do it. It's fun and a great experience as well. And who knows? You might even win.

7.

Woman: I'd like to talk to you about Diego, the new exchange student. He doesn't seem to be getting along with many of the students. I think he's pretty shy. Why don't you all try to become friends with him? Would you mind sitting with him at lunch and talking to him? I'd appreciate it if you'd do that. He really needs someone to hang out with.

8.

Man: As most of you know, light moves incredibly quickly. To be exact, it moves about 300,000 meters per second. That's known as the speed of light. As far as we know, it's impossible to exceed the speed of light. But our guest tonight, Dr. Lewis Farber, has some ideas about how it might be done. Dr. Farber, welcome to our show.

9.

Woman: People say that Christopher Columbus discovered the New World. However, he definitely wasn't the first person from Europe or Asia to reach either North or South America. It has been proven that the Vikings made it to parts of Canada by around the year 1000. And some people even believe that the Romans arrived in the New World centuries earlier. Let me explain ...

10.–13.

Boy: April, I need to talk to you for a moment.

Girl: Sure, Tom. What is it?

Boy: I heard you're interested in joining the school newspaper as a reporter. Is that true? Do you want to be a member of the staff?

Girl: Sure. I'd love to do that. My sister is a reporter for the local paper, and she tells me all kinds of stories

	about her job. It sounds fun, so, uh, I want to try it.
Boy:	You know I'm the editor of the paper, right?
Girl:	Yes, I'm aware of that. That means you have the power to give me a job, doesn't it?
Boy:	It sure does. And, to be honest, we need some reporters. Susan was a member of the staff until three days ago. But she had to quit for some reason. Ever since she quit, I've been looking for someone to replace her.
Girl:	I'd like to give it a shot.
Boy:	Great. I know you can write because I've seen your work before.
Girl:	You have? When did you do that?
Boy:	Remember a couple of years ago when we had to do that group project in English class? You and I were in the same group, and I read the paper that you wrote.
Girl:	Wow, I can't believe you remember it. It seems like that happened so long ago. Anyway, what do you want me to do for my first assignment? Do you want me to interview the new social studies teacher?
Boy:	No. Don't worry about that. I've already assigned that duty to Jim. Instead, I want you to cover tonight's football game. It starts at seven thirty, and it should last for a couple of hours. See if you can get some interviews after the game, especially if we win.
Girl:	No problem. I look forward to doing that.

14.–18.

Boy:	Ms. Whittle, you mentioned something about an extra-credit project in class today. Could you tell me a little about it?
Woman:	Okay. But why do you want to do it?
Boy:	Er ... I'm not pleased with my grade, so, uh, I figure that if I can get some bonus points, I might be able to pull off an A in your class.
Woman:	That's a good attitude to have, Bill. But, uh, I don't have much time to tell you about it because I've got class in a couple of minutes. Hmm ... And so do you I believe.
Boy:	That's correct. I have Mr. Thompson's class next.
Woman:	Well, you don't want to be late for his class. You know how he can be when students are even a few seconds late.
Boy:	Yeah. I know all about that.
Woman:	Anyway, let's get back to the matter at hand. The extra-credit project involves doing some work in the lab. I want you to think of an experiment that you'd like to do.
Boy:	What kind of experiment?
Woman:	Anything really. Read a couple of chemistry books in the library to get some ideas. But check with me for approval before you start. So, uh, basically, just do the experiment and then write a lab report on both the results and your interpretation of the results.
Boy:	That's it? Cool. Oh ... How many bonus points can I get for this?
Woman:	Anywhere from one to five. It depends on the quality of your work. Now get going. The bell is about to ring.

19.–22.

Boy 1:	Jimmy, are you going to try out for the baseball team again this year?
Boy 2:	Yeah. But, uh, I don't think I need to try out for the team. Coach has already told me that I'm going to be the starting second baseman.
Boy 1:	That's great. Congratulations.
Boy 2:	Thanks, Kevin. So, uh, why are you curious about the team?
Boy 1:	Well ... I've been giving some thought to trying out. I'm a pretty decent pitcher, so I think I've got a shot at making the team.

Boy 2:	If you're any good, you'll probably make it. Two of our best pitchers graduated last year, so we could definitely use a new player or two.
Boy 1:	That sounds good. So ... assuming that I make the team ... what is it like to be on the team?
Boy 2:	It's really cool. We play about twenty games a year ... more if we make the playoffs. Half are home games, and half are road games.
Boy 1:	How far away are the road games?
Boy 2:	Hmm ... I'd say most of them are within an hour's drive of the school. But there are a couple of schools ... White Plains and Gadsden I think ... that are about two hours away. That's a long ride on the school bus.
Boy 1:	Huh. I didn't know that.
Boy 2:	Yeah. It's no fun riding home on the bus if you lose one of those games.
Boy 1:	I can imagine. How does being on the team affect your schoolwork, Jimmy?
Boy 2:	It's rather hard when you've got a test the day after an away game. But I try to do my best, so my grades are good. I don't know if you work part time or not, but you won't be able to do that if you're on the team and want to keep your grades up.

23.–26.

Girl:	I am so overloaded with work. I have no idea what I'm going to do.
Boy:	I know what you mean. The teachers seem to be giving us a lot of homework these days. I'm totally swamped as well.
Girl:	Yeah, but you don't do any extracurricular activities, do you?
Boy:	Not this year. My parents want me to focus solely on my grades since they aren't as good as they should be. So they won't let me play basketball or join any clubs.
Girl:	That's too bad.
Boy:	Yeah. I wish they'd reconsider, but they won't. Anyway, what extracurricular activities are you doing that have you so busy?
Girl:	Well, I'm a member of the math team. And I also write for the school newspaper and work on the school yearbook committee.
Boy:	Wow, that's a lot. Which of those three activities keeps you the most occupied?
Girl:	Right now, it's the school newspaper. I have to write at least one article a week for it. The math team isn't too bad. All we do is go to math contests every once in a while. For example, we've got a contest this Saturday.
Boy:	That's cool. How about the yearbook?
Girl:	We're doing some preliminary meetings now. The bulk of the work will be in the spring. But we're still meeting at least once a week.
Boy:	Good luck with all that. It seems like your schedule is packed.

27.–30.

Male Teacher:	Can anyone tell me what a current is? Alice, do you know?
Girl:	I think it's like when the water in the ocean moves like a river. I mean, uh, the current seems to move differently than the water around it.
Man:	That's not a bad definition of a current, Alice. Thank you. Oceans and seas have currents. Like Alice said, they're like rivers that move in larger bodies of water. There are both warm-water and cold-water currents. There are currents all around the world. Some even have names. Do any of you happen to know the name of one? Fred, your hand is up.
Boy:	The Gulf Stream is a current. I know that because it flows right by our city. In fact, my dad and I take our boat out to fish in the Gulf Stream when we have the time.
Man:	Well done, Fred. That was the answer I was looking for. I'm sure most of you have heard of the Gulf

Stream. But you might not know what exactly it is. So let me give you a few facts about it.

The Gulf Stream is one of the world's largest and longest ocean currents. Look at the map here ... It extends from the Gulf of Mexico ... and passes Florida and the eastern coast of North America as it heads northward ... It crosses the Atlantic Ocean and goes to Europe ... There, it divides into two main streams. One heads south toward Africa ... The other moves north past England and Western Europe and then goes toward Norway.

As for the Gulf Stream itself, it's about 100 kilometers wide. It moves at a rate of two and a half meters per second. It mainly moves eastward and northward because of the wind conditions where it originates. The wind, you see, helps move the water. The Gulf Stream starts with very warm water, but, as the wind pushes it, the water starts cooling off. By the time the water reaches Europe, it's much warmer ... uh, sorry. I mean cooler ... It's much cooler than it was when it left the Gulf of Mexico. Alice?

Girl:	I heard that the Gulf Stream affects the climates of different places. Is that true?
Man:	It sure is. And that's what I want to tell you about now.

31.–33.

Male Teacher: In the early 1800s, Texas was a part of Mexico. However, as many Americans began to move westward, lots of them migrated to Texas. After a few years, they had established their own communities. These settlers had no desire to belong to Mexico. Instead, they sought to be independent. Understandably, the Mexicans objected to this. After all, which country wants to lose land that it controls? Anyway, in 1835, some fighting broke out between the American settlers and Mexican soldiers. For the most part, the Americans won those battles. Then, in early 1836, the Mexicans sent a large army into Texas. At that time, the Texans occupied an old Spanish church mission in San Antonio that was called the Alamo.

The Mexican army surrounded the Alamo and laid siege to it on February 23, 1836. The Mexicans had around 3,000 men and were led by Santa Anna. The Texans, meanwhile, only had about 250 men. They were led by Colonel William Travis. The famous frontiersmen James Bowie and Davy Crockett were at the Alamo as well. I'm sure you've heard of both men.

The siege lasted until March 6. On March 5, Santa Anna ordered his soldiers to move into position for an all-out assault on the Alamo the next day. In the morning on the sixth, the attack began. The Texans were good shots and killed a large number of Mexicans, who were out in the open. But there were too many Mexican soldiers. The Mexicans breached the walls, broke into the Alamo, and killed all of the men there. It was a stunning defeat for the Texans. However, they used this loss to inspire them to victory. "Remember the Alamo" became the battle cry of the Texans. They soon defeated Santa Anna's army and even captured him. After that, Texas split apart from Mexico and became an independent nation.

34.–37.

Woman Teacher: Australia has lots of unusual mammals, such as the kangaroo and the koala. We're going to get to them in a bit. But, for a couple of minutes, I'd like to tell you about another unique animal that lives there. It's called the dingo. The dingo is a predator that's similar to a dog. I guess you could say it's more like a wild dog. It's believed that the dingo migrated to Australia from Southeast Asia thousands of years ago since there are wild dogs similar to the dingo in some parts of Southeast Asia.

Anyway, the dingo lives mainly in the interior of Australia, which is called the Outback. It has short fur that's reddish brown in color, but, uh, its underside is more whitish in color. The dingo has short, pointed ears and a long tail. As for its size, it averages around thirty kilograms in weight. It can live for up to twenty years. As I already mentioned, the dingo is a predator. In fact, it's Australia's largest predator that lives solely on land. The dingo typically eats small mammals like, uh, like rabbits and rats. It also eats birds and reptiles, particularly lizards. The dingo has been known to attack livestock ... mainly sheep and cattle. There's an ongoing battle in Australia between farmers who want to kill the dingoes that attack their livestock and people who want to keep them alive. Dingoes occasionally attack humans and have, in a few rare cases, killed small children.

The dingo is a social animal that typically travels in packs of up to ten. In that way, I suppose it's like the wolf, another animal related to the dog. Female dingoes breed once a year and give birth to up to five pups at a time. The pups usually stay with their mother for up to eight months. Now, let me tell you a little about how dingoes communicate with each other. I think this is pretty interesting ...

38.–42.

Male Teacher: As I'm sure you know, there are eight planets in the solar system. What you might not be aware of, however, is that we can divide these planets into two distinct groups. Astronomers call them the inner and outer planets. Oh, uh, some also refer to them as terrestrial planets and Jovian planets, respectively. The inner planets are, naturally, those closest to the sun. They are Mercury, Venus, Earth, and Mars. The outer planets—or Jovian planets—are Jupiter, Saturn, Uranus, and Neptune.

The inner and outer planets have a number of characteristics that make them different from one another. I'm going to go over them for you now. First, the most obvious difference is their size. The inner planets are the four smallest while the outer planets are the four biggest. Jupiter is the largest, and Mercury is the smallest. Another obvious difference, if you think about it, is that the terrestrial planets orbit the sun much more quickly than the Jovian planets. Earth takes 365 days to orbit the sun. Mercury takes eighty-eight days, Venus 224, and Mars almost 687. Jupiter, however, takes twelve years to orbit the sun. And that's the fastest of the Jovians. Another clear difference is the number of moons that orbit them. Mercury and Venus have none, Earth has one, and Mars has two. The outer planets each have large numbers of moons. Let's see ... Neptune has thirteen, Uranus twenty-seven, Saturn sixty-two, and Jupiter at least sixty-three.

Okay ... So what about the less apparent differences ... ? One is their composition. The inner planets are rocky and have solid cores, which make them dense. The outer planets are mainly made of gases, aren't very solid, and aren't very dense. They're often called gas giants. Another difference is how quickly or slowly they rotate on their axes. The outer planets rotate quickly, which gives them short days. A day on Jupiter is about ten hours while Saturn's day is ten hours forty minutes long. Contrast that with Mercury, which takes more than fifty-eight days to rotate once. And Venus completes one revolution in 243 days. That's longer than a Venusian year.

Explanations

Listening Comprehension

1.　C；本题为细节题。根据原文 "I left my new smartphone on the bus today." 可知，本题答案选 C。

2.　A；本题为目的题。根据原文 "You have a knack for writing." 可知，老师认为女生有写作天赋，所以建议她为校报写文章，故本题答案选 A。

3.　A；本题为主旨题。该对话主要是两人在讨论男生丢失的自行车，所以本题答案选 A。

4.　D；本题为推断题。老师告诉学生，他应该告诉她霸凌者的名字。这样，学校就可以杜绝霸凌行为。根据学生的回答 "Yes, you're right." 可以推断，他将告诉老师霸凌者的名字。

5.　B；本题为推断题。根据原文 "You shouldn't have lied to her the first time." 可知，男生撒过谎，故本题答案选 B。

6.　C；本题为主旨题。对话中的两位女生主要在讨论拼写比赛，故本题答案选 C。

7.   C；本题为细节题。当提到新来的交换生 Diego 的时候，老师说："Why don't you all try to become friends with him?"，由此可知，老师让学生们和交换生做朋友，故本题答案选 C。

8.   A；本题为目的题。这段听力材料是为了引出 Dr. Farber 而做的介绍，故本题答案为 A。

9.   B；本题为推断题。根据原文"And some people even believe that the Romans arrived in the New World centuries earlier. Let me explain..."可知，接下来老师将介绍关于 Romans 的内容，故本题答案选 B。

10.   D；本题为细节题。根据男生说"You know I'm the editor of the paper, right?"可知，本题答案选 D。

11.   B；本题为推断题。for some reason 意为"出于某种原因"，由此可知男生并不知道 Susan 退出的原因，故本题答案选 B。

12.   A；本题为细节题。女生问男生怎么知道她的写作能力，男生回答说："Remember a couple of years ago when we had to do that group project in English class? You and I were in the same group, and I read the paper that you wrote."。由此可知，男生之前读过女生的论文，故本题答案选 A。

13.   C；本题为目的题。当谈到今晚的足球比赛时，男生说："Instead, I want you to cover tonight's football game."。由此可知，男生提及足球比赛的原因是想让女生报道该比赛，故本题答案选 C。

14.   B；本题为细节题。当谈到男生为什么想参与这个项目时，他说："I'm not pleased with my grade, so, uh, I figure that if I can get some bonus points, I might be able to pull off an A in your class."，由此可知，男生想提高自己的分数，故本题答案选 B。

15.   A；本题为推断题。当他们谈到 Mr. Thompson 时，老师建议学生说："You know how he can be when students are even a few seconds late."，对此学生回答说"Yeah. I know all about that."。由此可推断，学生可能在 Mr. Thompson 的课上迟到过，故本题答案选 A。

16.   D；本题为目的题。根据原文"Read a couple of chemistry books in the library to get some ideas."可知，老师建议学生去图书馆读一些化学方面的书籍寻找想法，故本题答案选 D。

17.   C；本题为细节题。根据原文"Anywhere from one to five. It depends on the quality of your work."可知，本题答案为 C。

18.   C；本题为推断题。根据对话内容可知，这句话的意思是铃声快要响了，学生上课要迟到了，故本题答案选 C。

19.   A；本题为主旨题。根据原文可知，两个男生主要在谈论学校棒球队的生活，故本题答案选 A。

20.   B；本题为细节题。根据原文"Two of our best pitchers graduated last year, so we could definitely use a new player or two."可知，本题答案选 B。

21.   B；本题为细节题。根据原文"I'd say most of them are within an hour's drive of the school."可知，本题答案为 B。

22.   C；本题为推断题。根据原文"But I try to do my best, so my grades are good. I don't know if you work part time or not, but you won't be able to do that if you're on the team and want to keep your grades up."可推断，Jimmy 没有兼职，因为他无法在保持成绩和参加棒球队的同时，兼顾兼职。故本题答案为 C。

23.   C；本题为主旨题。对话内容主要围绕着女生参加的课外活动展开，故本题答案为 C。

24.   B；本题为推断题。对话中男生提道："My parents want me to focus solely on my grades since they aren't as good as they should be. So they won't let me play basketball or join any clubs."，而后男生又说："I wish they'd reconsider, but they won't."。由此可推断，男生自己其实是想参与课外活动的，故本题答案为 B。

25.   B；本题为细节题。当男生问女生最忙的课外活动是什么时，她回答说："Right now, it's the school newspaper."。由此可知，本题答案为 B。

26.   A；本题为细节题。根据原文"The bulk of the work will be in the spring."可知，yearbook committee 的工作量将会在春天增加，故本题答案为 A。

27.   B；本题为主旨题。原文主要在谈论 the Gulf Stream，故本题答案选 B。

28.   C；本题为目的题。由原文可知，老师提出了一个关于 currents 的问题，男生的回答提到了 the Gulf Stream，故本题答案为 C。

29. A；本题为细节题。根据原文 "The Gulf Stream starts with very warm water, but, as the wind pushes it, the water starts cooling off." 可知，本题答案选 A。

30. A；本题为推断题。女生问了一个关于墨西哥湾流如何影响不同地方气候的问题。老师说："And that's what I want to tell you about now."。由此可知，他接下来可能会继续谈论这个问题，故本题答案选 A。

31. D；本题为主旨题。原文主要介绍了 Alamo 以及在那里发生的战斗，故本题答案选 D。

32. B；本题为推断题。根据原文 "These settlers had no desire to belong to Mexico. Instead, they sought to be independent. Understandably, the Mexicans objected to this. After all, which country wants to lose land that it controls?" 可知，本题答案选 B。

33. B；本题为目的题。根据原文 "The famous frontiersmen James Bowie and Davy Crockett were at the Alamo as well." 可知，本题答案为 B。

34. A；本题为目的题。文章主要介绍了关于澳洲野狗的一些事实，故本题答案为 A。

35. B；本题为推断题。根据原文 "It's believed that the dingo migrated to Australia from Southeast Asia thousands of years ago since there are wild dogs similar to the dingo in some parts of Southeast Asia." 可知，dingo 是从东南亚迁徙而来，故本题答案选 B。

36. D；本题为细节题。根据原文 "As I already mentioned, the dingo is a predator." 可知，本题答案选 D，predator 意为"捕食性动物"。

37. D；本题为细节题。根据原文 "The dingo is a social animal that typically travels in packs of up to ten. In that way, I suppose it's like the wolf, another animal related to the dog." 可知，本题答案为 D。

38. C；本题为主旨题。原文内容是关于太阳系内行星的介绍，故答案为 C。

39. A；本题为目的题。根据原文 "The inner and outer planets have a number of characteristics that make them different from one another. I'm going to go over them for you now." 可知，老师提及 outer space 的原因是为了和 inner space 进行比较，故本题答案为 A。

40. C；本题为细节题。根据原文 "Astronomers call them the inner and outer planets. Oh, uh, some also refer to them as terrestrial planets and Jovian planets, respectively." 可知，本题答案为 C。

41. A；本题为细节题。根据原文 "Neptune has thirteen, Uranus twenty-seven, Saturn sixty-two, and Jupiter at least sixty-three." 可知，本题答案为 A。

42. B；本题为推断题。根据原文可知 outer planets 都是 gas giants，而 Saturn 属于 outer planet，由此可以推断，它也是 gas giant。故本题答案为 B。

Language Form and Meaning

1. D；本题考查固定搭配。be pleased to do sth. 为固定搭配，意为"乐于做某事"，故本题答案为 D。

2. B；本题为词义辨析题。perform 意为"表演"，rehearse 意为"排练"，remember 意为"记得"，observe 意为"观察"，结合题意可知，本题答案为 B。

3. C；本题考查被动语态。戏剧和导演之间是被动关系，因此本题答案为 C。

4. A；本题考查固定搭配。固定搭配 be sure to do sth. 意为"确定做某事"；set aside some time 也是固定搭配，意为"留出一些时间"，故本题答案选 A。

5. C；本题为词义辨析题。register 意为"注册"，delay 意为"推迟"，suspend 意为"暂停"，detain 意为"扣留"。结合题意可知，学校在 4.6~4.17 这两周将没有课程，故本题答案为 C。

6. A；本题考查介词用法。原文想要表达的是"在不同领域的一些公司"，故应使用介词 in，由此可知，本题答案为 A。

7. C；本题考查定语从句。该空后面的时间状语为 in the future，助动词 may 有将来的含义，故本题答案为 C。

8. B；本题考查形容词的比较级。本题在比较去年和今年的活动，两者之间的比较应该使用比较级形式，故本题答案为B。

9. C；本题考查句意。题目中提到的 schedule 是需要遵守的，故应该使用 according to，由此可知，本题答案为C。

10. B；本题考查介词用法。根据题意可知，学生们将花时间在五个部门里参观，故应该使用介词 in，由此可知本题答案为B。

11. C；本题考查固定搭配。help sb. do sth. 意为"帮助某人做某事"，故本题应该填入一个动词原形，由此可知，本题答案为C。

12. A；本题考查宾语从句。由题意可知，从句中说的是未来的事情，故应该使用将来时。结合句意可知，本题答案为A。

13. A；本题考查固定搭配。交换学生的固定说法为 exchange student，故本题答案为A。

14. C；本题为词义辨析题。improve 意为"改进"，happen 意为"发生"，approach 意为"临近"，pass 意为"经过"，空格处想要表达的意思是假期临近，故本题答案为C。

15. D；本题考查定语从句。occasion 在这里指的是"……时候"，故从句应该使用 when 作为关系词，由此可知，本题答案为D。

16. A；本题为词义辨析题。invite sb. to do sth. 意为"邀请某人做某事"，require sb. to do sth. 意为"要求某人做某事"，let sb. to do sth. 意为"让某人做某事"，insist sb. to do sth. 意为"坚持让某人做某事"，结合题意，可知本题答案为A。

17. D；本题考查固定搭配。will + v. 意为"将……"，get to do sth. 意为"有机会做某事"，hang out with sb. 意为"与某人一起玩"，故本题答案为D。

18. B；本题考查形容词最高级。本空后面跟着的是一个可数名词的复数形式，由此可知应该使用"one of + 最高级"形式，表示"最……之一"的意思，故本题答案为B。

19. A；本题为词义辨析题。第一次体验某事可以用 get an introduction to sth. 表示。结合题意可知，Helgar 之前没有吃过美国家庭料理，故本题答案为A。

20. C；本题考查时态。事件发生在将来，所以应该使用将来时，故本题答案为C。

21. D；本题考查定语从句。先行词是地点，所以从句应该使用关系词 where，故本题答案为D。

22. A；本题考查词义辨析题。结合原文可知，接受家庭教育的学生大部分时间在家里学习，有时会去学校，故本题答案为A。primarily 意为"主要地"，solely 意为"单独地"，relatively 意为"相对地"，cautiously 意为"慎重地"。

23. C；本题考查单词词性。athletes 为名词，所以本空应该填入一个形容词，故本题答案为C。exceptional 意为"杰出的，卓越的"。

24. B；本题为词义辨析题。根据上下文可知，学生会问 homeschooler 很多问题，所以他们应该是很好奇的，故本空应该选 B。upset 意为"不高兴的"，worried 意为"担忧的"，hostile 意为"敌对的"。

25. A；本题考查动词时态。本句描述的是一般情况，所以应该使用一般现在时，故本题答案为A。

26. C；本题考查固定搭配。spend time with sb. 意为"花时间与某人在一起"，故本题答案为C。

27. B；本题为词义辨析题。revolution 意为"旋转；革命"，orbit 意为"轨道"，rotation 意为"旋转，转动"，atmosphere 意为"大气层"，根据句意可知，本题答案为B。

28. D；本题考查动词时态。时间状语为 since then，由此可知，这是一个从过去一直持续到现在的动作，所以应该使用现在完成进行时，故本题答案为D。

29. A；本题考查固定搭配。both A and B 意为"A 和 B 两者"，原文的意思是人们担心镜子的尺寸和质量两方面，故本题答案为A。

30. C；本题考查定语从句。that 在此被省略了，从句修饰先行词 mirror，故本题答案为C。

31. A；本题考查固定搭配。cause...to do... 意为"导致……做……"，故本题答案为A。

32. D；本题为词义辨析题。根据题意可知，本空应该填一个与资金有关的单词，故答案为 D。material 意为"材料"，account 意为"账户"，ingredient 意为"原料"，fund 意为"基金"。

33. B；本题考查固定搭配。as soon as possible 为固定搭配，意为"尽快地"，故本题答案为 B。

34. B；本题考查情态动词 can 的用法。作者在这里指的是未来可能发生的事，表达的是"我们能够继续了解"之意，故应该使用情态动词 can+continue to learn，所以本题答案为 B。

35. D；本题为词义辨析题。unique 意为"独特的"，known 意为"已知的"，entertaining 意为"使人愉快的"，hazy 意为"模糊的"，根据题意可知，本题答案为 D。

36. A；本题为词义辨析题。documented 意为"备有证明文件的"，applied 意为"应用的"，certified 意为"有合格证书的"，historical 意为"基于史实的"，根据上下文可知，本题答案为 A。

37. C；本题考查固定搭配。某项运动可以用"the sport of..."来表示，故本题答案选 C。

38. A；本题考查固定搭配。tend to be 意为"往往……"，结合题意可知，本题答案为 A。

39. D；本题考查句意。因为篮球是"一种比赛"，故 game 应该使用单数形式，再结合句意，可知答案应为 D。

40. B；本题考查定语从句。从句中使用的时间状语为 today，故 be 动词应该使用现在时，定语从句修饰 ones，故关系词应用 that，由此可知本题答案为 B。

41. D；本题为词义辨析题。skip 意为"跳过"，penalize 意为"处罚"，express 意为"表达"，halt 意为"停止，中断"，根据句意可知，因为作为篮筐的篮子有底，所以每次进球之后比赛都必须"中断"，故本题答案为 D。

42. A；本题为词义辨析题。origins 为名词，由此可知前面应该填一个形容词，故本题答案为 A。

Reading Comprehension

1. A；本题为主旨题。由全文第一句"Please read the following carefully as it describes my expectations of you during this class."可知，这篇文章主要在说老师对学生的要求，故本题答案为 A。B、C、D 均为具体的细节。

2. B；本题为推断题。原文提到 class discussions 占成绩的 10%，每个 test 占成绩的 20%，一共有四个 test，由此可以推测 homework assignment 最多占成绩的 10%，故答案选 B。选项 A、C、D 原文均未提及。

3. B；本题为细节题。文章提到会影响成绩的有 class discussion、homework assignment 以及 tests，没有提及 attendance（出勤率），故本题答案为 B。

4. D；本题为词义辨析题。inquiry 意为"询问"，根据前面的动词 answer 也能大概推测出单词的意思，故本题答案为 D。investigation 意为"调查，审查"，demand 意为"要求"，examination 意为"检查；审查"。

5. B；本题为词义辨析题。confess 意为"坦白，承认"，故答案选 B。blame 意为"责怪，归咎于"，常用搭配为 blame sb. for sth.，decide 意为"决定"，falsify 意为"伪造；篡改"。

6. C；本题为细节题。根据原文 ... you need to write down the important information that I mention in your notebooks. 可知，本题答案为 C。

7. D；本题考查作者意图。表格提到了今年一些俱乐部的变化，故本题答案为 D。

8. B；本题为词义辨析题。take note of 意为"注意，关注"，故本题答案为 B。

9. C；本题为推断题。从表格中可以看出 geography club 和 photograph club 的初次会议时间都是周四下午两点，根据"As these are the initial meetings, students who desire to join these clubs must be present; otherwise, they will not be allowed to join."这一要求可以推断出，学生无法同时参加这两个俱乐部。其余选项原文均未提及，故本题答案为 C。

10. A；本题为细节题。根据原文"In addition, the chess club and the hiking club have both been cancelled this year due to a lack of interest."可知，chess club 和 hiking club 今年都取消了，故本题答案为 A。

11. C；本题为词义辨析题。express 意为"表达"，demand 意为"强烈要求"，foresee 意为"预见"，show 意为"表明"，approve of 意为"赞成，同意"，故本题答案为 C。

12. B；本题为指代题。根据题意可知，they 应该指代的是前面提到的 both clubs，故本题答案选 B。

13. C；本题为主旨题。本文主要讨论的是一些当地的大学生寻找化石的相关内容，故本题答案选 C。

14. B；本题为词义辨析题。stumble upon 意为"偶然发现"，故本题答案为 B。trip on 意为"绊倒"，dig up 意为"挖出"，conduct research on 意为"对……进行研究"。

15. D；本题为指代题。them 在这句中指的是前面学生们发现的 some bones，故本题答案为 D。

16. B；本题为目的题。根据原文"Thanks to a generous grant from the Damke Foundation, the students were able to accompany the professor on his dig."可知，提及 Damke Foundation 是因为它出资让学生可以参与挖掘工作，故本题答案为 B。

17. C；本题为细节题。原文提到 Wendy Jacobs 是 a Donoho senior，由此可知，她是一名 Donoho 的大四学生，故本题答案为 C。

18. A；本题为细节题。根据原文"The students, all of whom intend to major in science at college, are looking forward to returning this coming weekend."可知，学生们打算下周回到挖掘地点，故本题答案为 A。

19. D；本题为主旨题。文章主要围绕着火星以及多少人相信火星上有生命体的内容展开，故本题答案为 D。

20. B；本题为推断题。根据原文"In the nineteenth century, there were finally telescopes made that could closely examine at the surface of the Red Planet. While looking at Mars, an Italian astronomer saw many straight channels on its surface."可知，Red Planet 指的是 Mars，故本题答案为 B。其他选项原文均未提及。

21. B；本题为词义辨析题。akin to 意为"类似，相当于"，useful to 意为"对……有用"，resemble 意为"类似，像"，imitated by 意为"被……模仿"，precisely like 意为"和……一模一样"，故本题答案为 B。

22. B；本题为修辞题。根据原文"The result of that highly publicized claim was that a great number of myths about Mars suddenly arose. For instance, H.G. Wells wrote *The War of the Worlds*, a book about a Martian invasion of Earth, in 1898."可知，作者提及 *The War of the Worlds* 的目的是支持前面"这一广为宣传的说法的结果是突然出现了大量关于火星的迷思"这一观点，故本题答案为 B。

23. D；本题为词义辨析题。ignite 意为"点燃；引发"，所以这句话的意思是"一张照片突然引发了人们对火星的兴趣"，故本题答案选 D。

24. A；本题为细节题。根据原文"In 1976, *Viking 1* took a snapshot of the Martian surface. In the picture was what appeared to be an enormous human face."可知，这张照片由 *Viking 1* 拍摄，而前面提到美国发射了一些卫星用于探索火星，*Viking 1* 就是其中之一，故本题答案为 A。

25. C；本题为细节题。根据原文"In 2001, however, the mystery of the Martian face was solved by *Mars Global Surveyor*. The pictures that it transmitted proved that the face was just a mesa, a type of geological formation."可知，原来人们以为的 Martian face 只不过是一种地质构造，故本题答案为 C。

26. C；本题为指代题。it 在句中指代的是把 Martian face 照片传送回来的 *Mars Global Surveyor*，故本题答案为 C。

27. B；本题为主旨题。整个故事主要是 Don 向 Jeremy 请教考试高分的秘诀，故本题答案为 B。

28. D；本题为细节题。根据原文"Don was feeling rather upset because he had gotten a 75 on his science test while Jeremy had received a 99."可知，Don 心情不好的原因是考试成绩不好，故本题答案为 D。

29. B；本题为词义辨析题。play dumb 意为"装傻，装蒜"，故本题答案为 B。

30. C；本题为推断题。Don 声称他学习很努力，Jeremy 指出 Don 曾在课上睡觉以及听音乐，由此可以推断，本题答案为 C。

31. D；本题为细节题。原文并未提及 Don 英语考试的分数，其他选项内容均与原文内容对应，故本题答案为 D。

32. B；本题为细节题。根据原文"If you take notes in class, pay attention, and then review your notes at home later the same night, you will be able to remember practically everything."可知，Jeremy 建议 Don 认真听课、做笔记、当天晚上复习笔记，这样几乎能记住所有的知识点，故本题答案为 B。

33. A；本题为词义辨析题。skeptical 意为"不相信的"，doubtful 意为"怀疑的"，amused 意为"愉悦的"，confused 意为"困惑的"，understanding 意为"能谅解的"，故本题答案为 A。

34. C；本题为推断题。由 Don 在最后说 "It's a deal." 可推断出，Don 将听从 Jeremy 的学习建议，其他选项原文均未提及，故本题答案为 C。

35. C；本题为主旨题。本文虽然提到了 Great Lakes 形成的原因，周边的城市以及占地面积，但是这些都是次要信息，这些信息都是为主旨——Great Lakes 的地理特征服务的，故本题答案为 C。

36. B；本题为细节题。根据原文 "The smallest of the group is Lake Ontario while Lake Superior is the largest." 可知，面积最大的是 Lake Superior，面积最小的是 Lake Ontario，故本题答案为 B。

37. A；本题为词义辨析题。recede 意为"渐渐退去"，retreat 意为"（水、雪或土地）范围缩小"，remove 意为"移开；废除"，revitalize 意为"使恢复生机"，result 意为"导致"，故本题答案为 A。

38. D；本题为细节题。关于 the Great Lake 形成的原因，原文的 "At the time of their creation, massive glaciers—some several kilometers thick—were retreating as they melted and the last ice age came to an end." "They were formed about 10,000 years ago due to the action of receding glaciers." "Then, the melting ice turned into water and filled in the holes with water." 分别对应选项 A、B、C。原文并没有提及雨雪的原因，故本题答案为 D。

39. C；本题为细节题。根据原文 "There are also around 35,000 islands in the lakes, yet most of them are quite small." 可知，本题答案选 C，同时判断选项 D 错误。选项 A 中的 240,000 指的是 Great Lakes 覆盖的面积，不是发现的岛屿数量，故排除。选项 B 中的 more than 400 meters 指的是 Great Lakes 中最深的深度，不是长度，故排除。

40. B；本题为词义辨析题。immense 意为"巨大的"，variable 意为"多样的"，huge 意为"庞大的"，considerate 意为"体贴的，考虑周到的"，relative 意为"相对的"，故本题答案为 B。

41. C；本题为修辞题。根据原文 "The entire system flows to the Atlantic Ocean by way of the St. Lawrence River in Canada." 可知，本题答案为 C。

42. C；本题为细节题。用题干中的 port cities 可定位到原文最后一行，由原文 "This has transformed many port cities into major transportation centers in Canada and the United States." 可知，本题答案为 C。

Practice Test 3

Answers

Listening Comprehension

1.~5.	BADAA	6.~10.	BBBBA	11.~15.	CABBA	16.~20.	CCBBB
21.~25.	DAACD	26.~30.	BAADD	31.~35.	BCACC	36.~40.	BDCCB
41.~42.	DC						

Language Form and Meaning

1.~5.	DBACD	6.~10.	ACBCB	11.~15.	CBABD	16.~20.	BCCAD
21.~25.	BADCB	26.~30.	BADAD	31.~35.	ABCAB	36.~40.	CAACB
41.~42.	CD						

Reading Comprehension

1.~5.	ACDBC	6.~10.	DBCAD	11.~15.	DADDA	16.~20.	BCCAC
21.~25.	BCACD	26.~30.	CADCC	31.~35.	DABCB	36.~40.	BCDCD
41.~42.	AB						

Scripts

1.

Boy:	Today is picture day. Which set do you intend to buy?
Girl:	I'm just going to purchase the standard set. I don't need to get the deluxe set.
Boy:	You don't? Why not?
Girl:	I've already got hundreds of pictures of myself on my smartphone. I don't want to pay for a bunch at school. That would be a waste of money.

2.

Girl:	Mr. Phillips, I think you made a mistake grading my test.
Man:	I did? Could you show me what I did wrong, Lucy?
Girl:	Sure. Take a look at number ten. I'm pretty sure I got the right answer, but you marked it wrong.
Man:	Hmm ... You're absolutely right. I'm so sorry. Thanks for bringing this to my attention.

3.

Girl 1:	Have you met the new girl yet?
Girl 2:	Yeah, she's quite nice. Her family lives next door to mine, so I met her a couple of days ago.
Girl 1:	Really? I didn't know that.
Girl 2:	Her name is Sarah. She likes volleyball and loves rock music. I think we're going to get along fine with her at school. Be sure to say hi to her sometime.

4.

Woman: Donny, do you know why you're in my office?

Boy: Yes, ma'am. Mr. Simmons caught me writing on the walls in the classroom.

Woman: That's a big problem, Donny. It causes extra work for the janitors. So you're going to spend the next week on detention helping them clean the school. Hopefully, it will teach you an important lesson.

5.

Girl: Mrs. Douglas, I simply can't learn Spanish. This class is too hard for me.

Woman: Don't give up, Emily. Learning a foreign language is never easy.

Girl: But I can't seem to remember any of these words. They all sound so, uh, so strange to me.

Woman: It's only the first week of school. I'm sure you'll get better as time passes. Just be more patient.

6.

Boy: Why weren't you at school yesterday? You missed the school picnic.

Girl: I know. I feel bad that I couldn't go, but I had to stay in bed all day yesterday. I felt awful.

Boy: At least you didn't miss any schoolwork. Still, everyone had a great time hanging out at the park. It would have been great if you had been there.

7.

Man: I'm proud to announce that our school has been selected as the best school in the city. Let me be the first to congratulate you on a job well done. There are fourteen other schools in the city, and we came out on top. But don't let this go to your heads. You need to keep up the good work and continue working hard.

8.

Girl: So, Mr. Feldman, can you tell our guests what a recession is?

Man: Sure, Gloria. Basically, a recession is an economic slowdown. This slowdown isn't measured in weeks though. It lasts at least a few months and could last even longer. Let me tell you what happens during a recession. First, unemployment goes up. As a result, fewer people have jobs.

9.

Man: This chart is known as the periodic table of elements. It lists all the elements known to man. This includes those that appear naturally and those that are manmade. Look at the individual boxes. Each has one or two large letters. These are the symbols for individual elements. For instance, hydrogen is represented by an H. Notice that there are numbers inside each box, too.

10.–13.

Man: Mary, why don't you stay here for a moment? I need to chat with you about something.

Girl: Sure thing, Mr. Kimball.

Man: I'm curious ... I asked a question in class that nobody could answer. Remember that?

Girl: Yes, sir, I do.

Man: Well, nobody answered it, but I'm pretty sure that you could have. I'm a good judge of students. After all, I've been teaching for more than two decades. And I could tell by the look in your eyes that you knew the answer. I'm right, aren't I?

Girl: Yes, you are. I knew the answer.

Man: So why didn't you speak up and say anything?

Girl:	Um ... I don't really enjoy speaking in front of others. I'm a little shy. I, um, I get kind of nervous if I have to talk in class.
Man:	I see. In that case, would it help if I called on you? I mean, instead of raising your hand and volunteering an answer, how about if I just ask you directly? Do you think that would be better?
Girl:	It might. I can't say for sure. I just have a hard time speaking up.
Man:	Okay. Let's try it the next time we have class. If it makes you feel uncomfortable, I won't do it anymore. But I'd like to see you speak more since I know you have a lot to contribute. So we'll give my idea a shot.
Girl:	Thanks, Mr. Kimball. I appreciate that.

14.–18.

Woman:	Ray, what are you doing here in the library after school? Don't you have soccer practice to attend?
Boy:	Actually, Mrs. Foss, I decided not to play on the team this year. I'm going to focus on my grades instead.
Woman:	Focus on your grades? But you're already getting all A's. In fact, I'm pretty sure that you've never gotten anything below an A⁻ since elementary school.
Boy:	Yes, ma'am. That's correct. But I want to make sure my grades don't drop this year. After all, I'm applying to a lot of top colleges.
Woman:	Ray, do you mind if I give you a little bit of advice?
Boy:	Not at all, ma'am. I'm always willing to accept advice, especially if it's free.
Woman:	Colleges—especially the best ones in the country—don't just want students who have good grades.
Boy:	They don't?
Woman:	Well, grades are important, of course. But most colleges are looking for well-rounded individuals. In other words, they want students who not only have good grades but who also participate in various extracurricular activities.
Boy:	I think I see what you're getting at.
Woman:	I hope so. What I'm trying to say is that if you don't play sports or don't belong to any clubs, no matter how good your grades are, you're going to have a harder time getting into an elite college.
Boy:	So ...
Woman:	Talk to Coach Patterson and see if he'll let you on the team.
Boy:	Yes, ma'am. I think I'll do that.

19.–22.

Girl:	David, how was driver's ed today? You got to drive on the road for the first time today, didn't you?
Boy:	Yeah, Beth, I did. But ... um ... it didn't go too well.
Girl:	You didn't crash the car or anything, did you? Oh, no. Please tell me you didn't.
Boy:	I didn't crash the car. But ...
Girl:	Okay. Spill it.
Boy:	I think I scared Ms. Hooper while I was driving.
Girl:	Ms. Hooper? Our teacher?
Boy:	Yeah. Here's what happened ... When I pulled out of the school parking lot, I guess I pressed down on the accelerator too hard. So the tires squealed pretty loudly. I'm surprised you didn't hear it from your classroom.
Girl:	Oh, so that's what that noise was.
Boy:	Ah, okay. Never mind. Anyway, as I left the school, I happened to pull out in front of a car that was going really fast, so it almost hit us. Fortunately, the driver managed to stop at the last moment. I was pretty shaken up by that, so I didn't notice that the first stoplight we came to was red. I drove right through it without even stopping. I can't believe I broke the law like that.

Girl:	You didn't.
Boy:	I did. I guess Ms. Hooper had had enough by then since she told me to pull over immediately. She made me sit in the passenger seat while she drove back to school. She berated me about my driving skills the entire trip back.
Girl:	I guess that you're not going to be driving in class again for a long time.
Boy:	That's what Ms. Hooper said.

23.–25.

Boy:	Mrs. Campbell, do you think I could have a word with you? I need to talk to you about something.
Woman:	Sure, Larry. Are you here about your grade on the book report?
Boy:	Yes, ma'am. Um ... I'm not really sure why I got a C⁺ on it. I mean, uh, I thought I followed your directions. This is the lowest grade I've ever gotten at school.
Woman:	Well, Larry, there were a lot of problems with your paper. I could have easily given you a lower grade, but it seemed obvious to me that you had tried hard while writing it.
Boy:	A lower grade? Um ...
Woman:	Did you bring the paper with you? I can show you a few things if you have it here.
Boy:	Yes, ma'am. I've got it right here. Just a minute ... Ah, here it is ...
Woman:	All right. Let's look ... Now, do you see this part? That's a run-on sentence. That's bad grammar, so you lost points for that.
Boy:	Okay.
Woman:	And you didn't use quotes here ... Right here, you used the wrong verb tense. You know, Larry, you really need to work on your grammar. You had so many of those mistakes on your paper.
Boy:	I guess I've never cared that much about grammar. It never seemed that important.
Woman:	You're going to have to get a new attitude toward it now. If your grammar isn't any good in my class, there's no way that you'll get an A or a B.
Boy:	I see. I'll start reviewing grammar as soon as school is done today.
Woman:	That's a good attitude. Good luck, Larry.

26.–29.

Woman Teacher:	We get most of our energy from fossil fuels, such as coal, oil, and natural gas. We use these fossil fuels to run machines, to operate cars, airplanes, and other vehicles, to heat our homes, and to make electricity. Unfortunately, fossil fuels won't last forever. Once we use them, they're gone. No one is really sure how big our supply of fossil fuels is. We may have enough to last for a few decades. Or we might have a supply that will last for several centuries. Anyway, since they are nonrenewable resources, we need to use them sparingly. We also need to come up with ways to save energy so that we can make our supplies last longer. So ... Any ideas?
Girl:	I think the best way to save energy is not to use it.
Woman:	You're going to have to explain that a little more clearly, Stephanie. Are you suggesting that we not use any energy at all?
Girl:	Uh, no, I'm not. I think I stated my idea poorly. I mean that we can do things like walk or ride bikes instead of driving cars. By acting that way, we can save gas.
Woman:	Yes, that makes sense. Chris?
Boy:	Since it gets pretty cold here in winter, we use lots of energy to heat our homes then. But, uh, if more people used wood to heat their homes, then we could save electricity. My family always has a fire going in the fireplace during winter. It keeps our home warm and doesn't waste any electricity.
Woman:	That's one possible solution, Chris. But think about this ... Imagine how many people there are in our city. Now, what would happen if all of them started burning wood during winter ... ? Yeah, pretty

soon, there wouldn't be any trees left for miles. See, class, this is a problem we face. We try to solve one problem, but the solutions we come up with can often lead to other ones.

Well, one option is to use more alternative energy sources. These include solar, wind, water, geothermal, and nuclear power. However, each of these types of energy has its own problems. Let's focus on solar power first. What are its benefits, and what are its drawbacks? Eric, your hand is up ...

30.–32.

Male Teacher: I'm sure most of you can tell me what a desert is. It's a really hot place that gets a small amount of water each year. That's right, isn't it ... ? Okay, I see lots of heads nodding. But let me tell you something ... That definition I just gave you is wrong. Let me give you the correct definition of a desert right now: It's a place that receives very little precipitation each year. Notice what I left off. I omitted the hot part. You see, the reason is that there are two main types of deserts: hot deserts and cold deserts. Hot deserts are the ones that most people normally think about. They are, for example, the Sahara Desert and the Arabian Desert. The temperatures there frequently get to be more than forty degrees Celsius. There are, however, cold deserts as well. The Gobi Desert in Mongolia and China is one example. So is Antarctica. Yes, that's right. Despite the cold weather in Antarctica, there is very little snowfall on most of the continent.

We can also classify deserts according to how much rainfall they receive. We call them extremely arid, arid, and semi-arid deserts. Arid, as I am sure you can guess by now, means "dry." Extremely arid deserts receive virtually no rainfall each year. The Atacama Desert of Chile is one of these. In some parts of that desert, it hasn't rained in more than 400 years. Incredible, huh? As for arid deserts, they receive fewer than 250 millimeters of rainfall each year. Most of the world's deserts fall into this category. Semi-arid deserts receive between 250 and 500 millimeters of rainfall annually. That's enough for short grasses and small plants to grow.

33.–37.

Male Announcer: We're back from our commercial break. And we're talking with gemologist Sandy Wellman. Professor Wellman teaches geology at the local college, and she has agreed to spend some time talking to us this evening. Before our last break, we discussed the local geology. One thing that Professor Wellman mentioned intrigued me. She said there used to be volcanic activity in this area. So, um, Professor Wellman, does that mean there might be diamonds in our area? If there are, please let me know where so that I can start digging for them.

Woman Professor: Peter, there may well be lots of diamonds in this region. Would you like for me to explain why?

Man: Please go ahead. I'm sure our listeners would love to hear this.

Woman: Thanks. You see, diamonds are simply carbon. They're formed deep within the Earth. Basically, the combination of extreme heat and pressure under the Earth's surface takes a lump of carbon, uh, like coal, and transforms it into a diamond.

Man: What's the connection between diamonds and volcanoes?

Woman: Well, as I said, diamonds are formed deep underground. But we often find them near the surface. How does that happen ... ? Most of the time, it happens due to volcanoes. Essentially, volcanic activity forces diamonds to the surface ... or, uh, at least close to it. For that reason, the majority of diamonds are discovered near places that were either volcanically active in the past or have active volcanoes.

Man: And we live in an area that once had active volcanoes, right?

Woman: That's correct. But the last volcanic eruption here happened millions of years ago. So we don't need to worry about any eruptions at all.

Man: That's a relief. So, if I understand you correctly, you're saying that all I need to do is go to the site of an extinct volcano and start digging. And then I'll be able to find some diamonds.

Woman: Oh, I am definitely not saying that, Peter. While some diamonds have been found in this area, it's not as simple as grabbing a shovel and digging them up. If it were, I'd already be rich. Let me tell you what you need to do if you really want to find some diamonds.

38.–42.

Male Teacher: When Robert E. Lee surrendered to Ulysses S. Grant on April 8, 1865, it pretty much meant that the Civil War had ended. Sure, there were some minor skirmishes fought after that, but the major battles were over. So, finally, after four years of bloodshed, peace could return to the land. There were celebrations all throughout the Union as people realized that the war had reached its conclusion.

Sadly, there would be one final major act of violence—one which changed the course of the entire country. On the evening of April 14, 1865, President Abraham Lincoln and his wife went to Ford's Theater in Washington, D.C. With the war over, Lincoln felt at liberty to spend an evening relaxing. During the performance, as he sat in an upper-level box near the stage, he was shot from behind. The assassin was an actor named John Wilkes Booth. He was a strong supporter of the Confederacy, which had lost the war.

Booth entered the door of the president's box, placed a pistol behind Lincoln's left ear, and pulled the trigger. He did so during a noisy moment in the play when the audience was laughing. As a result, few people heard the gunshot. Lincoln's wife Mary was sitting beside him and immediately saw what had happened. So did an army officer sitting with Lincoln. As Mary screamed, the army officer tried to stop Booth. But Booth stabbed the man in the arm with a knife twice. He then leapt to the stage, but he landed awkwardly and broke his leg. Ever the actor, Booth shouted, "Sic semper tyrannis." That's Latin for "thus always to tyrants". In the chaos that followed, Booth escaped from the theater and fled on his horse.

Meanwhile, Lincoln was dying. Two doctors in the audience attended him. When they saw his wound, they realized it was fatal. Lincoln was moved to a nearby house, where he died the next day on April 15, 1865.

As bad as the assassination was, it could have been worse. Booth was part of a large conspiracy to kill not only Lincoln but also Grant and several government leaders. Let me tell you what the original plan was.

Explanations

Listening Comprehension

1.   B；本题为细节题。根据原文"I'm just going to purchase the standard set."可知女生购买的是标准套餐，set 在这里意为"套餐"，deluxe set 意为"豪华套餐"，故本题答案为 B。

2.   A；本题为预测题。女生给老师展示了批卷的错误，由老师的回答"You're absolutely right. I'm so sorry. Thanks for bringing this to my attention."可知，老师承认了错误，接下来很有可能就是改正这个错误，故本题答案为 A。

3.   D；本题为主旨题。对话中两个人在讨论新来的学生，rock music 和 volleyball 都是 new student 的爱好，但不是主要的信息，故本题答案为 D。

4.   A；本题为细节题。根据原文"So you're going to spend the next week on detention helping them clean the school."可知，男生下周都要课后留校，帮助清洁工打扫卫生，故本题答案为 A。

5.   A；本题为修辞题。Emily 正在向老师诉说学习西班牙语的困扰，老师提到只是开学的第一周，再耐心一些。由此可知，老师提及 first week of school 是为了鼓励 Emily 不要灰心，故本题答案为 A。

6.   B；本题考查说话者的目的。由原文"Why weren't you at school yesterday? You missed the school picnic."可知，男生提及 picnic 的目的是告诉女生，她生病请假的时候错过了什么，故本题答案为 B。

7. B；本题考查说话者的目的。由原文 "Let me be the first to congratulate you on a job well done." 可知，这个通知的目的是宣布学校被选为 best school in the city，并恭喜学生们，故本题答案为 B。

8. B；本题为推断题。由原文 a recession is an economic slowdown 可知，本题答案为 B。

9. B；本题为预测题。由最后一句话 "Notice that there are numbers inside each box, too." 可推断，接下来老师可能会解释元素周期表里的这些数字，故本题答案为 B。

10. A；本题为主旨题。对话主要谈论的内容是女生知道问题的答案却没有在课堂上回应老师，由此可知，本题答案为 A。

11. C；本题为推断题。由 "I don't really enjoy speaking in front of others. I'm a little shy. I, um, I get kind of nervous if I have to talk in class." 可知，女生有点内向，如果在课堂上发言会紧张，由此可以推断出本题答案为 C。

12. A；本题为细节题。根据原文 "I, um, I get kind of nervous if I have to talk in class." 可知，本题答案为 A。

13. B；本题为预测题。由原文 "I mean, instead of raising your hand and volunteering an answer, how about if I just ask you directly?...Okay. Let's try it the next time we have class." 可知，下次上课老师会直接向女生提问，故本题答案为 B。

14. B；本题为细节题。当老师问到足球队时，男生回答说："I decided not to play on the team this year."。由此可知，本题答案为 B。

15. A；本题为语气推测题。从说话者的语气中能听出惊讶的情绪，再结合后文 "But you're already getting all A's." 可进一步确认，本题答案为 A。

16. C；本题为推断题。文中提到学生的成绩很好，但是未提及他的运动能力、学习多么努力以及是否在周末兼职，故本题答案为 C。

17. C；本题为修辞题。当得知男生为了保持成绩而不参加足球队时，老师说："Well, grades are important, of course. But most colleges are looking for well-rounded individuals. In other words, they want students who not only have good grades but who also participate in various extracurricular activities."。由此可知，老师提及顶级大学的原因是告知男生这些学校的招生标准，故本题答案为 C。

18. B；本题为预测题。根据原文 "Talk to Coach Patterson and see if he'll let you on the team." 以及男生的回应 "Yes, ma'am. I think I'll do that." 可知，接下来他可能会去和教练谈谈，希望加入足球队，故本题答案为 B。

19. B；本题为语气推测题。Spill it 在英语口语中是一种常用搭配，意思是"说吧"，故本题答案为 B。相关习语还有 spill the beans，意为"泄密，说漏嘴"。

20. B；本题为细节题。由原文 "I was pretty shaken up by that, so I didn't notice that the first stoplight we came to was red. I drove right through it without even stopping. I can't believe I broke the law like that." 可知，男生在第一个红绿灯的地方闯了红灯，故本题答案为 B。

21. D；本题为细节题。由原文 "I guess Ms. Hooper had had enough by then since she told me to pull over immediately. She made me sit in the passenger seat while she drove back to school." 可知，Ms. Hooper 是因为受不了男生的开车方式，所以自己把车开回了学校，故本题答案为 D。

22. A；本题为推断题。从对话中可以推断，男生正在学习开车，而且学习过程并不是很顺利，由此可知，本题答案为 A。

23. A；本题为主旨题。对话的主要内容是老师解释为什么会给出低分以及学生论文中的各种问题，故本题答案为 A。

24. C；本题为细节题。根据原文 "Larry, you really need to work on your grammar. You had so many of those mistakes on your paper." 可知，本题答案为 C。

25. D；本题为预测题。根据原文 "I'll start reviewing grammar as soon as school is done today." 可知，男生放学后将开始复习语法，故本题答案为 D。

26. B；本题为主旨题。老师从能源的来源以及用途引出化石燃料，接着提到这些燃料是不可再生能源，最后引出讨论的问题：如何通过节约能源的方式，更长久地使用能源。由此可知，本题答案为 B。

27. A；本题为细节题。根据原文"I mean that we can do things like walk or ride bikes instead of driving cars."可知，本题答案为 A。

28. A；本题为修辞题。根据原文"But, uh, if more people used wood to heat their homes, then we could save electricity. My family always has a fire going in the fireplace during winter. It keeps our home warm and doesn't waste any electricity."可知，本题答案为 A。

29. D；本题为推断题。根据原文"Well, one option is to use more alternative energy sources. These include solar, wind, water, geothermal, and nuclear power. However, each of these types of energy has its own problems."可知，解决问题的方案之一是使用更多的可替代能源，但是这些能源又有自己的问题，故本题答案选 D。

30. D；本题为主旨题。原文虽然提到了一些沙漠的名称，还有 hot desserts and cold desserts，但是这些都是具体细节，为"沙漠分类"这一主旨服务，故本题答案为 D。

31. B；本题为细节题。根据原文"There are, however, cold deserts as well. The Gobi Desert in Mongolia and China is one example."可知，Gobi Desert 属于 cold dessert，故本题答案为 B。

32. C；本题为推断题。由原文"Extremely arid deserts receive virtually no rainfall each year. The Atacama Desert of Chile is one of these. In some parts of that desert, it hasn't rained in more than 400 years."可知，Atacama Desert 全年几乎不下雨，而且有一些区域甚至 400 年都没有降水，由此可以推断本题答案为 C。

33. A；本题为主旨题。受访者主要从成分以及与火山的关系两方面解释了钻石形成的原因，故本题答案为 A。

34. C；本题为细节题。根据原文"Basically, the combination of extreme heat and pressure under the Earth's surface takes a lump of carbon, uh, like coal, and transforms it into a diamond."可知，本题答案为 C。

35. C；本题为修辞题。根据原文"For that reason, the majority of diamonds are discovered near places that were either volcanically active in the past or have active volcanoes."可知，提及火山是为了说明为什么火山周围容易发现钻石，故本题答案为 C。

36. B；本题考查说话者的目的。根据原文"So, if I understand you correctly, you're saying that all I need to do is go to the site of an extinct volcano and start digging. And then I'll be able to find some diamonds."可知，男子之所以认为当地可以找到钻石，是因为当地曾经发生过火山喷发，故本题答案为 B。

37. D；本题为推断题。由原文"While some diamonds have been found in this area, it's not as simple as grabbing a shovel and digging them up. If it were, I'd already be rich."可知，如果带着铁锹就能挖出钻石的话，女子早就致富了。由此可以推断，女子应该进行过一些挖掘活动，故本题答案为 D。

38. C；本题为主旨题。文章主要描述了南北战争结束之后，林肯遇刺的过程。故本题答案为 C。

39. C；本题为细节题。根据原文"On the evening of April 14, 1865, President Abraham Lincoln and his wife went to Ford's Theater in Washington, D.C. With the war over, Lincoln felt at liberty to spend an evening relaxing. During the performance, as he sat in an upper-level box near the stage, he was shot from behind."可知，林肯是在 Ford's Theater 的包厢里遇害的，故本题答案选 C。

40. B；本题为修辞题。结合原文"The assassin was an actor named John Wilkes Booth."以及之后对林肯遇刺细节的描述，可知提及 John Wilkes Booth 是为了描述他刺杀林肯的细节，故本题答案为 B。

41. D；本题为推断题。根据原文"Lincoln was moved to a nearby house, where he died the next day on April 15, 1865."可知，选项 D 正确。A、B、C 均未提及。

42. C；本题为预测题。根据老师的最后一句话"Let me tell you what the original plan was."可推断，接下来他将继续介绍课程相关内容。故本题答案为 C。

Language Form and Meaning

1. D；本题考查定语从句。根据句意，填空部分意为"计算机俱乐部正在计划的（活动）"，由此可知这里应该是定语从句省略了连词 that，故本题答案为 D。

2. B；本题为词义辨析题。and 前后为并列结构，根据 and 前面的 educational（*adj.* 有教育意义的）可知，本空应填入一个形容词，故本题答案为 B。

3. A；本题考查比较级。该句的意思是"我只是希望比去年的数学俱乐部更有趣"，所以本题应该填入一个表示"更有趣"的比较级形式，fun 的比较级为 more fun，因此本题答案为 A。

4. C；本题为词义辨析题。cancellation 意为"取消"，thrill 意为"激动，兴奋"，letdown 意为"失望"，challenge 意为"挑战"。根据句意"那个（数学）俱乐部太令人失望了"可知，本题答案为 C。

5. D；本题为词义辨析题。根据前文可知，有机体的生存依赖许多条件。由此推断下一句说的应该是 climate 就是这些条件之一，根据句意可知答案为 D。obstacle 意为"障碍"，appearance 意为"露面，外表"，complication 意为"复杂化；并发症"，determiner 意为"决定因素"。

6. A；本题为词义辨析题。结合后一空选项可知，整句话的意思是"在干热气候里成长的有机体比起在雨林，在沙漠里可能生存得更好"。thrive 意为"茁壮成长"，migrate 意为"迁徙"，detest 意为"憎恨"，submit 意为"提交"，因此本题答案为 A。

7. C；本题考查比较级。由填空处后面的 than 可知，本题考查的是比较级的使用，意思为"比……更有可能"，因此本题答案为 C。

8. B；本题考查定语从句。填空部分修饰的是前面的 another factor，所以动词应该使用第三人称单数形式，且时态应该使用一般现在时，故本题答案为 B。

9. C；本题考查被动语态。hold 在这里的意思是"举行"，修饰 elections，两者之间为被动关系，所以应该使用被动语态，故本题答案为 C。

10. B；本题为词义辨析题。该空修饰前面的 students，因此应填一个形容词，再根据后面的介词 in，可知本题答案为 B。interested in 意为"对……感兴趣的"，主语通常为人。

11. C；本题为词义辨析题。request 意为"要求"，delay 意为"延误"，prohibit 意为"禁止"，encourage 意为"鼓励"，根据句意可知，本题答案为 C。

12. B；本题考查定语从句。先行词为 student，故关系词应用 who，且动词应用第三人称单数形式，故本题答案为 B。

13. A；本题考查并列结构。此题目考查 and 前后两个结构并列的用法，此空的内容与前者 will start 结构并列，所以空格处也应该使用将来时，即 will end，但是因为前面已经出现了 will，因此这里可以省略，故本题答案为 A。

14. B；本题为词义辨析题。gather 意为"聚集"，contribute 意为"捐赠，做贡献"，buy 意为"购买"，collect 意为"收集"，故本题答案为 B。

15. D；本题考查句子结构。句意为"我们感谢所有给烘焙义卖的捐赠"。donation to 为固定搭配，意为"给……的捐赠"，故本题答案为 D。

16. B；本题考查连词。这句接下来开始介绍义卖会的相关细节，apparently 意为"明显地"，"as for the...itself"意为"至于……本身"，in accordance with 意为"与……一致"，nonetheless 意为"然而"，故本题答案为 B。

17. C；本题为词义辨析题。result 意为"结果"，approval 意为"批准，许可"，objective 意为"目标"，reminder 意为"提醒人的事物"。结合句意可知，本题答案为 C。

18. C；本题考查比较级。本题考查 as...as... 结构的常见搭配：as + *adj.* + *n.* + as，故本题答案为 C。

19. A；本题为词义辨析题。desperate 意为"极严重的"，divisive 意为"有争议的"，derisive 意为"嘲笑的"，discounted 意为"已折扣的"。in desperate need of 为固定搭配，意为"迫切需要"。故本题答案为 A。

20. D；本题考查固定搭配。desire to do 意为"决定做某事"，故本题答案为 D。

21. B；本题考查定语从句。先行词是前面的 genres，故关系词应该用 which。根据句意可知空格处的意思是"其中一种是科幻类"，故本题答案为 B。

22. A；本题为词义辨析题。element 意为"要素"，ingredient 意为"原料，材料"，constituent 意为"成分"，piece 意为"部件"，故本题答案为 A。

23. D；本题考查定语从句。先行词为 fantastic creatures，故关系词应用 which。根据句意"它们可能拥有神奇的力量"可知，本题答案为 D。

24. C；本题为词义辨析题。该空修饰 world，应该选择一个形容词，故答案为 imaginary，意为"想象的，虚构的"。

25. B；本题考查句子结构。该句的主语是 Middle Earth，"the world...books"为插入语，因此填空处的意思是"这样一个虚构的地方"，故答案为 B。

26. B；本题考查句子结构。填空处的意思为"可能存在的其他种族"，among other races 意为"在其他种族之中"，故本题答案为 B。

27. A；本题为词义辨析题。conflict 意为"矛盾"，debate 意为"辩论"，competition 意为"竞争"，warfare 意为"战争"，故本题答案为 A。

28. D；本题考查动词不定式。该填空部分考查动词不定式表目的的用法，所以应该使用 to do something 的结构，故选 D。

29. A；本题为词义辨析题。inform 意为"通知，告知"，announce 意为"宣布，公布"，insist 意为"坚持"，alarm 意为"使不安，使恐慌"，故本题答案为 A。

30. D；本题考查句子结构。由前文可知，Mr. Richard 的教学时间还有两周，所以搬回得克萨斯州是将来发生的事情，故答案选 D，用现在进行时表将来。

31. A；本题考查比较级。本题目考查形容词、副词的比较级用法，常用的比较级结构为"more + *adj.* + than"，故本题答案为 A。

32. B；本题为词义辨析题。swift 意为"迅速的"，thorough 意为"彻底的，全面的"，reduced 意为"减少的"，verified 意为"证实的"，故本题答案为 B。

33. C；本题考查固定搭配。agree to do sth. 意为"同意做某事"，故本题答案为 C。

34. A；本题考查同位语从句。先行词为 Mrs. Parker，所以关系词应用 who，再根据时间状语 two years ago 可知，本空应用过去时，故本题答案为 A。

35. B；本题考查句子结构。a choice of 为固定搭配，意为"选择的机会"。此外，students 和 given 之间是被动关系，需要使用被动语态，故本题答案为 B。

36. C；本题考查句意。have to do 为固定搭配，意为"必须做……"，结合后半句"但是今年他们可以使用电脑"可知，前半句的意思应该是"他们必须手写文章"，故本题答案为 C。

37. A；本题为词义辨析题。rate 意为"评价，评定"，guarantee 意为"确保，担保"，compose 意为"撰写，组成"，criticize 意为"批评，评论"，故本题答案为 A。

38. A；本题考查修饰语。consist 为不及物动词修饰 panel，此题使用现在分词形式作定语，故本题答案为 A。

39. C；本题为词义辨析题。detach 意为"使分离"，forgotten 意为"忘记"，omit 意为"省去"，repeal 意为"废除，废止"。结合句意"为了防止评分有失偏颇，论文将省去学生的名字"可知，本题答案为 C。

40. B；本题为词义辨析题。本题考查 entitle 的用法，此处应该使用该词的过去分词形式 entitled，意为"名为……"，故本题答案为 B。

41. C；本题为词义辨析题。submit to a contest 和 enter a contest 都意为"参加竞赛"，但是 enter to a contest 的说法是错误的，故本题答案为 C。

42. D；本题为词义辨析题。partial 意为"部分的；偏袒的"，appropriate 意为"合适的"，considerable 意为"相当重要的"，eligible 意为"有资格的"。be eligible for sth./to do sth. 为固定搭配，意为"有资格做……"。故本题答案为 D。

Reading Comprehension

1. A；本题为主旨题。文章主要介绍了 Carter's Department Store 销售的产品以及开学季的打折活动，故本题答案为 A。

2. C；本题为词义辨析题。stock up on 意为"囤货，购买大量……"，utilize 意为"利用，使用"，consider 意为"考虑"，purchase 意为"购买"，save 意为"救助，储蓄；保留"，故本题答案为 C。

3. D；本题为修辞题。根据原文"We also carry art supplies, such as paint, paintbrushes, and easels."可知，提及这些具体的工具是为了说明商店里售卖的绘画产品，故本题答案为 D。

4. B；本题为细节题。广告提到了 Carter's Department Store 售卖的各种 school supplies 以及开学季的打折信息，故本题答案为 B。其他选项原文均未提及。

5. C；本题为细节题。由原文 electronic goods are available at 40% discounts 可知，电子产品的折扣为 40%，而 notebook computer 是电子产品的一种，故折扣也为 40%，所以本题答案为 C。

6. D；本题为词义辨析题。whopping 意为"巨大的"，surprising 意为"令人惊讶的"，unlikely 意为"不太可能的"，reduced 意为"减少的"，enormous 意为"巨大的"，所以本题答案为 D。

7. B；本题为主旨题。通知主要提及的是关于科学课程的两个变化：课程费用的变化以及学生必须自己购买必备的安全装备，由此可知本题答案为 B。

8. C；本题为细节题。原文提到 physiology students must pay $275，可知本题答案为 C。

9. A；本题为细节题。根据原文"The reason for this is that there has been a general increase in the prices of the supplies needed for each class."可知，课程费用上涨的原因是所需材料的价格上涨了，故本题答案为 A。

10. D；本题为词义辨析题。requisite 意为"必须的"，safest 意为"最安全的"，minimum 意为"最少的；最小的"，obligated 意为"有义务的"，necessary 意为"必要的"，故本题答案为 D。

11. D；本题为指代题。which 指的是学生要 hold on to（抓住，不失去……）的对象，结合上下文可知，which 指代的是前文提到的 their own items，故本题答案为 D。

12. A；本题为推断题。原文提到，在过去两周内，已经有四副眼镜和两件实验服丢失，由此可推断，学校实验室的一些器材被盗了，故本题答案为 A。

13. D；本题考查作者意图。本通知的内容包括关于举行 spring festival 的信息以及呼吁家长们提供帮助，所以本题答案为 D。

14. D；本题为词义辨析题。engender 意为"产生，引起"，amplify 意为"扩大"，appreciate 意为"欣赏"，clarify 意为"明确"，create 意为"创造"，故本题答案为 D。

15. A；本题为推断题。由原文"The first is to engender a sense of community between the school and the residents of the neighborhood."可知，学校举行 spring festival 是为了让学校和该地区的居民建立联系，那么可以合理推测出学校可能坐落在住宅区里，故本题答案为 A。

16. B；本题为词义辨析题。consult 意为"咨询，查询"，edit 意为"编辑"，check 意为"查询；核对"，regard 意为"把……看作"，print 意为"打印；刊登"，故本题答案为 B。

17. C；本题为细节题。第二段提到节日活动将会在 school gym、auditorium 以及 football field 举行，除此之外，没有提到会在 classrooms 里举办活动，故本题答案为 C。

18. C；本题为细节题。由最后一段的"We need at least twenty-five volunteers to help out during the festival. If you can spare even one or two hours of your time, we would appreciate it."可知，学校呼吁家长能充当志愿者提供帮助，故本题答案为 C。

19. A；本题为推断题。由原文"Coral polyps appear to be small plants to many people, but they are in actuality a type of marine life."可知，很多人以为 coral polyps 是植物，故本题答案为 A。

20. C；本题为细节题。由原文"They grow in clusters and secrete a substance made of calcium carbonate that protects their bodies."可知，珊瑚虫成群生长，会分泌一种碳化钙物质保护自己的身体，故本题答案为 C。

21. B；本题为指代题。这句话中的代词 them 可以在珊瑚中找到很多食物，所以 them 指代的就是前一句话中的名词复数 sea creatures。故本题答案为 B。

22. C；本题为词义辨析题。voracious 意为"贪婪的"，stealthy 意为"鬼鬼祟祟的；秘密的"，gigantic 意为"巨大的"，ravenous 意为"贪婪的"，vicious 意为"凶险的；恶毒的"，故本题答案为 C。

23. A；本题为词义辨析题。sanctuary 意为"避难所，庇护所"，haven 意为"避难所；港口"，estuary 意为"河口"，aquarium 意为"水族馆"，container 意为"容器"，故本题答案为 A。

24. C；本题为细节题。第 15~16 行提到"The water that coral resides in must also be shallow since it needs access to sunlight in order to survive."，由此可知珊瑚的生存必须需要阳光，故本题答案为 C。

25. D；本题为词义辨析题。eschew 意为"避免；避开"，employ 意为"雇用；利用"，prefer 意为"更喜爱"，demean 意为"贬低……的身份"，avoid 意为"避免"，故本题答案为 D。

26. C；本题为细节题。文章提到的人为给珊瑚造成的伤害有：往水里排放化学物质的人为污染以及人类本身造成的破坏，如渔民使用爆炸物捕鱼，同时也给珊瑚造成了伤害；还有人切下珊瑚，用来制作珠宝或者用于家庭水族箱中。但是并未提及为了水族馆进行捕鱼，故本题答案为 C。

27. A；本题为主旨题。本文内容围绕着 Sherlock Holmes 展开，先后讲述了这个角色的由来、他破案的方式以及他的宿敌 Professor Moriarty。由此可推断，文章的主题应该是 Sherlock Holmes 的简要介绍，故本题答案为 A。

28. D；本题为细节题。原文提到 Sir Arthur Conan Doyle 从 1887~1927 年间一直在创作关于 Sherlock Holmes 的故事，故选项 D 正确。A、B、C 的内容原文均未提及。

29. C；本题为修辞题。根据原文"Among the most famous of all the works featuring Holmes are *The Hound of the Baskervilles*, *The Blue Carbuncle*, and *A Scandal in Bohemia*."可知，作者提及 *The Hound of the Baskervilles* 是为了给出关于福尔摩斯著名故事的例子，故本题答案为 C。其他选项原文均未提及。

30. C；本题为细节题。根据原文"One of the reasons that Sherlock Holmes was so popular concerns the method he employs to solve his cases: logic."可知，本题答案为 C。

31. D；本题为词义辨析题。nemesis 意为"宿敌，死对头"，competitor 意为"竞争者"，peer 意为"同等地位的人"，partner 意为"搭档，同伴"，rival 意为"竞争对手，敌人"，故本题答案为 D。

32. A；本题为词义辨析题。refrain from 意为"避免；不做……"，stop 意为"停止"，resume 意为"（中断后）重新开始"，postpone 意为"推迟"，continue 意为"继续"，故本题答案为 A。

33. B；本题为推断题。根据原文"While Holmes often solves cases that are unrelated to one another, he has a nemesis with whom he comes into both direct and indirect conflict in several stories. That person is Professor Moriarty, the leader of a crime ring in London."可知，Professor Moriarty 在一些故事中和福尔摩斯有正面和非正面的冲突，故本题答案为 B。

34. C；本题为细节题。根据原文"In one of the stories, *The Final Problem*, Holmes and Moriarty fight one another and fall to their deaths by plunging down a steep cliff near a waterfall. When he wrote that story, Doyle had tired of Holmes and wanted to kill off the character."可知，Sir Arthur Conan Doyle 在故事中杀死 Sherlock Holmes 的原因是已经厌倦了这个角色，故本题答案为 C。

35. B；本题为主旨题。文章主要讲述了 solar eclipse（日食）和 lunar eclipse（月食）两种现象，故本题答案为 B。

36. B；本题为词义辨析题。spectacular 意为"壮观的"，distinct 意为"不同的；清楚的"，impressive 意为"令人印象深刻的"，lost lasting 意为"失去持久的"，common 意为"普通的"，故本题答案为 B。

37. C；本题为指代题。it 指代的是从地面看上去和太阳一样大的物体，由此可以推断，it 指代的是文前的 moon，故本题答案为 C。

38. D；本题为词义辨析题。obscure 意为"遮掩，遮蔽"，transpose 意为"调换，顺序颠倒"，illuminate 意为"照亮，解释"，perceive 意为"理解；察觉"，block 意为"遮住；挡住"，故本题答案为 D。

39. C；本题为细节题。根据原文"While the sun is much larger than the moon, the relative nearness of the moon to Earth makes it appear to be the same size as the sun when viewed from the ground. Thus, when the sun, Earth, and moon are

37

perfectly aligned, the moon appears to cover the entire sun." 可知，虽然太阳比月球大得多，但是因为月球距离地球更近，所以从地面看，月球和太阳的大小看上去差不多，故本题答案为 C。

40. D；本题为细节题。原文第三段最后一句提到裸眼观看日食会对眼睛造成伤害，故 A 选项排除。第三段倒数第二句提到日食持续时间仅为几分钟，故 B 选项排除。第二段提到日食可能是 total 或者 partial，故 C 选项排除。而文章并没有提到日食发生的频率，故本题答案为 D。

41. A；本题为细节题。根据原文 "There are two different types of lunar eclipses. Taken together, the result is that lunar eclipses happen more frequently than solar eclipses." 可知，月食发生频率比日食更高，故本题答案为 A。

42. B；本题为推断题。根据 "People must also take care when viewing a solar eclipse since looking directly at it can cause damage—including blindness—to their eyes." 可知，裸眼观看日食会对眼睛造成伤害，再结合原文 "There is no harm in directly observing a lunar eclipse either, so looking at one will not damage a person's eyes." 可知，月食不会对眼睛造成伤害，故本题答案为 B。

Practice Test 4

Answers

Listening Comprehension

1.~5.	CBBAB	6.~10.	AACCB	11.~15.	ADDCA	16.~20.	CBDDA
21.~25.	CBACB	26.~30.	BDBCC	31.~35.	DBADC	36.~40.	DABBC
41.~42.	AC						

Language Form and Meaning

1.~5.	DABBD	6.~10.	ACBBD	11.~15.	AACAC	16.~20.	DADCC
21.~25.	ADABB	26.~30.	DDBAD	31.~35.	CCBBA	36.~40.	DBAAB
41.~42.	CA						

Reading Comprehension

1.~5.	BACDC	6.~10.	BCBBA	11.~15.	CACAC	16.~20.	DBCAD
21.~25.	CCAAD	26.~30.	CCDDA	31.~35.	DBADC	36.~40.	BADAB
41.~42.	CB						

Scripts

1.

Boy: Have you finished writing your report for history class yet?

Girl: Actually, I haven't even started doing any research on it. I have been too busy working on my English paper.

Boy: You haven't started? But the paper is due tomorrow. You'd better hurry.

Girl: I know. I guess I'll head to the library after school's done today.

2.

Girl: Mr. Patterson, Kevin told me that you wanted to see me.

Man: That's right, Amy. You didn't turn in your homework this morning. Did you forget to complete it?

Girl: Uh ... Actually, I left it at home this morning. Should I call my mother and ask her to bring it to school?

Man: No, don't do that. But please submit it first thing tomorrow morning.

3.

Girl: Hey, that's a nice bike you're riding. When did you get it?

Boy: My parents gave it to me yesterday.

Girl: Yesterday? But isn't your birthday two months from now? What was the occasion?

Boy: They didn't give it to me as a birthday present. They gave it to me since I got all A's last semester. I suppose it's kind of a reward for doing well.

4.

Boy: How did you do on the exam? I got an 88.
Girl: I totally bombed it. I can't believe that just happened to me.
Boy: You can't be serious, can you? I thought that you studied for the test the entire weekend.
Girl: I did, but, when the test started, I suddenly forgot everything I had learned.

5.

Girl: How are you going to get home this afternoon?
Boy: My mom is picking me up around 3:30. How come?
Girl: Would you mind if I caught a ride home with you? My parents are too busy to come to get me today.
Boy: No problem. You live right down the street from me.

6.

Man: Gina, I saw you passing notes again in class today. You really have to stop doing that.
Girl: I'm sorry, Mr. Sanders.
Man: That's the second time this week I've had to talk to you about your behavior. The next time it happens, you're going to get detention for three days.
Girl: Yes, sir. I won't do it again.

7.

Woman: Class, I would like to talk to you about the science fair. It's going to be held from November third to the fifth. That's six weeks from now. Everyone needs to participate in the science fair this year. I'd like you all to choose your topics by next week. If you need any help, just ask. I can help you select something.

8.

Man: We're going to have a new athletic team this year. I think that a lot of you might be interested in participating on it. It's the cross country team. Cross country is a running sport, but you don't run on a track. Instead, you run long distances outdoors. If anyone is interested, let me know. I can give you some more information.

9.

Man: There are both physical changes and chemical changes. A physical change can be something as simple as ripping a paper into two pieces. It can also be boiling water to change it from a liquid state to a gaseous one. But chemical changes are different. They change the actual molecules in a substance. Let me give you some examples of chemical changes ...

10.–13.

Boy: Sandy, I'd like to congratulate you on winning the election. It's so amazing you just got voted student body president.
Girl: Thanks for saying that, Tom. Honestly, I can't believe I won the election. I was positive Randy was going to win. The results were a pleasant surprise for me though.
Boy: Yeah, that's what a lot of people thought since he's so popular. But, uh, apparently more people wanted you to do the job.

Girl:	I guess so.
Boy:	Anyway, uh, now that you just got elected, what are you planning to do as president? Do you have any big plans for the student body this year?
Girl:	I sure do. First of all, I intend to do my best to keep every single one of my campaign promises. I'm going to start by focusing on the food selection in the cafeteria this year.
Boy:	That would be great. The quality of the food has really gone down the past few months. I've been bringing my own lunch lately because I can't stand eating the food there anymore.
Girl:	I know exactly what you're talking about. That's why I'm going to look into it.
Boy:	That would be great. Good luck.
Girl:	Thanks.
Boy:	While you're handling the cafeteria, are you planning to take care of any of your other campaign promises as well?
Girl:	I don't want to do too much at once. Basically, I need to get used to my new position. When I'm more comfortable in a month or two, I think I'll work on fulfilling my other campaign promises.

14.–16.

Woman Teacher:	Greg, would you mind staying for a moment, please? There's something I need to speak with you about before you head to your next class.
Boy:	No problem, Mrs. Whittaker. What do you want to talk to me about?
Woman:	Your recent homework ... It hasn't been particularly good the past couple of weeks. I'm worried that you're not going to do well on our upcoming test. Is there anything I need to know about?
Boy:	Um ... Not really. I guess I'm just having a hard time understanding the material. Geometry is sort of difficult for me.
Woman:	I see. Well, I have a suggestion for you ...
Boy:	Yes, ma'am?
Woman:	I believe you ought to join a study group. Are you aware that there are two separate geometry study groups here at school?
Boy:	There are?
Woman:	Indeed there are. However, it appears that you, uh, as well as most of the other students in the class, are unaware of them. Anyway, I believe you should consider joining one. They're led by seniors who get excellent grades in math. I'm positive that attending a few study sessions will let you improve the quality of your work. So what do you think?
Boy:	I guess I could give it a shot. But, um ... when do they meet? I have football practice as soon as school ends, so ...
Woman:	One of the groups meets after school. But the other gets together during the study hall period following lunch. Why don't you go there today? The group meets in room 214. I can let the group leader know you're going.
Boy:	Sure thing. Thanks for letting me know about the group, Mrs. Whittaker.

17.–21.

Girl:	Mr. Simmons, do you have a moment?
Male Teacher:	Oh, hi, Carol. It's nice to see you back at school today. I heard you were really ill last week. Are you feeling better now?
Girl:	Yes, sir. I had a bad case of the flu for a few days, but I got better over the weekend. Thanks for asking.
Man:	That's good to hear. So ... may I assume you're here to talk about all of the work you missed last week?
Girl:	That's right, Mr. Simmons. Since I was absent for four days, I must have missed a lot.

Man:	You did. But you're doing an outstanding job in my class, so I'm positive that you won't be behind the other students for too long. It shouldn't take you very much time to catch up with everyone else.
Girl:	I hope not.
Man:	Okay. The first thing you need to do is get notes from one of the students in class. We covered all of chapter four in class last week. We studied ancient civilizations in the Americas. I recommend that you ask, hmm ... Julie or Mark for their notes. They probably take the best notes of all the students.
Girl:	All right. Mark and I have a couple of other classes together, so I'll speak with him later in the day.
Man:	Sounds good.
Girl:	Did you give us any assignments? Do I have any homework to turn in?
Man:	Yes, you do. I assigned your class a report to write. It's due tomorrow ... but don't worry. I don't expect you to turn it in by then. Hold on ... Here ... Take this. This is the sheet that explains what you need to write about. Why don't you give me your report on, um ... How does Monday morning sound to you?
Girl:	Perfect. I can complete it by then.
Man:	Excellent. Okay, um, I think we've covered everything.
Girl:	Thanks, Mr. Simmons. Oh, the bell's going to ring soon. I don't want to make Mrs. Angleton mad by being late.
Man:	You'd better get going then.

22.–25.

Boy:	Molly, you look like you're deep in thought about something.
Girl:	Huh ...?
Boy:	I said that you look like you're thinking about something ... Are you okay?
Girl:	Oh, yeah. Sorry, Brent. I'm, uh, I'm just trying to figure out what to do about this semester.
Boy:	What do you mean?
Girl:	My parents have been encouraging me to join a lot of clubs this semester. They want me to do as many extracurricular activities as possible. They claim it will make my college applications look more attractive.
Boy:	I suppose so. Which activities are you considering?
Girl:	I'm already a member of the Spanish club and the science club. I'm on the math team, and I play softball as well.
Boy:	It seems like your plate is already full.
Girl:	That's exactly what I told my parents. However, they insist that I can do one or two more activities. They want me to join the band, but I simply don't have enough time for that. So I've narrowed my choices down to the computer club and the track team. Which of those two do you think I should do?
Boy:	It depends. You'll have fun if you run track, but you'll have to practice every day and go to track meets, too. That will be pretty time consuming. I'm on the track team, so I know how much work is involved. On the other hand, the computer club seldom meets, and the members don't really do much. If you join the computer club, it won't require a great deal of effort on your part.
Girl:	Hmm ... I'm already overworked. I think I'll join the computer club.
Boy:	That's exactly what I'd do.
Girl:	Yeah, that way, I can keep my parents happy, and I won't have a big increase in my workload.

26.–29.

Woman Announcer:	Good evening, listeners. This is Karen Pierson, and I'm the host of Current Events here on WQMR. I've got a very special guest for you tonight. I'm going to be talking with Professor Pratt Harris. He teaches archaeology at Westmoreland University. Good evening, Professor.
Male Professor:	Good evening, Karen. Thank you for having me on your show.

Woman:	The pleasure is all mine. Now, Professor ... We asked you to be with us today because of the news coming from nearby Watertown. Why don't you tell us about it?
Man:	Sure. It appears that three young boys were out walking in the forest near Watertown a couple of days ago. One of them stumbled upon a previously unknown cave. The boys, of course, couldn't restrain their natural curiosity, so they investigated the cave. Inside, they found some works of art painted on the walls.
Woman:	Cave art. I believe that's the first example of cave art ever found in our area, isn't it?
Man:	That's correct, Karen. A large number of Native American tribes are known to have lived here in the past. But none of the tribes that lived in this region in the past few centuries made any cave art. As a result, we ... uh, that would be my colleagues and I at the university ... we believe this cave art could be thousands of years old.
Woman:	Is there any way to determine the age of the paintings?
Man:	Yes, there is. We can use carbon dating methods on both the paintings and the artifacts that were found in the cave. You see, uh, not only are there works of art on the walls, but there are also many artifacts, uh, such as pottery, in the cave. It's quite an impressive archaeological discovery. In fact, I'm pretty sure that, by the time we discover everything there is to be known about the cave, it will be one of the most important archaeological sites in the entire country.
Woman:	That's a bold statement, Professor. And I'd like you to defend it. But, first, we're going to take a short commercial break, and then we'll continue talking with Professor Harris.

30.–34.

Male Teacher:	Everyone please turn to page 101. We're going to learn about Sir Isaac Newton next. You know who he is, right? Jane?
Girl:	He was one of the greatest scientists of all time. He discovered gravity, and he did work in several other fields, um, including mathematics and optics.
Man:	Well done, Jane. Newton was a brilliant scientist, and he's one of my favorite people in history. I simply love talking about him and his discoveries. One of his greatest contributions to humanity was his coming up with the three laws of motion. Let me give them to you in brief right now.
	The first law of motion states that every object is either in a state of rest or in uniform motion in a straight line unless an external force acts upon it. This means that a thing either remains still or moves in one direction until something causes it to stop doing that. Look at this ball on my desk. It's not moving. But ... I push it, and it starts to roll. It keeps rolling until it hits the book right ... about ... now. And then it stops. That's Newton's first law of motion in action.
	Now, um, the second law of motion. It's slightly more complicated. Newton said that the relationship between an object's mass and acceleration and its applied force can be summed up by the formula $F = MA$. Let me write that on the board ... F stands for force. M stands for mass. And A stands for acceleration. To put it simply, the velocity, um, or speed, of a moving object is accelerated when a new force is applied to it. Here's a simple example ... Press the gas pedal on a car, and it accelerates.
	As for the third law of motion ... Newton said that for every action, there is an equal and opposite reaction. What does that mean ... ? If one object hits another object, equal forces will act on them ... but the forces will move in opposite directions. Think about a rocket. When its engine ignites, the burning gases in the engine move downward. As a result, the rocket moves upward. Now, let me show you a short video that will give you some more examples of all three laws of motion ...

35.–38.

Woman Teacher:	I'd like to chat about stress. This is something that can affect people's well-being in many ways. But what exactly is stress ... ? It's a difficult question to answer since people tend to define stress in different ways. Let's take a look at some of the physical effects of stress first. What happens when a

	person experiences stress?
Boy 1:	Some people get headaches. My heart tends to beat faster, and my blood pressure rises, too.
Girl:	Yeah, and some people have specific responses to stress. For example, my sister bites her fingernails when she is stressed out. Other people sweat a lot.
Woman:	That's right, Lucy. Some people have trouble breathing, and others' legs and hands start shaking. Additionally, in some cases, a person's personality may undergo a change. For instance, some people act rudely when they're stressed out. Others shout, make demands, and act quite, well, quite poorly. Now, tell me ... What causes stress?
Boy 2:	School. And homework.
Woman:	Be serious, Brad.
Boy 2:	I wasn't trying to be funny, Ms. Carter. School and homework probably cause stress for everyone in the class. At least they do for me. Um ... people's jobs and their everyday lives can give them stress, too.
Woman:	That's a better answer. Thanks. People often experience stress when they have no control over something. Think about it ... Sitting in traffic jams can be stressful. You can't control the traffic. So there's nothing you can do to make the cars move faster. Thus your feeling of helplessness can transform into stress. What other problems cause stress?
Girl:	Not having enough time to do something. And money. I think money, er, a lack of money, can cause stress, too.
Woman:	Those are good points. Okay. What can people do about stress ... ? How can they get rid of it ... ? First, for those of you like Brad who suffer stress because of school, you can get your work done faster. That means you shouldn't wait to do your homework until ten minutes before class begins. You should do it earlier. In other words, solve the problems that are causing you stress. Any other ideas?
Boy 1:	Exercise works for me. When I get stressed out, I play basketball or go jogging. That always takes my mind off my problems and relieves my stress.

39.–42.

Male Teacher:	Centuries ago, miners made use of primitive railway systems. They utilized wooden tracks that carts ran on. The miners loaded ore onto the carts. Then, they wheeled the carts out of the mines. Most of these tracks were underground. But some ran aboveground as well. The miners could therefore transport heavy loads of ore somewhat easily. Of course, these carts were either pushed by people or pulled by horses or other animals. There weren't any engines at that time. This method of moving heavy objects was most commonly employed in Germany, Britain, and some other places in Europe.

Using people to push wagons or horses to pull them isn't very efficient though. People and horses get tired and can't travel long distances without resting. So people sought new sources of power to move their carts. The steam engine, which was perfected in Britain in the late 1700s, was the ideal solution. Some people immediately recognized the potential that the steam engine had for transportation.

As a result, these individuals tried using steam engines to pull wagons on rails. This was first accomplished in England in 1804. By the 1820s, a lot of people were experimenting with various types of engines and vehicles. In 1825, British engineer George Stevenson invented a train engine that he called Locomotion. It ran on the first public railway system in the world.

Over the next few years, railways were built all over Britain. Most only ran short distances. But they were so successful that long-distance railways began getting built. The first major railway line opened in 1830. It was the Liverpool to Manchester line in Britain. The owners made money by charging fees for transporting both cargo and passengers.

By 1860, Britain had more than 16,000 kilometers of railways. It wasn't the only place that had trains. All over Europe and the United States, people were building railroads. Trains came to dominate land transportation in the nineteenth century. Now, let me give you a few details about railroads in the United States. I think you'll find these facts quite interesting.

Explanations

Listening Comprehension

1. C；本题为主旨题。本对话由男生询问女生是否完成了明天即将要交的历史报告开始，女生表示由于忙于英语论文，还没有开始写历史报告，打算放学后去图书馆写，故本对话的主题为历史报告，答案为 C。

2. B；本题为预测题。由原文 "But please submit it first thing tomorrow morning." 可以推测，女孩明天一早将提交作业。故本题答案为 B。

3. B；本题为细节题。根据原文 "They gave it to me since I got all A's last semester. I suppose it's kind of a reward for doing well." 可知，男孩的父母给他买自行车是他上个学期拿了全 A 的奖励，故本题答案为 B。

4. A；本题为推断题。由原文 "I totally bombed it." 可以推断女孩考得并不好，bomb a test 意为 "考砸了"。如果这个表达考生并不知道，也可以从 "when the test started, I suddenly forgot everything I had learned" 推测出答案。故本题答案为 A。

5. B；本题为主旨题。对话提到女生的父母太忙所以无法来接她放学，因此她询问男生是否能送她一程，故对话的主要内容是女生怎么回家，答案为 B。

6. A；本题为推断题。由对话可知，女生多次在课堂上传递纸条，老师表示如果再发现女生有这样的行为，她将被课后留校，所以女生需要注意自己在课堂上的表现。故本题答案为 A。

7. A；本题考查说话者意图。这是一则关于 science fair 的通知，包括举行的时间、参加要求以及老师布置的任务，故这则通知的目的是提供关于 science fair 的相关信息，本题答案为 A。

8. C；本题为主旨题。该通知提到了一个新的体育队——cross country team 的组建信息以及该运动的介绍，故本题答案为 C。

9. C；本题为细节题。关于化学变化，男士提到 "They change the actual molecules in a substance."，故本题答案为 C。

10. B；本题为主旨题。男生首先恭喜女生当选学校主席，然后两人讨论了女生当选后的计划，故本题答案为 B。

11. A；本题为修辞题。根据原文 "Honestly, I can't believe I won the election. I was positive Randy was going to win." 可知，女生提及 Randy 是因为她以为 Randy 会当选学校主席，而自己会输给 Randy，故本题答案为 A。

12. D；本题为细节题。由原文 "The quality of the food has really gone down the past few months. I've been bringing my own lunch lately because I can't stand eating the food there anymore." 可知，男生觉得学校食堂的菜品质量下降严重，故本题答案为 D。

13. D；本题为语义题。当男生问女生："While you're handling the cafeteria, are you planning to take care of any of your other campaign promises as well?" 时，女生回答道："I don't want to do too much at once."，由此可知女生不想一次做太多改变，打算先从食堂问题开始处理，故本题答案为 D。

14. C；本题为细节题。由原文 "Your recent homework...It hasn't been particularly good the past couple of weeks." 可知，男生最近的作业完成得不太好，故本题答案为 C。

15. A；本题为推断题。根据原文 "I'm positive that attending a few study sessions will let you improve the quality of your work." 可知，老师认为参加学习小组能提高男生的成绩，故本题答案为 A。

16. C；本题为预测题。当老师建议男生今天午餐后去 214 教室参加学习小组时，男生回答道："Sure thing."。由此可知男生午餐后会去参加学习小组聚会，故本题答案为 C。

17. B；本题为主旨题。本对话发生在老师和学生之间，主题是女生因为生病缺课向老师询问自己拉下的课程和作业，故本题答案为 B。

18. D；本题为细节题。根据原文 "I had a bad case of the flu for a few days..." 可知，女生缺课的原因是得了流感，故本题答案为 D。

19. D；本题为推断题。当老师建议女生向 Julie 或者 Mark 借用笔记时，女生回答说："Mark and I have a couple of other classes together, so I'll speak with him later in the day."，由此可知，女生将问 Mark 借用笔记，本题答案为 D。

20. A；本题为细节题。根据 "Here ... Take this. This is the sheet that explains what you need to write about." 可知，老师给了女生一张关于作业的表格，故本题答案为 A。

21. C；本题为预测题。由女生最后说 "Oh, the bell's going to ring soon. I don't want to make Mrs. Angleton mad by being late." 可知，接下来她将去赶下一堂课，故本题答案为 C。

22. B；本题考查说话者意图。根据原文 "My parents have been encouraging me to join a lot of clubs this semester. They want me to do as many extracurricular activities as possible." 可知，女生谈及课外活动的原因是她的父母希望她能尽量多地参加各种俱乐部，故本题答案为 B。

23. A；本题为语义题。plate is full 意为 "某人的时间或者精力已经全部用于某项工作，无法再承担其他事情"，再结合上下文可知，女生已经参加了很多课外活动，故本题答案为 A。

24. C；本题为修辞题。男生提及田径队的时候说，"..., but you'll have to practice every day and go to track meets, too. That will be pretty time consuming. I'm on the track team, so I know how much work is involved."，由此可知田径队会占据大量的时间，故本题答案为 C。

25. B；本题为细节题。由原文 "I think I'll join the computer club." 可知，女生决定加入计算机俱乐部。

26. B；本题为修辞题。根据原文 "It appears that three young boys were out walking in the forest near Watertown a couple of days ago. One of them stumbled upon a previously unknown cave." 可知，教授提及 Watertown 的原因是它是洞穴所在地，故本题答案为 B。

27. D；本题为细节题。根据原文 "As a result, we ... uh, that would be my colleagues and I at the university ... we believe this cave art could be thousands of years old." 可知，最新发现的洞穴艺术可能是上千年前制作的，故本题答案为 D。

28. B；本题为细节题。根据原文 "You see, uh, not only are there works of art on the walls, but there are also many artifacts, uh, such as pottery, in the cave." 可知，一起被发现的还有陶器，故本题答案为 B。

29. C；本题为推断题。根据教授的发言 "In fact, I'm pretty sure that, by the time we discover everything there is to be known about the cave, it will be one of the most important archaeological sites in the entire country." 可推断，这个洞穴将会是全国最重要的考古遗址之一，故本题答案为 C。

30. C；本题为主旨题。讲座主要描述了牛顿的三大运动定律的具体内容，故本题答案为 C。

31. D；本题为推断题。当提到牛顿本人时，老师说道："Newton was a brilliant scientist, and he's one of my favorite people in history. I simply love talking about him and his discoveries."，由此可知，老师对牛顿的成就很熟悉，故本题答案为 D。

32. B；本题为细节题。讲述第一运动定律时，根据原文 "Look at this ball on my desk. It's not moving. But ... I push it, and it starts to roll. It keeps rolling until it hits the book right ... about ... now. And then it stops." 可知，老师用球作为演示的道具，故本题答案为 B。

33. A；本题为细节题。根据原文 "As for the third law of motion ... Newton said that for every action, there is an equal and opposite reaction." 可知，第三定律的内容是每一个力都有一个与之方向相反，大小相等的反作用力。故本题答案为 A。

34. D；本题为预测题。根据最后一句话 "Now, let me show you a short video that will give you some more examples of all three laws of motion ..." 可知，接下来老师将播放一段视频，展示更多关于三大运动定律的例子。故本题答案为 D。

35. C；本题为修辞题。当说到人们对压力的反应时，女生说："Yeah, and some people have specific responses to stress. For example, my sister bites her fingernails when she is stressed out."，因此她提及自己的妹妹是为了说明她妹妹对压力的反应，故本题答案为 C。

36. D；本题为语义题。Be serious 意为 "严肃点"，结合学生的回答 "I wasn't trying to be funny, Ms. Carter." 可知，老师认为学生的回答是在开玩笑。故本题答案为 D。

37. A；本题为细节题。根据原文 "Sitting in traffic jams can be stressful. You can't control the traffic. So there's nothing you can do to make the cars move faster. Thus your feeling of helplessness can transform into stress." 可知，交通堵塞会造成压力的原因是你无法控制交通，只能无助地坐在车里什么也干不了，故本题答案为A。

38. B；本题考查说话者意图。当谈到如何处理压力时，老师说如果和 Brad 一样觉得学校导致了压力，可以提前完成作业，不要等到最后一刻再开始。所以老师建议学生尽早完成作业的原因是这样可以缓解压力，故本题答案为B。

39. B；本题为主旨题。讲座讲述了铁路的历史以及其发展过程，故本题答案为B。

40. C；本题为细节题。根据原文 "Of course, these carts were either pushed by people or pulled by horses or animals." 可知，在木制轨道上的车是由人力或者马力驱动的。故本题答案为C。

41. A；本题为细节题。根据原文 "In 1825, British engineer George Stevenson invented a train engine that he called Locomotion." 可知，George Stevenson 发明了一种火车引擎，本题答案为A。

42. C；本题为推断题。根据最后一段中的 "By 1860, Britain had more than 16,000 kilometers of railways. It wasn't the only place that had trains. All over Europe and the United States, people were building railroads." 可知，除了英国，欧洲和美国也在建造铁路，故本题答案为C。

Language Form and Meaning

1. D；本题考查固定搭配。intend to do sth. 为固定搭配，意为"打算做某事"，故本题答案为D。

2. A；本题考查句子结构。从句中使用了表示将来的 if，所以助动词应该用 could，所填空意为"如果我们能成为队友"，故本题答案为A。

3. B；本题考查词义辨析。individual 意为"单独的；个人的"，organized 意为"有组织的；系统的"，respected 意为"受人尊重的"，extended 意为"扩展的；延长的"。结合上下文可知，本空应该填一个和游泳这项运动相匹配的形容词，故本题答案为B。

4. B；本题考查词义辨析。这封信的目的是向已经在游泳队的朋友询问如何加入该队的建议，在前文中也提到了 pointers，这个单词的意思是"提示；建议"，与选项中的 tips 意思相近。evidence 意为"证据"，clue 意为"线索"，prompt 意为"提词；提示"，故本题答案为B。

5. D；本题考查词义辨析。unfortunate 意为"不幸的"，scholastic 意为"学业的，学术的"，apparent 意为"显而易见的"，sheltered 意为"受保护的"。结合上下文可知，本空应该填入一个带有正面含义的形容词，这个词是后文 nice homes and enjoy food 的同义替换，也是前文 poor or homeless 的反义词，故答案为D。

6. A；本题考查比较级。本空的意思是"尽可能多的食物"，应该使用"as + *adj.* + *n.* + as"的形式，故本题答案为A。

7. C；本题考查句意。整句的意思是"通过在收容所或者食物银行当志愿者，我们可以看见其他社会成员是如何生活的"，两个从句共用主语 we，we 和 volunteer 之间为主动关系，所以本题答案为C。

8. B；本题考查固定搭配。learn by doing sth. 意为"通过做……学习"，故本题答案为B。

9. B；本题考查词义辨析。type of 意为"类型"，与 kind of 为同义词，根据题意可知本题答案为B。

10. D；本题考查固定搭配。get the most out of 为固定搭配，意为"充分利用；最大限度地利用"，故本题答案为D。

11. A；本题考查状语从句。两个从句共用一个主语 we，we 代表 academy，situated 意为"坐落在……，位于……"，引导状语从句，表示学校的位置，故本题答案为A。

12. A；本题考查固定搭配。have what it takes to do sth. 意为"有做……的能力"，故本题答案为A。

13. C；本题考查词义辨析。空格处应该填一个修饰前面 talk 的词，故本题答案为C，意为"关于……的"。

14. A；本题考查词义辨析。behind 意为"落后"，故本题应该填一个名词，作为落后的对象，故本题答案为A。

15. C；本题考查比较级。根据上下文可知，目前已经进度已经落后，所以需要（比现在的进度）"更快地"工作，much faster 后面省略了 than we have been working，故本题答案为C。

16. D；本题考查词义辨析。whimsically 意为"异想天开地，古怪地"，periodically 意为"定期地"，consequently 意为"因此"，apparently 意为"明显地"，结合上下文可知，本题答案为 D。

17. A；本题考查现在完成时。根据上下文可知，别的小组都已经快要完成作业了，而"我们"却几乎还没有开始，所以应该使用现在完成时表示到目前为止的动作，故本题答案为 A。

18. D；本题考查词义辨析。assignment 意为"作业"，exam 意为"考试"，experiment 意为"实验"，research 意为"调查"。根据空后的地点 library 可知，本题答案为 D。

19. C；本题考查宾语从句。根据上下文可以推断，本句句意应该是"我不记得你是否有篮球练习"，故本题答案为 C。

20. C；本题考查时间状语。根据句意可知，空格处的意思是"一放学就……"，英文可以是 as soon as school finishes 或者 once school finishes，故本题答案为 C。

21. A；本题考查比较级。本空的意思是"比……更吸引人"，所以应该使用"more + adj."的结构，故本题答案为 A。

22. D；本题考查定语从句。先行词为 figure of speech，关系词可以使用 that 或者 which，从句中作者讨论的是"可以"使用的修辞手法，故应该使用 can 而不是 will。

23. A；本题考查现在进行时。该句讨论的是作者在写句子的时候正在使用的时态，再结合空前的 is，可知应该使用"be + v.-ing"的形式，表示现在进行时，故本题答案为 A。

24. B；本题考查词义辨析。该句在对比 alliteration 和 assonance 两种修辞手法，故应该使用表示转折的连词。because 和 therefore 表示因果关系，whereas 表示转折，moreover 表示递进，故本题答案为 B。

25. B；本题考查并列结构。one 与前文的 an example 为同义替换，an example of alliteration 和 one of assonance 结构相似，后者省略了 example，故本题答案为 B。

26. D；本题考查词义辨析。superb 意为"极佳的"，creative 意为"有创意的"，long 意为"长篇的"，dull 意为"枯燥无聊的"。结合后文可知，该句的意思是把无聊的文章变得更有趣，故本题答案为 D。

27. D；本题考查词义辨析。reciprocate 意为"报答，回报"，appreciate 意为"欣赏；感谢"，renovate 意为"修复，翻新"，congratulate 意为"祝贺"。根据下文可知，女子排球队进入了州锦标赛，因此要表示祝贺，故本题答案为 D。

28. B；本题考查动词形式。由 defeated 可知，打败 Walker High School 是发生在过去的事情，而获得参赛资格也是过去的事情，所以应该使用一般过去时，故本题答案为 B。

29. A；本题考查词义辨析。upcoming 意为"即将到来的"，arriving 意为"到达的"，various 意为"各种各样的"，recent 意为"最近的"（已经发生了的）。根据后一句可知，比赛将在这个周末举行，故本题答案为 A。

30. D；本题考查固定搭配。come to an end 意为"结束"，而且这是发生在将来的事情，所以还应该使用将来时，故本题答案为 D。

31. C；本题考查被动语态。be ranked 意为"排在第几"，排名和主语之间为被动关系，所以应该使用被动语态，故本题答案为 C。

32. C；本题考查定语从句。定语从句修饰 Davenport，且中间用逗号隔开，所以关系词只能使用 which，故本题答案为 C。

33. B；本题考查条件状语从句。本题考查 let sb. know if 的结构，意为"如果……，请告知……"，故本题答案为 B。

34. B；本题考查词义辨析。appeal 意为"呼吁；申诉"，grant 意为"授予，给予"；wish sb. luck 为固定搭配，意为"祝……好运"。故本题答案为 B。

35. A；本题考查词义辨析。legend 意为"传说；传奇故事"，civilization 意为"文明"，art 意为"艺术"，sculpture 意为"雕像"。myth 和 legend 常常搭配使用，故本题答案为 A。

36. D；本题考查固定搭配。"There is no such thing as..."为固定句型，意为"没有……这样的事物"，故本题答案为 D。

37. B；本题考查固定搭配。lack sth. to do sth. 为固定搭配，意为"缺少干……的……"，故本题答案为 B。

38. A；本题考查宾语从句。从句的意思是"当月球运动到太阳之前，是什么造成了日食"，所以从句的关系词应该用 what，故本题答案为 A。

39. A；本题考查句子结构。本空应该填入 involve 的一个宾语，some sort of = some kind / type of，意为"某种"，故本题答案为 A。

40. B；本题考查词义辨析。根据 heavenly bodies 可知，空内应该填入一个复数名词，故本题答案为 B。

41. C；本题考查词义辨析。egg 意为"卵；蛋"，sample 意为"样本，样品"，fossil 意为"化石"，studies 意为"研究"。下一句中提到了 bones，而选项中只有 fossils 包含骨头，故本题答案为 C。

42. A；本题考查词义辨析。gigantic 意为"巨大的"，extreme 意为"极度的，极端的"，miniature 意为"微型的，小型的"，underground 意为"地下的"。此句中的 bones 的主体是 dragons and other large monsters，故本题答案为 A。

Reading Comprehension

1. B；本题为主旨题。本文是一个总一分的结构，第一段最后一句"However, there are a couple of changes you ought to be conscious of."给出全文主旨，之后分两段说明了具体的变化，所以本文主要介绍了学校体育队的一些变化。故本题答案为 B。

2. A；本题为词义辨析题。start 意为"开始"，consider 意为"考虑"，delay 意为"延迟"，repeat 意为"重复"，embark upon 意为"开始一项新的事情"，故本题答案为 A。

3. C；本题为词义辨析题。transfer 意为"转移；搬迁"，move 意为"移动；搬家"，quit 意为"离开（工作岗位）"，expect 意为"期待；预计"。根据下文可知，Coach Jenkins 去了别的地方工作，可推断 resign 意为"辞职"，故本题答案为 C。

4. D；本题为推断题。根据原文 Coach Jenkins resigned to take a job elsewhere 可知，Coach Jenkins 将辞职去别的地方工作。由此可推断，他将去别的学校工作，故本题答案为 D。

5. C；本题为细节题。根据原文"He has been replaced by Jeremy Sloan. Coach Sloan will be the head coach of the boys' football and basketball teams."可知，Coach Sloan 是接替 Coach Jenkins 的人选，他将是男子足球队和篮球队的总教练。故本题答案为 C。

6. B；本题为细节题。根据原文"Therefore, we regret that the girls' softball season has been cancelled."可知，本赛季的女子垒球比赛被取消了，故本题答案为 B。

7. C；本题考查作者意图。由第一段最后一句"On account of that, I would like to list which clothes are acceptable and which are not."可知，通知的主要内容是学校的穿着要求。接下来分别说明了男女生的穿着要求以及违反要求的后果，故选项 C 最能概括通知内容。

8. B；本题为细节题。根据原文"These shirts must have collars since all boys have to wear neckties as well."可知，男生必须佩戴领带，故本题答案为 B。

9. B；本题为词义辨析题。advise 意为"告知；建议"，forbidden 意为"禁止"，register 意为"登记，注册"，request 意为"要求，请求"，故和 prohibit（禁止；阻止）意思相近的答案为 B。

10. A；本题为指代题。them 指代的是多次违反穿衣要求而被送去校长办公室的人，也就是前一句中提到的 students，故本题的答案为 A。

11. C；本题为推断题。由通知中列出的惩罚可知，Tina Wimberley 预计会有违反规则的人，故本题答案为 C。A 和 B 原文均未提及，而文中提到一些休闲的衣物都不符合穿衣要求，故 D 选项错误。

12. A；本题为词义辨析题。adhere to 意为"遵守，坚持"，think about 意为"思考"，agree with 意为"同意"，be proud of 意为"为……感到自豪"，故本题答案为 A。

13. C；本题为主旨题。故事主要讲的是 Eric 和 Martin 着急完成作业，然后赶去参加比赛的内容，完成作业所占的篇幅更多，故本题答案为 C。

14. A；本题为细节题。根据原文"As members of the football team, they had to be on the bus no later than three twenty. Their team was playing an away game later in the evening and had to leave very soon in order to get to the site of the game on time."可知，Eric 和 Martin 是足球队的成员，他们坐车的目的是去客场踢足球比赛，故本题答案为 A。

15. C；本题为词义辨析题。compliment 意为"赞美"，penalize 意为"惩罚，处罚"，scold 意为"责骂，训斥"，insult 意为"侮辱"，故与 berate（严责；申斥）意思最相近的选项为 C。

16. D；本题为指代题。it 指代的是 Coach Jackson 旁边的一个名词单数，结合上下文可知，it 就是 bus，本题答案为 D。

17. B；本题为细节题。原文并未提及 Eric 和 Martin 是否换上了足球比赛制服，故本题答案为 B。

18. C；本题为主旨题。文章提到了人类制造的各种木制品，并对其中几种进行了详细介绍。故本题答案为 C。

19. A；本题为词义辨析题。embed 意为"深信；把……插入"，disturb 意为"打扰，妨碍"，initiate 意为"发起，开始实施"，consistent 意为"持续的；始终如一的"，故与 ingrain（使……根深蒂固）意思最接近的选项为 A。

20. D；本题为细节题。根据原文"Humans have additionally tended to create both religious and ceremonial objects from wood. In fact, all around the world, countless cultures have made use of ceremonial wood carvings."可知，人类倾向使用木头创造宗教和仪式物品，故本题答案为 D。

21. C；本题为词义辨析题。sacred to 意为"对……神圣的"，important to 意为"对……重要的"，hunted by 意为"被……困扰"，revered by 意为"被……尊敬"，necessary for 意为"对……必要的"，故本题答案为 C。

22. C；本题为细节题。根据原文"People in many cultures in Asia, Africa, and North America have made ceremonial wooden masks."可知，在亚洲、非洲和北美洲都有人制造仪式用的木制面具，故本题答案为 C。

23. A；本题为修辞题。根据原文"While masks tend to be fairly small, other wood carvings can be enormous. Among the largest of all ceremonial wood carvings is the totem pole."可知，作者提到图腾柱是为了说明除了小型的面具之外，还有一些大型的木雕品，故本题答案为 A。

24. A；本题为指代题。they 可以用来纪念重要的历史事件，结合上文可知，they 指代的就是前文提到的 totem poles，故本题答案为 A。

25. D；本题为推断题。原文提到木制品包括小型的面具和大型的图腾柱，由此可以推断，wood carving 有不同的尺寸。其他选项原文均未提及，故本题答案为 D。

26. C；本题为细节题。最后一段提到了图腾柱的用途、外观以及制造者，除此之外，还提到了图腾柱是用完整的树木制造的，但是并没有具体说是哪种树，故本题答案为 C。

27. C；本题为主旨题。文章主要描述了四种关于月球形成的假设，故本题答案为 C。

28. D；本题为细节题。原文提到月球是离地球最近的天体，与选项 D 意思相同。选项 C 具有一定的迷惑性，但是注意 virtually 的意思是"几乎"，而 always 意为"总是，每次都是"，二者在频率上有区别，故排除 C 选项。

29. D；本题为词义辨析题。known 意为"已知的；知名的"，determine 意为"决定"，thought 意为"认为，觉得"，presume 意为"假设；推定"，故和 estimate（估计；判断）意思接近的是选项 D。

30. A；本题为词义辨析题。hit 意为"撞击"，pass 意为"经过"，interfere with 意为"干扰，阻碍"，affect 意为"影响"，与 crash into（撞到……上）意思最接近的是选项 A。

31. D；本题为细节题。根据原文"The most widely accepted idea is the collision theory."可知，collision theory 是最广为接受的猜想，故本题答案为 D。选项 A 并未提及；选项 B 偷换概念，原文说是一个和火星一样大小的物体与地球发生了撞击，而不是火星本身撞击了地球；选项 C 说地球曾经有多个卫星，而原文说地球最开始曾经没有卫星，故排除。

32. B；本题为细节题。根据原文"Another theory is that Earth and the moon formed at the exact same time billions of years ago. However, many astronomers discount this theory. They point out that Earth and the moon are comprised of different substances. They claim that if the two bodies were formed at the same time, then they should be composed of the same materials."可知，许多天文学家发现地球和月球是由不同物质组成的，如果它们是同时形成的话，成分应该一样，所以他们不认为两者是同时形成的。故本题答案为 B。

33. A；本题为词义辨析题。suggest 意为"提议，建议"，insist 意为"坚持"，promise 意为"承诺，保证"，deny 意为"否认"，故与 propose（建议，提议）意思最接近的是选项 A。

34. D；本题为指代题。这句话的意思是：第四个理论称，it 在最初形成时，地球的转动速度比现在快得多。结合上下文可知，it 指代的是后半句中的地球，故本题答案为 D。

35. C；本题为细节题。原文第一段提到了采集狩猎者不种地也不饲养动物，而是通过打猎，设置陷阱，捕鱼以及采集水果、蔬菜等来获得食物。由此可知，本题答案为 C。

36. B；本题为词义辨析题。more cautious 意为"更谨慎的"；choosier 意为"更挑剔的"，原形是 choosy；smarter 意为"更聪明的"；more exotic 意为"更奇异的"；pickier 的原形是 picky，意思是"挑剔的"，故本题答案为 B。

37. A；本题为推断题。根据原文"While there are still places on the Earth where some people starve, it is no longer a major problem like it was in the past."可知，虽然现在一些地方仍存在饥饿问题，但是已经比过去好很多了，由此可以推断出，过去饥饿是一个大问题，故本题答案为 A。

38. D；本题为细节题。根据原文"Since most meat is high in protein, vegetarians must replace this lost nutrient by eating other types of food. For the most part, they can eat fish, soy products, and various kinds of beans to get the nourishment they require."可知，素食主义者会从鱼、豆制品以及各种豆类中获取蛋白质，故本题答案为 D。

39. A；本题为词义辨析题。choose 意为"选择"，require 意为"要求做（某事）"，prepare 意为"做好准备"，abandon 意为"放弃；抛弃"，故和 opt for（选择）意思接近的选项为 A。

40. B；本题为修辞题。文章提到了多种素食主义者的生活方式，他们对肉的定义有不同的标准。选项 A、C、D 原文均未提及，故本题答案为 B。

41. C；本题为词义辨析题。acceptable 意为"可以接受的"，unclean 意为"不纯洁的"，cruel 意为"残忍的"，unnecessary 意为"不必要的"，故和 inhumane（残忍的；无人情味的）意思接近的选项为 C。

42. B；本题为细节题。根据原文最后一段可知，大部分人选择素食主义的原因有两个：一是他们认为吃肉不健康，而且吃肉会导致肥胖、心脏病以及其他的健康问题；二是一些人不想伤害动物，他们认为为了食物杀死动物是残忍的。故本题答案为 B。

Practice Test 5

Answers

Listening Comprehension

1.~5. BCDAD	6.~10. BBDCB	11.~15. DABCD	16.~20. DBACB
21.~25. ACBDB	26.~30. ACABB	31.~35. CCBAB	36.~40. DCDAC
41.~42. AB			

Language Form and Meaning

1.~5. BAADC	6.~10. BDBDB	11.~15. ABAAB	16.~20. BACBD
21.~25. DBDAD	26.~30. ACBCD	31.~35. CBBDD	36.~40. CAADB
41.~42. CA			

Reading Comprehension

1.~5. CADAC	6.~10. AABDD	11.~15. CBCAB	16.~20. CCBDB
21.~25. CDBAC	26.~30. CBDAD	31.~35. CCCAC	36.~40. DDBBC
41.~42. DB			

Scripts

1.

Boy: I love looking at all of the paintings here. They are so well done.

Girl: I'm amazed. I've never been here before.

Boy: You should come back in the future. There are different paintings on display every month.

Girl: I had no idea. Let me know the next time you decide to return here.

Boy: Sure. I can do that.

2.

Boy 1: Did you hear that we might have a pop test in history class today?

Boy 2: Are you serious? How do you know that?

Boy 1: Weren't you listening at the end of class yesterday? Mr. Warren told us that he highly recommended we read the material before class. That always means he's going to test us on it.

Boy 2: Uh-oh. I didn't do the reading.

3.

Woman: Kevin, you haven't been speaking up much in class lately. You were doing that a lot at the beginning of the semester. What's up?

Boy: I guess I'm having some trouble with the new material. Everything we studied at the start of the semester was easy, but the newest stuff is harder.

Woman: Feel free to ask questions in class if you don't understand something.

4.

Man: Jeff, I need to talk to you about the science club since you're the president.
Boy: Sure. What do you need to know, Mr. Kipley?
Man: When are you planning on having a club meeting? You've got to reserve a room ahead of time to do that.
Boy: Oh ... I didn't realize that. I guess I'd better find out what rooms are available next week then.

5.

Girl: You seemed to be concentrating a lot after you finished lunch. What were you working on?
Boy: Oh, I had an idea about a science project. I wanted to write down everything I thought of so that I didn't forget it.
Girl: That's smart thinking. It's no fun to come up with a great idea only to forget it a few moments later.

6.

Woman: Andrea, do you remember that you're supposed to give your presentation tomorrow?
Girl: Yes, ma'am. I haven't forgotten about it.
Woman: Great. Do you need me to prepare anything before you give it?
Girl: Actually, yes. I'm going to show some slides, so I will need to use the projector. I hope that's all right with you.

7.

Man: When you're in the laboratory, you need to remember one important rule: Safety first. You will do nothing dangerous while you are in this lab. Everyone must wear safety goggles and a lab coat at all times. Whenever you are working with chemicals, you must wear gloves. You must also follow my directions exactly as I give them to you. All right. Let's get started.

8.

Woman: Writers often use various figures of speech. These can considerably improve the quality of their writing. A simile is one common figure of speech. A simile is a comparison between two things that uses either "like" or "as." For instance, "he's as brave as a lion" is a simile. So is "my love is like a rose." How about coming up with two similes right now?

9.

Woman: Everyone please be careful when walking down the hall. The janitors waxed the floor last night, and it appears to be a little slippery. One of the receptionists fell down and hurt herself earlier. We'd hate to see the same thing happen to any of you. There is not to be any running in the halls. Walk slowly but surely until the floor isn't so slick.

10.–13.

Male Principal: Good morning, Molly. Please have a seat in this chair ... As the principal of this school, I'd like to be the first person to welcome you here.
Girl: Thank you, sir. I'm very glad to be a new student at Briarwood.
Man: I'm happy to hear that. Now, before you attend your first class, do you have any questions for me?
Girl: Not right now, sir. I'm sure I'll have some questions later, but, um ... I-I-I guess I don't really know

	what to ask at the moment.
Man:	All right. In that case, let me tell you a little bit about what we expect from you at this school.
Girl:	Sure.
Man:	First of all, here at Briarwood, we take the honor code very seriously. So there is to be no cheating. That means no cheating on homework, tests, presentations, or other assignments. In addition, we frown upon lying here.
Girl:	I understand.
Man:	Good. Students who cheat or lie are severely punished. Do it twice, and we will kick you out. But you seem like a nice young lady, so I'm sure we won't have any problems like that with you.
Girl:	I hope not, sir. Is there anything else?
Man:	Yes, there's one more thing before you go to class. Please understand that you can talk to me anytime you have questions or problems. I know it's not easy being a transfer student in the middle of the semester. It might take you a while to adjust here. But I want to see you succeed, so please come to my office if there is anything bothering you.
Girl:	Okay. If I have any problems, I'll be sure to talk to you about them.

14.–17.

Girl:	I'm really not looking forward to going on tomorrow's field trip. It's going to be so boring.
Boy:	Why do you say that? I think it will be fun to go to city hall tomorrow.
Girl:	You've got to be kidding me.
Boy:	Not at all. I mean, um, first of all, we are going to get to meet the mayor. And he's even going to talk to us for half an hour or so.
Girl:	Um ... So what?
Boy:	He's the mayor. He's the most important person in our city.
Girl:	Oh, right. I just remembered that you're interested in politics. I, on the other hand, couldn't care less about anything connected with politics. But I guess that explains why you're so eager to go on the field trip.
Boy:	Yeah, exactly. I know all about Mayor Robinson, so I can't wait to hear him speak. In fact, I heard that he's going to take questions from us. There are a couple of things I'm eager to ask him.
Girl:	Well, I'm glad you're excited about this trip. As for me, I'd much rather go on a field trip somewhere else.
Boy:	Like where?
Girl:	We went to the hospital last year. I thought that was pretty cool. We got to see a bunch of doctors in action. Getting to watch some of that eye operation was so awesome.
Boy:	Ah, I didn't like that field trip at all. In fact, I hate hospitals. I start to get sweaty and dizzy anytime I get near them. I think I'm allergic to doctors or something.
Girl:	Oh, well. I guess everyone has different tastes.

18.–22.

Boy:	Thanks for explaining that problem to me, Mrs. Peters. I think I understand the material a lot better now.
Woman Teacher:	It's my pleasure, James. I'm glad I could help you out.
Boy:	Anyway, I guess I should leave. I have P.E. class now.
Woman:	Oh, James ... Hold on a minute. There's something I've been meaning to ask you.
Boy:	What's that?
Woman:	In the past three weeks or so, you've started speaking up in class. You were so quiet last year and in the first month of the semester. But now you are contributing a lot during class.
Boy:	Ah, right ...

Woman:	Well, I'm curious ... What sparked this change?
Boy:	Hmm ... I guess I have more confidence now. I mean, uh, my grades have been improving in all of my classes this semester since I started studying every day. So, uh, I guess I know more answers than I used to.
Woman:	Right.
Boy:	In the past, I kept quiet because I ... Um, to be honest, I never knew the answers to any of the teachers' questions. And I didn't really understand the material either. Now that I'm trying harder, I find that I can answer the questions. So, uh, I suppose I just want to show that I know the answers.
Woman:	Good for you, James. I must say that I—and several of your other instructors—am very impressed with how you've changed recently. Be sure to keep up the good work. And talk as much as you want in my class. I love it when students volunteer answers.
Boy:	Thanks for the vote of confidence. I was actually, uh, a little worried that you thought I was speaking too much.
Woman:	Not at all. I wish I could get most of the other students to speak half as much as you in class. It would make for livelier discussions.

23.–26.

Girl:	I'm so relieved that we've only got one more class to go until the weekend.
Boy:	You're telling me. It's been a long week.
Girl:	That's true. So, uh, do you have any plans for the weekend?
Boy:	Actually, I do. I've got to go to my part-time job on both Saturday and Sunday.
Girl:	I didn't know you work part time. When did you start doing that?
Boy:	I just landed the job two weeks ago. I work as a cashier at the supermarket down the street. You know, Danielson's. It's a decent job. I make about eight dollars an hour, and I only have to work on weekends. But I do a five-hour shift every Saturday and an eight-hour shift every Sunday.
Girl:	Wow. Those are long shifts. Still, it must be nice to make money.
Boy:	It is. My parents want me to start saving for college because they have no desire to pay for the entire cost of tuition.
Girl:	That's too bad for you, but I understand them as well. As a matter of fact, I think I'm going to have to find a part-time job myself.
Boy:	Find a job? But don't you already have one? You work at ... um, one of those clothing stores in the mall, don't you?
Girl:	I did, but I quit before school began. I wanted to focus on my studies this semester.
Boy:	How has that been going for you?
Girl:	Quite well. I'm getting all A's at the moment. That's why I'm thinking of getting another job. There are only a few weeks left in the semester, so I don't think that working now will harm my grades too badly.
Boy:	You know ... you might want to wait until the semester is over. You'd feel awful if you bombed a final exam because you couldn't study the night before it since you were working.
Girl:	Hmm ... I see what you mean. You may be right. That would be depressing, wouldn't it? I guess I can wait a little while longer to start working again.

27.–29.

| Woman Teacher: | One of the most important things the Founding Fathers did was to create the Electoral College. This meant that the president of the country would not be decided by the popular vote. Instead, each state was given a certain number of representatives in the Electoral College. The number of electors each state got was determined by how many representatives it had in Congress. The winner of the popular vote in a state would then receive all of that state's votes in the Electoral College. Jason? |

Boy:	That doesn't seem right to me. After all, the United States is a democracy. So the winner of the popular vote should become the president.
Woman:	Actually, Jason, you're wrong about one thing. The U.S. is not a democracy. It's a republic. There's a difference. Can anyone tell me what the difference is? Mary, why don't you try?
Girl:	In a real democracy, everyone would get to vote on, well, everything I guess. In a republic, the people elect representatives. These representatives then vote on matters according to the will of the people who elected them. Uh, well, they're supposed to do that. They don't always though.
Woman:	Well said, Mary.
Boy:	But I still think that the president should be elected by the popular vote. So, uh, now I'm curious. Why did the Founding Fathers create the Electoral College? I think it's totally useless. I don't understand why they made it.
Woman:	That's a good question, Jason. Basically, they were worried that the large states would dominate the small ones. You see, when there were only thirteen states, some were large while others were small. The Founding Fathers realized that the large states—large by population that is—could easily control the small ones if the presidential election were determined by the popular vote. So they created the Electoral College. That would enable the small states to have more influence in presidential elections. Thus they wouldn't always be subjected to the will of the people in the larger states.

30.–33.

Male Teacher:	One of the greatest warriors and leaders who ever lived was Genghis Khan. He was born in Mongolia around 1162 and died in 1227. His birth name was Temujin. Growing up, he had a difficult childhood. His father was killed when he was ten. Temujin then became the leader of his family. He married when he was sixteen, and his wife bore him four sons. When he was young, many Mongol tribes were constantly fighting one another. Temujin rose in the ranks and eventually became the leader of his tribe. Then, he made alliances with other tribes. He went to war against the tribes that didn't ally with him. When he conquered them, he allowed those tribes to join his. Thus Temujin's tribe grew in both size and stature.
	By 1206, when he was in his early forties, Temujin was considered the ruler of all the Mongols. It was then that he took the title Genghis Khan. That title, by the way, means "universal ruler." With an army of more than 100,000 men, he decided to conquer more territory. He was extremely successful. The Mongols mostly fought from horseback. And Genghis Khan's soldiers had a reputation for being exceptional and ruthless warriors. In many cases, cities simply surrendered without putting up a fight. The reason was that, if they fought and lost, Genghis Khan would order the massacre of everyone in the city.
	Genghis Khan first conquered much of the land that's in northern China today. Then, they moved westward, where they quickly overran much of central Asia. They conquered the land that's modern-day Pakistan and Afghanistan. Next, they moved north to Russia and seized many of its southern lands. Finally, in 1225, Genghis Khan, who was by then an old man in his sixties, returned to Mongolia. In 1227, he went on another military campaign. It's said that he fell from his horse and died while campaigning. During his life, Genghis Khan conquered more land than anyone else in history.
	That's a quick overview of his life. Now, let me go into more detail on some of his battles and conquests. I think you'll find this rather interesting.

34.–37.

Woman Teacher:	Unfortunately, viruses kill millions of people worldwide each and every year. Prior to the advent of modern medicine, the situation in the past was much worse though. Nowadays, many viruses that were once killers are under control. A century ago, smallpox and polio, two types of viruses, killed

or maimed huge numbers of people. But, for the most part, they have both been eradicated. This happened thanks to vaccines.

A vaccine is a type of medicine that basically triggers an immune response in a person. There are a couple of different types of vaccines. One involves the injecting of a weakened form of the virus into a person's body. Since it is weak, the body can develop antibodies to fight off and kill the virus. This enables the person to become immune to that particular virus. Thus, in the future, if that virus should attempt to enter the person's body, his immune system will kill it. The person will therefore never suffer from the effects of that virus.

Boy: Mrs. Porter, when do people get vaccines?

Woman: It depends. A lot of vaccines are given when a baby is first born or in the early years of childhood. Other vaccines are given later in life. And there are some vaccines that, depending on where the person lives, are not necessary at all. Furthermore, when a person gets vaccinated depends on the vaccine itself. Sometimes, uh, a single vaccination can protect a person for the rest of his life. Other times, it only provides protection for a limited number of years. So, um, a person may need to get vaccinated for certain viruses about once a decade. Oh, and just so you know, um, some of the vaccines that most people get are for smallpox, chickenpox, measles, mumps, influenza, diphtheria, and polio.

The first vaccinations were made for smallpox in the late 1700s. Edward Jenner, a British doctor and scientist, developed a smallpox vaccine from cowpox, a similar virus that affected cattle. Despite the importance of his work, it took decades for his vaccine to be accepted. Finally, in the 1840s, the British government started a widespread smallpox vaccination program based on Jenner's work. By the mid-1900s, smallpox had virtually disappeared from the world.

38.–42.

Woman Teacher: I think that's enough about bays. So, um, let's move on to another body of water. This is one of the more interesting ones we're going to study. I'm referring to estuaries. Now, an estuary ... Um, that's E-S-T-U-A-R-Y ... an estuary is a body of water that forms where a river enters an ocean. It's typically wide and has aspects of both the river and the ocean. You might think that an estuary is simply the mouth of a river, but it's actually a separate body of water. For instance, an estuary has a combination of fresh river water and salty ocean water. An estuary can be affected by ocean tides, too. In addition, sediment carried downriver often settles in an estuary. One result of this is that estuaries often have land formations. Thus they are frequently considered wetlands rather than merely bodies of water.

There are many types of estuaries. Let me show you some pictures up here on the screen. This estuary has a wedge shape ... It's narrow where the river enters it and very wide ... see ... very wide where the estuary meets the ocean. Other estuaries are almost like lakes ... They have barriers where they meet the ocean. This barrier looks like a long finger of land ... The land may be sandy ... and even have beaches. Small channels in the barrier allow the water in the estuary to enter the ocean. Other estuaries were formed by glaciers in rocky coastal regions ... They're narrow, they have steep sides, and they are very deep.

Historically, estuaries have been places where many humans have settled. The reason is that the rivers leading to them could provide people with fresh water. Simultaneously, being close to the ocean provided fish and other animals for people to eat as well as direct access to trade routes. Some of the biggest cities in the world happen to be located on estuaries. New York City, for example, is located on the estuary of the Hudson River.

Explanations

Listening Comprehension

1. B；本题为推断题。对话中两人正在欣赏一些绘画作品，根据原文 "There are different paintings on display every month." 可推断，对话发生的地点应该是一个画廊，故本题答案为 B。

2. C；本题为主旨题。对话中两人正在谈论今天可能会有突击测试，接着其中一个男生说他并没有看书，由此可知，对话主题为突击测试，故本题答案为 C。

3. D；本题为细节题。当老师问男生为什么最近都不怎么在课上发言时，他回答说，"I guess I'm having some trouble with the new material. Everything we studied at the start of the semester was easy, but the newest stuff is harder."。由此可知，男生觉得新东西更难，故本题答案为 D。

4. A；本题为推断题。通过老师提醒男生提前预订房间，以及男生回答说要去看看下周有哪些房间可以预订可推断，男生将在下周举行科学俱乐部会议，故本题答案为 A。

5. D；本题为语气题。"That's smart thinking." 表示女生对男生的赞同，结合上下可知，女生认为男生及时记下想法的举动很聪明。故本题答案为 D。

6. B；本题为推断题。老师问女生是否需要她帮忙准备什么，女生回答说需要用到投影仪，由此可以推断，老师将为女生准备投影仪，故本题答案为 B。

7. B；本题为主旨题。老师在通知中强调了实验室的安全问题，并展开说明了需要采取的一些措施，故这则通知的主旨是如何在实验室中保证安全。

8. D；本题为细节题。根据原文 "How about coming up with two similes right now?" 可知，老师想让学生举一些 simile（明喻）的例子，故答案为 D。

9. C；本题为修辞题。这则通知的主要目的是告诉学生在大堂里走路时要小心，因为地板被打了蜡，接着还提到已经有人滑倒摔伤。再结合原文 "We'd hate to see the same thing happen to any of you." 可知，提及 slippery floor 的目的是提醒学生不要受伤，故本题答案为 C。

10. B；本题为主旨题。校长先对女生表示欢迎，接着介绍了一些学校对学生的要求。根据原文 "Let me tell you a little bit about what we expect from you at this school." 可知，校长在告诉女生学校对她的要求，故本题答案为 B。

11. D；本题为细节题。根据原文 "Students who cheat or lie are severely punished. Do it twice, and we will kick you out." 可知，作弊或者撒谎两次的学生会被赶出学校，故本题答案为 D。

12. A；本题为推断题。根据原文 "I know it's not easy being a transfer student in the middle of the semester." 可知，女生是在学期中间转学来的，故本题答案为 A。

13. B；本题为预测题。对话一开始校长说道，"Now, before you attend your first class, do you have any questions for me?"，由此可知接下来女生要去上第一节课。对话结束前校长再一次说道，"Yes, there's one more thing before you go to class."。由此可知，本题答案为 B。

14. C；本题为主旨题。对话讨论的主题是明天的户外教学活动，男生和女生分别说了自己对该活动的看法，故本题答案为 C。

15. D；本题为语气题。"You've got to be kidding me?" 意为 "你在开玩笑吧？"，再结合上下文可知，女生并不喜欢这次户外教学活动，相反男生很喜欢，同时还可以结合女生的语气推测，她的情绪是惊讶的。

16. D；本题为预测题。根据原文 "In fact, I heard that he's going to take questions from us. There are a couple of things I'm eager to ask him." 可知，男生可能会向市长提问，故本题答案为 D。

17. B；本题为细节题。根据原文 "In fact, I hate hospitals." 可知，男生不喜欢医院，故本题答案为 B。

18. A；本题为主旨题。对话主要是老师发现男生最近上课发言变得很积极，询问他为什么会有这么大的转变。故本题答案为 A。

19. C；本题为细节题。根据原文"Now that I'm trying harder, I find that I can answer the questions. So, uh, I suppose I just want to show that I know the answers."可知，男生课上发言变得积极的原因是他想展现出自己知道问题的答案，故本题答案为C。

20. B；本题为修辞题。根据原文"I must say that I—and several of your other instructors—am very impressed with how you've changed recently."可知，其他老师也对男生的变化很满意，故本题答案为B。

21. A；本题为推断题。根据原文"I wish I could get most of the other students to speak half as much as you in class."可知，老师希望别的学生发言的积极程度能达到男生的一半就很好了，由此推断，其他学生在课上发言不是很积极，故本题答案为A。

22. C；本题为预测题。根据对话开始男生说"Anyway, I guess I should leave. I have P.E. class now."可知，接下来他将去上体育课，故本题答案为C。

23. B；本题为语气题。"You're telling me."是男生对女生前一句话的反馈，表示对"本周还剩一节课就到周末"这一事实的赞同，故本题答案为B。

24. D；本题为细节题。根据原文"I work as a cashier at the supermarket down the street."可知，男生在一家超市当收银员，故本题答案为D。

25. B；本题为细节题。根据原文 but I quit before school began. 可知，女生在开学前辞职了，故本题答案为B。

26. A；本题考查说话者意图。根据原文"You know ... you might want to wait until the semester is over. You'd feel awful if you bombed a final exam because you couldn't study the night before it since you were working."可知，男生建议女生本学期结束以后再兼职，防止因为没有时间复习而考砸了期末考试，故本题答案为A。

27. C；本题考查说话者意图。对话讨论的是选举团以及其在美国政治中扮演的角色，故本题答案为C。

28. A；本题为细节题。根据原文"The U.S. is not a democracy. It's a republic."可知，老师表示美国不是一个民主国家，而是一个共和国，故本题答案为A。

29. B；本题为修辞题。当谈到 Electoral College 时，男生说道："Why did the Founding Fathers create the Electoral College? I think it's totally useless. I don't understand why they made it."。由此可知，男生认为 Electoral College 的设立没有用处，故本题答案为B。

30. B；本题为主旨题。原文讲述了成吉思汗的生平，故本题答案为B。

31. C；本题为细节题。根据原文"He went to war against the tribes that didn't ally with him. When he conquered them, he allowed those tribes to join his. Thus Temujin's tribe grew in both size and stature."可知，成吉思汗通过吞并战败的部落来壮大自己的部落，故本题答案为C。

32. C；本题为修辞题。根据原文"Genghis Khan first conquered much of the land that's in northern China today."可知，成吉思汗曾经征服了现在中国北部的大部分区域，故本题答案为C。

33. B；本题为预测题。根据倒数第二句"Now, let me go into more detail on some of his battles and conquests."可知，接下来老师将继续讲述一些战役的细节，故本题答案为B。

34. A；本题为细节题。根据原文"A century ago, smallpox and polio, two types of viruses, killed or maimed huge numbers of people."可知，老师提到在一个世纪之前，很多人因为天花和脊髓灰质炎而丧命或致残，故本题答案为A。

35. B；本题考查说话者意图。男生先问道："Mrs. Porter, when do people get vaccines?"，之后老师对这个问题做出了回答，所以本题答案为B。

36. D；本题为推断题。根据原文"And there are some vaccines that, depending on where the person lives, are not necessary at all."可知，某些疫苗是否注射，取决于人们生活的地方。由此可以推断，不同地方的人可能注射不同的疫苗，故本题答案为D。

37. C；本题为细节题。根据原文"Edward Jenner, a British doctor and scientist, developed a smallpox vaccine from cowpox, a similar virus that affected cattle."可知，Edward Jenner 是发明天花疫苗的英国医生和科学家，故本题答案为C。

38. D；本题为主旨题。文章主要讲了 estuary（河口，江口）的特点、种类以及它常常被人们作为定居点的原因，故选项 D 与主旨相符。

39. A；本题为细节题。老师说道："In addition, sediment carried downriver often settles in an estuary. One result of this is that estuaries often have land formations."河流里的沉积物往往会在河口淤积，所以河口常常会形成陆地构造，故本题答案为 A。

40. C；本题为推断题。根据原文"There are many types of estuaries. Let me show you some pictures up here on the screen."可知，河口有很多，接着老师还以图片为例，对其中一些进行了介绍，由此推断它们看上去是有区别的，故本题答案为 C。

41. A；本题为细节题。根据原文"Other estuaries were formed by glaciers in rocky coastal regions ... They're narrow, they have steep sides, and they are very deep."可知，由冰川形成的河口很窄，而且有陡峭的河岸，深度很深，故本题答案为 A。

42. B；本题为修辞题。根据原文"New York City, for example, is located on the estuary of the Hudson River."可知，提及纽约是为了举例支持"一些大城市就位于河口"的论点，故本题答案为 B。

Language Form and Meaning

1. B；本题考查动词形式。根据前一句可知现在是完成年度历史项目的时间，项目为将来要完成的事情，故这一句应该使用一般将来时。

2. A；本题考查固定搭配。desire to do sth. 意为"渴望做……"，故本题答案为 A。

3. A；本题为词义辨析题。alter 意为"改变，改动"，cancel 意为"取消"，rearrange 意为"重新整理，改变（位置、时间、顺序）"，postpone 意为"推迟"。根据题意可知，这句话的意思是"一旦决定了搭档就不能更改"，故本题答案为 A。

4. D；本题考查宾语从句。整个从句充当介词 of 的宾语，从句中的 projects 指的是学生们还未做出来的项目，所以应该使用将来时态，should 可以表示将来，故本题答案为 D。

5. C；本题为词义辨析题。apply 意为"申请"，register 意为"登记；注册"，attend 意为"出席，去（学校）"，consider 意为"考虑"。结合上下文可知，作者考虑的是上哪所大学，而不是申请哪所大学，而且申请大学是 apply to，本题缺少介词 to，故排除 A 选项。

6. B；本题考查句子结构。由下文可知，作者并不想去他父亲的学校，但是他的父母想让他去，故本题答案为 B。

7. D；本题考查比较级。作者在比较他不想去的学校和想去的学校，所以需要使用比较级，故本题答案为 D。

8. B；本题考查动词形式。奖学金和得奖人之间是被动关系，得奖人"被"授予了奖学金，故本题应该使用被动语态，答案为 B。

9. D；本题为词义辨析题。remove 意为"移开；脱下"，enforce 意为"实施；强迫"，stress 意为"强调；焦虑"，value 意为"尊重，重视"，根据题意可知，本题答案为 D。

10. B；本题考查比较级。此处应该使用最高级，而且是复数形式，故本题答案为 B。

11. A；本题考查时态。全篇时态为一般现在时，本题中 and 前后为 enjoy doing 的并列结构，即 enjoy spending time outdoors and being active，故本题答案为 A。

12. B；本题为词义辨析题。broaden one's horizons 为固定搭配，意为"开阔眼界"，故本题答案为 B。

13. A；本题为词义辨析题。advice 为名词，意为"忠告，建议"；advise 为动词，意为"通知；建议"；advisement 为名词，意为"深思熟虑；劝告"；advisory 为形容词，意为"顾问的"。本空意为询问他人意见，故应该选 advice。

14. A；本题考查句子结构。Tim 正在思考一个眼下的问题，所以应该使用现在进行时，故本题答案为 A。

15. B；本题考查固定搭配。put pressure on sb. to do sth. 意为"给某人施压做某事"，故本题答案为 B。

16. B；本题考查句子结构。此前描述的是去年的篮球比赛，故主语应该为 it，而且要使用一般过去时，故本题答案为 B。

17. A；本题为词义辨析题。allowance 意为"津贴；补贴"，scholarship 意为"奖学金"，endowment 意为"捐款"，grant 意为"拨款；补助金"，cut off one's allowance 意为"不再给予补贴"，再结合空前的 parents 可知，本题答案为 A。

18. C；本题为词义辨析题。condition 意为"状态"，resumption 意为"重新开始"，situation 意为"情况"，imposition 意为"实施"，in sb.'s situation 意为"在某人的情况下"，故本题答案为 C。

19. B；本题考查比较级。作者说比起其他朋友的意见，更相信"你"的意见，所以本题应该使用比较级 more than，故本题答案为 B。

20. D；本题考查宾语从句。本句结构为"tell sb. + 宾语从句"，sb. 是间接宾语，直接宾语由该宾语从句充当，句意为"请告诉我你认为我该怎么做"，故本题答案为 D。

21. D；本题考查比较级。"one of the + 形容词最高级"为固定搭配，意为"最……之一"，所以本题应该使用最高级，答案为 D。

22. B；本题考查句子结构。句意为"直到他去世的时候……"，描述他去世这一特定时间之前的事情，故本题答案为 B。

23. D；本题为词义辨析题。reply 意为"回答，答复"，treat 意为"对待；治疗"，approach 意为"靠近；处理"，predict 意为"预言"，根据句意可知，本题答案为 D。

24. A；本题为词义辨析题。direct 为形容词，意为"直接的"；directive 为形容词，意为"指导的"；direction 为名词，意为"方向"；directly 为副词，意为"直接地"。此处需要填一个形容词修饰名词 result，故本题答案为 A。

25. D；本题考查固定搭配。"something of a + n."为固定搭配，意为"某人在某种程度上算是……"，故本题答案为 D。

26. A；本题为词义辨析题。accomplish 意为"完成，实现"，regard 意为"认为，把……看作"，approach 意为"靠近"，instruct 意为"教授，指导"，故本题答案为 A。

27. C；本题为同位语从句。从句为 his mother 的同位语，且时态应该为过去时，故本题答案为 C。

28. B；本题为词义辨析题。portray 意为"描绘，描写"，develop 意为"逐渐形成；发展"，satisfy 意为"使满意；满足"，structure 意为"计划，组织"，develop an interest 意为"逐渐产生兴趣"，故本题答案为 B。

29. C；本题考查修饰语。该短语应该是一个名词短语，作 start 的宾语，根据上下文可知，文章讨论的是一个 project，故本题答案为 C。

30. D；本题考查句子结构。后半句的主语为 the Beaumont Academy，故可以排除 A、B 两个选项。Thanks to... 意为"多亏了"，符合题意，故本题答案为 D。

31. C；本题为词义辨析题。reprove 意为"责骂；谴责"，restructure 意为"调整结构"，renovate 意为"修复，翻新"，renege 意为"食言，违约"，根据上下文可知，本题答案为 C。

32. B；本题考查句子结构。根据下文可知，本句讲的是剩余资金的用途，故本题答案为 B。

33. B；本题为词义辨析题。cafeteria 意为"食堂"，facility 意为"设施"，stadium 意为"体育场"，library 意为"图书馆"。结合下文推测，能提升整个学习环境的应该是设施，其他选项都过于片面，本题答案为 B。

34. D；本题为词义辨析题。apparent 意为"显而易见的"，order 意为"命令；订购"，finance 意为"提供资金"，complete 意为"完成，结束"，结合上下文可知，本题答案为 D。

35. D；本题为词义辨析题。creator 意为"创作者"，family 意为"家庭，家族"，example 意为"例子；典型"，style 意为"样式；风格"，故本题答案为 D。

36. C；本题考查句子结构。本句描述的是人们在过去如何制作壁画，所以本空的意思应是"在过去不同的时期里"，故本题答案为 C。

37. A；本题考查比较级。由 among 可知，本题比较的对象为两个以上，所以应该使用形容词最高级，故本题答案为 A。

38. A；本题为词义辨析题。apply 意为"申请；涂"，dry 意为"（使）变干"，paint 意为"上油漆，涂颜料"，mix 意为"混合"。apply to 为固定搭配，意为"把……涂在……"，故本题答案为 A。

39. D；本题考查动词形式。壁画只能"被完成"，因此动词 complete 应该使用被动语态，故本题答案为 D。

40. B；本题为词义辨析题。enjoy 意为"享受"，avoid 意为"避免；回避"，request 意为"要求，请求"，plan 意为"计划；打算"。结合上文可知，壁画制作十分费时，所以艺术家们都会避免制作壁画，故本题答案为 B。

41. C；本题为词义辨析题。attempt 意为"努力，尝试"，study 意为"学习；研究"，resort 意为"诉诸，求助于"，train 意为"培训，训练"。结合上下文可知，那些想更快地完成壁画的人会转而选择其他技术，故本题答案为 C。

42. A；本题考查修饰语。way of doing sth. 为固定搭配，意为"做……的方式"，故本题答案为 A。

Reading Comprehension

1. C；本题考查作者意图。由第一句"All students who are enrolled in history and social studies classes this year should be aware of the following changes."可知，本则通知的目的是告知学生历史和社会学课程有变化，故本题答案为 C。

2. A；本题为细节题。根据原文"We are making them because of the sudden departure of Mr. Sellers, who taught American history."可知，Mr. Sellers 离开了学校，与选项 A 意思一致。

3. D；本题为细节题。根据表格第四行第三列可知，教授 California State History 的老师是 Ms. Henderson，不是 Mr. Nelson，故本题答案为 D。

4. A；本题为细节题。由原文"Please be aware that the class times have not undergone any changes at all."可知，上课时间没有变化，故本题答案为 A。

5. C；本题为词义辨析题。out of one's control 意为"不受某人控制"，所以划线部分的意思是"这件事的发生学校无能为力"，与选项 C 的意思一致。

6. A；本题为推断题。由最后一句话"The school will also hire a new history teacher by next semester so that our current teachers will not be so overworked."可知，学校将在下一个学期聘用新的历史老师，这样就不会让目前的老师过度劳累。由此可推断出，目前为止还没有找到替代的老师，故本题答案为 A。

7. A；本题考查作者意图。这封信说明了 AP 课程的难度和作业量之大，并且给出了一些关于 AP 课程的建议，与选项 A 意思一致。

8. B；本题为细节题。根据原文"I hope you understand that the workload in an AP class is much greater than the workload in a standard class."可知，AP 课程的作业量比一般课程大得多，故选项 B 正确。接下来一句继续说道，选择 AP 课程是为了获得大学学分，但是并没有提到是否由大学教授授课，课程难度也没有和大学课程进行对比，故选项 C、D 错误。

9. D；本题为推断题。根据原文"In fact, you will have up to twice the normal amount of work in each AP class that you are taking. Please take this into consideration when signing up for extracurricular activities or working part time."可知，由于 AP 课程的作业量是普通课程的两倍之多，所以在报名课外活动或者参加兼职时需要考虑自己的时间是否充足。由此可以推断出，作者的意思是参加 AP 课程的学生可能没有时间进行课外活动或者兼职，故本题答案为 D。

10. D；本题为词义辨析题。excessive 意为"过度的"，serious 意为"严重的，严肃的"，monotonous 意为"单调乏味的"，stimulating 意为"令人兴奋的"，extreme 意为"极度的；过分的"，故与原文意思最接近的是选项 D。

11. C；本题为推断题。由原文"If you find the work to be excessive, you may speak with either Mr. Reginald or me anytime. Just visit his or my office, and we will help you to the best of our ability."可知，Mr. Reginald 和作者的职位应该是相似的，再根据信件的落款 Guidance Counselor 可以推断，Mr. Reginald 应该也是一名 Guidance Counselor，故本题答案为 C。

12. B；本题为细节题。根据原文"If you find the work to be excessive, you may speak with either Mr. Reginald or me anytime."可知，如果学生有课程上的问题，可以找老师沟通，故本题答案为 B。

13. C；本题为词义辨析题。qualified 意为"有资格的"，sanction 意为"对……实施制裁"，request 意为"要求，请求"，eligible 意为"符合条件的"，responsible 意为"负责的"，故本题答案为 C。

14. A；本题为推断题。根据原文"Remember that teenagers are involved in more accidents than people in any other age group in the country."可知，青少年发生事故的概率高于其他年龄层，由此推断，选项 A 正确。

15. B；本题为词义辨析题。significantly 意为"显著地；相当数量地"，possibly 意为"可能，或许"，considerably 意为"非常，相当多地"，apparently 意为"据说，显然"，persistently 意为"坚持地"，故本题答案为 B。

16. C；本题为修辞题。根据原文"Last, but surely not least, when you finish the course, you will qualify for discounts of up to 25% on your driver's insurance."可知，作者提及司机保险是因为完成课程可以有优惠，故本题答案为 C。

17. C；本题为细节题。文章提到参加课程的三个好处是：学习如何开自动挡和手动挡的车，学习如何安全驾驶以及可以优惠购买司机保险。除此之外，只提到了可以大大减少事故的发生概率，但是并没有说参加课程可以防止事故的发生，故本题答案为 C。

18. B；本题为细节题。根据最后一句"All of our contact information is available at the bottom of this ad."可知，联系信息在广告下方，故本题答案为 B。

19. D；本题为主旨题。文章第一段提到了在美国的亚利桑那州也有季风，第二段描述了该地区季风形成的两大原因，第三段讲述了亚利桑那州季风的多发季节，最后一段提到有一些气象专家认为亚利桑那州的天气情况并不符合季风特征。由此可知，季风和亚利桑那州是本文的主旨，故本题答案为 D。

20. B；本题为细节题。根据原文"During the summer months, the wind in Arizona suddenly changes direction. It stops blowing from the west or northwest and instead begins to blow from a southern or southeastern direction."可知，亚利桑那州夏天的风向会突然改变，从由西边或者西北边吹来改为由南边或东南边吹来，故本题答案为 B。

21. C；本题为细节题。由原文"The result is that the wind brings moist air from the Gulf of California and the Gulf of Mexico to Arizona."可知，湿润的空气随着风从加利福尼亚湾和墨西哥湾来到亚利桑那州，故本题答案为 C。

22. D；本题为词义辨析题。recurring 意为"循环的，反复的"，short-term 意为"短期的"，lengthy 意为"长时间的"，random 意为"随机的，任意的"，habitual 意为"惯常的"。结合后文可知，可能有段时间完全没有雷暴，也有可能几天连续出现雷暴天气，所以选项 D 与原文意思最接近。

23. B；本题为推断题。根据原文"The monsoon season starts in Arizona in June. Thunderstorms are common occurrences from then until sometime between July and September."可知，雷暴常常从六月开始，结束时间在七月和九月之间的某个时间。由此可推断，雷暴结束的时间并不固定，故本题答案为 B。

24. A；本题为细节题。根据原文"Local residents refer to the rainy periods as bursts and the periods without rain as breaks."可知，当地居民把下雨的时候称为 bursts，把没有雨的时候称为 breaks，故本题答案为 A。

25. C；本题为词义辨析题。to some degree 意为"在某种程度上，稍微"，由此可知，风没有完全转向，只是在一定程度上（partially）转向了，故本题答案为 C。

26. C；本题为指代题。their 指代的是前面的 some meteorologists，再加上选项中有 mind 的只有选项 C。

27. B；本题为主旨题。文章主要介绍了喷泉形成的要素以及喷泉喷发的步骤，Old Faithful 只是起到抛砖引玉的作用，并不是文章主要描述的内容，故本题答案为 B。

28. D；本题为词义辨析题。spew 意为"喷出"，heat 意为"加热"，pour 意为"倒出"，push 意为"推，按"，spray 意为"喷洒"，故本题答案为 D。

29. A；本题为词义辨析题。radiate 意为"辐射，向周围伸展"，spread out 意为"散开"，shine 意为"发光，照耀"，melt 意为"熔化，融化"，disappear 意为"消失"，故本题答案为 A。

30. D；本题为指代题。These 指代的是像房子里的管道系统的一些东西，由此可知，本题答案为前一句中的"cracks, tunnels, and chambers"，故本题答案为 D。

31. C；本题为细节题。文章中提到了喷泉存在的三个要素：该地区要有地下热源、地下水以及地下洞庭和隧道。原文并没有提及火山的岩浆，故本题答案为 C。

32. C；本题为细节题。根据原文"In order for a geyser to erupt, the following steps take place. First, water starts gathering in an underground chamber."可知，喷泉喷发的第一步是水开始在地下聚集，故本题答案为 C。

33. C；本题为指代题。it 指代的东西会随着水离开热源而冷却，故 it 就是前半句中的 water，本题答案为 C。

34. A；本题为推断题。根据原文"Some geysers, such as Old Faithful, erupt on a regular basis. Others erupt more seldom

whenever the conditions are right." 可知，Old Faithful 的喷发是有规律的，结合喷泉喷发的步骤可推断，Old Faithful 地下持续有水聚集，故本题答案为 A。

35. C；本题为主旨题。文章主要围绕着 Rorke's Drift 之战，描述了其缘由、过程以及结果，故本题答案为 C。

36. D；本题为指代题。根据本句谓语可知，These 指代的是居住在南非的两个部落，故其指代的是前一句中的 the Natal and Zulu。

37. D；本题为词义辨析题。competent 意为"能干的，能胜任的"，traditional 意为"传统的"，elected 意为"当选的"，warlike 意为"好战的"，skilled 意为"有技能的"，故本题答案为 D。

38. B；本题为修辞题。根据原文"The onset of the war saw the British suffering a great loss at the Battle of Islandlwana."可知，作者提及 Battle of Islandlwana 是为了说明英国人和 Zulus 之间的开始之战，故本题答案为 B。

39. B；本题为细节题。根据原文"The Zulus then marched on Rorke's Drift, which was located nearby. The station was defended by about 300 men; half were British while the other half consisted of colonial troops. The men were led by Lieutenant John Chard, a British engineer."可知，当 Zulus 抵达 Rorke's Drift 时，英国的保卫人员有 300 人，由一半英国人和一半殖民部队组成，这些人由 John Chard 领导，故本题答案为 B。

40. C；本题为词义辨析题。stout 意为"顽强的"，strategic 意为"战略的"，extensive 意为"广泛的"，strong 意为"强烈的"，high 意为"高的"，故本题答案为 C。

41. D；本题为词义辨析题。breach 意为"攻破，破坏"，burn 意为"燃烧；烧毁"，climb over 意为"爬过去"，approach 意为"靠近"，break 意为"破坏"，故本题答案为 D。

42. B；本题为细节题。最后一段提到在本次战争中 Zulus 预计有 1000 名的伤亡人员；有 11 名保卫者获得了维多利亚十字勋章，以及正因为是 Rorke's Drift 的保卫者拖住了 Zulus，才给英国增援部队的到达争取了宝贵的时间，所以 A、C、D 正确。原文并没有提到 Zulus 认为自己是胜利者，反之他们其实是战败的一方，故本题答案为 B。

Practice Test 6

Answers

Listening Comprehension

1.~5.	CDDCB	6.~10.	DADBB	11.~15.	CABDB	16.~20.	CBACA
21.~25.	BABBA	26.~30.	CCACB	31.~35.	DABAB	36.~40.	DCAAB
41.~42.	BD						

Language Form and Meaning

1.~5.	CDBBA	6.~10.	DABCB	11.~15.	AAACC	16.~20.	BAADC
21.~25.	ACACD	26.~30.	DBADD	31.~35.	ACBAA	36.~40.	BDBCD
41.~42.	AC						

Reading Comprehension

1.~5.	CADDC	6.~10.	CBBAB	11.~15.	DCADA	16.~20.	CACDA
21.~25.	CDDCB	26.~30.	DACDA	31.~35.	BDACA	36.~40.	CBBAD
41.~42.	BD						

Scripts

1.

Boy 1:	Rick, did you see that Coach Young posted a list of all the players who made the basketball team?
Boy 2:	No way, Allen. Did we make it?
Boy 1:	We sure did. We're both on the varsity team, and practice starts at 3:30 today. Isn't that awesome? Clark didn't make it though. He's going to be on the junior varsity team.
Boy 2:	That's too bad for him.

2.

Woman:	Molly, you were late for class again this morning. That's the third time this week you've arrived at school after the bell.
Girl:	Sorry, Ms. Mason. I come to school with my younger sister, and she has trouble getting up in the morning.
Woman:	Well, I'd worry more about myself than her if I were you.

3.

Boy:	Ms. Daniels, is it too late for me to do an extra-credit project for class?
Woman:	No, I believe there's still enough time for you to do something. What are you thinking of doing?
Boy:	I was hoping to write a report on one of Shakespeare's plays.
Woman:	That sounds fine. Make sure I have it no later than next Monday at three o'clock.

4.

Girl:	Jason, you're left-handed, aren't you?
Boy:	That's right. Why do you ask?
Girl:	You've got a cast on your left hand, so I'm wondering how you're going to take notes.
Boy:	I don't think I'll be able to.
Girl:	In that case, why don't I give you copies of the notes I take in each class? That will keep you from falling too far behind.

5.

Boy:	Do I really have to stay after school today, Mr. Robinson?
Man:	I'm afraid so, John. You were disrupting my class by speaking to other students and passing notes. So you are on detention both today and tomorrow.
Boy:	Tomorrow? But I have plans tomorrow as soon as school ends.
Man:	You're going to have to change them. And I suggest that you change your behavior as well.

6.

Girl:	I hope the school decides to let us buy our textbooks on e-readers next year.
Boy:	So do I. Carrying around all these books is no fun at all. I nearly hurt my back the other day because my backpack was so heavy.
Girl:	We'll be able to save money as well since e-books are a lot cheaper than paper books.

7.

Man:	Next Monday will be the first day of your class presentations. Since they should be eight to ten minutes long, we'll have enough time for five presentations each day. We have twenty-two students, which means that the presentations will last all week. I've made a list of the order in which you'll give your presentations. Let me read it for you now.

8.

Woman:	If you're ever late for school in the morning, you need to do the following. Do not go to your classroom. Instead, come to my office. You need to sign in at my desk. You also need to let me know why you are late. If you can bring a note from your parents, that would be great.

9.

Woman:	May I have your attention, please? This Thursday and Friday, the school cafeteria is going to be closed. So you will have lunch in your homerooms. You need to be sure to bring a lunch from home on those two days. Don't forget to bring a drink as well since all of the school's vending machines are in the cafeteria.

10.–13.

Boy:	I'm really glad that I decided to join the school band this year.
Girl:	So am I. This is my third year in the band, and I must say it's the best one of all. I think the fact that we have a new band director is great. Mr. Conaway is much better than Mr. Jessie ever was.
Boy:	I can't comment on that since I never got a chance to meet Mr. Jessie. But it sounds like every band member who knew both of them agrees with you.
Girl:	Trust me. Mr. Conaway is a huge improvement. He's a talented conductor. And he's also an excellent teacher. I feel that I've improved a lot as a flutist this past year.

Boy:	Yeah. I think Mr. Conaway is definitely a good teacher. He has taught me a few things about the trumpet that I never knew. And I've been playing it for, hmm ... for at least six years now.
Girl:	That long, huh? Anyway ... are you ready for the spring concert we're putting on next week?
Boy:	I think so. I've learned most of the songs we're going to play. There are still a couple of pieces that are giving me problems though.
Girl:	I'm pretty much the same as you. But I'm getting more comfortable with the difficult pieces. I don't anticipate having any problems by the time we hold the concert.
Boy:	I hope we don't have any. Everyone in my family is planning to be there, so I'd hate to put on a poor performance in front of them.
Girl:	That would be bad, wouldn't it?
Boy:	Well, we'd better get to band practice now. Hopefully, we can work out our problems today.
Girl:	You said it. Let's get going.

14.–17.

Male Coach:	Matt, are you going to be trying out for the basketball team this year?
Boy:	I'm not sure yet, Coach. My parents don't particularly want me to play ball this year though.
Man:	What? You were one of the first players off the bench last year. You did a good job last year, and I'm counting on you to be a starter this season.
Boy:	Thanks for saying that, Coach.
Man:	So you're going to try out then, right? We need as many quality players as possible if we want to have a winning season.
Boy:	I'll tell my parents what you said. And then I'll try to convince them that they should let me play on the team.
Man:	That's good to hear.
Boy:	Thanks.
Man:	If you don't mind my asking ... Why don't your parents want you to play? If I remember correctly, they both attended every game last year. A lot of parents don't support their children like that. Many don't even bother attending a single game.
Boy:	Oh, they support me in everything I do. They're good like that.
Man:	Then what's the problem? I don't get it.
Boy:	My grades in the first quarter weren't as good as they had expected them to be. I got a couple of low grades in, um, in math and science. So my parents want me to dedicate myself more to my studies. That's why they're not too keen on letting me join the team.
Man:	I see. Well, Matt, you study harder and get those grades up. Then, I'm sure your parents will see fit to let you play on my team.
Boy:	Yes, sir. I'll do my best.

18.–22.

Girl:	Mr. Gibson, are you busy right now?
Male Teacher:	I'm just grading these history tests, Mindy.
Girl:	Oh ... So then should I come back to speak with you sometime later?
Man:	Oh, no. Sorry. I didn't mean that. I was just ... Sorry. I get spaced out sometimes when I'm grading papers. Please come into my office and grab a seat.
Girl:	Thanks, Mr. Gibson.
Man:	What do you want to talk about, Mindy?
Girl:	It's the research paper we have to do.
Man:	What about it?
Girl:	Um ... I've never written a long paper before. You told us that it has to be twenty pages long. And, um,

we need to have a bibliography so that we can cite all of our sources. To be honest, I've never done any of this before. So I don't have a clue as to what I should be doing.

Man: Ah, I see ... Okay. For a research paper, you need to get your information from several different sources. I hope you use at least five sources, but I would prefer that you use more. These sources can be books, magazine articles, information from websites, and so on.

Girl: Okay. But what about the bibliography? And footnotes?

Man: Every time you use information from another source in your paper, you need to make a footnote. This provides information about the work from which you got your information. At the end of the paper, you should write a bibliography. Simply put, it's a list of the sources that you used to write your paper. If you look at that big handout I gave you yesterday, you'll see how to make both footnotes and a bibliography. So ... does that help?

Girl: A lot. Thanks for clearing that up. If I have any more questions while I'm writing my paper, can I come back here and ask you?

Man: Of course you can. That's what I'm here for: to help you learn.

`23.-26.`

Girl: George, have you figured out your schedule for next semester yet?

Boy: There's not too much to think about, is there?

Girl: What do you mean by that?

Boy: I mean that we don't even have a choice for several of our classes. Let's see ... We're required to take English. We have to take history, too. And we have to enroll in P.E. as well.

Girl: Oh, yeah. I see your point. But what about math?

Boy: What about it? I'm taking geometry next year. That's what you're going to be taking as well, isn't it?

Girl: That's right. And I'm taking Spanish 3 next semester.

Boy: Not me. So I guess our schedules will be different there. I'm taking French 3 instead. I wish I had taken Spanish, but it's too late for me to change now.

Girl: Are you going to take biology or physics?

Boy: Definitely physics. I don't enjoy biology. Plus, I love math, and physics has a good deal of math in it.

Girl: That's the same reason I'm going to take physics as well.

Boy: So there really isn't that much for us to decide on, is there?

Girl: Wait. We have to take one more class. We can choose from art, music, computer science, and economics. I can't make up my mind between music and economics. I'm leaning toward economics, but I really enjoy taking classes with Ms. Jenkins, the music teacher.

Boy: She is a lot of fun, isn't she? But, as for me, I'm going to sign up for the computer science class. That's what I'm hoping to major in when I go to college.

`27.-30.`

Woman Teacher: Let's turn our attention to the human ear. The ear has two primary functions: hearing and balance. There are two ears. One is on each side of the head. The ear has three main parts. Take a look at the picture on page fifty-eight in your textbooks. See it ... ? The three main parts are the outer ear ... the middle ear ... and the inner ear ... The ear is also, as you can see, made up of skin, membranes, bones, nerves, and blood vessels.

The part of the ear that is visible is called the pinna. Notice that it has two N's in the spelling. The pinna is a part of the outer ear. It helps collect sound waves as they move through the ear. This tube here ... is called the external auditory canal. It leads from the pinna to the tympanic membrane. Most people know it as the eardrum. Anyway, uh, sound waves hit the tympanic membrane. This causes vibrations that are transferred to the middle ear.

Take a look at the middle ear. There are three small bones here ... here ... and here. These bones help transfer the sound waves from the outer ear to the inner ear. That's pretty much the role of the middle ear. Simple, huh?

As for the inner ear ... There are three main parts: the cochlea ... the vestibule ... and three semicircular canals ... The cochlea collects the sound waves that come from the middle ear. It's spiral shaped as you can see from the picture. Inside the cochlea are fluids that transfer sound waves to a nerve. This nerve is connected to the brain. The brain then interprets the sounds. The other two parts—the vestibule and the three semicircular canals—are used for balance. They're filled with fluids and help us maintain a sense of balance whenever we move.

31.–34.

Woman Teacher: Marsupials are among the oddest of all the families of animals. They're mammals such as opossums, kangaroos, wombats, koalas, and wallabies. As you might have guessed from the list I just gave you, the vast majority of marsupials live in Australia. Many others are found in South America. As for here in North America ... Well, the only marsupial native to this continent is the opossum.

Boy: How are marsupials different from other mammals? Uh, I mean, what makes them special?

Woman: The primary difference concerns how they give birth. Almost every female mammal has a placenta in her womb. The baby—or babies—develops and grows in the womb and gets nourishment from the placenta. A marsupial, however, doesn't have a placenta.

Instead, a marsupial's womb is more like, um, an egg. A baby marsupial only lives in its mother's womb for a short time. In the womb is a substance that's sort of like an egg yolk. Well, once the baby is born, it crawls into its mother's pouch. Ah, yeah ... That's another characteristic of marsupials. Every female marsupial has a pouch in the front of her body. This pocket-like area is where her nipples are. So, uh, the baby crawls into the pouch, latches on to a nipple, and starts feeding on its mother's milk. Depending on the species, the baby will stay in the pouch for weeks or months until it's mature enough to survive on its own.

Nowadays, as I mentioned, marsupials primarily live in Australia and South America. DNA testing has shown that they actually originated in South America. However, marsupial fossils have been found on every continent. Thus they were once much more widespread. So here's a question: What happened that caused them to die out on the other continents? And here's another question: Why do they thrive in Australia? As for the answers to those two questions, no one is really sure. But many experts believe it has to do with how marsupials give birth. Marsupial females are only pregnant for a short time.

And pregnant females are vulnerable in many ways. So, in the harsh, hot climate of Australia, it's possible that marsupial females were able to survive more easily than other female mammals.

35.–38.

Male Teacher: In my opinion, the most beautiful part of the country is the Southwest. I'm referring specifically to the land in the states of Arizona, New Mexico, Utah, and Colorado. If you ever get a chance to go there, you should. One reason that the region is so amazing is that there are a large number of different land features there. You all know about the Grand Canyon in Arizona. Canyons are quite impressive. But, before we discuss them, I want to cover three other land features. They are buttes, mesas, and plateaus. Cathy, your hand is up. Do you have a question?

Girl: Yes, Mr. Wilkinson, I do. I thought that buttes, mesas, and plateaus are pretty much the same. I mean, um, they are, aren't they? All three of them are just raised areas of land.

Man: Well ... You're correct to some extent, Cathy. All three of them are similar. But they also have some distinct differences. Why don't I tell you about them right now?

Basically, class, Cathy is right about one thing: Buttes, mesas, and plateaus are all land formations that are higher in elevation than their surrounding areas. They also have steep sides. Oh, and they all have relatively flat tops. Nevertheless, despite these similarities, they have differences as well.

Let's start with buttes. Buttes are the smallest of the three features. They are also, uh, in my opinion, the most spectacular. A butte is basically the remains of a mesa after most of the mesa has been eroded away. Buttes have extremely steep sides that can rise hundreds of feet above the ground. They usually have flat tops, but they can have pointed tops at times. That's due, uh, to the effects of erosion.

As for mesas, they are larger than buttes and are not as steep or high as them. Furthermore, there's one major difference between mesas and buttes. Mesas have standing water on their tops. This is typically in the form of a lake or pond. Buttes, on the other hand, lack water. If you ask some people in the west, they will say that if you can graze cattle on the land, it's a mesa. If you can't do that, it's a butte.

39.–42.

Male Teacher: Okay, so, uh, Napoleon's armies were still successful on the battlefield. However, the allied coalition captured Paris in March 1814. At that time, Napoleon's generals gave up. They basically told him that they—and their armies—would not follow him anymore. So, on April 11, 1814, Napoleon abdicated at Fontainebleau, France. When I say that he abdicated, I mean that he gave up his throne and all the power that went with it. The allied forces decided to send Napoleon into exile. They chose to send him to the island of Elba, which is, uh, in the Mediterranean Sea.

Napoleon went to Elba and remained there for ten months. His wife and son didn't accompany him there. And, while he was on the island, he heard rumors that there were plans to exile him to a place far from Europe. Given Napoleon's personality, there was no way that he was going to sit around and do nothing. On February 26, 1815, he escaped from Elba. This began the period in history known as the Hundred Days. Napoleon returned to France, won some soldiers to his side, and marched on Paris. As he did so, more soldiers and citizens joined him.

Soon, the allied forces realized that Napoleon had returned and was going to cause more trouble. They returned to the field of battle. While many Frenchmen had high hopes for Napoleon, he did not manage to remain in power. In June, Napoleon was defeated by the Duke of Wellington at the Battle of Waterloo. Once again, he was sent into exile.

This time, he wasn't allowed to remain anywhere near Europe. He was instead sent to the island of St. Helena.

Girl: Where's that? I've never even heard of it.

Man: Take a look at the map. It's way down here in the South Atlantic Ocean. It's, uh, it's pretty much in the middle of nowhere. Napoleon was also treated more like a prisoner rather than an emperor. He was kept in a house and permitted few freedoms. A few people from France joined him in exile, but he was constantly guarded by both British soldiers and the British navy to prevent him from escaping.

Explanations

Listening Comprehension

1. C；本题为预测题。对话中两位男生都成功入选了篮球代表队，根据原文 practice starts at 3:30 today 可推测，下午他们要参加训练，故本题答案为 C。

2. D；本题为修辞题。对话中老师因为女生第三次迟到而批评了她，根据原文 "I come to school with my younger sister, and she has trouble getting up in the morning." 可知，女生提及她妹妹是为了把迟到的原因归咎于妹妹的晚起，故本题答案为 D。

3. D；本题为推断题。男生正在向老师询问可以获得额外学分项目的相关信息，鉴于这个项目可以获得额外的学分，可以推测，男生想提高自己的学分，故本题答案为 D。

4. C；本题为细节题。根据原文"In that case, why don't I give you copies of the notes I take in each class?"可知，女生提出可以把她的课堂笔记复印给男生，故本题答案为 C。

5. B；本题为主旨题。男生因为在课上说话并且传纸条被课后留堂，男生试图和老师协商取消留堂，但是被拒绝了。因此对话的主题是男生被留堂的这一惩罚，故本题答案为 B。

6. D；本题为主旨题。对话中谈论了教科书的电子版本的好处——更轻、更便宜，以及比起纸质书，他们更愿意购买电子书，故本题答案为 D。

7. A；本题考查作者意图。通知提到了每个课堂展示的时长、所有学生做完展示需要的时间以及学生展示的顺序，故通知的目的是提供关于课堂展示的信息，答案为 A。

8. D；本题为细节题。根据原文"Do not go to your classroom. Instead, come to my office."可知，如果迟到了，不要直接去教室，而是要先去学校秘书的办公室。故本题答案为 D。

9. B；本题考查作者意图。通知告知了本周四和周五学校餐厅将暂时关闭，需要学生们自行携带午饭，故选项 B 符合题意。

10. B；本题为修辞题。根据原文"Mr. Conaway is much better than Mr. Jessie ever was."可知，女生提及 Mr. Jessie 是为了对比两位老师，故本题答案为 B。

11. C；本题为细节题。根据原文"I feel that I've improved a lot as a flutist this past year."可知，女生会的乐器是长笛，故本题答案为 C。

12. A；本题为推断题。根据原文"Everyone in my family is planning to be there, so I'd hate to put on a poor performance in front of them."可知，男生的家人都会去春季音乐会，有可能是他发出的邀请，故本题答案为 A。

13. B；本题为预测题。对话最后男生说"Well, we'd better get to band practice now."，女生则表示"You said it. Let's get going."。由此可推测，接下来他们将去参加乐队练习，故本题答案为 B。

14. D；本题为主旨题。对话主要是教练和男生在讨论男生是否参加篮球队选拔一事，故本题答案为 D。

15. B；本题为推断题。根据原文 and I'm counting on you to be a starter this season. 可知，教练认为男生有可能在本赛季成为首发队员。starter 表示队伍中较为优秀的运动员，故本题答案为 B。

16. C；本题为细节题。根据原文"My parents don't particularly want me to play ball this year though."可知，男生的父母不太愿意让男生今年参加篮球队，故选项 C 正确。

17. B；本题为修辞题。根据原文"I got a couple of low grades in, um, in math and science."可知，男生在数学和科学两门课上拿了低分，故选项 B 正确。

18. A；本题为主旨题。女生正在向老师咨询关于 research paper 的写作方法，包括如何写参考文献和脚注等问题，故本题的主旨是如何撰写研究论文，答案 A 符合题意。

19. C；本题为语气题。space out 意为"发呆，走神"，故这句话的意思是老师还没有反应过来女生对他说的话，选项 C 符合题意。

20. A；本题为细节题。根据原文"I hope you use at least five sources, but I would prefer that you use more."可知，老师希望女生的研究论文引用五处以上的信息来源，选项 A 符合题意。

21. B；本题为细节题。根据原文"If you look at that big handout I gave you yesterday, you'll see how to make both footnotes and a bibliography."可知，女生可以从昨天的讲义上了解脚注和参考文献的撰写方式，故本题答案为 B。

22. A；本题为推断题。在对话中，老师给女生提供了许多帮助，在对话结尾还表示，如果女生还有其他问题可以再来办公室找他。由此可以推断，老师十分乐于帮助女生，故选项 A 符合题意。

23. B；本题为主旨题。对话中，男生和女生在讨论下个学期的选课事宜，故选项 B 符合题意。

24. B；本题为细节题。根据原文"I wish I had taken Spanish, but it's too late for me to change now."可知，男生提到自己本想选西班牙语课，而现在要换课已经太迟了，表现出了自己没有选西班牙语的遗憾，故本题答案为 B。

25. A；本题为推断题。根据原文"Plus, I love math, and physics has a good deal of math in it."可知，男生喜欢数学，故本题答案为 A。

26. C；本题为细节题。根据原文 "But, as for me, I'm going to sign up for the computer science class. That's what I'm hoping to major in when I go to college." 可知，男生的大学专业想选计算机，故本题答案为 C。

27. C；本题为主旨题。在讲座中老师主要讲到了耳朵的三个组成部分以及每个部分扮演的角色，故选项 C 最能概括所讲内容。

28. A；本题为修辞题。根据原文 "Take a look at the picture on page fifty-eight in your textbooks." 可知，老师提到课本是为了让学生们看图，故本题答案为 A。

29. C；本题为细节题。根据原文 "The pinna is a part of the outer ear. It helps collect sound waves as they move through the ear." 可知，pinna 是外耳的一部分，作用是收集声波，故选项 C 符合题意。

30. B；本题为细节题。根据原文 "The other two parts—the vestibule and the three semicircular canals—are used for balance. They're filled with fluids and help us maintain a sense of balance whenever we move." 可知，vestibule（前庭）以及 the three semicircular canals（半规管）是用来保持平衡的，故本题答案为 B。

31. D；本题为细节题。根据原文 "As you might have guessed from the list I just gave you, the vast majority of marsupials live in Australia." 可知，marsupial（有袋类动物）主要生活在澳大利亚，故本题答案为 D。

32. A；本题为修辞题。根据原文 "As for here in North America ... Well, the only marsupial native to this continent is the opossum." 可知，作者提到 opossum 是因为它是北美洲本土唯一的有袋类动物，故本题答案为 A。

33. B；本题为细节题。根据原文 "Almost every female mammal has a placenta in her womb. The baby—or babies—develops and grows in the womb and gets nourishment from the placenta. A marsupial, however, doesn't have a placenta." 可知，几乎所有的雌性哺乳类动物都有胎盘，但是雌性的有袋类动物没有，故本题答案为 B。

34. A；本题为推断题。根据原文 "Nowadays, as I mentioned, marsupials primarily live in Australia and South America. DNA testing has shown that they actually originated in South America. However, marsupial fossils have been found on every continent. Thus they were once much more widespread." 可知，DNA 测试显示有袋类动物最初源于南美洲，现在主要生活在澳大利亚和南美洲，但是它们的化石却遍布各大洲。由此可推测，它们过去的数量比现在更多，故本题答案为 A。

35. B；本题为主旨题。老师提到了三种地理特征，并着重描述了其中两种——buttes 和 mesas 的特征，故选项 B 最能概括主题。

36. D；本题为推断题。根据原文 "In my opinion, the most beautiful part of the country is the Southwest. I'm referring specifically to the land in the states of Arizona, New Mexico, Utah, and Colorado. If you ever get a chance to go there, you should." 可知，老师认为全国西南部最美，并且推荐没有去过的人去那里看看。由此可以推断，他应该去过并且亲自领略了那里的美景，故本题答案为 D。

37. C；本题为细节题。根据原文 "Buttes have extremely steep sides that can rise hundreds of feet above the ground." 可知，孤山有陡峭的斜坡，可以高出地面数百英尺，因此本题答案为 C。

38. A；本题为预测题。讲座一开始老师说他将介绍三种地理特征，现在已经讲了其中两种，由此可推测，接下来他将继续讲述第三种——plateaus 的特征，故本题答案为 A。

39. A；本题为主旨题。老师在讲座里主要讲的是拿破仑政权的末期，以及那段时期拿破仑的经历，故本题答案为 A。

40. B；本题为细节题。根据原文 "The allied forces decided to send Napoleon into exile. They chose to send him to the island of Elba, which is, uh, in the Mediterranean Sea." 可知，第一次流放的时候，拿破仑被送去了地中海上的厄尔巴岛，故本题答案为 B。

41. B；本题为细节题。根据原文 "On February 26, 1815, he escaped from Elba. This began the period in history known as the Hundred Days." 可知，百日王朝开始于拿破仑逃离厄尔巴岛之时，故本题答案为 B。

42. D；本题为修辞题。提到拿破仑第二次被流放的 St. Helena 时，学生表示从没有听过那个地方，老师说道，"Take a look at the map. It's way down here in the South Atlantic Ocean."。由此可知，老师提到地图是为了向学生展示 St. Helena 的具体位置，故本题答案为 D。

Language Form and Meaning

1. C；本题考查词义辨析。send 意为"邮寄，发送"，throw 意为"投，扔"，cast 意为"投票"，write 意为"写作，编写"。cast ballot 为固定搭配，意为"投票"，故本题答案为 C。

2. D；本题考查介词用法。结合上下文可知，投票涉及 Caroline 和 Mark 两个人，两人之间介词应该使用 between，故本题答案为 D。

3. B；本题考查定语从句。整个定语从句修饰先行词 speech，关系词可以是 that 或者 which，而 A 选项中 amazed 后面缺少 by，故不选，因此本题答案为 B。

4. B；本题考查词义辨析。concerned 意为"担心的"，serious 意为"严肃的"，ambitious 意为"有抱负的"，considerate 意为"体贴的"。前一句说 Mark 是一个喜剧人，前后语气有转折，所以本题应该选一个和喜剧人意思相反的词，故答案为 B。

5. A；本题考查修饰语。本空为 party 的修饰语，consisting 为现在分词作定语，修饰 party，故本题答案为 A。注意，consist 这个单词本身为不及物动词，且只用于一般时态，也不用于被动结构。

6. D；本题考查句子结构。Following 为现在分词作时间状语，表示在晚饭后这个时间将观看电影，故本题答案为 D。

7. A；本题考查词义辨析。guest 意为"客人"，movie 意为"电影"，program 意为"节目；项目"，dessert 意为"甜品"，结合上下文可知，接下来将介绍一位客人，故答案为 A。

8. B；本题考查句子结构。本句建议学生报名这项特别的活动，表达建议或者邀请的时候应该使用祈使语气，故本题答案为 B。

9. C；本题考查动词时态。由前文可知，作者描述的是过去发生的事情，故应该使用一般过去时 rushed。

10. B；本题考查比较级。此处作者在对比过去和现在的状态，并且现在的状态好多了，所以应该使用比较级 much better。

11. A；本题考查时态。此处陈述的是经常性和习惯性的事情，即 Caroline 笔记记得很好，故应该使用一般现在时。

12. A；本题考查词义辨析。lend 意为"借出，借给"，tell 意为"告知"，borrow 意为"借入"，transfer 意为"转移"，结合句意可知，本题答案为 A。

13. A；本题考查句子结构。结合句意可知，chaperone（监护人）就是发出通知的人，在介绍自己职责的时候，一般使用介词 As，且和后半句的主语一致，故本题答案为 A。

14. C；本题考查词义辨析。trip 意为"旅行，旅游"，flight 意为"航班；飞行"，abroad 意为"在国外"，country 意为"国家"，结合句意可知，这是一趟出国旅游，故本题答案为 C。

15. C；本题考查词义辨析。our 为形容词性物主代词，意为"我们的"，后面应该填一个名词，故本题答案为 C。

16. B；本题考查情态动词。此处老师正在提醒学生近期要注射的疫苗，故应该使用情态动词 should。should 作情态动词时，表示建议、劝告或义务，常用来表示在现在或未来某个时间点应该做的事情。

17. A；本题考查介词。a list of 意为"……的清单"，故此处应该使用介词 of。

18. A；本题考查句子结构。根据下文可知，这样就能保证你有所有可能用得上的东西，故本空应该填 every item。

19. D；本题考查词义辨析。regard 意为"认为"，promise 意为"承诺，保证"，await 意为"等待，期待"，ensure 意为"确保，保证"，结合句意，本题答案为 D。

20. C；本题考查词义辨析。remember 意为"记得"，think 意为"认为，觉得"，hesitate 意为"犹豫"，attempt 意为"努力，尝试"。do not hesitate to do sth. 为固定搭配，意为"不要犹豫，尽管……"，故本题答案为 C。

21. A；本题考查词义辨析。employ sb. as 意为"雇用某人为……"，as 后面应该是名词，故本题答案为 A。

22. C；本题考查词义辨析。contract 意为"合同"，money 意为"钱"，compensation 意为"报酬，薪水"，currency 意为"货币"，结合句意可知，本题答案为 C。

23. A；本题考查句子结构。根据句意可知，作者统计了目前为止已经确定合作的公司数量，故应该选一个表示"目前"这个时间的表述，故本题答案为 A。

24. C；本题考查时态。本句描述的是正在发生的动作，故应该使用现在进行时。

25. D；本题考查宾语从句。which 为 of 的宾语，构成介宾结构，从句修饰先行词 firms，故本题答案为 D。

26. D；本题考查句子结构。作者正在描述谈判结束后发生的事情，once 意为"一……就"，与 after 意思相近，故本题答案为 D。

27. B；本题考查词义辨析。requested 意为"要求的"，mandatory 意为"强制性的"，implemented 意为"应用的"，deliberate 意为"故意的"，结合下一句"学生也可以忽略"可知，本题答案为 B。

28. A；本题考查词义辨析。competition 意为"竞争者，对手"，application 意为"申请"，interview 意为"面试"，registration 意为"登记，注册"，an advantage over 意为"比……有优势"，根据句意可知，本题答案为 A。

29. D；本题考查固定搭配。lie with 为固定搭配，意为"在于"，故本题答案为 D。

30. D；本题考查词义辨析。参加运动用 participate in 或者 join，根据空后的介词 in，可知答案为 D。

31. A；本题考查句子结构。since 引导的原因状语从句的主语是 volleyball 和 basketball，故主语应该为表示复数的 they，故本题答案为 A。

32. C；本题考查句子结构。前一句提到了天气好的时候人们会打棒球，根据这一题的后半句可知，填空处说的是天气不好的时候，during 表示"在……期间"，故本题答案为 C。

33. B；本题考查词义辨析。本空前面是介词 in，应填单词为介词的宾语，in length 为固定搭配，意为"在长度上"，故本题答案为 B。

34. A；本题考查词义辨析。concentrated 意为"集中的"，focused 意为"专注的"，stressed 意为"焦虑的"，adorned 意为"被修饰的"，根据句意，本题答案为 A。

35. A；本题考查固定搭配。come to one's mind 为固定搭配，意为"出现在脑海里"，故本题答案为 A。

36. B；本题考查定语从句。定语从句修饰先行词 island，故关系词用 which。

37. D；本题考查时态。本句描述的是发生在过去的事情，故应该使用一般过去时，答案为 D。

38. B；本题考查词义辨析。relevant 意为"有关的"，notorious 意为"臭名昭著的"，uncaught 意为"未被抓的"，harmless 意为"无害的"，根据句意可知，本题答案为 B。

39. C；本题考查让步状语从句。even though 引导让步状语从句，意为"虽然有几次越狱的尝试"，且因为发生在过去，所以应该使用一般过去时，故本题答案为 C。

40. D；本题考查词义辨析。condemn 意为"谴责"，execute 意为"处决"，rehabilitate 意为"休养生息"，recapture 意为"重新捕获"，根据句意，本题答案为 D。

41. A；本题考查比较级。本题比较了恶魔岛以及其他旧金山的有名景点，两者之间的比较需要使用"比较级 more+ *adj.* + than"，故本题答案为 A。

42. C；本题考查词义辨析。focus 意为"重点"，destination 意为"目的地"，setting 意为"场景"，location 意为"地点"，结合句意，本题答案为 C。

Reading Comprehension

1. C；本题为主旨题。本通知的主要内容是因为恶劣天气，运动日被取消了，故选项 C 最能概括主旨。

2. A；本题为指代题。该句出现了两个 it，指代的都是同一个单数名词。根据句意可知，it 会在周四晚到达该市，而且将逗留好几天，故 it 指代的是前一句中的 a severe storm front。

3. D；本题考查词义辨析。anticipate 意为"预期，预料"，appear 意为"出现"，worry 意为"担心"，deny 意为"拒绝承认"，predict 意为"预计，预言"，故本题答案为 D。

4. D；本题为细节题。第一段第三句提到风暴锋面将于周四晚抵达该城市，而且会逗留好几天，接着第四句提到"The storm is expected to drop several inches of rain once it begins."，由此可推断，周五的天气是风暴锋面导致的大雨，选项 D 正确。

5. C；本题为推断题。根据原文 ...most sports day activities are held outdoors 可知，大部分运动日的活动都在室外举行，由此可推断，也有一些在室内举行的活动，故选项 C 正确。

6. C；本题为细节题。根据原文 "Since teachers may not have prepared lesson plans for classes during that time, they may feel free to watch movies or to do other similar activities in their classes." 可知，原本是活动日的周五，因为活动取消，老师们可以安排观看电影或者其他类似的活动，故选项 C 正确。

7. B；本题考查词义辨析。compulsory for 意为 "对……来说是强制性的"，advise 意为 "提出建议"，be required for 意为 "对……来说是必需的"，be stated by 意为 "由……陈述"，insist upon 意为 "坚持"，故本题答案为 B。

8. B；本题为主旨题。文章介绍了 Centerville High School 的一位学生获得的各种奖项与荣誉，故选项 B 最能概括文章主旨。

9. A；本题考查词义辨析。outdone oneself 意为 "超过自己原来的水平"，与选项 A 含义相符。

10. B；本题为指代题。Ms. Barton 在 it 中获得了冠军，由此可知，it 指代的是前面提到的拼写比赛，故本题答案为 B。

11. D；本题考查词义辨析。setback 意为 "挫折"，victory 意为 "胜利"，competition 意为 "竞争；比赛"，entertainment 意为 "娱乐"，loss 意为 "失败"，故本题答案为 D。

12. C；本题为推断题。根据原文 "Writing about her life as an immigrant, Ms. Barton captured first place." 可知，Ms. Barton 是一位移民，故选项 C 和原文相符。

13. A；本题为细节题。当 Ms. Barton 被问到下一步的计划时，她说： "I'm on my school's math team, and we have a big tournament coming up. With luck, our team will do well."由此可知,她接下来将参加数学比赛,故本题答案为 A。

14. D；本题为修辞题。根据原文 "Modern-day airplanes are mostly jets." 可知，作者提及 jets 是为了说明目前最常见的飞机类型，故本题答案为 D。

15. A；本题考查词义辨析。propel 意为 "推进，驱动"，drive 意为 "驾驶"，encourage 意为 "鼓励"，ignite 意为 "点燃"，pull 意为 "拉，拽"，结合句意可知，选项 A 与原文最接近。

16. C；本题为细节题。第三段提到了螺旋桨的数量以及它与发动机相连接，第四段提到了螺旋桨的形状，故选项 A、B、D 均有提及。文章并没有提到螺旋桨的大小，故本题答案为 C。

17. A；本题为细节题。根据原文 "In doing so, the propeller can create lift as well as thrust. These two factors enable a propeller first to move an airplane forward and then to help it get off the ground." 可知，螺旋桨通过制造升力和推力使飞机起飞，故本题答案为 A。

18. C；本题考查词义辨析。initial 意为 "最初的"，experimental 意为 "实验性的"，successful 意为 "成功的"，first 意为 "首次的"，practice 意为 "练习"，故本题答案为 C。

19. D；本题为推断题。根据原文 "The first airplanes relied upon propellers to fly. In fact, it was not until a few decades after the Wright brothers' initial flight that advanced jet airplanes were made." 可知，最初的飞机依靠螺旋桨起飞，在怀特兄弟的第一架飞机诞生的几十年之后才出现了更先进的飞机，所以可以推断怀特兄弟最初制造的飞机也有螺旋桨，故本题答案为 D。

20. A；本题为主旨题。文章介绍了水獭的各种特征，故选项 A 最能概括文章内容。

21. C；本题为修辞题。根据原文 "They are found mostly in North and South America, Europe, and Asia." 可知，作者提及 "North and South America, Europe, and Asia" 是为了说明目前已发现的水獭的栖息地，故本题答案为 C。

22. D；本题为细节题。第一段第五句提到，水獭尾巴很长，选项 C 符合原文。下一句提到它们四肢很短，而且是蹼足，选项 B 符合原文，故选项 D 为答案。

23. D；本题为细节题。根据原文 "Otters reach maturity fairly quickly and begin to mate when they are two years of age." 可知，水獭两岁就开始交配，由此可推测选项 D 正确。

24. C；本题考查词义辨析。dependent upon 意为 "依赖于"，suspicious of 意为 "对……持怀疑态度"，attach to 意为 "附着于"，reliant on 意为 "依赖于"，aware of 意为 "意识到"，故本题答案为 C。

25. B；本题为推断题。根据第三段内容可知，水獭是天生的游泳能手，所以它们很容易就能学会游泳。但是尽管如此，幼年水獭在一岁之前都会和妈妈在一起，直到学会如何自行捕猎才会离开妈妈，自己独自生活。由此可推测，捕猎比游泳更难，故本题答案为 B。

26. D；本题为指代题。those 指代的是并非是水獭觅食第一选择的那些动物，即前半句中提到的 "reptiles, amphibians, and birds"。故本题答案为 D。

27. A；本题为修辞题。根据原文 "Further out at sea, killer whales frequently hunt them." 可知，killer whale 是水獭在海里的掠食者，故本题答案为 A。

28. C；本题考查词义辨析。take a toll on 意为 "对……产生负面影响"，由此可知划线部分的意思是水獭总体数量下降，故选项 C 符合原文。

29. D；本题为细节题。由第四段第一句可知，水獭捕食鱼类和甲壳类动物，因此，甲壳类动物不是水獭的掠食者，反之，水獭是它们的掠食者，故本题答案为 D。

30. A；本题为主旨题。文章主要介绍了什么是摄影记者以及他们的工作内容，故选项 A 最能概括文章主旨。

31. B；本题为修辞题。根据原文 "Dorothea Lange was an American photojournalist. She became famous for the pictures she took during the Great Depression in the United States in the 1930s." 可知，提及 Dorothea Lange 是为了说明她因为拍摄美国大萧条时期的照片而出名，故本题答案为 B。

32. D；本题为细节题。根据原文 "Eddie Adams gained renown for his pictures taken during the Vietnam War." 可知，Eddie Adams 以拍摄越南战争时期的照片而闻名，故本题答案为 D。

33. A；本题考查词义辨析。influential 意为 "有影响力的"，significant 意为 "重要的，意义重大的"，appropriate 意为 "合适的"，respected 意为 "受人尊重的"，famous 意为 "著名的"，故本题答案为 A。

34. C；本题为推断题。根据原文 "Due to the influence of photojournalists in modern society, a large number of people have entered the field." 可知，摄影记者在社会上有一定的影响力，由此可推断，选项 C 正确。

35. A；本题为细节题。根据原文 "In some cases, photographs taken by paparazzi can sell for hundreds of thousands of dollars." 可知，在一些情况下，记者拍摄的照片能卖到成百上千美元，故选项 A 正确。

36. C；本题考查词义辨析。pervasiveness 意为 "普遍性"，cheapness 意为 "便宜，廉价"，quality 意为 "质量"，commonnesss 意为 "普遍，常见"，popularity 意为 "流行，受欢迎"，故本题答案为 C。

37. B；本题为主旨题。文章描述了第一次环球旅行，该次旅行是由 Ferdinand Magellan 的几位船员完成的，选项 B 最符合文章主旨。

38. B；本题为细节题。第一段提到，大航海时代起源于欧洲的 15 世纪，欧洲人首先去到了非洲，然后通过印度洋来到了亚洲，在世纪末，还去了美洲。全文没有提及澳大利亚，故本题答案为 B。

39. A；本题考查词义辨析。circumnavigate 意为 "环航"，go around 意为 "绕行"，explore 意为 "探索，考察"，learn about 意为 "了解"，map 意为 "地图"，故本题答案为 A。

40. D；本题为细节题。原文第三段提到，1950 年 11 月，Magellan 终于找到了进入太平洋的路线。但在寻找过程中，他的一艘船撞上了沙滩并且撞毁了。由此可知，选项 D 正确。

41. B；本题考查词义辨析。engage in trade 意为 "从事贸易"，故本题答案为 B。

42. D；本题为指代题。Magellan 船队的航行是由西班牙国王赞助的，因为西班牙和葡萄牙正在交战，所以抓获他们的只能是葡萄牙人，故 them 指代的就是葡萄牙人，故本题答案为 D。

Practice Test 7

Answers

Listening Comprehension

1.~5. CBCAD	6.~10. ABCBC	11.~15. CBDDA	16.~20. BCACB
21.~25. ABBBA	26.~30. CBCCB	31.~35. CCACA	36.~40. CBBAB
41.~42. DB			

Language Form and Meaning

1.~5. DCAAC	6.~10. ABABD	11.~15. BBBDA	16.~20. BDDCA
21.~25. ADDBC	26.~30. CABDB	31.~35. CDABD	36.~40. BCABA
41.~42. AA			

Reading Comprehension

1.~5. BDDBC	6.~10. DCBAB	11.~15. BBDAA	16.~20. DCCAC
21.~25. CBACB	26.~30. DCBCB	31.~35. DBDDD	36.~40. BCDBA
41.~42. DD			

Scripts

1.

Boy:	Are you going to attend the tutorial that Mr. Sanders is giving during study hall?
Girl:	Definitely. I want to make sure I understand the material for the test he's going to give. I've heard that his tests are really tough.
Boy:	That's exactly what I've heard as well. I'm going to be sure to pay close attention during the tutorial.

2.

Man:	Sam, you still haven't turned in your essay. When can I expect to receive it?
Boy:	Sorry, Mr. Crawford, but I've been too busy with my French assignment to complete it. Do you mind if I turn it in tomorrow?
Man:	Well, you can give it to me then, but you're going to lose five points for tardiness. You've had a week to work on it.

3.

Girl:	Mr. Walker, have you graded our exams yet?
Man:	I'm afraid not, Alice. I've already checked the exams for the students in first period, but I haven't gotten to your class's tests yet.
Girl:	Oh ... When do you think you'll get them back to us?
Man:	Hmm ... I expect to return them to your class no later than this Thursday.

4.

Girl:	Chris, do you happen to have your science notebook on you now?
Boy:	No, I don't. I left it in my locker. How come?
Girl:	Would you mind if I copied your notes from today's class? I left my notebook at home, so I didn't take any today.
Boy:	No problem. I'll give it to you after next period ends.

5.

Man:	Jacqueline, I thought your poem was really creative. How did you come up with the idea for it?
Girl:	Um ... It just came to me in a flash of inspiration.
Man:	Well, I hope you have more instances like that. I was impressed by what you wrote. Keep up the good work.
Girl:	Thanks for saying that, Mr. Duncan.

6.

Boy:	I like that new student. Uh, you know, Jeff. He seems like a good guy.
Girl:	Tell me about it. I spoke with him during break today.
Boy:	Apparently, he and his family recently moved here from Florida.
Girl:	That's what he told me. Life here will be a little different than what he's used to, but I'm sure he'll get along well.

7.

Woman:	Listen up, everyone. I went over the homework assignments you submitted yesterday, and it's pretty clear that most of you didn't understand the material. There were a lot of wrong answers to the problems. I thought I had explained everything clearly, but, uh, apparently I didn't. So we're going to go back over the material to make sure you all understand it.

8.

Man:	There's one more thing I need to discuss. It's my policy on pop quizzes. I like to give at least one per week. Anytime I give a pop quiz, it will be at the start of class. Each quiz will be worth ten points, so it counts toward your final grade. If you do the reading, you're pretty much guaranteed to get a perfect score.

9.

Man:	Next Friday, we're going to have the school's annual field day. It's going to last all day long, so there won't be any classes at all. Instead, we'll play games, eat a picnic lunch, and have lots of fun. All of your parents are invited as well, so be sure to let them know about the date.

10.–13.

Girl:	Hey, Greg. I see you just finished up soccer practice. Volleyball practice ended for me only a few minutes ago.
Boy:	That's great. How is the team looking this year? Do you think you'll have a winning record?
Girl:	Oh, we definitely expect to do well. All of the starters from last year's squad are returning, and that team only lost three games all year. If you ask me, I'd say we have a great shot at winning the state championship.
Boy:	That's awesome news. I hope the team meets expectations.

Girl:	So, uh, what about the soccer team? How do you guys expect to do?
Boy:	We're hoping to have a winning record. But, um ... I don't know if I am going to be a part of the team this year.
Girl:	Huh? Tryouts are already over, and you made the team. Coach Murphy isn't going to cut you now, is he? After all, you're a starter.
Boy:	No, it's not that. It's just that I'm having trouble keeping my grades up right now. I'm taking two advanced placement classes—in math and history—and you know how much work they are. Since the team either practices or plays every day, I'm losing a lot of valuable study time.
Girl:	You shouldn't quit though. It's your senior year. This is your last chance to be on the team.
Boy:	But what about my grades?
Girl:	Hmm ... We're in the same AP classes, right? Why don't we get together after practice every day and study? I could invite a couple other members of the team to join our study group. They get good grades. So we could help each other.
Boy:	That just might work. What do you say to having our first meeting tomorrow?
Girl:	It sounds perfect. I'll talk to Jenny and Karen later tonight.

14.–17.

Woman:	Jeff, you said that you wanted to talk to me about something. Do you have a moment to chat right now?
Boy:	Yes, ma'am. I think I've got a few moments before my next class.
Woman:	Great. So what's going on? Is everything okay in class?
Boy:	Class is going great. I think I understand most of the material we're learning. But, uh, I have a question about our upcoming lab assignment.
Woman:	You're talking about the one where we dissect some animals, right?
Boy:	Yes, that's the one. You see ... uh, I'm a little squeamish, and I'm not quite sure how I'm going to react to cutting up animals. Do I have to do this assignment?
Woman:	First of all, I wouldn't worry too much. After all, it's not like we're going to be dissecting dogs, cats, or any other cute animals. For our first lab assignment, we're simply going to cut up a few worms.
Boy:	Worms? That's it?
Woman:	That's it. You don't have a problem with worms, do you?
Boy:	No, not at all. In fact, I use worms as bait every time I go fishing. I don't think I'll have any problems with the lab in that case.
Woman:	That's great to hear. But do me a favor ... If you have a problem dissecting something else in the future, just tell me. I can excuse you if you really think you can't do it. About two or three students opt out of doing it each year, so it's not a big deal.
Boy:	That's good to know. Thanks for telling me that.

18.–22.

Girl:	Mr. Cussler, Tommy just told me that you wanted to speak with me about something. He wasn't pulling my leg, was he?
Man:	No, he wasn't. I know Tommy is something of a joker, but he was telling you the truth. I did ask him to find you for me.
Girl:	Well, uh, here I am.
Man:	Indeed. Anyway, it's about your science project. You were supposed to submit the status report on it to me yesterday, but you never did that. What's going on?
Girl:	Oh, the status report. I totally forgot to email it to you. I've been so busy with classes and other things that it slipped my mind.
Man:	That's all right. I understand. Well, uh, since you're here, why don't you just give me the status report

now? If I remember correctly ... you are doing some sort of chemistry experiment in your father's laboratory at work, right?

Girl: That's right.

Man: How's it going?

Girl: The lab work is pretty much all finished. I got some interesting results. They weren't quite the results that I had predicted, but they're still unique.

Man: Okay. And how about the report you're going to write? How's progress on it going?

Girl: Actually, uh ... I haven't even started on it yet. I know there are only two more weeks until it's due, so I'm going to get to work on it tomorrow. Is that all right?

Man: I suppose that's fine for now. But be sure to send me a status report next Monday. I need to know how you're doing with that report.

Girl: Sure. I can handle that.

23.–26.

Boy: Betsy, you don't look happy right now. Is something the matter?

Girl: Yeah, I've got a big problem. I am completely overwhelmed by all of my work. I'm probably going to fail the history test we have this Thursday, too. I simply can't seem to remember any of the information for it.

Boy: I'm sure that if you keep studying, you'll do well on it.

Girl: That's easy for you to say. You always get good grades in school. It's a lot harder for me though.

Boy: You just need to try hard. That's all I do.

Girl: You must have a few tips that you can give me. Go ahead and fill me in. What should I do to improve my grades?

Boy: Well, why don't you tell me where you usually study?

Girl: I pretty much study in my bedroom. I lie down on my bed and do most of my studying and homework there.

Boy: Okay. That's your first mistake. You should never lie down while you're studying. All that does is make you sleepy. It's harder for you to remember things if you're trying to keep from falling asleep. Instead, sit at a desk. And you might want to play some soft music like, uh, classical music while you study.

Girl: Classical music? Are you serious? I always play rock music when I'm studying.

Boy: That's another mistake. Why don't you turn the music off? And don't watch TV either. You need to focus solely on the material you're studying. Oh, and one more thing ... Don't log on to the Internet while you're studying. You'll just get distracted. And you'll waste tons of time checking your email and your blog.

Girl: Yeah, that seems to happen to me a lot. Anyway, thanks. I'll try out your suggestions when I study later tonight. I hope they work.

27.–30.

Male Teacher: People often talk about one major event in human history that led to civilization. I'm talking about the discovery of agriculture. Once humans learned how to farm, they were able to settle down, build villages and towns, and, uh, basically create civilizations. But there's another event that helped humans considerably. Does anyone have a guess ... ?

Girl: Learning how to write?

Man: Well, yes, that was important, but it's not what I'm thinking about. I'm talking about the domestication of animals. There are a huge number of animals on the planet. But, throughout all human history, only a relative handful of them have been domesticated. People have tried domesticating many animals, but it's just not possible in most cases.

It's likely that the first animal which humans domesticated was the dog. No one knows for sure when this happened. But we can make an educated guess. DNA testing tells us that dogs and wolves are related. Sometime in the past, they separated into two distinct species. It probably happened around, oh, 100,000 years ago. Some experts believe it occurred in East Asia while others claim it took place in the Middle East. We don't know for sure though.

How did dogs and humans come to have such a close relationship? The most popular theory claims that they provided mutual benefits for one another. Dogs protected humans from animals and other humans. They also helped people hunt. In return, humans provided dogs with steady supplies of food. They also gave dogs relatively safe places to live. Over time, the two developed an extremely close relationship.

Girl: Do we know when the first dog was tamed?

Man: No, but, again, we can make an educated guess. There's a site in Germany where human and dog skeletons were found buried together. Those bones date back to around 14,000 years ago. A similar site in China has bones that date to 7,500 years ago. At a dig site in Siberia that's around 6,200 years old, a dog was found buried next to many humans in a cemetery. All three of those finds show how highly regarded dogs were in their communities. So we can infer that dogs had been domesticated in those places due to where they were buried.

31.–34.

Woman Teacher: One of the strangest-looking animals in the world is the anteater. Take a look at this picture of it up on the screen here ... The most obvious physical feature is the long snout, uh, or nose. The anteater uses its snout to dig in the ground for ants and termites, its two favorite foods. This animal you're looking at here is a giant anteater. It can grow to almost two meters in length. But a lot of that is its snout and big, bushy tail. So its body isn't that large. There are two other anteater species. They are the silky anteater and the southern tamandua. Both are a bit smaller than the giant anteater. Yes, Brenda? Your hand is up ... ?

Girl: Where does the giant anteater live?

Woman: It resides mostly in Central and South America. Its territory ranges from Mexico to northern Brazil.

Now, uh, how about some of its other physical characteristics ... ? Again, focus on the screen ... It has stiff, bristly fur that's brown or gray in color. Sometimes its fur can be so dark that it's almost black. Now, look at the snout. Notice that its mouth is at the very end of it. Cool, huh ... ? The anteater lacks teeth, but it has a very long tongue that can extend far from its mouth. Also, observe its paws. Each paw has very long, sharp claws. The anteater uses them to get inside an anthill or termite mound. Then, it uses its tongue to find ants and termites and to eat them. In case you're curious ... a single anteater can consume up to 35,000 ants in one day. Now that's a big appetite.

The giant anteater usually lives alone. It can be territorial at times, yet, as a general rule, it's rather docile. Pumas and jaguars sometimes hunt it, but it has few other natural enemies. Now, uh, how about watching a short video of an anteater attacking a termite mound? I think you'll find this fascinating.

35.–38.

Woman Teacher: It's going to be cold tonight. In fact, it's going to be so cold that we're supposed to get the first frost of the year. Now, uh, I know you've all heard that word before. But what exactly does it mean? What is frost ... ? Simply put, it's a type of frozen water. When the air has too much water vapor, it condenses. Then, it gets deposited on many surfaces, including, uh, including the ground, plants, cars, and windows. If the temperature is cold enough, the water vapor freezes and thereby forms frost. Frost always appears to be white in color. The reason is that the frost crystals contain air.

There are different types of frost. Let me tell you about three of them. Hoarfrost is one. That's H-O-A-R by the way. It resembles loose ice crystals. It can form on the ground or on virtually any object.

It often appears in the morning after a cold, clear night. It manifests when water vapor condenses on a very cold surface. What happens is that the water vapor freezes on contact.

A second type of frost is rime frost. Er, spell that R-I-M-E. There's a picture of it in your books on page 194. Take a look ... Note the ice crystals that are around the flower petals. It forms when icy wind blows and water vapor freezes on flowers, plants, and tree branches. Pretty, isn't it ... ? Oh, uh, I should make an important point about frost before we continue. One big problem with frost is that it can kill plants. If farmers plant their crops too early in the spring, a late frost can cause lots of damage, and many plants can die. In fall, if there's an early frost—like tonight's expected one—farmers need to harvest their crops to keep them from suffering any damage.

Now, uh, a third type of frost is fern frost. It's sometimes called window frost. There's a picture of it in your books as well. It resembles the leaves of a fern, doesn't it? This type of frost forms when you have a window pane that's very warm on the inside and very cold on the outside.

39.–42.

Woman Teacher: I know almost all of you have smartphones. And many of you have laptop computers as well, right? Go ahead and take out your smartphones if you have them with you ... Don't use them of course. Just take them out ... Look at them for a moment ... What do you think is special about them? Len?

Boy: They're so small. My dad showed me a picture of the first cell phone he ever owned. It was enormous. Oh, and it wasn't powerful at all.

Woman: Len is absolutely correct, class. Smartphones today are incredibly powerful devices that are also small. So are your laptop computers. But, uh, how about the first computers ... ? Do any of you know how big they were ... ? Nobody even wants to guess ... ? Okay. Let me show you. Turn to page 356 in your books ... Do you see that? That's ENIAC. It was one of the first computers ever invented. Do you see how large it was?

ENIAC was invented in 1946. It took up 167 square meters of floor space. That's about as big as an average four-bedroom house in this neighborhood. It weighed thirty tons. Tons. It was huge. It ran on vacuum tubes, of which it had more than 17,000. Just replacing the vacuum tubes as they quit working was practically a full-time chore. Oh, and as for its computing power ... The calculators that you use in your math class are much more powerful than ENIAC ever was.

Why am I telling you this ... ? Well, I want you to realize how technology often progresses. Improvements in technology tend to go from large to small ... from weak to strong ... and from slow to fast. We're going to cover the history of computers today. And I want you to focus on three words: smaller, stronger, and faster. Okay. We're going to begin with a man named Alan Turing ...

Explanations

Listening Comprehension

1. C；本题为主旨题。在整个对话中，男生和女生讨论了他们要去参加的桑德斯先生的辅导课程。故答案为 C。

2. B；本题为细节题。根据原文 ... but you're going to lose five points for tardiness. 可知，男生会因为晚交而丢掉五分。

3. C；本题为细节题。根据原文 "I expect to return them to your class no later than this Thursday." 可知，老师最晚周四会将试卷返给女生。

4. A；本题为预测题。女生向男生借科学课笔记，男生回答说："I'll give it to you after next period ends."。由此可知，男生在下一个课间结束后会借给女生他的笔记本。

5. D；本题为目的题。在对话中，老师告诉学生他认为她的诗 was really creative 并且他说 "was impressed by what you wrote."。由此可知，老师是在赞扬学生诗作的创造性。

6. A；本题为语气题。在对话中，女生回答男生："Tell me about it."，表示同意。由此可知他们对新学生有相同的观点。

7. B；本题为目的题。老师告诉学生由于他们没有理解课程的资料，因此她要求大家重新学习。由此可知，这则通知的目的是向学生解释为何要重新学习资料。

8. C；本题为主旨题。在通知中，老师解释了他进行突击测验的政策。故答案为 C。

9. B；本题为目的题。在听力音频中，校长正在向学生们说明学校一年一度的野外活动日会发生什么。

10. C；本题为主旨题。在对话中，学生们主要讨论男生这学期的学习问题。故答案为 C。

11. C；本题为细节题。根据原文 "All of the starters from last year's squad are returning." 可知，排球队去年的所有首发队员都将回归。

12. B；本题为细节题。在对话中男生说他有 AP 数学和 AP 历史两门课，然后女生说："We're in the same AP classes, right?"，由此可知，他们一起上 AP 历史课。

13. D；本题为推断题。首先女生说她可以邀请团队中的其他几个成员加入学习小组，之后她又表示 "I'll talk to Jenny and Karen later tonight."。由此可以推断出，Jenny 和 Karen 是排球队的队员。

14. D；本题为主旨题。对话中两个人主要谈论的是男生对即将到来的实验室任务的感受。故答案为 D。

15. A；本题为细节题。男生对老师说："I'm a little squeamish, and I'm not quite sure how I'm going to react to cutting up animals."。squeamish 意为"神经脆弱的；易心烦意乱的"，由此可知，男生可能会因为解剖动物而感到恶心。

16. B；本题为语气题。由于男生钓鱼时会用虫子当鱼饵，所以他在暗示他可以把虫子切碎。

17. C；本题为推断题。在对话的最后，老师表示："If you have a problem dissecting something else in the future, just tell me."，由此可以推断出，老师暗示学生们将在本学期晚些时候解剖虫子以外的动物。

18. A；本题为主旨题。在整个对话中，女生和老师主要谈论她在科学项目上的进展情况。故答案为 A。

19. C；本题为推断题。在对话中，学生说："Mr. Cussler, Tommy just told me that you wanted to speak with me about something. He wasn't pulling my leg, was he?"，pull someone's leg 表示"戏弄某人"。由此可以推断出女生暗示她认为 Tommy 在对她耍花招。

20. B；本题为细节题。根据原文 "Oh, the status report. I totally forgot to email it to you." 可知，她忘记把报告用电子邮件发给老师了。

21. A；本题为目的题。在对话中，老师问学生："How's it going?"，以了解她的实验室工作，然后学生回答了他的问题。

22. B；本题为细节题。根据原文 "But be sure to send me a status report next Monday." 可知，老师要求女生在下周一前交报告。

23. B；本题为目的题。根据原文 "I'm probably going to fail the history test we have this Thursday, too." 可知，女生提及历史考试是来表示她认为自己有可能挂科。

24. B；本题为细节题。在对话中，女生说她会躺在床上学习。继而男生回答道："You should never lie down while you're studying."，由此可知，男生告诉女生不要躺着学习。

25. A；本题为推断题。在对话中，男生让女生在学习时听古典乐。女生说："Classical music? Are you serious?"。需要仔细听女生的语气，从她的语气可以推断出她非常不喜欢古典乐。之后，她还表示她喜欢听摇滚乐。由此可以推断，她不喜欢古典乐。

26. C；本题为预测题。根据原文 "I'll try out your suggestions when I study later tonight." 可以推断出，女生晚上会试一试男生给她的学习建议。

27. B；本题为主旨题。在本段录音中，老师主要谈论狗的驯化问题。故答案为 B。

28. C；本题为推断题。根据原文 "There are a huge number of animals on the planet. But, throughout all human history, only a relative handful of them have been domesticated. People have tried domesticating many animals, but it's just not

possible in most cases." 可以推断出，老师暗示驯养动物很难。

29. C；本题为目的题。根据原文 "DNA testing tells us that dogs and wolves are related. Sometime in the past, they separated into two distinct species. It probably happened around, oh, 100,000 years ago." 可知，老师提及 DNA 测试是为了说明狗和狼成了不同的物种。

30. B；本题为细节题。老师推断说关于狗和人类拥有亲密的关系的一个最流行的理论是：狗和人类产生了互惠互利的关系。

31. C；本题为主旨题。老师在课堂上主要谈论了巨型食蚁兽的特征。故答案为 C。

32. C；本题为细节题。关于巨型食蚁兽，老师说："Now, look at the snout. Notice that its mouth is at the very end of it."，由此可知，它的嘴在它的口鼻部的最末端。

33. A；本题为推断题。老师提及了 "The giant anteater usually lives alone. It can be territorial at times, yet, as a general rule, it's rather docile."。territorial 意为"领土的，地盘性的"，如果描述一种动物的特征为 territorial，那就表示它会在其他动物侵犯它的领地时进行攻击。由此可以推断，老师暗示巨型食蚁兽会在其他动物进入它的领地时发起攻击。

34. C；本题为预测题。在讲座结束时，老师对学生说："Now, uh, how about watching a short video of an anteater attacking a termite mound?"，由此可以预测，接下来老师会在课上播放一段巨型食蚁兽的视频。

35. A；本题为细节题。关于白霜，老师提到 "It often appears in the morning after a cold, clear night."，由此可知，白霜经常出现在早晨。

36. C；本题为目的题。谈及冰霜时，老师告诉学生："There's a picture of it in your books on page 194. Take a look..."，由此可知，老师建议学生看课本的目的是看冰霜的图片。

37. B；本题为目的题。根据原文 "One big problem with frost is that it can kill plants. If farmers plant their crops too early in the spring, a late frost can cause lots of damage, and many plants can die. In fall, if there's an early frost—like tonight's expected one—farmers need to harvest their crops to keep them from suffering any damage." 可知，老师提到农民是为了说明霜冻是如何影响农民种植的作物的。

38. B；本题为推断题。关于蕨类植物霜，老师提道："This type of frost forms when you have a window pane that's very warm on the inside and very cold on the outside."，由此可以推断出，蕨类植物霜是在冷空气和暖空气共同存在的情况下形成的。

39. A；本题为主旨题。老师主要谈论了历史上的第一台电脑，包括其大小和名称，故答案为 A。

40. B；本题为细节题。关于 ENIAC，老师说："It took up 167 square meters of floor space. That's about as big as an average four-bedroom house in this neighborhood."，由此可知，ENICA 的体积和一座房子差不多。

41. D；本题为目的题。根据原文 "Oh, and as for its computing power... The calculators that you use in your math class are much more powerful than ENIAC ever was." 可知，老师提及计算器的目的是比较它与 ENIAC 的计算能力。

42. B；本题为预测题。根据原文 "We're going to cover the history of computers today. And I want you to focus on three words: smaller, stronger, and faster. Okay. We're going to begin with a man named Alan Turing." 可以预测，接下来她会继续进行她的讲座。

Language Form and Meaning

1. D；本题考查固定搭配。be available for 意为"可用于……的"，由于该通知是发给学生的，所以要选择 you 作为宾语的选项。故答案为 D。

2. C；本题考查定语从句。定语从句修饰 options，省略关系词 that。此外，该句子描述未来的活动，所以 may choose 作动词。故答案为 C。

3. A；本题考查固定搭配。dress pants 意为"正装长裤"，故答案为 A。

4. A；本题为词义辨析题。improper 意为"不适当的"；approved 意为"被正式接受的"；formal 意为"正式的"；purchased 意为"已经购买的"。故答案为 A。

5. C；本题为词义辨析题。sincerely 意为"真诚地"；repeatedly 意为"重复地"；practically 意为"差不多，几乎，实际地"；apparently 意为"显而易见地"。由此可知，本题答案为 C。

6. A；本题考查动词时态。句子描述过去发生的事情，由此排除选项 B 和 C。选项 D 为过去完成时，表示在另一个过去行动之前就已经完成了的动作。而根据该句的时态，前面出现的动词 understood 为一般过去时，后面的动词时态应一致。故本题答案为 A。

7. B；本题考查宾语从句。根据句意可知，应选择表达"答案为 0"的选项。主句中 aware 为动词，后面的从句为 aware 的宾语，选项 B 中的 that 引导宾语从句。

8. A；本题考查固定搭配。根据句意可知，学生在问朋友是否有空闲时间。而表示"空闲时间"的表达就是"a spare moment"。故答案为 A。

9. B；本题为词义辨析题。schedule 意为"安排，预定"；cancel 意为"取消"；resume 意为"重新开始"；delay 意为"延迟，推迟"。故答案为 B。

10. D；本题考查固定搭配。根据上下文可知，前半句提出的是另一个选择，因此需使用"instead of + *v.*-ing"的搭配。

11. B；本题考查时态。根据上下文可知，句子时态为一般将来时，故答案为 B。

12. B；本题考查单词形式。根据原文，or 连接两个并列的名词，前面的 questions 为复数形式，因此后面的名词也应该为复数形式。故答案为 B。

13. B；本题考查动词形式。"resort to + *v.*-ing"意为"诉诸，采取……的行动"，故答案为 B。

14. D；本题为词义辨析题。request 意为"要求"；imitate 意为"模仿，仿效"；preserve 意为"保留；保存；保护"；copy 意为"抄写；复制；作弊"。故答案为 D。

15. A；本题为词义辨析题。excessively 意为"过分地，过度地"；reputedly 意为"据说"；conservatively 意为"保守地，谨慎地，适当地"；restrictively 意为"限制地"。故答案为 A。

16. B；本题考查固定搭配。表示"从……方面"时，应使用固定搭配 in...way。故答案为 B。

17. D；本题考查宾语从句。why 引导宾语从句，用于寻求解释。故答案为 D。

18. D；本题为词义辨析题。extreme 表示"极端的，极度的"；negligent 表示"疏忽的"；virtual 表示"虚拟的"；light 表示"轻的"。故答案为 D。

19. C；本题考查句子结构。根据上下文可知，and 连接的两个分句都是表示对作弊学生惩罚的建议，再根据前半句中的 ought to 可判断，后半句应该使用同样表示建议的 should。故答案选 C。

20. A；本题考查形容词比较级。本题应该选 severe 的比较级 more severe 作为答案，故答案为 A。

21. A；本题考查同位语。根据上下文可知，答案应为 Dr. Enrico Prado 的同位语，应该是一个名词短语。故答案为 A。

22. D；本题考查比较级。根据句意，当作家有一本新书出版时，通常用 the latest 来表达，意为"最新作品"。故答案为 D。

23. D；本题为词义辨析题。nonfiction 意为"非虚构文学"；presumptuous 意为"自负的，专横的"；traditional 意为"传统的"；global 意为"全球的"。故答案为 D。

24. B；本题为词义辨析题。attendance 意为"出席，参加"；highlight 意为"最好的部分，强调"；show 意为"演出"；convenience 意为"方便"。故答案为 B。

25. C；本题考查单词形式。根据上下文可知，该处修饰后面的名词 King Arthur，答案应为形容词形式。故答案为 C。

26. C；本题考查句子时态。根据上下文可知，该句应为一般将来时。故答案为 C。

27. A；本题考查句间关系。whereas 表示对比，前半句 Parents and local citizens are welcome to attend 表达的意思是家长和当地居民不需要强制参加，后半句的意思与之相反，故答案为 A。

28. B；本题考查形容词比较级。"形容词比较级 + than"意为"比……更……"，所以本题应该选 high 的比较级 higher 作为答案，故答案为 B。

29. D；本题考查句子结构。and 后面的分句中的 they 指代前半句中的 positions，根据句意可知，本空意思为"它们是如何影响人们的生活"，因此答案为 D。

30. B；本题为词义辨析题。sliced 是 slice 的被动语态，意为"被切"；divided 是 divide 的被动语态，意为"被分开，被分成……份"；cut 是 cut 的被动语态，意为"切，剪"；repeated 是 repeat 的被动语态，意为"重复"。故答案为 B。

31. C；本题考查后置定语。非谓语动词作后置定语修饰 sky，省略了 that is。

32. D；本题为词义辨析题。register 意为"注册，登记"；pester 意为"打扰，纠缠"；suggest 意为"建议"；consider 意为"认为，视为"。根据上下文可知，答案为 D。

33. A；本题考查句子结构。非谓语动词作状语，因此答案为 A。

34. B；本题为词义辨析题。refute 意为"反驳，驳斥"；predict 意为"预测"；enable 意为"使能够，使实现"；assume 意为"假设"。根据上下文可知，答案为 B。

35. D；本题考查比较级和最高级。根据 one of 可知，本题应选择 important 的最高级形式，因此答案为 D。

36. B；本题考查句子结构。Unlike 在句首，表示对比，意为"不像是……"。故本题答案为 B。

37. C；本题为词义辨析题。portray 意为"描绘"；appear 意为"出现"；behave 意为"表现"；result 意为"结果"。根据上下文可知，答案为 C。

38. A；本题考查动词的时态。根据上半句中的 held 可以判断，答案应为动词的一般过去时。因此本题答案为 A。

39. B；本题考查句子结构。根据下文"For instance, he was..."可知，he 为本句主语的代词，因此本句主语应为 King，故答案选 B。

40. A；本题考查单词形式。根据 other 可知，本题答案应为名词形式。故答案为 A。

41. A；本题考查强调句。It was 和 that 之间是被强调的部分，in part 意为"部分地"，thanks to 意为"归因于，幸亏"。答案为 A。

42. A；本题为词义辨析题。award 意为"授予，奖励"；trade 意为"交易，营业"；nominate 意为"提名"；donate 意为"捐赠"。根据上下文可知，答案为 A。

Reading Comprehension

1. B；本题为主旨题。该文章主要是一篇和新来的科学老师的一次对话记录。故答案为 B。

2. D；本题为推断题。根据原文"She was kind enough to sit down for an interview with *The Quill and Paper*."可以推断出，*The Quill and Paper* 是报纸的名字。故答案为 D。

3. D；本题为细节题。根据原文 ... she double-majored in chemistry and biology as an undergraduate while simultaneously getting a minor in physics. 可知，她的两个主修专业和一个辅修专业都在科学领域，所以她在本科时确实专注于科学。故答案为 D。

4. B；本题考查固定搭配。当提到 spark someone's interest 时，表示某人对做一些活动感兴趣和好奇。故答案为 B。

5. C；本题为推断题。根据原文"Finally, Ms. Burgess added that she welcomes student participation in her classes."可以推断出，老师希望学生可以在课上积极发言，故答案为 C。

6. D；本题为词义辨析题。consistently 意为"一贯地，始终如一地"；recently 意为"最近"；reportedly 意为"据报道，据传说"；expressly 意为"明确地，清楚地，特意地"。由此可知，expressly 是 specifically 的同义词。故答案为 D。

7. C；本题为细节题。本文为一则发给学生的通知。根据原文"Therefore they are looking to replace their paid tutors with volunteers."可知，当地小学正在物色学生成为他们的新导师。因此答案为 C。

8. B；本题为指代题。根据上下文可知，it 指代前面的 transportation。故答案为 B。

9. A；本题为细节题。根据原文 "A teacher here can provide transportation to your school and home if you require it." 可知，他们不要求学生们自己去辅导学校，学校提供交通工具。因此答案为 A。

10. B；本题为推断题。根据原文 "To qualify as a tutor, you must have an A average in the subject you wish to teach. You must also be of good character and be willing to work with young children." 可知，学生必须具备成为导师的资格，这意味着并非所有学生都有资格成为导师。因此答案为 B。

11. B；本题为词义辨析题。recommend to 意为"推荐给……"；excuse from 意为"免除……"；request by 意为"要求，请求"；appoint to 意为"指派到……"。由此可知，excused from 与题目中的 exempted from 意思相近。故答案为 B。

12. B；本题为主旨题。这篇文章主要是关于木星的伽利略卫星的介绍。故答案为 B。

13. D；本题为细节题。根据原文 "Jupiter has at least sixty-three moons and may have more waiting to be discovered." 可知，木星至少有 63 颗卫星，可能还有更多的卫星有待发现。故答案为 D。

14. A；本题为目的题。根据原文 "Together, these four moons are called Galilean moons. The reason is that they were discovered by Galileo Galilei in 1610." 可知，这四颗卫星之所以被称为伽利略卫星，是因为它们是伽利略在 1610 年发现的。故答案为 A。

15. A；本题为推断题。首先，文章中提到 "In fact, one is larger than the planet Mercury while the other three are bigger than Pluto."。之后，文章中又说 "The largest of the Galilean moons is Ganymede."。由此可以推断出木卫三比水星大。故答案为 A。

16. D；本题为词义辨析题。engaging 意为"有趣的，迷人的"；seductive 意为"诱人的，性感的"；mysterious 意为"神秘的"；appealing 意为"吸引人的"。由此可知，appealing 是题干中 enticing 的同义词。故答案为 D。

17. C；本题为指代题。根据上下文可知，it 指代前半句中的 a thick layer of ice。故答案为 C。

18. C；本题为细节题。根据原文 "For instance, Io is one of the most volcanically active bodies in the solar system." 可知，木卫一是太阳系中火山活动最活跃的天体之一。故答案为 C。

19. A；本题为主旨题。这篇文章主要讲了化石对现代科学家的重要性。故答案为 A。

20. C；本题考查词义辨析。apply with 意为"应用"；bury at 意为"埋在……"；cover with 意为"被……遮盖"；remove from 意为"从……移除"。由此可知，covered with 与题干中 encased in 的意思相近。故答案为 C。

21. C；本题为指代题。根据上下文可知，they 指代前面的 the fossils。故答案为 C。

22. B；本题为细节题。根据原文 "In the case of plants, most fossils are simply impressions of the leaves or stems that are set in stone." 可知，大多数植物化石都不是完整的标本。故答案为 B。

23. A；本题为细节题。在文章中，作者完全没有提到恐龙是如何死亡的。故答案为 A。

24. C；本题为细节题。根据原文 "These permitted scientists to develop something called the geological time scale. It provides a detailed picture of life on the Earth throughout different periods of time." 可知，地质时间尺提供了地球上不同时期生命的详细图像。故答案为 C。

25. B；本题为推断题。根据原文 "For instance, dinosaurs first appeared around 250 million years ago and then vanished around sixty-five million years ago. Ever since then, mammals have dominated the planet." 中提到恐龙 "vanished around sixty-five million years ago" 可以推断，现在地球上没有恐龙存在。故答案为 B。

26. D；本题考查词义辨析。abandon 意为"放弃，抛弃"；live with 意为"与……一起生活，适应……"；survive on 意为"以……为生"；rule 意为"统治，控制"。由此可知，ruled 与题干中的 dominated 为同义词。故答案为 D。

27. C；本题为主旨题。这篇文章描述了人们正在使用的一些新型替代能源发动机。故答案为 C。

28. B；本题考查词义辨析。remove 意为"去除，移开"；change 意为"改变"；appear 意为"出现"；respond 意为"回复"。由此可知，change 是题干中 switch 的同义词。故答案为 B。

29. C；本题为推断题。根据原文"Nowadays, many engines are used to power cars and other forms of transportation. These vehicles most commonly have an internal combustion engine and rely upon gasoline for power. However, there are several types of engines that can use alternative energy sources. Many people are trying to switch to them because gasoline, which is a fossil fuel, creates pollution and is also a nonrenewable resource."可知，最常见的 gasoline 是化石燃料的一种，而替代能源不如化石燃料常见。故答案为 C。

30. B；本题为目的题。根据原文"Biofuels are fuels that are made from biological material, such as corn, soybeans, and sugarcane."可知，作者在文章中提到玉米、大豆和甘蔗，是因为它们是制作燃料的生物材料。故答案为 B。

31. D；本题为细节题。根据原文"In fact, most of the cars in Brazil have engines that can operate on either gasoline or biofuel."可知，巴西大多数汽车的发动机都可以使用汽油或生物燃料。故答案为 D。

32. B；本题为细节题。根据原文"The electric engine is utilized for city driving."可知，电动发动机可用于城市驾驶。故答案为 B。

33. D；本题考查词义辨析。resume 意为"重新开始，继续"；repel 意为"排斥，驱逐"；reveal 意为"揭示，透露"；refresh 意为"刷新，充电，恢复精力"。由此可知，refreshes 是题干中 recharges 的同义词。故答案为 D。

34. D；本题为细节题。原文中没有提到更换氢发动机电池有多容易或有多困难。故答案为 D。

35. D；本题为主旨题。文章主要讲的是罗马帝国的灭亡。故答案为 D。

36. B；本题考查词义辨析。regard 意为"关注，尊重"；purpose 意为"目的，使命"；assumption 意为"假设，猜想"；role 意为"角色"。由此可知，purpose 是题干中 intention 的同义词。故答案为 B。

37. C；本题为细节题。根据原文"There were many reasons that the Roman Empire fell."可知，罗马帝国灭亡的原因有很多。故答案为 C。

38. D；本题考查单词在原文中的含义。题干中 turmoil 的含义是"混乱"，与选项 D 中的 disorder 为同义词。

39. B；本题为细节题。根据原文"The Romans began to depend upon foreigners to man the armies that they kept on the borders of the empire."可知，罗马人开始依赖外国人来管理他们在帝国边界上的军队。故答案为 B。

40. A；本题为细节题。根据原文"Emperor Diocletian split the Roman Empire into two halves in the late fourth century."可知，戴克里先皇帝在四世纪末将罗马帝国一分为二。故答案为 A。

41. D；本题为目的题。作者在原文中提到，"The Eastern Roman Empire, which later became known as the Byzantine Empire, started to flourish. Its emperor ruled from the city Constantinople, which was built by Emperor Constantine I."，之后作者对东罗马帝国与西罗马帝国进行了对比。故答案为 D。

42. D；本题为指代题。根据上下文可知，He 指代前文中的 Odoacer。故答案为 D。

Practice Test 8

Answers

Listening Comprehension

1.~5. ACBCB	6.~10. DCBAD	11.~15. ACBCB	16.~20. CCDBC
21.~25. DBCAA	26.~30. ACAAC	31.~35. BDCDA	36.~40. DBBBA
41.~42. CC			

Language Form and Meaning

1.~5. DBBBD	6.~10. AADBA	11.~15. DCADC	16.~20. ABDAC
21.~25. BDCCB	26.~30. AACCB	31.~35. DDBCC	36.~40. AACDB
41.~42. AC			

Reading Comprehension

1.~5. CBBBC	6.~10. DBADC	11.~15. BDABA	16.~20. CDADA
21.~25. DADCB	26.~30. DDAAB	31.~35. AABDC	36.~40. ABBDA
41.~42. CD			

Scripts

1.

Boy:	Alice, I heard all about the math contest over the weekend. Way to go.
Girl:	Thanks for saying that. But I pretty much got lucky. I just happened to write down most of the answers before anyone else did.
Boy:	Don't be so modest. You got the highest score at the contest. Everyone says you were incredible and led the team to victory.

2.

Boy:	Mr. Jacobs, I have a question about my research topic. Is it all right if I write about hyenas?
Man:	Hyenas? Hmm ... I don't believe we studied them. And I specifically mentioned that your reports should be about an animal we covered in class.
Boy:	Oh, right. I had forgotten about that. I guess I'll come up with something else then.
Man:	Thank you.

3.

Girl:	How many colleges are you planning to apply to this year?
Boy:	I haven't made up my mind, but I'll probably apply to at least ten.
Girl:	Why so many? I'm only applying to three schools.
Boy:	I'm not sure where I want to go, so I want to apply to every place that I'm even remotely interested in.

4.

Boy: Sarah, you missed the bus this morning. What happened to you?

Girl: I stayed up late last night studying for our science test, so I got up too late to take the bus this morning.

Boy: Oh, I see. How did you manage to get here on time then?

Girl: My mother drove and dropped me off on her way to work.

5.

Girl: I can't believe you fell asleep in the middle of Mrs. Haught's class.

Boy: Well, I was so tired I could barely keep my eyes open in her class.

Girl: You'd better start going to bed earlier.

Boy: I know. Could you believe how mad she got at me? I was so embarrassed when she started chastising me in front of everyone else.

6.

Girl: Mr. Thompson, would you mind filling this out for me, please?

Man: Um ... What exactly is that?

Girl: Oh, sorry. I'm applying for a special summer program at the local college. So I need two letters of recommendation. I'm hoping you'll write one of them for me.

Man: Of course. It would be my pleasure. I'll give it back to you by tomorrow.

7.

Man: Everyone, please listen closely. We can't have gym class out on the field today since it's being watered now. Instead, we're going to have class in the gym. Everyone please take five minutes to change into your gym clothes. Then, we're going to do some warm-up activities. After that, we'll get a couple of basketball and volleyball games going.

8.

Woman: I want you to know that we're going to be holding elections for student government two weeks from today. The available positions are president, vice president, and secretary-treasurer. Student government is lots of fun and a great experience. I hope several of you decide to run for office. If you want to do so, please talk to me anytime this week.

9.

Woman: John Paul Jones is among my favorite people in American history. He was a member of the Continental Navy during the American Revolution. He was the captain of the *Bonhomme Richard*. During a battle with the English ship Serapis, he uttered one of the war's most famous quotes. When asked if he was ready to surrender, he responded, "I have not yet begun to fight."

10.–13.

Boy: That was a fun class we just had, wasn't it?

Girl: It sure was, Jim. I can't believe how entertaining it was.

Boy: Yeah, and Mr. Jackson said some really nice things about you as well.

Girl: I know. Can you believe what he said? I was completely shocked since he doesn't usually openly praise students like that.

Boy: Yeah, I guess you must have written an amazing paper. What exactly did you write about?

Girl:	Oh, it was nothing special. I just wrote my thoughts about how computers are likely to change society even more in the future. I imagine that Mr. Jackson must have agreed with what I wrote since he liked my essay that much.
Boy:	I suppose you're right. Well, congratulations on doing such a good job with your paper.
Girl:	Do you mind if I ask what you got on your paper?
Boy:	No, not at all. I got a 91. I did fairly well—not as well as you though. However, I was hoping to get at least a 95 since that would help me increase my grade. I'm trying to get from a B⁺ to an A⁻ by the end of the semester. But I don't know if I'll be able to do it.
Girl:	I'm sure you can. All you have to do is ace the final exam. It's worth, uh, twenty-five percent of our final grade.
Boy:	That's true. But I almost never do well on final exams because I have to study for so many tests at once. Still, I'm going to go home and start studying for the exam tonight. I simply have to raise my grade.
Girl:	Best of luck, Jim. I hope you can do it.

14.–17.

Man:	Janet, I need to have a word with you, please.
Girl:	Sure, Mr. Wilkinson. What's going on?
Man:	I'm interested in knowing when you're going to do your presentation. I know you have been trying to catch up with all of your work since you broke your arm, but all of your classmates did their presentations two weeks ago. I'd say that it's about time you did yours.
Girl:	Oh, all right. How does next week sound?
Man:	Not so good. I was thinking more along the lines of tomorrow.
Girl:	Tomorrow? B-b-but ... I couldn't possibly do that.
Man:	Janet, you've been back at school for a week. All of the teachers have been really easy going about letting you take your time doing makeup work. But, um, if you ask me, you're being too slow about this.
Girl:	I still don't think tomorrow is possible.
Man:	Then you can do it the day after tomorrow. That's Thursday. You can give your presentation as soon as class begins.
Girl:	Yes, sir. But I don't know if I'll do a good job or not.
Man:	I'm sure you'll do fine. I have confidence in you. You get good grades in all of your classes. Besides, it's only a five-minute presentation. It's not like you have to do that much preparation for it.
Girl:	I suppose you're right, sir. Okay. I'll definitely be ready to give my presentation first thing on Thursday morning.

18.–21.

Woman:	Good morning, Kevin. Are you ready to go to the museum for our field trip today?
Boy:	I guess so.
Woman:	What's the matter? Don't you want to go on the trip? I thought you'd enjoy getting out of school for the day.
Boy:	Oh, sure. It's always nice to do something other than just sit in class and listen to lectures. Uh ... no offense, of course.
Woman:	None taken.
Boy:	Anyway, uh ... I guess what I mean is that we always go to the museum. At least, we've gone on field trips to the museum for the past three years. And that's kind of boring, um, especially since the exhibits at the museum never seem to change. So we just look at the same things every year.
Woman:	Hmm ... You may have a point there. What do you suggest we do then?

Boy:	I suppose the easiest suggestion is for us to go somewhere else.
Woman:	Such as?
Boy:	Well ... if we want to go on a science field trip, we could visit the local university. Maybe a professor or two could show us around a laboratory. As for history, we could visit one of the old Civil War battlefield sites near here. And, um ... oh, I can't think of any more places off the top of my head.
Woman:	Those are two good ones you gave me. I'll talk to the other teachers about it while we're on the bus. Maybe we can arrange a trip to one of those places ... uh, or some other place ... later in the semester. But, for now, why don't you get on the bus? And try to enjoy the museum. Okay?
Boy:	Yes, ma'am. I'll do my best.

22.–25.

Boy:	I'm going to take a study break for a moment, Cynthia. I'm just about ready to fall asleep. I need to do something to wake myself up.
Girl:	Dylan, the test is in two days. And this is the third study break you've taken in the past hour. If you keep on taking breaks, we're not going to get enough studying done. And that's going to affect my grade, too.
Boy:	I can't help it. I'm so tired right now.
Girl:	Well, that's no surprise.
Boy:	Huh? What is that supposed to mean?
Girl:	I'm talking about the way that you live.
Boy:	I'm totally not following you. What do you mean about the way that I live?
Girl:	First of all, look at that food you're eating. You've got a bag of chips and a can of cola sitting on your desk. You simply can't consume all of that junk food and expect to have enough energy to study.
Boy:	So, uh, what am I supposed to do then?
Girl:	You need to eat healthier food. Look ... I'm not talking about eating bran muffins and stuff like that. But you need to have more fruits and vegetables in your diet. And cut out all of those trips to fast-food restaurants.
Boy:	But I love fast food. How is not eating at fast-food restaurants going to help me?
Girl:	Eating healthy food will provide your body with more nutrition. That way, you'll have more energy. So you won't get sleepy and yawn all the time while we're studying. Oh, here's something else you need to do.
Boy:	What's that?
Girl:	Exercise. I don't think I've ever seen you do any exercise other than during gym class. And you only give a half-hearted effort then. Here, uh, let me tell you a few things you can do to get into better shape ...

26.–29.

Male Announcer:	Hello, everyone. Welcome back to another episode of The David Mason Hour. I'm your host, David Mason, and we're live on KSTR radio. Tonight, our first guest isn't from this country. Instead, he's from across the Atlantic Ocean. His name is Ian Abernathy, and he's an exchange student from Scotland. Good evening, Ian.
Boy:	Good evening to you, Mr. Mason.
Man:	Ian, you've been here for the past three months. And during that time, you've made quite an impression on your fellow students. In fact, one of the things you've done is that you started a rugby club at your school. Now, uh, I don't know much about rugby. In fact, I don't know anything about it except that it's similar to football. Uh, I guess you call it American football in Scotland, right?
Boy:	That's right, Mr. Mason. I guess rugby and football have some similarities. Actually, uh, football developed from rugby.

Man:	That's fascinating. I never knew that. Would you happen to know about the history of rugby? Could you tell us a bit about it?
Boy:	I'll do my best. Rugby started in England sometime during the 1800s. It developed from the sport of soccer. People had been playing soccer throughout England for centuries. Then, one day, some students at the Rugby School ... uh, that's one of the oldest public schools in England ... some students decided to play a version of soccer in which they picked up the ball and carried it.
Man:	When did this happen?
Boy:	No one knows for sure. According to legend, it happened in 1823. A student named William Webb Ellis picked up the ball and ran forward with it. Whatever the case, the new style became popular. So, uh, people all around the country began playing it. The first rules for the game of rugby were written down in 1845. And the game continued to evolve throughout the 1800s. Um, I'm not boring you, am I? Shall I go on?
Man:	By all means. Please continue. I find this fascinating. And I'm sure our listeners do, too.

30.–34.

Woman Teacher:	In today's class, we're going to talk about plants. Now, uh, there are two main types of plants. Can anyone tell me what they are? Greg, why don't you try?
Boy:	Um ... Conifers and deciduous trees, right?
Woman:	Those are two types of trees, Greg. But trees are only one type of plant. I'm talking about all plants in general. Does anyone else want to try ... ? Hazel, your hand is up. What are the two main types of plants?
Girl:	I believe they are vascular and nonvascular plants.
Woman:	That's correct. Well done. First, I'm going to tell you about these plants in brief. Then, I'm going to show you some pictures to see if you can identify which kind of plant each one is.
	Okay. We'll start with vascular plants. Vascular plants have root systems and internal systems that allow them to move water and nutrients to different parts. Most vascular plants have roots, stems, branches, leaves, and flowers. They also typically have either flowers or nuts with seeds. Vascular plants come in a variety of sizes. They can be tiny flowers. And they can be enormous trees. As you've probably guessed, vascular plants make up the vast majority of plant species.
	As for nonvascular plants ... Well, um, they lack the internal transport systems that vascular plants have. Botanists classify nonvascular plants as bryophytes. That's a hard word to spell, but you can find it on the handout I gave at the end of yesterday's class ... Yes, Greg?
Boy:	I understand what vascular plants are. But what kinds of plants are nonvascular ones? I'm a little confused.
Woman:	Let me see ... Mosses are nonvascular plants. So are hornworts and liverworts. Don't worry if you don't know what those two plants are. I'm going to show you some pictures of them in a moment. All right?
	As for some other characteristics of nonvascular plants ... They do not produce flowers or seeds. Instead, they reproduce through the use of spores. Nonvascular plants are often limited in size. As a rule, they don't grow higher than twenty centimeters. They're also found mainly in moist habitats. That enables all their parts to absorb water from their surroundings. Now, let's get to those pictures ...

35.–38.

Woman Teacher:	Look at the screen, please. Check out these works of art. Here is the first one ... Here is the second one ... A third ... And a fourth ... Nice, aren't they? Bill, can you tell me what they're called?
Boy:	They're not murals. But, um, I think that the name for them begins with an M.
Woman:	You're right on both counts. They're not murals. And the word does begin with an M. Can someone help Bill?
Boy:	Wait. I've got it. They're mosaics.

Woman:	Nice. I'm glad you remembered that. Mosaics are a very old type of art. They're my favorite type of art as well. As you can see from this picture up here ... mosaics consist of many small pieces of material that are grouped together to form a picture. We call these small pieces tesserae ... That's T-E-S-S-E-R-A-E. In case you're curious, the word comes from the Latin language. It's the term used by the ancient Romans, who frequently made mosaics.
	Traditionally, a tessera ... er, that's the singular form, by the way ... a tessera was made of glass or stone. However, in the past, people used seashells, ivory, gems, and various metals. Many modern mosaic artists use ceramics. A tessera can be made in any shape, but squares are the most common.
	This is how an artist makes a mosaic. First, the artist finds some kind of surface. It could be something small, such as a vase. Or it could be a large surface, like a floor or wall. Then, the artist decides what the work of art will look like. After that, the artist glues the tesserae to make the picture. There are two main ways artists do the gluing. For small mosaics, the artist glues the tesserae to the object one at a time. For large mosaics, most artists glue the tesserae to paper and then glue the paper to the large surface.
	That's enough about mosaics. Now, let's make our own. I've prepared some paper, glue, and tesserae for you. Let's get to work and see what kinds of mosaics you can come up with.

39.–42.

Male Teacher:	In our area, most farmers harvest their crops from late summer to early fall. When the farmers do that, they suddenly have an enormous amount of food. So ... can anyone tell me what one of their problems is?
Girl:	They have to get all of that food to the market before it spoils. Otherwise, they won't make any money.
Man:	That's right. And how can they keep the food from spoiling?
Boy:	They have to preserve it some way.
Man:	Such as?
Boy:	My dad stores the grain we harvest in a couple of silos. The silos keep the moisture out, so the grain doesn't go bad. Other farmers dry their produce in the sun. That's what raisin farmers do.
Man:	Good, but you're all missing an obvious one.
Girl:	I've got it. Refrigeration. Farmers use it for both the crops they grow and the animals they slaughter.
Man:	That's correct, Beth. Nowadays, we don't think much about food preservation. Well, farmers think about it a lot. But most regular people don't consider it at all. However, since ancient times, one of the biggest problems humans have faced has been how to preserve their food. This is especially true for meat. People tried many different refrigeration methods ... Uh, no. That's not right. I mean preservation methods. People tried many different preservation methods throughout history. They dried food. They salted it. They buried it in the ground. They froze it in ice. They pickled it. Then, fortunately, refrigeration was invented. Do any of you know when that happened?
Boy:	It was during the nineteenth century.
Man:	Correct. The first refrigeration machines were built in the 1840s. Prior to the invention of refrigeration, people kept meat outdoors during winter. Others used big blocks of ice in ice boxes in their homes. But, thanks to refrigeration, people could keep their food cool—and preserved—all year round in any climate.
	Refrigeration was an instant success. Railroad companies built refrigerated cars to transport frozen meat and other food. By the 1870s, refrigeration ships were sailing the oceans. In the early twentieth century, refrigeration technology began to improve greatly. Home refrigeration machines became available to the wealthy. Then, in 1927, General Electric started making the first mass-produced refrigerator in the United States.

Listening Comprehension

1. A；本题为主旨题。在谈话的大部分时间里，男生和女生都在谈论女生在数学竞赛中的表现。故答案为 A。

2. C；本题为推断题。在对话中，男生说他想写关于鬣狗的文章，但老师说他们在课堂上没有研究鬣狗。根据男生接下来的回答 "I guess I'll come up with something else then." 可以判断，男生不会写关于鬣狗的文章。故答案为 C。

3. B；本题为细节题。根据原文 "I'm only applying to three schools." 可知，女生仅申请三所学校。故答案为 B。

4. C；本题为细节题。根据原文 "My mother drove and dropped me off on her way to work." 可知，女生乘坐汽车上学。故答案为 C。

5. B；本题为目的题。在对话中，女生说："I can't believe you fell asleep in the middle of Mrs. Haught's class."，紧接着她给出了对这件事的评价："You'd better start going to bed earlier."，由此可知，女生提起 Mrs. Haught 是为了指出男生在课上睡觉的行为。故答案为 B。

6. D；本题为语气题。女孩让老师给她写一封推荐信，老师回答说："It would be my pleasure."，意思是"我很乐意这样做"。由此可以推断出，老师对女生的评价很好。故答案为 D。

7. C；本题为目的题。在录音中，老师宣布学生们在体育课上要做什么。故答案为 C。

8. B；本题为目的题。根据原文 "Student government is lots of fun and a great experience." 可以推断，老师建议学生竞选的原因是学生可能会喜欢参与到学生会中。故答案为 B。

9. A；本题为主旨题。在录音中，老师主要谈论了约翰·保罗·琼斯这个人。故答案为 A。

10. D；本题为语气题。由于老师给了女生很好的评价，于是女生问男生："Can you believe what he said?"。由此可以判断，因为老师称赞了她，她可能感到很高兴。故答案为 D。

11. A；本题为细节题。根据原文 "I imagine that Mr. Jackson must have agreed with what I wrote since he liked my essay that much." 可知，女生认为老师同意她写的观点。故答案为 A。

12. C；本题为推断题。根据原文 "I got a 91. I did fairly well—not as well as you though." 可以推断，女生的成绩比男生高。而男生的成绩是 91 分，也就是 A，所以女生的成绩至少也是 A。

13. B；本题为推断题。根据原文 "Still, I'm going to go home and start studying for the exam tonight." 可知，男生今晚要回家复习。故答案为 B。

14. C；本题为主旨题。整个对话中，女生和老师主要讨论了女生要做的课堂陈述。故答案为 C。

15. B；本题为细节题。根据原文 "I know you have been trying to catch up with all of your work since you broke your arm, but all of your classmates did their presentations two weeks ago." 可知，女生摔断了胳膊。故答案为 B。

16. C；本题为推断题。根据原文 "All of the teachers have been really easy going about letting you take your time doing makeup work." 可以推断，老师们对女生很宽容，所以她还没有完成她的作业。故答案为 C。

17. C；本题为细节题。根据原文 "Then you can do it the day after tomorrow. That's Thursday." 可知，老师要求女生周四完成作业。故答案为 C。

18. D；本题为主旨题。对话主要讨论了男生对实地考察缺乏热情，以及为什么他对此没有感到兴奋。故答案为 D。

19. B；本题为语气题。在对话中，男生说他很高兴可以不在学校听讲座。然后他向老师道歉，老师回答："None taken."，由此可知，男生的评论并没有冒犯老师。故答案为 B。

20. C；本题为细节题。根据原文 "Well ... if we want to go on a science field trip, we could visit the local university." 可知，男生建议去当地大学进行实地考察。故答案为 C。

21. D；本题为推断题。根据原文最后 "But, for now, why don't you get on the bus?" 可以推断，男生接下来要乘车去博物馆。故答案为 D。

22. B；本题为推断题。根据原文 "And this is the third study break you've taken in the past hour. If you keep on taking breaks, we're not going to get enough studying done. And that's going to affect my grade, too." 可以推断，他们正在一起学习。故答案为 B。

23. C；本题为目的题。根据原文 "And cut out all of those trips to fast-food restaurants." 可知，女生建议男生不要去快餐店。故答案为 C。

24. A；本题为细节题。在对话中，女生多次提到男生需要吃有益健康的食物。故答案为 A。

25. A；本题为推断题。根据原文 "Exercise. I don't think I've ever seen you do any exercise other than during gym class. And you only give a half-hearted effort then. Here, uh, let me tell you a few things you can do to get into better shape." 可以推断，接下来女生会给男生一些锻炼的建议。故答案为 A。

26. A；本题为主旨题。男生主要介绍了英式橄榄球运动的发展情况。故答案为 A。

27. C；本题为细节题。根据原文 "Rugby started in England sometime during the 1800s." 可知，英式橄榄球起源于英格兰。故答案为 C。

28. A；本题为目的题。根据原文 "A student named William Webb Ellis picked up the ball and ran forward with it." 可知，威廉·韦布·埃利斯是第一个拿起球跑的人，因此他创造了英式橄榄球运动。故答案为 A。

29. A；本题为推断题。男生先问："Shall I go on?"，接着主持人说："By all means. Please continue."，由此可以推断，男生会继续讲关于英式橄榄球的事。故答案为 A。

30. C；本题为主旨题。老师主要讲了两种植物，有维管植物和无维管植物。故答案为 C。

31. B；本题为目的题。在谈论有维管植物时，老师讲了它的主要特征。故答案为 B。

32. D；本题为细节题。根据原文 "Mosses are nonvascular plants." 可知，答案为 D。

33. C；本题为细节题。根据原文 "Instead, they reproduce through the use of spores." 可知，答案为 C。

34. D；本题为推断题。根据原 "Now, let's get to those pictures." 可以推断，接下来老师会向学生展示一些图片。故答案为 D。

35. A；本题为推断题。根据原文 "They're my favorite type of art as well." 中的 as well 可以判断，比起绘画，老师更喜欢马赛克拼花艺术。

36. D；本题为目的题。老师提及 tesserae 是为了说明艺术家在制作马赛克时如何使用它们。故答案为 D。

37. B；本题为细节题。根据原文 "Many modern mosaic artists use ceramics." 可知，许多现代马赛克艺术家都使用陶瓷。故答案为 B。

38. B；本题为细节题。根据原文 "Or it could be a large surface, like a floor or wall." 可知，艺术家也会在一个大的表面，比如地板或者墙上做马赛克。故答案为 B。

39. B；本题为主旨题。原文主要讨论了人们使用的各种食品保存方法。故答案为 B。

40. A；本题为推断题。男生说："My dad stores the grain we harvest in a couple of silos."，之后他还提到了 other farmers。由此可以推断，男生可能住在农场里。故答案为 A。

41. C；本题为目的题。关于筒仓，男孩介绍了它是如何保存食物的。故答案为 C。

42. C；本题为细节题。根据原文 "The first refrigeration machines were built in the 1840s." 可知，第一台制冷机制造于 19 世纪 40 年代。故答案为 C。

Language Form and Meaning

1. D；本题考查句子结构。根据上文中的 a minor problem 可以推断，男孩的父母都不能送他去上学。几个选项中，one of 的含义是 "两者之一……"，both of 的含义是 "两者都……"，either of 的含义是 "两者中的任意一个……"，neither of 的含义是 "两者都不"。故答案为 D。

2. B；本题考查动词时态。根据上下文可知，男生在描述未来发生的事，所以应该选择一般将来时。故答案为 B。

3. B；本题为词义辨析题。hint 意为"提示，暗示"；idea 意为"主意，想法"；belief 意为"信仰"；thought 意为"思想"。have no idea 是固定搭配，意为"对……一无所知"。故答案为 B。

4. B；本题考查句子结构。首先从上下文可知，本句为疑问句，因此可以排除选项 A 和 D。"Would you mind doing?"句型通常用于面对陌生人或是较为正式的场合，用于表达委婉、客气的主观意愿。故本题答案为 B。

5. D；本题考查时态。根据上半句 the thunderstorm that happened over the weekend 可知，本句描述的是过去发生的事情，故时态应为一般过去时。故答案为 D。

6. A；本题为词义辨析题。sustain 意为"遭受，蒙受"；withstand 意为"抵住，经受住"；retain 意为"保持，保留"；replace 意为"代替"。根据句意可知，答案为 A。

7. A；本题考查句子结构。根据上下文可知，并不知道食堂会关闭多久，因此学生在得到通知之前都必须自己带午饭。选项 A 中，until 作为连接从句的连词放在句首，表示强调。

8. D；本题考查单词形式。根据上下文可知，此处应填入一个修饰名词 lunches 的形容词。因此答案为 D，boxed 的意思是"盒装的"。

9. B；本题是词义辨析题。audition 意为"试镜，试唱"；tryout 意为"（争取入队资格的）角逐赛，选拔赛"；rehearsal 意为"排练"；exercise 意为"练习"。根据上下文可知，答案为 B。

10. A；本题考查固定搭配。do one's best to do sth. 的意思是"尽力做某事"，故答案为 A。

11. D；本题考查单词形式。and 是连接词，前面是名词 speed，因为此处也应该选择一个名词。故答案为 D，endurance 的意思是"耐力"。

12. C；本题考查宾语从句。believe 后面接由 that 引导的宾语从句，故答案为 C。

13. A；本题考查宾语从句。what 引导宾语从句，也在从句中充当句子成分，它的含义是"……的人／事／物"，因此 what 不能够被省略。

14. D；本题为词义辨析题。decide 意为"决定"；think 意为"想，思考"；consider 意为"考虑"。前三个选项都为动词的现在进行时，而 D 选项 willing 是形容词，意为"愿意的"，be willing to do 是固定搭配，意为"愿意去做"。故答案为 D。

15. C；本题考查方式状语。根据句意可知，此处应选择一个介词短语，表示方式。故答案为 C，介词短语在句首，表示强调。

16. A；本题考查动词形式。use that money 后面应该接动词的不定式 to do，因此答案为 A。

17. B；本题考查修饰语。本句主语是 I，此处应选择 become 的宾语，故答案为 B。a member of 为固定搭配，意思是"……的成员"。

18. D；本题为词义辨析题。lecture 意为"讲课，讲授"；provide 意为"提供"；research 意为"研究"；sponsor 意为"赞助，资助"。根据上下文可知，答案为 D。

19. A；本题考查修饰语。and 连接两个并列的结构，根据前面的 spend time learning the piano 可知，and 后面也应该是动词的 doing 形式，因此可排除选项 B 和 C。根据句意，可以排除选项 D，因此答案为 A。

20. C；本题考查句子结构。I hope that + 宾语从句，根据后面的 has 可知，宾语从句的主语为单数。故答案为 C。

21. B；本题考查单词形式。根据前面的 a 可知，此处应选择名词形式，故答案为 B。shortage 意为"短缺"。

22. D；本题为词义辨析题。repeal 意为"废除，撤销"；implode 意为"内爆，突然崩溃"；experience 意为"经历，体验"；increase 意为"增加"。根据上下文可知，答案为 D。

23. C；本题考查词义辨析题。restricted 意为"受限制的，有限的"；confined 意为"受限制的，狭窄而围起来的"；frustrated 意为"沮丧的，失意的，懊恼的"；detained 意为"扣留的"。根据上下文可知，答案为 C。

24. C；本题考查动词时态。根据上下文可知，此处应为一般现在时。故答案为 C。

25. B；本题考查句子结构。so 引导一个表示结果的句子，时态应与前半句一致，因此应选现在进行时，表示正在做出退休的决定。故答案为 B。

26. A；本题考查固定搭配。根据上下文可知，"not...until..." 为固定搭配，意思是"直到……才……"，该句的意思是"许多人倾向选择那些不会让他们在学校待到三十出头的职业道路"。故答案为 A。

27. A；本题为词义辨析题。practice 意为"实践，练习"，treat 意为"治疗，招待"；diagnose 意为"诊断"；establish 意为"确立"。practice medicine 为固定搭配，意为"从事医学工作"，答案为 A。

28. C；本题考查状语从句。根据上下文可知，后半句为主句，前面需要选择一个状语从句，故答案为 C。

29. C；本题为词义辨析题。encourage 意为"鼓励，激励"；endorse 意为"支持，认可，赞同"；endeavor 意为"努力，尽力"；enjoy 意为"享受"。根据上下文可知，答案为 C。

30. B；本题考查比较级。"形容词比较级 + than" 意为"比……更……"，所以本题答案为 B。

31. D；本题考查定语从句。先行词是 students，因此关系词应为 who，且定语从句的谓语应为复数形式。故答案为 D。

32. D；本题为词义辨析题。gift 意为"礼物"；fine 意为"罚款"；grant 意为"（政府、机构的）拨款"；tuition 意为"学费"。根据上下文可知，答案为 D。

33. B；本题考查情态动词。根据下文的 "The money that we receive will..." 可知，此处应为一般将来时。would like to 表示意愿，故答案为 B。

34. C；本题考查介词短语。根据句意可知，需要奖学金的应该是来自低收入家庭的学生，from 表示"来自"，故答案为 C。

35. C；本题为词义辨析题。cost 意为"使损失，使丧失"；spend 意为"花费，度过"；afford 意为"承担得起，买得起"；purchase 意为"购买"。根据上下文可知，答案为 C。

36. A；本题考查比较级。根据上下文可知，with 后面应该接一个名词短语，advanced 的比较级是 more advanced。故答案为 A。

37. A；本题考查动词形式。根据句子时态可知，此处应为一般现在时。而且先行词 musicians 为复数形式，因此动词应该使用原形形式。故答案为 A。

38. C；本题为词义辨析题。listen 意为"听"；participate 意为"参加"；represent 意为"代表，表现"；appoint 意为"任命，委派"。根据上下文可知，答案为 C。

39. D；本题为词义辨析题。include 意为"包括，包含"；involve 意为"涉及，参与"；contain 意为"包含，含有"；consist 意为"由……组成"。strings 在这里意为"弦乐器"，根据上下文可知，答案为 D。

40. B；本题考查定语从句。根据主句的时态和句意，此处也应为一般现在时。故答案为 B。

41. A；本题考查句子结构。根据上下文可知，此处的主语应为 musicians。再看四个选项的意思，可知应该选择被动语态。故答案为 A。

42. C；本题为词义辨析题。stern 意为"船尾"；border 意为"边界"；rear 意为"后部，背部"；front 意为"前部，前面"。打击乐器一般位于交响乐团的后方，故答案为 C。

Reading Comprehension

1. C；本题为目的题。阅读全文后可知，这封信的作者描述了一个特别的项目，她认为她的朋友应该申请。故答案为 C。

2. B；本题为细节题。根据原文 "I am curious as to whether or not you are still planning to go on that skiing trip with your family this winter vacation." 可知，托马斯在寒假有可能和家人一起去滑雪。故答案为 B。

3. B；本题为推断题。根据在 "Apparently, Westfield State University, our local college, is going to hold an art seminar for thirty students." 中的 our local college 可以判断，这是一所当地的大学，可能在她家附近。故答案为 B。

4. B；本题为细节题。根据原文 "Apparently, Westfield State University, our local college, is going to hold an art seminar for thirty students." 可知，Westfield State University 将为三十名学生举办艺术研讨会，但并没有提及研讨会会持续多久。故答案为 B。

5. C；本题为细节题。根据原文 "However, you have to apply for a position. You can do that by submitting a sample of your work." 可知，可以通过提交作品样本来申请参加研讨会。故答案为 C。

6. D；本题为词义辨析题。omit 意为 "省略，忽略"；ignore 意为 "忽视"；forget 意为 "忘记"；miss 意为 "错过"。由此可知，miss 是题干中 pass up 的同义词。故答案为 D。

7. B；本题为推断题。根据原文中 once-in-a-lifetime event 可知，本次研讨会是千载难逢的机会。由此可以推断，作者在暗示托马斯以后不会再遇到类似的机会了。故答案为 B。

8. A；本题为目的题。阅读全文后可知，该公告主要内容是告知学生一名教师为何不再任教，并且提供了接替她的教师的信息。故答案为 A。

9. D；本题为细节题。根据原文 "Ms. Melvin suffered some serious injuries in a car crash over the weekend." 可知，Ms. Melvin 在车祸中受了重伤。故答案为 D。

10. C；本题为词义辨析题。appreciative 意为 "感激的，欣赏的"；determined 意为 "下定决心的"；positive 意为 "积极的"；convinced 意为 "被说服的"。由此可知，positive 是题干中 optimistic 的同义词。故答案为 C。

11. B；本题为词义辨析题。thank 意为 "感谢"，greet 意为 "欢迎，打招呼"；admit 意为 "承认，准许"；approve of 意为 "同意，允许"。由此可知，greet 是题干中 welcome 的同义词。故答案为 B。

12. D；本题为推断题。根据原文 "Mr. Potter was highly recommended by the principal of Centerville High School." 可以推断，波特先生的校长对他的工作表现应该是很满意的。故答案为 D。

13. A；本题为细节题。在原文中，校长建议学生："We expect you to be on your best behavior during the final month of the semester and to treat Mr. Potter as you do all of our other faculty members."。由此可知，校长希望学生们能像对待所有其他教员一样友好地对待波特先生。故答案为 A。

14. B；本题为主旨题。这篇文章描述了关于针灸的各种信息。故答案为 B。

15. A；本题为推断题。根据原文 "It was developed in China well over one thousand years ago..." 可以推断，针灸是在中国发展起来的。故答案为 A。

16. C；本题为细节题。根据原文 "Acupuncture involves the inserting of multiple needles into the body." 可知，针灸包括将多个针插入体内。故答案为 C。

17. D；本题为细节题。根据原文 "It is also becoming more common and attracting new patients in Europe and North America." 可知，针灸在欧洲和北美也越来越普遍，吸引了新的患者来尝试。故答案为 D。

18. A；本题为词义辨析题。useless 意为 "无用的，无效的"；doubtful 意为 "可疑的，不确定的"；abnormal 意为 "不正常的"；fraudulent 意为 "欺诈的，欺骗的"。由此可知，useless 和题干中的 ineffective 是同义词，故答案为 A。

19. D；本题为指代题。根据上下文可知，ones 指代前面的 studies，故答案为 D。

20. A；本题为主旨题。这篇文章主要讲了螳螂的特征。故答案为 A。

21. D；本题为细节题。文章中提到了一些螳螂捕食的动物，但没有讨论哪些动物捕食螳螂。故答案为 D。

22. A；本题为词汇题。blinding 的意思是 "使人视线模糊的"，blinding speed 可以引申为 "速度飞快"，故答案为 A。

23. D；本题为目的题。根据原文 "It eats other insects, especially moths, crickets, grasshoppers, and flies." 可知，作者提到这些昆虫的目的是描述螳螂的猎物有哪些。

24. C；本题为词汇题。struggling 的意思是"挣扎的"，由此可知这里说的是被螳螂抓住的昆虫在挣扎着试图逃脱，因此答案为 C。

25. B；本题为细节题。根据原文"They are small, have no wings, and cannot reproduce. Gradually, they transform into adult praying mantises."可知，螳螂幼虫体型小，没有翅膀，无法繁殖。故答案为 B。

26. D；本题为主旨题。本文主要讲了学校科学博览会上发生的事情。故答案为 D。

27. D；本题为词义辨析题。appearance 意为"外貌，外观"；outline 意为"轮廓，概述"；expectation 意为"预期，期待"；result 意为"结果"。由此可知，results 是题干中 outcomes 的同义词。故答案为 D。

28. A；本题为指代题。根据上下文可知，their 指代做出最终决定的 the judges，故答案为 A。

29. A；本题为细节题。根据原文"This is clearly the best science fair we've ever had."可知，Mr. Morrison 认为这届科学博览会无疑是目前为止最好的一届。故答案为 A。

30. B；本题为细节题。根据原文"So let's congratulate Sarah Rafael for the research that she did on bacteria."可知，Sarah Rafael 在博览会上展示了在细菌方面所做的研究。故答案为 B。

31. A；本题为推断题。根据原文"He designed and programmed his own computer game, which I know many of you had fun with. Let's congratulate Tim Simpson, the second-place winner."可知，Tim Simpson 设计的电脑游戏是大家可以玩的。故答案为 A。

32. A；本题为词义辨析题。magnificent 意为"宏伟的，壮观的，令人印象深刻的"；original 意为"起初的，独创的"；unmatched 意为"无双的"；imaginative 意为"富有想象力的"。由此可知，magnificent 和题干中的 breathtaking 为同义词，故答案为 A。

33. B；本题为主旨题。这篇文章重点介绍了各种类型的化学反应以及它们是如何发生的。故答案为 B。

34. D；本题为细节题。根据原文"In all cases, however, when there is a chemical reaction, a new compound is formed."可知，在任何情况下发生化学反应，都会形成一种新的化合物。故答案为 D。

35. C；本题为细节题。根据原文"There are six main types of chemical reactions. They are combustion, synthesis, decomposition, single-displacement, double-displacement, and acid-base reactions."可知，有六种主要的化学反应，而 physical reaction 并不属于化学反应。故答案为 C。

36. A；本题为词义辨析题。medium 意为"介质，媒介"；sponsor 意为"发起者，倡导者"；conversion 意为"转化，转变"；tool 意为"工具"。由此可知，medium 是题干中 catalyst 的同义词。故答案为 A。

37. B；本题为细节题。根据原文"Combustion happens when oxygen combines with another compound. When this occurs, heat and fire are produced. A catalyst, such as a spark, is needed for combustion to take place. One example of this is when gas and oxygen burn in a car's engine. The spark plugs in the engine provide the fire necessary to initiate the chemical reaction."可知，作者以汽车发动机中的汽油和氧气燃烧为例，解释发动机中的火花塞提供了启动化学反应所需的火，当氧气与另一种化合物结合时，就会发生燃烧。故答案为 B。

38. B；本题为目的题。根据原文"As for synthesis, it happens when two elements or compounds combine to form a new compound. For example, hydrogen and oxygen can unite to form water, and sodium and chlorine can come together to form salt."可知，作者举例氢和氧可以结合形成水，钠和氯可以结合形成盐，以此说明两种元素或化合物结合发生反应会形成一种新化合物。故答案为 B。

39. D；本题为指代题。根据上下文可知，it 指代上一句中的 decomposition。故答案为 D。

40. A；本题为词义辨析题。part 意为"部分，组成部分"；atom 意为"原子"；trait 意为"特征"；kind 意为"类别，分类"。由此可知，parts 和题干中的 components 为同义词。故答案为 A。

41. C；本题为词义辨析题。reveal 意为"揭示"；commit to 意为"承诺，承担责任"；trade 意为"交易，买卖"；join 意为"加入"。由此可知，trade 和题干中的 swap 是同义词。故答案为 C。

42. D；本题为细节题。根据原文"Last of all, acid-base reactions occur when an acid and base are combined. After exchanging protons, the two compounds form water as well as some kind of salt."可知，当酸和碱结合时，会发生酸碱反应。在交换质子后，这两种化合物会形成水和某种盐。故答案为 D。

Practice Test 9

Listening Comprehension

1.~5. BBDBA   6.~10. DBCBB   11.~15. ADBBD   16.~20. CCABB
21.~25. CBADD   26.~30. BDBCC   31.~35. DBACC   36.~40. ADDBD
41.~42. BB

Language Form and Meaning

1.~5. BCADC   6.~10. AACAC   11.~15. CABDD   16.~20. CCADA
21.~25. BCADC   26.~30. DABBB   31.~35. DAABD   36.~40. CABDA
41.~42. CD

Reading Comprehension

1.~5. CBADC   6.~10. BBBAC   11.~15. DBABD   16.~20. BACAC
21.~25. CCDDB   26.~30. CBACD   31.~35. CCBDA   36.~40. CBADA
41.~42. BB

Scripts

1.

Boy:	Did you do any of the reading for our social studies class?
Girl:	I read about half of the material. I'm planning to go over the rest during lunchtime.
Boy:	Do you think it's absolutely necessary to read everything before class?
Girl:	I think so. It definitely helps me understand the material Ms. Reardon teaches. And I don't mind doing the reading anyway.

2.

Girl 1:	You joined a couple of clubs this semester, right? I think I remember you said that.
Girl 2:	That's correct. I'm in the science club as well as the Spanish club. Oh, we have a meeting today if that's why you're asking.
Girl 1:	A meeting? Which club?
Girl 2:	The Spanish club. We're planning to get together in room 108 after school ends.

3.

Man:	Robert, you did a great job researching your history paper. I thought you made some good arguments in it. But ...
Boy:	But what?

Man:	Your paper had numerous grammar and spelling mistakes. You really need to proofread your work before submitting it. Ask one of your parents to help you.
Boy:	All right. I'll do that in the future.

4.

Girl:	Mr. Mayfield, um, about the homework that's due tomorrow. May I get an extension on it, please?
Man:	Why? You look healthy to me, Sandra.
Girl:	Oh, I'm fine. But the softball team has an away game tonight. So I won't be home until really late.
Man:	All right. Turn it in the day after tomorrow. But submit it first thing in the morning.
Girl:	Thanks.

5.

Boy:	Sue, I heard you want to talk to me about something. What's going on?
Girl:	Yeah, I was wondering if you understand the science homework. I can't figure it out at all.
Boy:	I know how to do it, but I don't have time to explain it now. How about giving me a call this evening?
Girl:	Sure. I can handle that. Thanks.

6.

Woman:	Dave, I gave you a B⁻ on your speech.
Boy:	That's not very good. What can I do to improve my performance?
Woman:	A few things. First, try to make more eye contact with your audience. Second, don't pause so much in between sentences. Third, try to speak clearly and in a more confident voice. Do those things, and you can get an A.

7.

Woman:	I believe most of you heard about the accident yesterday. Please be more careful when crossing the street. Only cross the street at the crosswalk. And be sure to look both ways before you leave the sidewalk. Do that even if the light is already red. Some drivers don't pay attention and run red lights. Your safety needs to be of the utmost importance.

8.

Man:	Two terms that people often get confused are latitude and longitude. These are imaginary lines that go east-west and north-south. I know many of you don't think they're important. But, on the contrary, they're incredibly vital for finding your location, especially if you're on a body of water or in a desert or forest. Now, let me tell you the difference between them.

9.

Man:	The bell's going to ring in just a minute, so let's stop for today. Let me remind you that your essays are due tomorrow. They should be between 800 and 1,000 words long. They can be typewritten or handwritten. Either way is fine with me. But all essays must employ the five-paragraph style. Any essays that don't use this method will receive failing grades.

10.–13.

Girl:	Mr. Lewis, the paper you just handed back had "see me" written on it.
Man:	Ah, yes, Lucy. That's right. I definitely need to talk to you about your essay.
Girl:	How come? There was only one mistake on it, so I assume I got a decent grade.

Man:	That's correct. In fact, you got a 99 on it. But your grade isn't the reason I want to speak with you about your paper.
Girl:	Uh-huh.
Man:	Are you aware of the city essay-writing competition that's coming up? It's going to be held approximately one month from now.
Girl:	I think I remember hearing something about the competition. But that's pretty much it.
Man:	Well, I think you ought to take part in the competition.
Girl:	Oh, sure. Do I just need to submit this essay? That should be fairly easy to do.
Man:	To be honest, it's not that simple. There is an actual competition you have to attend. The students who are competing in it are given a choice of two topics to write on. Then, they have one hour to write their essays. Once they're done, they submit their essays to the judges. The judges then determine who the winner of the contest is.
Girl:	So, um, I'd have a limited amount of time to write my essay. I see. Um ... That sounds like it's kind of difficult. I don't know if I can do it.
Man:	I'm sure you can. Your writing skills are good enough. You proved that to me with the essay you're holding there. Anyway, I'm currently helping three of your classmates prepare for the contest. If you want to join us, we meet in this classroom from three to four after school every day. What do you think?
Girl:	I guess I can give it a shot. I'll see you later today then.

14.–17.

Boy:	What are you planning to do after graduation?
Girl:	Hmm ... In the immediate future, I'm going to look for some part-time employment during the summer. I need to start saving money.
Boy:	Oh, I'm not talking about that. I mean, uh, are you going to go to college or do something else?
Girl:	I'm heading straight to college. I really wish I could travel abroad for a few months like a couple of my friends are doing. But doing that is simply out of my price range.
Boy:	I know exactly what you mean. As for me, I'm going to go to college. I'm just not sure which one since I haven't heard back from all of the places that I applied to yet.
Girl:	Same here. I'm still waiting to get letters from four places.
Boy:	What do you intend to major in?
Girl:	I am giving serious consideration to majoring in Chemistry. I love studying science, so I'd like to continue doing that. I just want to make sure I can take a lot of laboratory classes. For me, there's nothing more fun than doing experiments in the lab.
Boy:	I wish I were the same as you. I enjoy science like, uh, physics and biology, but I'm not particularly good at it. And I'm awful at math as well.
Girl:	In that case, what do you think you're going to major in?
Boy:	I have no idea. I guess I'm going to experiment by taking classes in several departments during my freshman year. I'll figure out what I like and what I'm good at, and then I'll make a decision on a major when I'm a sophomore.
Girl:	That sounds like a good plan to me.

18.–21.

Woman:	Hi, Jeremy. Is there something you want to speak about with me?
Boy:	Yes, ma'am. I'm curious why I got such a poor grade on my research paper. After all, I followed your directions. I had, uh, nine different sources for my work. That was what you wanted, wasn't it?
Woman:	Yes, Jeremy, I wanted you to have a variety of sources for your paper. However, the problem with your work was the sources you used. You had a large number of incorrect statements in your paper. When I

	checked your sources, I saw that you had gotten that incorrect information from them.
Boy:	Really?
Woman:	Yes. Really.
Boy:	But those websites looked so professional. The articles even had footnotes. I can't believe they had a bunch of wrong information.
Woman:	Jeremy, you've probably heard this before, but let me repeat it to you: Don't trust everything that you read on the Internet. You simply can't do that.
Boy:	Well, uh, how do I know which sources are legitimate then?
Woman:	That's a good question. In general, look for websites associated with schools and government agencies. They tend to deal mostly with facts. So do the websites of most magazines, journals, and newspapers.
Boy:	I see. But what if those websites get something wrong?
Woman:	You ought to confirm all of your facts by checking at least two or three different websites. If multiple websites give the same details, then the chances are high that the information is correct. There's also something else you can do.
Boy:	What's that?
Woman:	Use books. The library has plenty of encyclopedias and other reference books available. Try using them sometime. It might take you longer than searching the Internet, but the reference books in the library are invaluable. You can find out just about anything you need to know from them.

22.–25.

Boy:	Jane, how was your summer?
Girl:	It was good, but it's also nice to be back at school. I'm ready to start our last year of high school.
Boy:	I know what you mean. I feel the same way. Hey, I heard that you started playing a musical instrument over the summer. Is the rumor true?
Girl:	It sure is. I took flute lessons nearly every day.
Boy:	Are you going to join the school orchestra? We could definitely use another flutist or two.
Girl:	That's precisely what I'm planning to do. I learned a lot this summer, but I think it would benefit me if I were to join the orchestra. Do you know when auditions are going to be held?
Boy:	Er ... I don't think we have anything like tryouts. It's pretty much like this: If you want to join the orchestra and can play an instrument, you're in.
Girl:	Oh ... Is the orchestra not very serious if pretty much anyone can play in it?
Boy:	No, no. It's not like that. We only have twenty-five members. I'm not quite sure why our numbers are that low since there are so many students at our school. Well, uh, actually, I think the reason is that the previous band instructor wasn't very popular.
Girl:	How is the new guy?
Boy:	He's great. We all love him. But I guess the other students don't know anything about him yet. Perhaps, once everyone learns more about him, some more students will join the orchestra.
Girl:	I think I'd better hurry up and become a member then.
Boy:	I suppose so. Why don't you talk to the director after lunch? His name is Mr. Spartan, and his office is in room 203. Just introduce yourself to him. He's a nice guy, so there's nothing to be worried about.
Girl:	Great. I'll do that. And I look forward to our first practice session together.

26.–29.

Male Teacher:	After the Wright brothers made their first flight in 1903, numerous people began experimenting with powered flight. As a result, there were swift improvements in airplanes. Basically, airplanes became faster, safer, and larger.
	However, it wasn't until 1947 that one crucial milestone in the history of flight was achieved. It

took place on October 14, 1947. On that day, Chuck Yeager, who was a captain in the United States Air Force, piloted an experimental aircraft called the Bell X-1. His plane was powered by a special type of rocket fuel. Anyway, Yeager and his plane were airlifted high into the atmosphere by a B-29 Superfortress ... uh, that was an enormous bomber which was first manufactured during World War II ... well, the B-29 dropped the X-1, Yeager fired up the engines, and the plane quickly sped away. Soon afterward, Yeager reached a speed of Mach 1.06. And people on the ground heard the first manmade sonic boom. That's right. Chuck Yeager had just broken the sound barrier.

Now, uh, I made that feat sound really simple. But it wasn't. It took a, well, a tremendous amount of effort to break the sound barrier. In fact, people weren't even sure that it was possible. There were many scientists who believed it would act as a sort of physical barrier and therefore couldn't be exceeded. Obviously, um, they were wrong about that and lots of other things. But that's why people do experiments: to determine if something is possible or not.

Anyway, as soon as people realized it was possible to break the sound barrier, many different things happened. Obviously, one of them was that military aircraft became much faster. Today, a lot of them regularly exceed the speed of sound. Some can go two, three, or even four times faster than the speed of sound. In addition, civilian aircraft that could break the sound barrier were constructed. The first of these to be used as a passenger plane was the Tupolev Tu-144. It was a Soviet aircraft that flew for the first time in 1968. A few years later, in 1976, the French and British built the Concorde. It was a supersonic passenger plane that made regular flights from London and Paris to New York.

30.–34.

Woman Teacher: Check out the pictures on page thirty-one of your textbooks, please ... As you can see, there are three pictures. One is of some flowers. Another is of some trees. And the third is of some bushes. Flowers, trees, and bushes are all plants. Just by looking at them, it's obvious that they have many differences. For instance, um, they differ in size, appearance, and color. Yet all of these plants have similar parts. The three main parts of plants are ... Anyone?

Girl: I know. They are roots, stems, and leaves.

Woman: Correct. Of course, plants have more than three parts. But roots, stems, and leaves are their three primary parts. The roots are found at the bottoms of plants. They enter the ground and help anchor plants to the soil. As a result, this prevents plants from being blown away by the wind or getting swept away by flooding water. What else do roots do?

Boy: They absorb water and various nutrients from the ground.

Woman: Well done, Tommy. I'm glad you all seem to be on the ball today. Roots can take in both water and nutrients from the soil. Then, they transport them aboveground to the other parts of the plants. Oh, and one more thing about roots before we continue. You should be aware that the root systems of plants vary. Some are quite small. For instance, you can easily pull many flowers out of the ground by their roots. Others, especially trees, have extensive root systems. Some, such as pine trees, have something called a taproot. This is a root that grows straight down ... often quite deeply ... and makes a plant very hard to uproot. Many plants have root systems that spread widely. This is particularly common with desert plants. The roots of desert plants can extend very far in all directions in order to absorb as much water as possible in their dry environments.

Next up is the stem. The stem extends from the roots above the ground. It is typically long and slender. It is quite strong since it needs to support the rest of the plant. The plant's leaves branch off from it. So, uh, what exactly does the stem do? Anyone ... ? No? Okay. Let me tell you then.

35.–38.

Woman Teacher: Okay. So those are roughly the time periods when modern humans came to occupy the Earth's continents. As I just mentioned, Africa was where we believe modern humans, uh, Homo sapiens, evolved. This happened around 150,000 years ago. I also stated that the first modern humans are believed to have left Africa sometime around 70,000 years ago. Now, let me get this discussion started by asking a simple question: Why do you think modern humans left Africa ... ? Who wants to go first?

Boy: I'll try, Mrs. McKinney. Well, I know the first humans were hunter-gatherers. So most of them followed herds of animals around and hunted them. I suppose it's possible that some of those herds migrated out of Africa and headed into the Middle East and other lands.

Girl: But the Middle East is mostly a desert environment. Why would large herds of animals wander into the desert? There wouldn't be any food or water for them. That doesn't make any sense to me.

Woman: Not necessarily, Shannon. Think about it like this ... Is the climate in this region the same as it was, say, fifty years ago?

Girl: Fifty years ago? Wasn't there some huge drought then that lasted a few years? There's definitely no drought here these days. It rains all the time ... Oh ... I see your point.

Woman: Exactly. Climates change. Much of the Middle East is desert now, but it wasn't always the case. 70,000 years ago, it's possible that the Middle East was as green and fertile as this area here.

Boy: Hey, maybe that's another reason that the first humans left Africa ... climate. Perhaps a drought in some part of Africa forced them to leave the continent. And I suppose that war could be another reason.

Woman: That's right. Humans lived in small tribes then. It's entirely possible that defeated tribes left Africa in search of a new homeland. The winners would have stayed while the losers might have had no choice but to depart. Okay. I've heard three good reasons. But I want more. What other possible reasons could there have been for a mass migration?

39.–42.

Male Teacher: We can divide English literature into several periods. The earliest is known as Old English. This refers to works of literature that were written prior to, hmm ... around 1100 or so. Old English, by the way, is extremely different from modern English. In fact, if you read some Old English poetry, there's virtually no way you'd understand more than a handful of words. The most well-known work of literature from that period is *Beowulf.* I'm sure all of you have at least heard of it. It's an epic poem that tells the tale of the hero Beowulf and his battles against various monsters.

Well, unfortunately, we're not going to study any Old English literature this year. You'll have to wait until next year to do that. But we are going to study some works from the next period in English literature. The second period is known as Middle English. During that time, the English language was undergoing a lot of changes. It started to look more like modern English. However, Middle English is still hard to decipher. Uh, don't worry, by the way. We're not going to read anything in Middle English. We're going to read versions that have been rendered into modern English.

Anyway, uh, Geoffrey Chaucer was one of the most notable writers during this period. Ah, it lasted from around 1100 to 1500. After that, the next period is Renaissance literature. But we won't cover it for a while. So, um, back to Middle English ...

As I was saying, Geoffrey Chaucer was a famous Middle English poet. He wrote *The Canterbury Tales*. There were also many works by anonymous authors during that time. *Pearl* is one. *Sir Gawain and the Green Knight* is another. Oh, and I think this is something that will interest you ... A lot of the literature written in this period features King Arthur and his knights. For example, in the late 1400s, Sir Thomas Mallory published a famous work on King Arthur. It was called *Le Morte d'Arthur*. That's French for "the death of Arthur." We're going to read some excerpts from it. In fact, we're going to read several poems about King Arthur. I love these works, and I'm sure you'll enjoy them as well.

Explanations

Listening Comprehension

1.　B；本题为推断题。在对话中，两位学生正在谈论社会研究课的阅读材料，根据原文 "It definitely helps me understand the material Ms. Reardon teachers." 可以推断，Ms. Reardon 是社会研究课的老师。

2.　B；本题为细节题。根据原文 "We're planning to get together in room 108 after school ends." 可知，她们计划放学后在 108 房间聚会。故答案为 B。

3.　D；本题为目的题。老师建议学生让父母帮他校对作业，这样他们就能帮他找出作业中的错误。故答案为 D。

4.　B；本题为目的题。在对话中，女生说："May I get an extension on it, please?" 并且解释了原因："But the softball team has an away game tonight."。由此可知，女生和老师谈论家庭作业的原因是她想要延期。故答案为 B。

5.　A；本题为预测题。在对话中，男生建议："How about giving me a call this evening?"。女生表示同意。由此可以预测，女生晚上会给男生打电话。故答案为 A。

6.　D；本题为主旨题。在对话中，男生问老师："What can I do to improve my performance?"，然后老师解释了提高成绩需要做什么。故答案为 D。

7.　B；本题为目的题。在听力原文中，老师正在为学生们提供一些过马路的安全提示。故答案为 B。

8.　C；本题为预测题。根据原文 "Now, let me tell you the difference between them." 可以推断，接下来他可能继续和学生讲述两者的不同。故答案为 C。

9.　B；本题为主旨题。在录音中，老师主要谈论了学生作文的提交时间以及希望他们如何写作文。故答案为 B。

10.　B；本题为细节题。在对话中，老师告诉女生："In fact, you got a 99 on it.", 由此可知女生的论文得了 99 分。故答案为 B。

11.　A；本题为语气题。在对话中，老师问女生是否知道写作比赛，女生回答说："I think I remember hearing something about the competition.", 从女生的语气可以推断，她对比赛知之甚少。故答案为 A。

12.　D；本题为推断题。在对话中，老师说道："Well, I think you ought to take part in the competition.", 他还提及："Your writing skills are good enough. You proved that to me with the essay you're holding there.", 由此可知，女生的写作能力足以参赛。故答案为 D。

13.　B；本题为预测题。在对话中，老师提到放学后他将在教室帮助其他学生准备比赛，他邀请女生也参加。根据原文 "I guess I can give it a shot. I'll see you later today then." 可以预测，女生在放学后要去教室见老师。故答案为 B。

14.　B；本题为主旨题。从整个对话可知，两位学生正在谈论他们的大学计划。故答案为 B。

15.　D；本题为推断题。根据原文 "I really wish I could travel abroad for a few months like a couple of my friends are doing. But doing that is simply out of my price range." 可以推断，女生暗示她负担不起出国旅行的费用，因为这超出了她能支付的范围。故答案为 D。

16.　C；本题为细节题。根据原文 "I am giving serious consideration to majoring in Chemistry." 可知，女生正在考虑选化学专业。故答案为 C。

17.　C；本题为细节题。根据原文 "I'll figure out what I like and what I'm good at, and then I'll make a decision on a major when I'm a sophomore." 可知，男生计划在大二时再选专业。故答案为 C。

18.　A；本题为主旨题。从整个对话可知，男生与老师在讨论他写报告时使用的资料来源。故答案为 A。

19.　B；本题为细节题。根据原文 "You had a large number of incorrect statements in your paper." 可知，男生的报告中有大量不正确的陈述。故答案为 B。

20.　B；本题为目的题。根据原文 "In general, look for websites associated with schools and government agencies. They tend to deal mostly with facts." 可知，老师提到查找与学校和政府机构相关的网站是为了把这些网站推荐给男生，让他查证引用的陈述是否正确。故答案为 B。

21. C；本题为目的题。根据原文"The library has plenty of encyclopedias and other reference books available. Try using them sometime. It might take you longer than searching the Internet, but the reference books in the library are invaluable."可知，老师提到图书馆是为了告诉男生图书馆有很多百科全书和参考书，可以在那里查阅资料。故答案为C。

22. B；本题为细节题。根据原文"I took flute lessons nearly every day."可知，女生在暑假上了长笛课。故答案为B。

23. A；本题为推断题。在对话中，男生经常用we来指代学校管弦乐队。由此可以推断，男生暗示自己是管弦乐队的一员。因此，他应该会演奏乐器。故答案为A。

24. D；本题为细节题。根据原文"We only have twenty five members. I'm not quite sure why our numbers are that low since there are so many students at our school."可知，管弦乐队的人数不多。故答案为D。

25. D；本题为预测题。在对话中，男生告诉女生："Why don't you talk to the director after lunch? His name is Mr. Spartan, and his office is in room 203."，女生回答说："I'll do that."。由此可知，女生在午餐后会去斯巴达老师的办公室。故答案为D。

26. B；本题为主旨题。老师在讲话中主要谈到打破音障的问题。故答案为B。

27. D；本题为目的题。在讲话中，老师指出Bell X-1是第一架速度超过音速的飞机。由此可知，老师提到Bell X-1是为了指出第一架速度超过音速的飞机。故答案为D。

28. B；本题为推断题。根据原文"There were many scientists who believed it would act as a sort of physical barrier and therefore couldn't be exceeded. Obviously, um, they were wrong about that and lots of other things."可以推断，老师认为许多科学家的理论是错误的。故答案为B。

29. C；本题为细节题。根据原文"In addition, civilian aircraft that could break the sound barrier were constructed. The first of these to be used as a passenger plane was the Tupolev Tu-144."可知，第一架突破音速的客机是Tupolev Tu-144。故答案为C。

30. C；本题为主旨题。从整个对话可知，老师重点讲解了植物的根系。故答案为C。

31. D；本题为细节题。根据原文"Roots can take in both water and nutrients from the soil."可知，根可以从土壤中吸收水分和养分。故答案为D。

32. B；本题为细节题。根据原文"Some, such as pine trees, have something called a taproot. This is a root that grows straight down ... often quite deeply ... and makes a plant very hard to uproot."可知，松树这类植物有主根。故答案为B。

33. A；本题为目的题。根据原文"This is particularly common with desert plants. The roots of desert plants can extend very far in all directions in order to absorb as much water as possible in their dry environments."可知，老师提到沙漠植物是为了解释它们的根系。

34. C；本题为预测题。在对话的最后，老师问学生们是否知道植物的茎的作用，但并没有学生回答。然后她说："Okay. Let me tell you then."，由此可以预测，接下来老师可能会开始讲解植物的茎。

35. C；本题为主旨题。在讨论中，学生和老师给出了一些早期人类可能离开非洲的原因。故答案为C。

36. A；本题为目的题。在对话中，男生提到人们可能跟随成群的动物离开非洲进入中东地区，女生不同意他的说法。女生说："But the Middle East is mostly a desert environment. Why would large herds of animals wander into the desert? There wouldn't be any food or water for them. That doesn't make any sense to me."。由此可知，女生提出中东地区是沙漠环境的原因是为了反对男生的观点。故答案为A。

37. D；本题为推断题。根据原文"Much of the Middle East is desert now, but it wasn't always the case. 70,000 years ago, it's possible that the Middle East was as green and fertile as this area here."可以推断，老师暗示中东地区的气候多年来发生了变化。故答案为D。

38. D；本题为细节题。根据原文"It's entirely possible that defeated tribes left Africa in search of a new homeland. The winners would have stayed while the losers might have had no choice but to depart."可知，战败的部落可能为了寻找新的家园而离开了非洲。故答案为D。

39. B；本题为目的题。根据原文"The most well-known work of literature from that period is *Beowulf*."可知，《贝奥武夫》是古英语时期最著名的文学作品，老师提到《贝奥武夫》是为了说明它创作于古英语时期。故答案为B。

40. D；本题为推断题。老师首先告诉学生，他们很难理解古英语的单词。然后，他又指出："During that time, the English language was undergoing a lot of changes. It started to look more like modern English. However, Middle English is still hard to decipher."，意思是在那段时间里英语发生了很多变化，它开始变得看起来更像现代英语，然而中古英语仍然很难解读。由此可知，通过说中古英语看起来更像现代英语，老师暗示它比古英语更容易阅读。故答案为D。

41. B；本题为细节题。根据原文"As I was saying, Geoffrey Chaucer was a famous Middle English poet. He wrote *The Canterbury Tales*."可知，杰弗里·乔叟创作了《坎特伯雷故事集》。故答案为B。

42. B；本题为推断题。当谈到关于亚瑟王的中古英语作品时，老师说："I love these works, and I'm sure you'll enjoy them as well."，由此可以推断，老师喜欢中古英语诗歌。故答案为B。

Language Form and Meaning

1. B；本题考查固定搭配。decide to do sth. 为固定搭配，故答案为B。

2. C；本题为词义辨析题。necessity 意为"必需品"；workshop 意为"车间，讲习班，研讨会"；elective 意为"选修课程"；major 意为"专业"。根据上下文可知，答案为C。

3. A；本题为词义辨析题。enroll 意为"注册，服役，编入"；register 意为"登记，记录"；enlist 意为"入伍，从军"；participate 意为"参加，参与"。enroll in 意为"参加，选课"，故答案为A。

4. D；本题考查宾语从句。宾语从句的引导词包括：①连词：that(可省略)、whether、if；②代词：who、whose、what、which；③副词：when、where、how、why 等。B 选项的 why 表示原因，C 选项的 when 表示时间，均错误。D 选项的 which 表示"哪一个"，故答案为D。

5. C；本题考查宾语从句。从句中的主语是 the school。plan for 为固定搭配，意为"计划，为……作安排"。故答案为C。

6. A；本题考查比较级。形容词 competitive 的比较级是 more competitive，最高级是 the most competitive。根据句意可知，此处应选比较级，意为"使学生更具竞争力"。故答案为A。

7. A；本题为词义辨析题。resource 意为"资源，财力"；material 意为"资料，物质"；ability 意为"能力"；skill 意为"技巧，技能"。根据上下文可知，答案为A。

8. C；本题考查情态动词和动词的语态。根据句意可知，本句主语为 the renovations，动词 complete 应该使用被动语态，故排除 A 和 D。而且，句子在描述可能在将来完成的工作，而 B 选项 must have done 表示对过去的推测，并且正确的表达应为 must have been completed，故排除。故答案为C。

9. A；本题为词义辨析题。alter 意为"改变"；attune 意为"使协调，使合拍"；administer 意为"管理，施行"；arrange 意为"安排"。根据上下文可知，答案为A。

10. C；本题考查动词的变形。"动词＋ed"可以表示形容词，"动词＋ed"表示动作已经完成或者持续的状态，通常用来形容人的感受或情绪。licensed 意为"获准拥有的，得到正式许可的"，表示已经获得了许可。故答案为C。

11. C；本题考查动词不定式。find time to do sth. 是一个十分常见的结构，其中不定式作目的状语。故答案为C。

12. A；本题考查句子结构。根据句意可知，本句的主语应为 tests，故排除选项 B 和 D。本句为对未来的推测，must be done 表示必须要做什么事，故答案为A。

13. B；本题考查固定搭配。"It is time to do sth."是固定句型，意为"是……的时间"，故答案为B。

14. D；本题考查形容词的比较级。根据句意可知，句子要表达的是"希望你和其他人一样兴奋"。as...as 的意思是"和……一样"，故答案为D。

15. D；本题为词义辨析题。interview 意为"采访，面试"；transfer 意为"转移，转让"；attain 意为"达到，得到"；hire 意为"雇用，聘用"。根据上下文可知，答案为D。

16. C；本题考查形容词的最高级。根据句意可知，此处应该填入最高级。new 的最高级是 the newest，而最高级前已有物主代词时，不用 the，故答案为 C。

17. C；本题考查动词的时态。根据上下文可知，此处为对未来的期待和设想，应该使用一般将来时。故答案为 C。

18. A；本题为词义辨析题。positive 意为"积极的，肯定的"；concerned 意为"担忧的"；aware 意为"有……意识的"；alert 意为"警觉的"。根据上下文可知，答案为 A。

19. D；本题考查固定搭配。last of all 为固定搭配，一般用于文章末尾段落的段首，意为"最后"。故答案为 D。

20. A；本题考查定语从句。先行词 a school alumna 是一个人，定语从句的引导词应为 who，故答案为 A。

21. B；本题为词义辨析题。discover 意为"发现"；provide 意为"提供"；approve 意为"同意"；result 意为"结果，产生"。根据上下文可知，答案为 B。

22. C；本题考查动词的变形。根据上下文可知，句子的主语是 people。结合句意，这里说的是人们使用网络而感到快乐，应该使用 entertain 的被动语态，形容人或物的感受或情绪。因此答案为 C。

23. A；本题考查句子结构。根据上下文，本句的谓语是 is，为单数，所以主语也应该为单数形式，因此排除选项 B 和 C。动名词作主语的时候，谓语动词用单数，故答案为 A。

24. D；本题考查形容词的比较级和最高级。根据上下文可知，此处应填入 common 的最高级，即 the most common。故答案为 D。

25. C；本题考查插入语。要填入的部分充当句子中的插入语，as it is called 为非限定性定语从句。故答案为 C。

26. D；本题为词义辨析题。manufacture 意为"制造，生产"；stagger 意为"使错开，使震惊，蹒跚"；remove 意为"删除，移除"；decline 意为"拒绝"。根据上下文可知，答案为 D。

27. A；本题考查状语从句。根据上下文可知，此处为表示时间的状语从句，因此引导词应为 whenever，表示"每当，一……就……"。故答案为 A。

28. B；本题为词义辨析题。request 意为"要求，请求"；attempt 意为"尝试，试图"；demand 意为"要求，强烈需求"；challenge 意为"挑战"。故答案为 B。

29. B；本题考查句子结构。根据句意可知，由于缺席，所以 Karen 不能去野外考察。表示"能够"的情态动词是 can 和 could，故答案为 B。

30. B；本题为词义辨析题。agenda 意为"议程"；opposite 意为"相反的"；excitement 意为"激动"；guidance 意为"指导，引导"。根据上下文可知，答案为 B。

31. D；本题考查介词的用法。with 表示"具有"，句子的意思是"博物馆的一个展览展出了许多珍贵珠宝"。故答案为 D。

32. A；本题考查句子结构。句子的主语是 we，and 连接两个并列的动作，因此 and 之后的动词时态应与前面的 learned 一致。故答案为 A。

33. A；本题为词义辨析题。annually 意为"每年，一年一次"；separately 意为"单独地，分别地"；considerably 意为"相当多地，非常"；typically 意为"通常；典型地"。根据上下文可知，答案为 A。

34. B；本题考查固定搭配。根据上下文句意可知，此处应使用 there be 句型，表示"人或事物的存在"或"某地有某物"。故答案为 B。

35. D；本题考查动词时态。该句为宾语从句，根据下文的 May 31 this year 可知，从句所说的是未来将要发生的事，应使用一般将来时。故答案为 D。

36. C；本题为词义辨析题。interest 意为"兴趣，利益"；funding 意为"基金，资金"；attendance 意为"参加，出席"；facility 意为"设施，设备"。根据上下文可知，学校关闭的原因是学生减少，故答案为 C。

37. A；本题为词义辨析题。falling 意为"下落的，下降的"；steady 意为"平稳的，稳定的"；regular 意为"常规的，定期的"；receding 意为"逐渐远去的，减弱的"。根据上下文可知，答案为 A。

38. B；本题考查句子结构。此处为句子的插入语，作前面 Derrick Burgess 的同位语，因此可排除选项 C 和 D。a member of 的意思是"……的成员"，故答案为 B。

39. D；本题考查单词形式。根据句意可知，此处应填入名词形式，neighboring 是形容词，意思是"邻近的"，故排除。neighbor 和 neighbors 的意思是"邻居"，指人，可以排除。neighborhood 的意思是"邻域，街区"，故答案为 D。

40. A；本题考查句子结构。as 引导伴随状语从句，根据句意可知，这里表示一个从过去一直持续到现在且还将持续到将来的动作，应使用现在完成进行时。故答案为 A。

41. C；本题考查宾语从句。promise 后面应该连接一个由 that 引导的宾语从句，故答案为 C。

42. D；本题考查单词形式。A 选项的 close 作名词，意思是"（一段时间或活动的）结束，死胡同"。B 选项意为"关着的，（短时间）歇业的"，C 选项的 closeness 的意思是"亲密；严密"。根据句意，可排除这三个选项。D 选项的 closure 意为"（永久的）关闭，倒闭"。故答案为 D。

Reading Comprehension

1. C；本题为主旨题。这篇文章主要讲了学生志愿者俱乐部的成功。故答案为 C。

2. B；本题为词义辨析题。unique 意为"独特的，唯一的"；shocking 意为"令人惊讶的"；inspiring 意为"鼓舞人心的"；frightful 意为"可怕的，令人不愉快的"。由此可知，shocking 与题干中的 beyond belief 含义相同，都表示"令人惊讶的"，故答案为 B。

3. A；本题为细节题。根据原文"Nearly fifty percent of the entire student body joined the club."可知，将近 50% 的学生加入了这个俱乐部。故答案为 A。

4. D；本题为词义辨析题。discouraged 意为"泄气的，心灰意冷的"；unemployed 意为"失业的，待业的"；unmotivated 意为"没有动力的，动机不明的"；deprived 意为"贫困的，贫穷的"。由此可知，deprived 与题干中的 underprivileged 为同义词。故答案为 D。

5. C；本题为细节题。原文中没有提到志愿者俱乐部的任何学生与无家可归的人一起工作。故答案为 C。

6. B；本题为细节题。在原文中，温迪·福尔曼说："I couldn't be prouder of these students. It's great to see them doing something productive during their free time."。由此可知，她为这些学生感到无比自豪。故答案为 B。

7. B；本题为目的题。该通知主要针对学生参加户外教学必须向学校提交的一些表格。故答案为 B。

8. B；本题为词义辨析题。respond 意为"回答，回应"；agree 意为"同意"；stress 意为"使有压力"；obtain 意为"获得，存在"。由此可知，agree 和题干中的 consent 为同义词，故答案为 B。

9. A；本题为推断题。根据原文"All students who are not yet eighteen years of age must submit a permission slip signed by a parent or guardian."可知，该校也有一些学生年龄在十八岁或以上，而这些学生不必提交许可证。故答案为 A。

10. C；本题为指代题。根据上下文可知，it 指代前文中的 this proof，故答案为 C。

11. D；本题为细节题。根据原文"All students must also provide proof that they have medical insurance..."可知，所有学生必须提供他们有医疗保险的证明。故答案为 D。

12. B；本题为细节题。根据原文"Students are expected to listen to their teachers and to follow the rules and regulations of the places that they visit. Failure to do so will result in some sort of punishment, such as detention or suspension."可知，学生们应该听从老师，遵守参观的地方的规章制度，否则将受到惩罚。故答案为 B。

13. A；本题为主旨题。原文是一则通知，主要介绍了暑期的课程安排。故答案为 A。

14. B；本题为词汇辨析题。refundable 意为"可退还的"；minor 意为"少数的，轻微的"；cash 意为"现金"，是名词；required 意为"需要的，必修的"。由此可知，minor 和 nominal 为同义词，都表示"较小的，微不足道的"。故答案为 B。

15. D；本题为细节题。关于课程，根据原文 ...will meet every day from Monday to Friday from ten to noon. 可知，

课程授课时长为每周五天、每天两小时，因此每周总共上课十小时。故答案为 D。

16. B；本题为推断题。由于这三个课程都是同时举行的，因此可以推断学生只能参加其中一个。故答案为 B。

17. A；本题为细节题。原文中没有提到驾驶课，故答案为 A。

18. C；本题为指代题。根据上下文可知，them 指代前文中的 reservations，故答案为 C。

19. A；本题为词义辨析题。harmful 意为"有害的，导致损害的"；influential 意为"有影响力的"；constant 意为"不断的，固定的"；conditional 意为"有条件的"。由此可知，harmful 和题干中的 detrimental 为同义词。故答案为 A。

20. C；本题为推断题。根据原文 "In addition, the atmosphere provides life-giving oxygen for animals and carbon dioxide for plants." 可知，由于赋予生命的氧气是由大气层提供的，因此地球上的生命离不开大气层。故答案为 C。

21. C；本题为细节题。根据原文 "The troposphere is the layer of the atmosphere closest to the Earth's surface." 可知，对流层是大气层中最靠近地面的一部分，而动植物就生活在这片土地上。故答案为 C。

22. C；本题为目的题。根据原文 "The stratosphere extends from the troposphere to around fifty kilometers above sea level. It contains most of the rest of the atmosphere in addition to the ozone layer." 可知，除了臭氧层外，平流层还包含大气层的大部分其他部分。因此作者提到臭氧层是为了说明它是大气层的一部分。故答案为 C。

23. D；本题为指代题。根据上下文可知，This 指代前文中的 the ozone layer。故答案为 D。

24. D；本题为词义辨析题。explode 意为"爆炸"；ward off 意为"避开"；repel 意为"排斥，击退"；burn up 意为"烧毁，烧光"。由此可知，burned up 与题干中的 incinerated 为同义词。故答案为 D。

25. B；本题为细节题。根据原文 "The fourth layer is the thermosphere. It extends all the way up to 690 kilometers above sea level. It is where the aurora borealis, or northern lights, form." 可知，第四层是热层，极光或北极光就是在这里形成的。故答案为 B。

26. C；本题为细节题。根据原文 "Last is the exosphere. It extends thousands of kilometers above the ground until there is no longer an atmosphere but only outer space." 可知，外逸层在地面上延伸数千千米，直到不再有大气层，只有外太空为止。故答案为 C。

27. B；本题为主旨题。文章主要讲了托马斯·杰斐逊在撰写《独立宣言》中的作用。故答案为 B。

28. A；本题为指代题。根据上下文可知，them 指代前文中的 the American Founding Fathers。故答案为 A。

29. C；本题为细节题。根据原文 "He was responsible for the Louisiana Purchase, which more than doubled the size of the United States." 可知，托马斯·杰斐逊负责路易斯安那州的收购案，该案使美国的领土面积翻了一倍多。故答案为 C。

30. D；本题为目的题。在文章中作者指出，托马斯·杰斐逊曾就读于威廉玛丽学院。故答案为 D。

31. C；本题考查词义理解。detest 的意思是"讨厌，憎恶"，因此 most colonists detested the taxes 的意思是"大多数殖民地居民讨厌税收"。detest 与选项 C 的 hate 是同义词，故答案为 C。

32. C；本题为细节题。根据原文 "He felt very strongly about the importance of the American colonies being represented in Parliament. Since King George III of England refused to allow that, Jefferson spoke out strongly in favor of independence." 可知，杰斐逊非常强烈地感受到美国殖民地在议会中有代表的重要性，但英国国王乔治三世拒绝这样做。故答案为 C。

33. B；本题为词汇题。construct 意为"建造，修建"；seal 意为"确定，使……成定局"；decide 意为"决定"；consider 意为"考虑"。由此可知，sealed 和题干中的 cemented 为同义词。故答案为 B。

34. D；本题为推断题。根据原文 "Signed on July 4, 1776, it gave freedom to the American colonies and cemented Jefferson's place in history as one of the greatest supporters of the cause of freedom." 可以推断，《独立宣言》是托马斯·杰斐逊最大的成就之一。故答案为 D。

35. A；本题为主旨题。这篇文章主要讲了维京人的航海技术，并且他们可以进行长距离的航行。故答案为 A。

36. C；本题为细节题。根据原文 "Starting in the eighth century and continuing until around the tenth, the Vikings began moving out of their homelands. They sailed to the south and west. At first, they simply raided areas and then returned to their homes." 可知，从 8 世纪到 10 世纪左右，维京人开始向南和向西航行。起初他们只是突袭一些地区，然后就返回故乡。故答案为 C。

37. B；本题为细节题。根据原文 "They were built in what is known as the clinker style. Long planks were overlapped and held together with iron rivets. This made the hulls of the ships very strong..." 可知，熟料风格建造的船体是由长木板叠在一起，用铁铆钉固定的，这使得船体非常坚固。故答案为 B。

38. A；本题为词义辨析题。survive 意为"幸存，幸免于难"；penetrate 意为"渗入，穿透"；conquer 意为"征服"；divide 意为"分开，分裂"。由此可知，survive 和题干中的 withstand 是同义词，故答案为 A。

39. D；本题为细节题。文章中没有提到维京人在他们的军舰上作战。故答案为 D。

40. A；本题为细节题。根据原文 "First, they utilized the knowledge that had been gained by their forefathers and passed down from generation to generation. Thus the Vikings knew all the harbors, coves, islands, and rocks in their homelands." 可知，维京人利用从祖先那里获得并代代相传的知识，了解他们故乡的所有港口、海湾、岛屿和岩石。故答案为 A。

41. B；本题为目的题。在文章中，作者描述了维京人在水上使用太阳石导航的方式。由此可知作者提到 sunstone 是为了解释维京人如何用这种方式导航。故答案为 B。

42. B；本题为词义辨析题。cool 意为"凉爽的"，stormy 意为"有暴风雨的"；torrential 意为"倾泻的"；unlucky 意为"倒霉的"。由此可知，stormy 和题干中的 inclement 都可以表示"狂风暴雨的"。故答案为 B。

Master Word List for the TOEFL Junior

Master Word List
for the TOEFL Junior

antler *(n.)* a horn on an animal, such as a deer
A deer's **antlers** start growing in spring and stop getting larger in summer.

apologize *(v.)* to say that one is sorry for something
You had better **apologize** to Betty for being so rude to her.

appearance *(n.)* how something looks
Everyone was startled by Jenny's **appearance** when she cut her hair.

assign *(v.)* to give out, such as homework
Mr. Thompson likes to **assign** group projects to the students.

athletics *(n.)* sports
A lot of the students at the school participate in **athletics**.

auditorium *(n.)* a building in which speeches are given or performances are held
The speech is going to be held in the **auditorium** in just a couple of hours.

bonus *(n.)* something extra
If you write another report, you can earn some **bonus** points.

cancel *(v.)* to end; to call off
Because of all the rain, the school **cancelled** the picnic.

competition *(n.)* an organized contest between two or more teams
There is going to be a chess **competition** this Friday after school.

complete *(v.)* to finish; to end
How much time do you need to **complete** that report?

decent *(adj.)* all right; adequate; neither good nor bad
Kevin always does a **decent** job, but he does not excel in his classes.

defeat *(v.)* to win against
Our soccer team **defeated** the other school's team by a score of three to one.

depression *(n.)* extreme sadness
Some students suffer from **depression** because of the constant demands their parents place on them.

device *(n.)* an object, most often something that is manmade; a piece of equipment
Always handle electronic **devices** with care since they can be fragile.

disaster *(n.)* a tragedy
There was nearly a huge **disaster** when the train crashed.

enormous *(adj.)* very large; huge
One of the most **enormous** of all animals is the rhinoceros.

essay *(n.)* a piece of writing in which the writer gives his or her opinion
Have you decided what you are going to write your **essay** on?

exception *(n.)* someone or something to which the normal rules do not apply
Ms. Wimberly does not make any **exceptions** for students who turn in their work late.

exclusively *(adv.)* solely; completely
David is **exclusively** interested in computers and spends all his time learning about them.

expert *(n.)* a person with a great deal of knowledge on a topic
I would like to become an **expert** at foreign languages.

extension *(n.)* extra time to complete a project or to do something
James received an **extension** on his paper from Mr. Wood.

feat *(n.)* a great deed or accomplishment
It was an amazing **feat** for the team to come from behind to win the game.

focus *(v.)* to concentrate
You need to **focus** on your work and not get distracted by watching television.

forage *(v.)* to search for food, particularly vegetation
Many forest animals **forage** for food all throughout the year.

forecast *(n.)* a prediction for the future
The weather **forecast** is calling for sunny skies and hot temperatures.

founder *(n.)* a person who creates or starts something
Donna Falco is the **founder** of that company.

genius *(n.)* a very intelligent person
Even though he is a **genius**, he does poorly at school since he is so lazy.

gruesome *(adj.)* bloody; horrible
There was a **gruesome** scene when the lions attacked the zebra.

hang out to be doing nothing special at some place; to spend time with others
Many teens like to **hang out** at the shopping mall and talk to their friends.

mayor *(n.)* the elected leader of a city
No one is sure who is going to win this year's race for **mayor**.

mistake *(n.)* an error
If you check your work twice, you should be able to find most of your **mistakes**.

participate *(v.)* to take part in
Many students like to **participate** in various clubs and after-school activities.

partner *(n.)* a person with whom one does something together
Thomas and Karen are lab **partners** in their chemistry class.

realize *(v.)* to recognize; to understand
The students suddenly **realized** they only had five minutes to complete the test.

reject *(v.)* to turn down; to say no to
I will **reject** your offer unless you make it better.

remainder *(n.)* something that is left over
You can choose which clothes you want from the **remainder** in the pile over there.

remind *(v.)* to tell a person not to forget something
Please **remind** me to finish my homework by this evening.

rip *(v.)* to tear
If you are not careful, you are going to **rip** your blue jeans.

select *(v.)* to choose
The students need to **select** a topic for their reports by Friday.

sponsor *(v.)* to pay money in support of something; to support
Many local companies help **sponsor** the school's football team.

structure *(n.)* a building; an organization
The **structure** is getting older and is in bad need of repairs.

stunned *(adj.)* shocked
Mr. Martin was **stunned** when Jessica gave him a fifty-page report.

submit *(v.)* to turn in
Most teachers insist that their students **submit** their homework when class begins.

taut *(adj.)* tight; stiff; extended
Pull the rope until it is **taut**, and then tie it to the tree.

terrible *(adj.)* awful; very bad
To most students, anything below a C is a **terrible** grade.

theory *(n.)* an idea about something; a hypothesis
Once you come up with a **theory**, it is necessary to test it to see if it can be proven false.

tryout *(n.)* an audition for a sports team
Tryouts for the baseball team are going to be held on Thursday and Friday.

virtually *(adv.)* nearly; almost
There were **virtually** no empty seats in the auditorium during the school play.

unintentionally *(adv.)* accidentally; not on purpose
I **unintentionally** ran into Sue and knocked her to the ground.

wisely *(adv.)* in a clever manner; smartly; cleverly
Sarah **wisely** decided to write her paper before she went to the movies with her friends.

Practice Test 2

accompany *(v.)* to go along with another
Three teachers will **accompany** the students on the field trip.

assault *(n.)* an attack
The **assault** on the enemy's base was successful.

assignment *(n.)* a work or school project
The **assignment** in English class is to write a five-page essay.

assume *(v.)* to believe to be true
Do not **assume** that everything you read on the Internet is true.

attitude *(n.)* a manner; an approach
Some students with bad **attitudes** often get into a lot of trouble.

bonus *(n.)* something extra
By writing another lab report, Amy was able to get some **bonus** points.

bully *(v.)* to pick on someone smaller or weaker than oneself
When students **bully** others, the teachers should put a stop to it.

canal *(n.)* a manmade waterway connecting two bodies of water
Thanks to the new **canal**, ships can travel between the two cities more quickly than before.

comparison *(n.)* an attempt to show how two people, places, or things are either similar or different
Most children dislike when their parents make **comparisons** between them and their siblings.

core *(n.)* a center
The Earth's **core** lies deep beneath the crust and the mantle.

distortion *(n.)* a change; an alteration
Because the lens had a crack in it, there was some **distortion** in the images it produced.

editor *(n.)* a person who corrects written mistakes
The **editor** fixed the article and prepared it for publication.

embarrassed *(adj.)* shy, uncomfortable or ashamed
I was **embarrassed** when I fell asleep in the middle of the exam.

glacier *(n.)* a large mass of compacted ice and snow
There are many places in the world where **glaciers** are expanding and getting larger.

graduate *(v.)* to complete a course of study at a school
After Don **graduates**, he intends to take a year off before going to college.

grant *(n.)* a donation of money
Thanks to a **grant** from a local company, the school can afford to buy some new computers.

hazy *(adj.)* unclear
The directions on the test were **hazy**, so the students asked the teacher what they meant.

initial *(adj.)* first; starting
My **initial** impression of Jane as being kind was totally wrong.

interference *(n.)* an intrusion
Due to atmospheric **interference**, there was no cell phone service in the area.

intern *(n.)* a person who works at a low-level job for the purpose of gaining experience and knowledge
He is going to work at the company as an **intern** this summer.

interpretation *(n.)* an explanation; an understanding
What is your **interpretation** of the events that happened last night?

interview *(n.)* a question-and-answer session with an individual
George sat down for an **interview** with the president of the company.

knack *(n.)* a talent or ability to do something
Jason has a **knack** for getting into trouble.

laboratory *(n.)* a place where scientific experiments are conducted
Be sure to clean up the **laboratory** after you complete your experiment.

livestock *(n.)* animals that farmers raise, including cows, sheep, and chickens
The farmer puts his **livestock** into the barn every night.

manufacture *(v.)* to make
That company **manufactures** all kinds of electronic products.

migrate *(v.)* to wander from one place to another
Some people **migrate** from city to city in search of good jobs.

object *(v.)* to oppose; to be against
I **object** to your constant use of bad language.

obvious *(adj.)* apparent; clear
If you read the material, then the answer to this question should be **obvious**.

orbit *(v.)* to move around a large object in a circle
All of the planets in the solar system **orbit** the sun.

originate *(v.)* to come from; to start from
The idea for our science project **originated** during a conversation we had last week.

participation *(n.)* a contribution; the act of taking part in something
The **participation** of students in extracurricular activities is very important.

pop test a short test that is given by surprise
Kevin got a perfect score on the **pop test** since he had studied the material the night before.

predator *(n.)* a hunter
Wolves are some of the most dangerous **predators** in the forest.

profession *(n.)* a career; a line of work
Many students think they need to choose a **profession** early in their lives.

replacement *(n.)* a substitute
Because Peter lost his textbook, he needed a **replacement**.

reporter *(n.)* a journalist; a person who writes for a newspaper
There were two **reporters** covering the story for the newspaper.

reserve *(v.)* to save; to set aside
Please **reserve** the book for me until I can get to the library to check it out.

response *(n.)* an answer; a reply
Ed made no **response** when the teacher asked him why he had cheated on the test.

revolution *(n.)* a complete rotation
It takes Earth 365 days to complete one **revolution** of the sun.

semester *(n.)* one of two terms in a school year
During the spring **semester**, Erica's grades improved a great deal.

snapshot *(n.)* a picture taken with a camera
Could you take a **snapshot** of us while we stand over there, please?

surround *(v.)* to encircle; to make a circle around someone or something
The army **surrounded** the city and would not let anyone out of it.

spelling bee a competition in which individuals must spell words correctly
David won the **spelling bee** in a competition against 100 other students.

telescope *(n.)* a tool used to get closer looks at distant objects
They used a **telescope** to look at Venus, Mars, and Jupiter last night.

terrestrial *(adj.)* relating to the Earth
It could be possible for humans to live on a **terrestrial** planet someday.

theft *(n.)* a robbery
There was a **theft** at the school, which greatly upset the students.

tremendously *(adv.)* greatly
The principal is **tremendously** pleased with how the students are performing.

urge *(n.)* a desire to do something
Lee had a sudden **urge** to eat something sweet.

ward *(n.)* a section of a hospital in which patients are kept
There are three patients in that **ward**, and the nurses are watching them carefully.

advice *(n.)* an opinion given to another person
If you need some **advice**, feel free to talk to the guidance counselor, Mr. Thomas.

aligned *(adj.)* in line with
Three planets are going to be **aligned** with one another this evening.

alteration *(n.)* a change; an adjustment
You need to make a few **alterations** in this paper.

alternative *(adj.)* other; another
Linda tried an **alternative** approach when she wrote her latest essay.

appreciate *(v.)* to welcome; to be thankful for
The students **appreciate** how hard Ms. Lewis tries in her classes.

attend *(v.)* to go to, as in class
It is necessary to **attend** all of your classes so that you can learn as much as possible.

awful *(adj.)* terrible; horrible
Chris felt **awful** when he learned that he had gotten an F on his midterm exam.

behavior *(n.)* how one acts
Please improve your **behavior** and stop talking during class.

berate *(v.)* to yell at; to scold
Mr. Peters **berated** the students who did not turn in their homework on time.

biased *(adj.)* prejudiced; having a strong opinion about someone or something
Many reporters claim to be neutral but are instead incredibly **biased**.

blindness *(n.)* an inability to see
Some people with color **blindness** cannot see certain colors, such as red and green.

celestial *(adj.)* relating to outer space; heavenly
There are many **celestial** bodies, such as the planets, orbiting the sun.

complain *(v.)* to speak badly about someone or something
Carrie often **complains** about the amount of work she has to do.

conclusion *(n.)* an end
The play is going to come to its **conclusion** in about five minutes.

consider *(v.)* to think about
I would like you to **consider** my suggestion.

conspiracy *(n.)* a plot; a scheme, often for something illegal
The police broke up a **conspiracy** against the president.

contribute *(v.)* to add to something
All students need to **contribute** by speaking during class discussions.

crash *(v.)* to wreck
Try to avoid **crashing** the car when you are driving.

detect *(v.)* to find
Can you **detect** any problems in this paper?

detention *(n.)* a type of punishment in which a student must stay after school
Joe got **detention** for two days for speaking rudely to his math teacher.

discount *(n.)* a reduction in price
You can get some good **discounts** by shopping at stores that are having sales.

donation *(n.)* a gift, often of money
Everyone is encouraged to make a small **donation** to charity.

eligible *(adj.)* qualified to do something; suitable
Don will be **eligible** to play basketball if he can improve his grade in science.

essentially *(adv.)* basically; fundamentally
There are **essentially** no problems at all with her report.

extracurricular *(adj.)* after-school
Some students are involved in a large number of **extracurricular** activities.

extreme *(adj.)* intense; great; very large
In cases of **extreme** violence, the police must be called.

fatal *(adj.)* deadly; lethal
There was a **fatal** car accident last night that was caused by the icy road.

fund *(n.)* money
The club has enough **funds** to pay for its members to make a trip to the zoo.

hero *(n.)* a champion; a great warrior
In literature, stories about **heroes** are often popular.

intend *(v.)* to mean; to plan
Ron **intends** to try out for the school's soccer team this year.

intrigued *(adj.)* interested; curious about
She was **intrigued** by the thought of doing a project for extra credit.

janitor *(n.)* a person whose job is to clean
The **janitors** at the school work hard to keep the facilities clean.

letdown *(n.)* a disappointment
It was a **letdown** when the football team lost when the other team scored in the last minute.

nonrenewable *(adj.)* not able to be used again
We must conserve as many of our **nonrenewable** resources as possible.

option *(n.)* a choice
You have two **options**: Do the work now or do it later.

organism *(n.)* a living creature
There are all kinds of **organisms** that we cannot see without a microscope.

partial *(adj.)* somewhat; not completely; partly
You will get **partial** credit if your answer is not completely correct.

plunge *(v.)* to fall swiftly
The temperature **plunged** when a cold front suddenly blew in from the north.

recession *(n.)* an economic downturn; an extended period when the economy gets worse
Hopefully, the **recession** will end soon, and employment will begin to increase.

renovate *(v.)* to repair, such as a building
It is going to take three months to **renovate** the school's gym.

shy *(adj.)* timid; withdrawn; coy
Sandra is extremely **shy**, so she rarely speaks to anyone.

skirmish *(n.)* a minor battle
The soldiers fought a **skirmish** during which two of them were hurt.

solely *(adv.)* only
John is **solely** responsible for his grade in that class.

squeal *(v.)* to make a high-pitched noise
The pigs began to **squeal** when the farmer entered the barn.

symbol *(n.)* a sign
The archaeologists did not understand what the **symbols** on the pot meant.

tyrant *(n.)* a dictator; an unelected person who rules in a cruel and often violent manner
The **tyrant** treated the people of his country badly.

unanimously *(adv.)* as one; collectively
The students voted **unanimously** to watch a movie in class the next day.

undertake *(v.)* to do; to attempt; to try
We are about to **undertake** a very difficult task.

vary *(v.)* to be different
Try to **vary** the words that you use so that your writing will be better.

vibrant *(adj.)* lively; striking
The **vibrant** atmosphere made the party more exciting.

Practice Test 4

absent *(adj.)* not present
Jason was **absent** from school three times this week.

appealing *(adj.)* attractive; interesting
The company made an **appealing** offer to Mr. Denton.

application *(n.)* a request to be accepted to a place, such as a school or business
Your **application** must be submitted no later than January 1.

approximately *(adv.)* about; around; close to
There are **approximately** 550 students who attend that high school.

artifact *(n.)* a relic, often from a past civilization or culture
There may be several valuable **artifacts** buried in those ruins.

beat *(v.)* to defeat; to win against, as in a game or a battle
We hope that our soccer team **beats** its opponent in the game tonight.

boil *(v.)* to heat a liquid to a point where it begins to turn into a gas
Water **boils** at 100 degrees Celsius.

bold *(adj.)* brave; courageous
You are **bold** for trying to learn how to skydive.

bomb *(v.)* to fail, as in a test
I cannot believe that I **bombed** the science test I took yesterday.

brilliant *(adj.)* intelligent; smart; bright
One of the most **brilliant** students in the class is Rick.

carve *(v.)* to cut with a knife
Some people like to **carve** tiny figures from blocks of wood.

century *(n.)* a period of 100 years
There will be many great advances during the twenty-first **century**.

colleague *(n.)* a coworker
Sarah gets along well with nearly all of her **colleagues**.

conscious *(adj.)* aware
Eric was concentrating so hard that he was not **conscious** of the people around him.

cover *(v.)* to go over; to discuss; to talk about
We are going to **cover** pages 102 to 105 in the book this afternoon.

curiosity *(n.)* interest in something that is often excessive
She has a natural **curiosity** that makes her try to understand how machines work.

define *(v.)* to give the meaning of
Could you please **define** this word since I do not know what it means?

detractor *(n.)* a person who opposes or disagrees with another
The manager will have a meeting with several **detractors** who dislike the new plan.

distorted *(adj.)* unclear; hazy; indistinct
The mirror produced a **distorted** image because of the crack in it.

dominate *(v.)* to rule over; to control
The Roman Empire **dominated** much of Europe for a few hundred years.

dress code a rule or rules for what clothes to wear, often at a school or business
The **dress code** at this private school is very strict.

dull *(adj.)* boring; drab; of little or no interest
Mrs. Martin's economics class is usually really **dull**.

efficient *(adj.)* able; capable; making good use of time
Please tell me the most **efficient** way to study for the test.

encourage *(v.)* to support; to cheer for
The fans **encouraged** the players on the field to do their best.

entire *(adj.)* total; complete; all
During the **entire** class, you are not allowed to speak to anyone else.

forget *(v.)* not to remember; to fail to recall something
Robert sometimes **forgets** to bring a pen with him to class.

frightening *(adj.)* scary
Encountering a bear in the forest is **frightening** for most people.

fulfill *(v.)* to complete
You must **fulfill** your part of the agreement, or I will get upset.

hurry *(v.)* to move quickly
We had better **hurry** so that we do not miss the train.

ill *(adj.)* sick
I feel **ill**, so I need to stay home for the rest of the day.

investigate *(v.)* to look into; to study
The police are **investigating** the scene of the crime to try to find some clues.

participate *(v.)* to take part in
Most students **participate** in one or two after-school activities.

pointer *(n.)* a tip; a hint; advice
Mr. Burgess always gives the students some **pointers** on how to prepare for their test.

primitive *(adj.)* basic; simple; uncomplicated
Even **primitive** tribes know how to use fire and how to make clothing.

relieve *(v.)* to ease; to make one feel better
If you take this medicine, it should **relieve** your pain.

restrain *(v.)* to keep from doing something; to hold back
You had better **restrain** your dog so that it does not bite anyone.

reward *(n.)* a prize, such as money, for doing something successfully
There is a **reward** for anyone who helps the police find the criminal.

ring *(v.)* to sound a bell; to cause a bell to make a sound
When the bell **rings**, it means that it is time for class.

rush *(v.)* to hurry; to move quickly
The students are **rushing** to their classrooms in order not to be late.

shake *(v.)* to move something back and forth, often very quickly
If you **shake** the mixture, the two ingredients will combine with one another.

sheltered *(adj.)* protected; privileged
Students from rich families often live **sheltered** lives.

shout *(v.)* to yell; to speak in a very loud voice
You had better not **shout**, or else Ms. Kimball will get angry.

significance *(n.)* importance
Who can tell me the **significance** of the word written on the board?

student body all of the students at a school
The entire **student body** always meets in the auditorium on Monday morning.

suppose *(v.)* to guess; to make a prediction
I **suppose** that the answer to the question is seven.

support *(v.)* to assist; to help; to provide aid
They volunteer at the hospital to **support** the doctors and nurses.

teammate *(n.)* a person who is on the same team as another
Doug is popular with his **teammates** since he is not a selfish player.

transform *(v.)* to change; to alter
A caterpillar **transforms** into a butterfly while it is inside a cocoon.

velocity *(n.)* speed
The cars are moving at a high **velocity**.

violate *(v.)* to break a rule or law
If you **violate** any of his rules, you will get detention or some other form of punishment.

Practice Test 5

abandon *(v.)* to give up; to depart
A true friend never **abandons** another person in need.

alliance *(n.)* a union between two or more people or groups; a coalition
The nations formed an **alliance** when they were threatened with the possibility of war.

allowance *(n.)* spending money that a parent gives a child on a regular basis
She receives her **allowance** from her parents every Sunday.

annual *(adj.)* yearly; happening every year
The festival is an **annual** event that is held in May.

anticipate *(v.)* to expect that something will happen
I do not **anticipate** having any problems with the report.

avoid *(v.)* to stay away from a person or place; to keep from doing something
You need to **avoid** bothering any of your teachers, or you will get in trouble.

barrier *(n.)* an obstruction; a fence; something that prevents a person from doing an action
There is a stone **barrier** that prevents anyone from going further.

bravery *(n.)* courage
Those soldiers were noted for their **bravery** during the battle.

campaign *(n.)* an effort by a politician to win an election
The presidential **campaign** lasts for several months and costs millions of dollars.

cashier *(n.)* a store clerk; a person who accepts payments at a store or place of business
Take the items to the **cashier**, who will tell you how much you owe.

cheat *(v.)* to use improper or illegal methods to do something
If you **cheat** on the test, you will get a zero on it.

concentrate *(v.)* to focus on
We need to **concentrate** in order to understand this material.

conquer *(v.)* to defeat, often in battle
The invaders' armies **conquered** everyone who opposed them.

consult *(v.)* to look at; to check
Consult your schedule in case you do not remember which class you have.

counselor *(n.)* a person who provides advice
The school **counselor** will keep everything that you say private.

crack *(n.)* a break; a fracture in something solid
There is a large **crack** in the wall that needs to be fixed.

departure *(n.)* a going away; an exit
The **departure** of the plane has been delayed by thirty-five minutes.

discount *(n.)* a reduction in price
You can get a **discount** every time you shop with a membership card.

display *(n.)* an exhibition; a showing
The rock **display** at the museum attracted a large number of visitors.

eager *(adj.)* willing to do something; enthusiastic; excited
The girls are **eager** to try out for the school's volleyball team.

elect *(v.)* to choose by voting
The students **elected** Allen the class president.

enable *(v.)* to permit; to let happen; to allow
This ID card will **enable** you to check out books from the library.

enroll *(v.)* to register for; to become a member of a group or organization; to sign up for a class

We can **enroll** in classes starting next Wednesday.

goggles *(n.)* a kind of protective eye covering
I always wear my **goggles** when I am doing chemistry experiments.

hyperactive *(adj.)* overly active; having too much energy
If you are too **hyperactive**, you might have some kind of a problem.

inject *(v.)* to insert; to put something into another thing
The doctor **injected** the patient with some medicine.

leftover *(adj.)* remaining
There is some **leftover** food in the refrigerator if you are hungry.

lively *(adj.)* energetic; full of life or energy
I cannot believe how **lively** the students are this afternoon.

massacre *(n.)* a mass murder, often of civilians or unarmed people
The enemy army committed a **massacre** of an entire village.

massive *(adj.)* huge; very large; enormous
There is a **massive** pile of garbage behind the building.

moist *(adj.)* damp; slightly wet
The laundry is still **moist**, so you need to put it in the dryer.

overrun *(v.)* to flood; to take over; to cover
The farmers' fields were **overrun** by millions of insects.

penetrate *(v.)* to go into, often by using force; to break into
The steel armor is so strong that nothing can **penetrate** it.

phenomenon *(n.)* an incident; an occurrence
That is an unexplained **phenomenon** that has confused people for years.

reduce *(v.)* to make smaller; to decrease in size; to lessen
You need to **reduce** the amount of money you spend since you are in debt.

revolutionize *(v.)* to change dramatically
The Internet **revolutionized** a number of aspects of modern life.

ruthless *(adj.)* cruel; showing no mercy
You must be **ruthless** if you want to be the winner.

seasonal *(adj.)* happening on a regular basis in a particular season
Seasonal changes in the weather happen every couple of months.

seize *(v.)* to take something by force
The government **seized** the man's home when he did not pay his taxes.

shift *(n.)* a change; an alteration
Recently, there has been a **shift** in public opinion concerning the matter.

slide *(n.)* a picture that can be shown on a projector
We often look at **slides** during biology class.

slippery *(adj.)* slick; oily
The floor is **slippery** since it has just been mopped.

spark *(v.)* to cause a fire to start; to flash; to ignite
What **sparked** Judy's sudden interest in math?

stuff *(n.)* something; an object or objects
Do not forget to pick up all this **stuff** and put it back where it belongs.

surrender *(v.)* to give up; to stop fighting; to quit
The soldiers vowed never to **surrender** and to keep fighting to the very end.

trigger *(v.)* to prompt; to start; to make happen
You can **trigger** a response in the animal by stimulating it.

trust *(v.)* to believe
Mr. Thompson **trusts** his students not to cheat on their exams.

tuition *(n.)* the money a person pays to attend a school or educational center
Tuition at many schools is rising too quickly nowadays.

unintelligent *(adj.)* stupid; dumb; not smart
He is an **unintelligent** boy who has no interest in school at all.

widespread *(adj.)* common; prevalent; happening over a wide area
The disease is **widespread** and is infecting many people.

Practice Test 6

abdicate *(v.)* to step down as a ruler; to quit ruling as a king or queen
When the king became too old to rule, he **abdicated** and let his son become the king.

bibliography *(n.)* a list of the sources that a writer uses for a written work
Be sure to write a **bibliography** for your research paper.

bleak *(adj.)* drab; dark; dreary; hopeless
The weather conditions today are **bleak**.

carnivore *(n.)* an animal that eats meat
Sharks are some of the most dangerous **carnivores** on the planet.

cite *(v.)* to quote another work; to refer to
You must **cite** all quotations that you use from other writers in your report.

coalition *(n.)* a group; an alliance
The **coalition** of nations came together during a time of war.

compensation *(n.)* payment for the work that a person does
If you work for someone, you must receive **compensation** for your efforts.

constantly *(adv.)* continually; at all times
Ted is **constantly** trying to improve himself by learning new skills.

decade *(n.)* a period of ten years
Kate has lived in more than five countries during the past decade.

den *(n.)* an animal's home, usually located underground; a lair
It can be dangerous for a person to try to enter an animal's **den**.

dispute *(n.)* an argument
I had a **dispute** with Greg, so now he is angry with me.

disrupt *(v.)* to interrupt; to cause a disturbance; to disturb
Students should not **disrupt** class by talking or causing other problems.

embassy *(n.)* a building that houses the ambassador of a country
Most **embassies** are located in the capital of the country they are in.

emperor *(n.)* the ruler of an empire
The **emperor** ordered his army to invade the nearby country.

employ *(v.)* to hire; to give a person a job
Who is the company going to **employ** to fill the manager position?

escapee *(n.)* a person who has escaped from a jail or prison
The prison **escapees** were all captured by the police.

eventually *(adv.)* after some time; finally
I hope that I can **eventually** attend one of the country's best colleges.

exceed *(v.)* to go beyond; to do better than one had expected
I **exceeded** my goal when I got a 99 on the exam.

execute *(v.)* to kill someone, often for having committed a crime
The state decided to **execute** the terrorist for his crimes.

exile *(n.)* the state of being forced to live away from one's home
While in **exile**, the man worked on his memoirs to write about his life.

feature *(n.)* a characteristic; an attribute; an identifying mark
Amy's loyalty to her friends is one of her most attractive **features**.

fluid *(n.)* a liquid
There is some sort of **fluid** dripping from the car's engine.

footnote *(n.)* a note at the bottom of a page that provides explanatory information
Footnotes can provide valuable information in a research paper.

fossil *(n.)* the preserved bone of a dead animal
I enjoy digging for **fossils** in a field located near my house.

geometry *(n.)* a branch of math that focuses on shapes and figures
The students agreed that they learned a lot in their **geometry** class.

grade *(v.)* to check papers or tests; to mark; to score
Mr. Carter does not have time to **grade** our tests this week.

graze *(v.)* to eat grass or other vegetation, such as what cows do
The cattle **graze** in the field during the day.

handout *(n.)* a printed paper that has information on it
Ms. Peters gave the students a **handout** with a couple of maps on it.

hesitate *(v.)* to pause; to be unsure or uncertain
If you **hesitate** too much, you may have problems making any decisions at all.

hospitalize *(v.)* to be kept at a hospital due to some kind of medical problem
Larry was **hospitalized** when he got into a serious car accident.

iconic *(adj.)* representative; famous; referring to an icon
Some of the world's most **iconic** photographs were published in *Life* magazine.

inclement *(adj.)* bad, as in the weather
Expect **inclement** weather for the next few days as snow will continue to fall.

notorious *(adj.)* infamous; well known for a bad reason
Brutus is one of history's most **notorious** individuals since he helped kill Julius Caesar.

nourishment *(n.)* food; sustenance; anything that provides energy to an organism
The **nourishment** provided by food keeps people alive.

personality *(n.)* a person's character or traits
You need to improve your **personality** by being nicer to people.

postpone *(v.)* to delay an event until a later time; to reschedule
We have to **postpone** the club meeting since we cannot find a room to hold it in.

primary *(adj.)* main; major
The **primary** purpose of today's class is to explain some economics terms.

prisoner *(n.)* a person being kept in a jail or prison; a captive
There are several policemen around the **prisoner** to keep him from escaping.

prize *(n.)* an award
The winner of the contest will receive a cash **prize**.

raised *(adj.)* elevated
The farmhouse is in a **raised** position that is higher than the rest of the land.

regret *(v.)* to feel bad about an action that one did in the past
I **regret** that I did not tell you about this problem earlier.

relatively *(adv.)* fairly; somewhat
Brian has a **relatively** good idea that you ought to hear.

renew *(v.)* to extend the due date or expiration date of something
Are you interested in **renewing** your magazine subscription?

rumor *(n.)* an unconfirmed story about someone or something

There were a lot of **rumors** at the high school about the new principal.

shallow *(adj.)* not deep; low
Stay in **shallow** water and do not swim too far away from shore.

steep *(adj.)* having sharp sides; high
The mountain is so **steep** that climbing it is extremely difficult.

substance *(n.)* the makeup of someone or something; composition; material
The students must determine the contents of the **substance** during their lab class.

thrive *(v.)* to do well; to excel; to prosper
If you try hard, you should be able to **thrive** at your new place of employment.

vibration *(n.)* movement; shaking
I can feel the **vibrations** when the car is moving.

zest *(n.)* zeal; enthusiasm
Mr. Patterson's **zest** for teaching makes the students interested in his class.

Practice Test 7

allegiance *(n.)* loyalty to a person or group
No one questions Tom's **allegiance** to his country.

approach *(n.)* a method; a way of doing something
The best **approach** is to use a computer to design the building.

assume *(v.)* to take over the leadership of a group
Mary **assumed** the manager's position when the previous manager retired.

biofuel *(n.)* a type of fuel made from some type of organic matter
Biofuel is often made from matter such as corn or sugarcane.

boycott *(n.)* a type of protest in which people refuse to use a service or to buy a company's products
The company gave the protesters what they wanted after a ten-week-long **boycott**.

breakdown *(n.)* an event when a machine stops working
The **breakdown** of the computer system made the company lose money.

breakthrough *(n.)* an advance; a discovery, often of great importance
The new product was made thanks to a **breakthrough** that happened in the lab.

cheater *(n.)* a person who cheats, such as on a test
The two **cheaters** were suspended from school and given failing grades.

condense *(v.)* to change from a gaseous to a liquid state
Water vapor **condenses** when the weather begins to get warmer.

consult *(v.)* to look at; to check
I need to **consult** my notes to give you the correct answer.

contemporary *(n.)* a person who lives at the same time as another
George Washington and John Adams were **contemporaries**.

corruption *(n.)* dishonesty; immoral behavior
The city of Chicago is known for its political **corruption**.

deposit *(v.)* to set something down on a surface; to deliver something and then leave
Amy **deposited** her books on her desk.

dissect *(v.)* to cut up; to cut into small pieces
The student is going to **dissect** a frog during his laboratory class.

disrupt *(v.)* to interrupt; to cause a disturbance; to disturb
The rude student continually **disrupted** the teacher's lecture.

elite *(n.)* a person who belongs to the highest class or group
Too many **elites** these days only care about increasing their personal wealth.

enticing *(adj.)* appealing
There is an **enticing** aroma coming from the kitchen.

exempt *(v.)* to excuse a person from doing something
The school **exempts** members of sports teams from taking gym class.

expressway *(n.)* an interstate; a thruway; a large highway with limited entrances and exits and no traffic lights
We plan to take the **expressway** the entire way across the country.

flash *(n.)* a sudden burst
I had a **flash** of inspiration that gave me the idea for my science project.

fraction *(n.)* a part; a section; a number that is expressed a/b
It took the computer a **fraction** of a second to do a search for that term.

frost *(n.)* a condition in which the weather is so cold that dew turns into a small covering of ice
The **frost** killed most of the oranges that were still on the trees.

horoscope *(n.)* a prediction about a person's future, often based on that individual's birthday
According to my **horoscope**, I am going to have good luck today.

joker *(n.)* a person who tells many jokes; a humorous person
Matt is such a **joker**, so he always makes people laugh.

manifest *(v.)* to appear; to form; to come into existence
The particles will **manifest** if you do the experiment properly.

mutual *(adj.)* common; shared
We have a **mutual** friend whom we both trust.

nonrenewable *(adj.)* not able to be used again
Coal and oil are two examples of **nonrenewable** sources of energy.

nonviolence *(n.)* peacefulness; the act of refusing to engage in violent behavior
Gandhi promoted **nonviolence** during his struggles against Great Britain.

overrun *(v.)* to flood; to take over; to cover
The yard was **overrun** with weeds when the family stopped caring for it.

overthrow *(v.)* to defeat; to take the place of, often through the use of violence
The colonists **overthrew** their masters and declared independence.

overwhelmed *(adj.)* overloaded; having too much of something
We were **overwhelmed** by all of the homework that Mr. Appleton assigned us.

pane *(n.)* glass, often that is used in windows
The boy threw the baseball and shattered a window **pane** with it.

penmanship *(n.)* handwriting; the art of writing by hand
More schools ought to teach their students to have good **penmanship**.

reign *(v.)* to rule over a land as a king or emperor
The king **reigned** for more than forty-five years.

renewable *(adj.)* able to be used again
Solar energy is one type of **renewable** energy.

replace *(v.)* to substitute one thing or person for another
I need to **replace** these old gloves with a new pair.

shot *(n.)* a chance; an attempt
Coach Bird gave Dave one more **shot** to make the team.

skeleton *(n.)* a complete set of bones for a human or animal
There is a picture of a human **skeleton** on page 198 in the book.

snout *(n.)* a large nose; a projection from an animal's face that contains its jaws and nose
The pig stuck its **snout** into the food and starting eating.

spark *(v.)* to cause a fire to start; to flash; to ignite
Mr. Kelvin managed to **spark** the student's interest in learning about history.

squad *(n.)* a team
The basketball **squad** must ride on the bus to get to the game.

squeamish *(adj.)* easily upset; easily made nauseous or sick
Cathy becomes very **squeamish** if she sees blood.

steady *(adj.)* constant; regular
If you have a **steady** income, you should be able to save money each month.

tardiness *(n.)* lateness; the act of being late
Tardiness is not accepted in Ms. Clarkson's class.

timeline *(n.)* a line that shows when various events occurred in the past
Look at the **timeline** to see when various historical events

occurred.

tissue *(n.)* a part of an organism that has numerous cells with the same function
He suffered some damage to his **tissues** in the car accident.

ton *(n.)* a measure of weight that amounts to 1,000 kilograms
The truck can carry several **tons** of equipment.

turmoil *(n.)* disorder; chaos
There was a lot of **turmoil** in the country during the revolution.

tutorial *(n.)* a special class in which a tutor gives extra instructions
Mr. Clifford always has a **tutorial** before the final exam.

yearbook *(n.)* an annual; a book published for high school or college students that shows pictures of various events from the previous year
Many students wanted to sign Tina's **yearbook**.

Practice Test 8

ace *(v.)* to do very well on something, such as an exam; to get a perfect or near-perfect grade
Sarah **aced** her science test and did not miss a single question.

acupuncturist *(n.)* a person who practices acupuncture
After I visited the **acupuncturist**, I felt much better.

ambush *(v.)* to hide and then attack someone or something
Many animals prefer to **ambush** their prey.

appreciate *(v.)* to welcome; to be thankful for
We **appreciate** all of the help that you have given us.

arrange *(v.)* to set up; to position; to place
Karen is going to **arrange** all of the furniture in her house today.

assemblage *(n.)* a group; a crowd
There was quite an **assemblage** of people at the park last weekend.

barb *(n.)* a sharp bristle found on an animal
The **barbs** on the animal allow it to protect itself from predators.

battlefield *(n.)* the site of a battle
There were hundreds of dead bodies lying on the **battlefield**.

bore *(v.)* to make someone uninterested; to cause a person to become bored
Everyone in the class was **bored** by the teacher's lecture.

branch *(n.)* the limb of the main stem of a plant, especially a tree
The bird built its nest on one of the **branches** of the tallest tree in the forest.

clap *(v.)* to applaud; to strike one's hands together to make a sound when one is pleased
All of the members of the audience **clapped** at the end of the performance.

combustion *(n.)* burning; the igniting or lighting of a fire
The **combustion** of the two compounds caused a fire to start.

conductor *(n.)* the leader of a band or orchestra; a director
Mr. Carter has been the school's band **conductor** for ten years.

decomposition *(n.)* the breakdown of a compound; the act of rotting
The **decomposition** of the body caused a horrible smell to be released.

displace *(v.)* to move; to shift
Several large rocks were **displaced** when the storm caused a serious flood.

distinguishing *(adj.)* notable
Lisa is interested in learning what Tim's **distinguishing** features are.

donation *(n.)* a gift, often of money
If you want to make a **donation**, we would appreciate it.

embarrassed *(adj.)* shy, uncomfortable or ashamed
I was **embarrassed** when I slipped and fell down on stage.

endeavor *(v.)* to try hard
You must **endeavor** to do your best in all situations.

endurance *(n.)* stamina; a person's ability to survive personal hardship
By exercising every day, you can increase your **endurance**.

episode *(n.)* a story; an incident; an event
Tell us about one of the most interesting **episodes** in the series.

follow *(v.)* to understand
Do you **follow** what I am trying to tell you?

halfhearted *(adj.)* unenthusiastic; lacking enthusiasm or interest
Amy gave a **halfhearted** effort at painting a picture during art class.

handout *(n.)* a printed paper that has information on it
Ms. Sullivan almost always gives her students **handouts**.

inclined *(adj.)* tending to be or act in some way
I am not **inclined** to assist you because of your bad attitude.

legend *(n.)* a story from the past that may or may not be true
There are many **legends** about King Arthur and his knights.

limited *(adj.)* restricted in size or amount
The sale is going to last for a **limited** time only.

mandible *(n.)* a biting organ found in some animals
The animal's powerful **mandibles** ripped the creature apart.

model *(adj.)* ideal; perfect
Larry is a **model** student who gets A's in all of his classes.

modest *(adj.)* humble; not egotistic or vain
She is so **modest** that she refused to accept an award for her hard work.

mural *(n.)* a painting on a wall
It took George two months to complete the work on his **mural**.

path *(n.)* a route; a trail
Be sure to take the **path** that goes straight up the mountain.

placebo *(n.)* something that a patient believes is medicine but which has no effect at all
Some patients were given aspirin while others received **placebos**.

pounce *(v.)* to leap suddenly
The cat **pounced** on the mouse as soon as it came out of its hole.

praise *(v.)* to compliment; to say nice things about someone or something
Be sure to **praise** your students when they do good work.

preparation *(n.)* the act of getting ready for something
All of our **preparations** for the concert are nearly complete.

prick *(v.)* to poke
The sharp needle **pricked** my skin and made me start bleeding.

relieve *(v.)* to ease
Brenda will be **relieved** when she hears the good news.

remotely *(adv.)* to a very slight degree
I am not **remotely** interested in working with him.

retire *(v.)* to stop working, often because of one's age
Mr. Jenkins plans to **retire** five years from now.

reverse *(n.)* the opposite
What I believe is the **reverse** of what you just said.

silo *(n.)* a large, cylindrical building in which grain is kept
The farmer will store all of his grain in those **silos** over there.

slaughter *(v.)* to kill animals for food; to kill in a brutal manner; to butcher
The ranchers **slaughter** large numbers of cattle every year.

spoil *(v.)* to go bad, as in food; to rot
If you leave the food out of the refrigerator, it will **spoil**.

surroundings *(n.)* an environment; an area
Be aware of your **surroundings** at all times.

telescope *(n.)* a tool used to get closer looks at distant objects
She used her **telescope** to observe Venus and Mars.

thunderstorm *(n.)* a heavy rainstorm with thunder and lightning.
Expect the **thunderstorm** to begin around three in the afternoon.

version *(n.)* a description; an account
Which **version** of the book is the teacher reading from?

workman *(n.)* a laborer; a person who does manual labor
The **workmen** repaired the house for the entire day.

yield *(v.)* to produce; to result in
Her research was a waste of time since it **yielded** no positive results.

accomplished *(adj.)* talented; having many skills; completed
Clara is one of the country's most **accomplished** writers.

admire *(v.)* to like very much; to respect
Many people **admire** Mr. Wilson because he is such an honest man.

airlift *(v.)* to transport someone or something by air
The military **airlifted** the necessary supplies to the soldiers.

alumna *(n.)* a female graduate of an educational institution
As an **alumna** of that college, Paula likes to support it with donations.

beach *(v.)* to land one's ship or boat on the shore
We **beached** the ship on the shore and then explored the island.

bomber *(n.)* an airplane built for the purpose of dropping bombs
The air force ordered many **bombers** to be built.

boom *(n.)* a loud noise; an explosive sound
Everyone was startled when they heard the loud **boom**.

confident *(adj.)* sure; certain
I am **confident** that I will do well in the class.

considerably *(adj.)* greatly; very much; noticeably
Jack is **considerably** thinner than the last time we saw him.

consideration *(n.)* thought; deliberation
After a lot of **consideration**, I have decided to take the job.

cove *(n.)* a sheltered area along the shore of a sea, lake, or river
Sail your ship into that **cove** if the sea becomes too rough.

crosswalk *(n.)* a designated part of a street where people may cross it
He told his children that they should only cross the street at the **crosswalk**.

decent *(adj.)* all right; adequate; neither good nor bad
The meal was **decent**, but there was nothing special about it.

decipher *(v.)* to figure out; to solve
Computers can easily **decipher** many secret codes these days.

elective *(n.)* a class that a student does not need in order to graduate
Janet is going to take two **electives** this semester.

element *(n.)* an aspect
There are some **elements** of the work that we do not understand.

entrée *(n.)* a main course
The diners are about ready to order their **entrées** from the waiter.

encyclopedia *(n.)* a reference book that contains short articles about a wide variety of topics
There are a number of online **encyclopedias** that people can consult.

epic *(adj.)* heroic
Tony loves to read **epic** poems such as the Iliad and Odyssey.

excerpt *(n.)* a short passage from a large work; an extract
After reading an online **excerpt** of the book, Sue decided to purchase it.

experimental *(adj.)* new; based on an experiment
This is an **experimental** medical procedure that has not yet been approved.

footnote *(n.)* a note at the bottom of a page that provides explanatory information
A good research paper always contains **footnotes**.

forefather *(n.)* an ancestor
My **forefathers** came to this country more than 300 years ago.

further *(v.)* to advance; to promote
Ms. Thompson promised to **further** Jeff's career if he works with her.

handful *(n.)* a small number
A **handful** of students stayed late after school to study in the library.

handwritten *(adj.)* being written with a pen or pencil
Your papers need to be **handwritten**, not typed on a computer.

headmaster *(n.)* the person who is in charge of a private school
Mr. Sinclair, the **headmaster** of the school, has decided to retire.

immediate *(adj.)* instant; direct
There is a problem that needs your **immediate** attention.

knowledgeable *(adj.)* informed; having a lot of knowledge
Julie is one of the most **knowledgeable** people that I know.

legislative *(adj.)* lawmaking; relating to the legislature
Ms. Keller has a number of **legislative** duties to conduct today.

legitimate *(adj.)* legal; following the rules or laws
The king is considered the **legitimate** ruler of his country.

licensed *(adj.)* certified; approved; qualified
You should only visit a **licensed** doctor when you are sick.

mast *(n.)* a tall structure on a ship that can support a sail
If you climb to the top of the **mast**, you can see further.

meteor *(n.)* a small object, such as a rock or speck of dust, that has entered the Earth's atmosphere
We are all excited to see the **meteors** later tonight.

mutually *(adv.)* equally; commonly
Let's try to meet at a **mutually** acceptable time tomorrow.

oppressive *(adj.)* harsh; cruel; unfair
The reigns of most tyrants are **oppressive** times for the people of their countries.

pause *(v.)* to stop for a short period of time
You should **pause** for a moment before you continue.

plank *(n.)* a long, flat piece of wood, often used for construction; lumber
We need several **planks** in order to complete building the house.

professional *(adj.)* trained; skilled; having a certain occupation
Professional athletes can make millions of dollars a year.

raid *(v.)* to attack suddenly; to assault
The soldiers plan to **raid** the enemy camp at dawn.

render *(v.)* to change; to turn into
It is possible to **render** cream into butter if you stir it enough.

rumor *(n.)* an unconfirmed story about someone or something
You need to tell the truth because there are too many **rumors** about the incident.

seafaring *(n.)* traveling by sea or on the ocean
The tribe has a long **seafaring** tradition, so its members are comfortable on ships.

session *(n.)* a meeting; a gathering
There is a practice **session** at three for people who want to prepare for the exam.

shot *(n.)* a chance; an attempt
Joe gave his best **shot**, but he did not succeed.

slender *(adj.)* thin; slim
Cindy is so **slender** now that she exercises daily.

slip *(n.)* a small piece of paper that has information on it; a small form
Fill out this **slip** and then give it to your teacher.

sonic *(adj.)* relating to sound
A **sonic** boom is a very loud noise created when something breaks the sound barrier.

supersonic *(adj.)* faster than the speed of sound
The airline is considering purchasing some **supersonic** airplanes.

uproot *(v.)* to remove from the ground
Be careful that you do not damage the flowers when you **uproot** them.

TOEFL Junior
全真模考题
强化训练

韩国多乐园TOEFL Junior研发中心 编著

浙江教育出版社·杭州

音频

Introduction

Every year, as the world becomes more globalized, the importance of knowing the English language increases. As a result, it is crucial for students to be able to determine how well they know English. This is one of the reasons that standardized tests are so common.

TOEFL Junior is a relatively new standardized test. It is intended for middle school and high schools students who are learning English. The test serves a couple of purposes. First, it enables young learners of the English language to rate their abilities. They can therefore find out which aspects of the English language they are skilled in and which aspects they need to improve upon. Second, TOEFL Junior helps prepare young learners for the TOEFL test, which they may take at some time in the future.

The goal of this book is to provide students with practice tests that are as similar to the real TOEFL Junior tests as possible. In this way, this book can enable students to get the practice they need to excel on the TOEFL Junior test when they take it.

This book has been written so that young learners may prepare to take the TOEFL Junior test in either a classroom environment or by themselves. We hope that both young learners and instructors will find this book useful. By utilizing this book, young learners should be able both to increase their scores on the TOEFL Junior test and to improve their knowledge of the English language.

About This Book

This book consists of nine complete TOEFL Junior practice tests. Each test is divided into three parts: Listening Comprehension, Language Form and Meaning, and Reading Comprehension. Each of these three parts contains a various number of passages along with 42 questions. The passages and questions have been written so that they are similar in style and difficulty to the actual passages and questions that appear on the TOEFL Junior test.

Listening Comprehension

This section contains both short and long passages. Some of the passages are academic in nature while others are practical. After each short passage, which may be a conversation, announcement, or lecture, there is one question. After each long passage, which may be a conversation, lecture, or discussion, there are three to five questions. The question types include main idea, detail, inference, and rhetorical purpose questions.

Language Form and Meaning

This section contains both short and long passages. Some of the passages are academic. Meanwhile, other passages cover practical topics. The passages appear in a variety of styles. These include letters, emails, advertisements, diary entries, announcements, and articles. Each short passage has four blanks while the long passages have six to eight blanks. Learners must choose the correct word or phrase for each blank. The answer choices test learners' knowledge of sentence structure, grammar, and vocabulary.

Reading Comprehension

This section contains both short and long passages. Some of the passages are academic whereas others are about practical topics. The passages may be written as letters, emails, advertisements, diary entries, stories, announcements, and articles. After each passage, there are four to eleven questions. The question types vary, but they include main idea, detail, vocabulary, inference, reference, and rhetorical purpose questions.

About the TOEFL Junior Test

TOEFL Junior考试介绍

    TOEFL Junior考试是由美国教育考试服务中心（ETS）研发并在世界范围内推广的针对初中生的一项测评工具，用以衡量在以英语为媒介的教学环境中，11~17岁的中学生在学术和社交方面的英语水平。作为一项测评工具，它可以帮助考生申请美国初、高中，同时，多维度的标准化测评使得TOEFL Junior考试还能够为考生的进一步语言学习提供参考和指导。

    如果现有的托福考试是评估考生的英语技能，以适应大学水平，那么TOEFL Junior考试将评估考生的中学英语技能。此外，TOEFL Junior考试是对一般英语使用能力的评估，其内容并不只集中在特定课程上，考试内容分为Listening Comprehension（听力理解）、Language Form and Meaning（语言形式与含义）以及Reading Comprehension（阅读理解）三个部分。

考试结构

考试模块	文章长度（单词数）	文章总数	每篇文章的题目数	题目总数	时长（分钟）
Listening Comprehension	55~65	6~9	1	42	40
	210~360	8~10	3~5		
Language Form and Meaning	60~120	3	4	42	25
	120~170	4	6 or 8		
Reading Comprehension	120~200	2~3	4~7	42	50
	200~420	3~4	5~11		

模块考查内容

Listening Comprehension

    听力理解考查以下三种听力技能。

The ability to listen for basic interpersonal purposes

    考生应该能够理解学校中日常话题的对话。这包括理解对话的主题和主要内容的能力、根据说话者所讲的内容进行推理或预测的能力、理解对话目的的能力，以及识别某种语气或者强调某些用词的能力等。

The ability to listen for instructional purposes

    考生应该能够理解教师和其他教职工在非上课时间使用的话语。这可能包括课堂内外发生的对话，例如，现场学习或图书馆的情况以及指导，即通知、警告等内容。考生在听到这些内容时，必须能够理解信息的主题或要点，并具备根据说话者所讲的内容进行推理或预测的能力。

The ability to listen for academic purposes

    考生应该能够理解基于课程内容的讲座或讨论。这些讲座或讨论的内容多为学术主题，可能涉及复杂的句子结构。此外，考生必须能够理解主题和主要内容，并能够根据说话者所讲的内容进行推理或预测。最后，考生还需要理解说话人的说话目的和陈述中的修辞表达。

听力和阅读能力等对语言表达来说很重要，但与语法和词汇相关的能力也很重要。

与语法和词汇相关的技能很重要，因为不仅它们本身很重要，而且它们在提高沟通技巧方面还起着至关重要的作用。因此，考生不应只关注语法或词汇的形式方面，还应理解英语语法结构和掌握相关词汇知识。

Reading Comprehension

阅读理解考查以下两种阅读技能。

The ability to read and comprehend academic texts

考生应该能够阅读和理解涵盖各种学科的不同文本，例如艺术、人文和科学，再例如说明文、传记和论文。他们还应该能够阅读和理解在实际说英语的教室中使用的有一定难度的文本。在阅读这些文本时，考生必须能够理解主题及其相关性，能够从未直接揭示的内容中做出推断，并理解关键词汇。考生应该能够根据内容，了解作者的意图，理解文本的结构及基本的修辞表达。与听力一样，阅读部分不需要任何特定的背景知识，但平时的阅读经验有可能有助于考生理解学术内容中的新信息。

The ability to read and comprehend nonacademic texts

在英语教育环境中，阅读学术内容是主要要求，但考生也应该能够阅读各种非学术内容。这可能包括电子邮件、信件、文章、学生作文、小册子、广告和时间表。在阅读非学术内容时，考生应该具有与阅读学术内容相同的理解水平，同时能够理解含有地道表达的文本。

蓝思指数

TOEFL Junior考试提供与考生的成绩对应的蓝思指数，考生可以以此为依据选择适合自己的书籍。蓝思指数是一种阅读能力指数，可指导特定读者阅读适合其水平的书籍，并且已经在TOEFL iBT考试中广泛使用。成千上万的英语学生和教师正在使用蓝思指数帮助他们提高阅读技能。

成绩

TOEFL Junior考试的成绩是由考生回答正确的题目数量决定的。答错不扣分。每个部分正确答案的数量会转换成一个数值，每个部分的最高分是300分。

考试模块	分数
Listening Comprehension	200~300
Language Form and Meaning	200~300
Reading Comprehension	200~300
总分	600~900

* 分数是通过ETS评分方法重新调整的，该方法考虑了问题的类型和难度，而不是简单地给每个问题打分。

考试报名

个人和团体可以登录http://www.toeflyss.cn/在线注册考试，也可以在此网站查询考试地点和考试日期。

Table of Contents

Practice
Test 1

Listening
Comprehension

听力音频

The listening section has 42 questions. Follow along as you listen to the directions to the listening section.

Directions

In this section of the test, you will hear talks and conversations. Each talk or conversation is followed by one question. Choose the best answer to each question and mark the letter of the correct answer on your answer sheet. You will hear each talk or conversation only one time.

Here is an example: 📢

What does the girl mean?

(A) She will meet the boy at band practice soon.

(B) She is not going to be a member of the band.

(C) She thinks that the band is no longer fun.

(D) She has been a member of the band for a year.

The correct answer is (B), "She is not going to be a member of the band."

Here is another example: 📢

What are the speakers talking about?

(A) Their classes

(B) Going on a trip

(C) Spring break

(D) An upcoming test

The correct answer is (C), "Spring break."

Go on to the next page, and the test will begin with question number one.

GO ON TO THE NEXT PAGE ⟫

1. What does the boy mean when he says: "So I'll have to take a pass on the game"?

   (A) He is going to play in the game.

   (B) He cannot attend today's game.

   (C) He will meet the girl before the game.

   (D) He is able to watch the game today.

2. Why does the teacher talk about the boy's grade?

   (A) To express her concern about his grade

   (B) To encourage him to study hard for the test

   (C) To praise him for submitting a good report

   (D) To compliment him for getting an A on his exam

3. What is the girl planning to do on the weekend?

   (A) Go cycling with her friends

   (B) Spend some time with the boy

   (C) Stay home and study

   (D) Check out the weather forecast

4. What will the boy probably do next?

   (A) Go to his meeting with Mr. Jacobs

   (B) Continue speaking with Jenny

   (C) Make a telephone call to Brian

   (D) Turn in his group project to the teacher

5. Why is the student discussing his essay with the teacher?

   (A) To insist that the teacher grade it again

   (B) To ask about a grammar mistake on it

   (C) To complain about the teacher's emphasis on facts

   (D) To express his confusion about his grade

6. What will the girl probably do next?

   (A) Finish eating her lunch

   (B) Solve some math problems

   (C) Look at the boy's homework

   (D) Skip their math class

7. What are the speakers mainly talking about?

   (A) Mr. Norton's class

   (B) Their grades at school

   (C) A test they just took

   (D) A question the boy asked in class

8. Why does the principal mention the winter storm?

   (A) To give the students a lesson on the weather

   (B) To claim that it will start tomorrow

   (C) To note the amount of snow that it dropped

   (D) To explain why she is cancelling classes

9. What is probably true about Dr. Walt Campbell?

   (A) He is a citizen of France.

   (B) He is the host of the radio program.

   (C) He has visited the site of the Battle of Waterloo.

   (D) He knows a lot about Napoleon.

GO ON TO THE NEXT PAGE

Now you will hear longer talks or conversations. Each talk or conversation will be followed by three or more questions. Choose the best answer to each question and mark the letter of the correct answer on your answer sheet. You will hear each talk or conversation only one time.

10. **What are the speakers mainly discussing?**

   (A) The boy's desire to get an extension
   (B) The topic of the paper the boy is writing
   (C) The boy's involvement in athletics
   (D) The type of research that the boy needs to conduct

11. **Why does the boy say that he is unable to finish his assignment on time?**

   (A) He cannot find the information that he needs.
   (B) He needs to study for a test in another class tonight.
   (C) His partner has not done enough work on the project.
   (D) He has not had enough time to do his work.

12. **What does the boy suggest about the soccer team?**

   (A) It has not lost any games yet this season.
   (B) There is going to be a game tonight.
   (C) Being on it takes up a lot of his time.
   (D) It needs to get some new members.

13. **What does the teacher tell the boy to do?**

   (A) Go to the library
   (B) Attend his next class
   (C) Skip soccer practice
   (D) Have a chat with Coach Grubbs

14. **What are the speakers mainly talking about?**

   (A) The girl's soccer team
   (B) The boy's attendance at the game
   (C) The girl's next game
   (D) The boy's desire to play soccer

15. **When will the girl's next soccer game be?**

   (A) This Friday
   (B) This Saturday
   (C) Next Tuesday
   (D) Next Thursday

16. **What can be inferred about the girl?**

   (A) She is interested in playing goalkeeper on her team.
   (B) She is not happy with the attendance at her games.
   (C) She suffered a minor injury in the last game.
   (D) She is the best player on the girls' soccer team.

17. **Why does the boy mention his friends?**

   (A) To ask how they can join the girls' soccer team
   (B) To say that they enjoyed watching the last soccer game
   (C) To tell the girl that they all wish the team good luck
   (D) To indicate that he will invite them to the next game

GO ON TO THE NEXT PAGE

18. How does the girl probably feel when she says: "A science fair? That's peculiar."

   (A) She is pleased.
   (B) She is upset.
   (C) She is confused.
   (D) She is interested.

19. Why does the boy mention the science fair?

   (A) To encourage the girl to enter it along with him
   (B) To claim that it is going to be held at the school
   (C) To state that he intends to win this year's competition
   (D) To tell the girl what he was speaking to a teacher about

20. In which subject is the boy doing research?

   (A) Chemistry
   (B) Physics
   (C) Biology
   (D) Geology

21. What does the boy mention about Mr. Stevenson?

   (A) He is the school's only science teacher.
   (B) He is doing research with the boy.
   (C) He designed the boy's science fair project.
   (D) He is thinking of teaching at another school in the city.

22. What can be inferred about the boy?

   (A) He intends to enter the science fair.
   (B) He is the top student at the school.
   (C) He is the girl's classmate.
   (D) He is better at sports than at science.

23. What are the speakers mainly discussing?

   (A) Visiting Italy
   (B) The girl's sister
   (C) Life as a student
   (D) Hanging out with their friends

24. What was the girl's sister doing in Italy?

   (A) She was studying as an exchange student.
   (B) She was taking a tour with some other students.
   (C) She was visiting the country's museums.
   (D) She was looking for a place to live there.

25. What can be inferred about the girl?

   (A) She wants to keep talking to the boy.
   (B) She feels jealous of her sister.
   (C) She is looking forward to seeing her sister.
   (D) She is learning how to speak Italian.

26. What will the girl do after school today?

   (A) Apply to become an exchange student
   (B) Hang out at the mall with her friends
   (C) Pick her sister up at the airport
   (D) Go home and complete her homework

GO ON TO THE NEXT PAGE

27. What is the teacher mainly talking about?

(A) Which foods flying squirrels prefer to eat

(B) The appearance of the flying squirrel

(C) Where most flying squirrels live

(D) The unique way flying squirrels can travel

28. What is the purpose of the membrane that the flying squirrel has?

(A) It allows the squirrel to control its body while in flight.

(B) It enables the squirrel to soar through the air.

(C) It lets the squirrel leap from tree to tree.

(D) It permits the squirrel to make very long jumps.

29. What will the teacher probably do next?

(A) Have one of the students read from a textbook

(B) Show a video that has flying squirrels in it

(C) Assign some homework to the students

(D) Give a physical description of the flying squirrel

30. What is the main idea of the talk?

(A) There are differences between pyramids and ziggurats.

(B) Egypt and Mesopotamia had great cultures.

(C) The pharaohs were important in ancient Egypt.

(D) People in ancient cultures practiced religion.

31. What does the teacher imply about ziggurats?

(A) They took many years to build.

(B) They look much nicer than the pyramids.

(C) They were built in both Mesopotamia and Egypt.

(D) They are less well known than pyramids.

32. How is a ziggurat different from a pyramid?

(A) It is much larger than most pyramids.

(B) It has a stepped look as it goes up.

(C) It is made of different types of stone.

(D) It has various types of artwork on it.

33. Why does the teacher talk about the pharaohs?

(A) To describe their role in Egyptian society

(B) To note that they built the pyramids

(C) To compare them with Mesopotamian rulers

(D) To claim that many were bad rulers

34. What is the teacher mainly talking about?

(A) The antlers that deer can grow

(B) How deer take care of their babies

(C) The characteristics of white-tailed deer

(D) What his opinion of deer is

35. What is probably true about the teacher?

(A) He recently made a visit to Australia.

(B) He enjoys going deer hunting.

(C) He lives in an area with many deer.

(D) He spends a lot of time outdoors.

36. What does the teacher imply when he says this: "That's H-A-R-T, not H-E-A-R-T"?

(A) He is making an important point about deer.

(B) Some students tend to misspell the word.

(C) The word he is spelling is a common one.

(D) He wants the students to listen carefully.

37. What does the teacher say about antlers?

(A) Both male and female deer grow them.

(B) They fall off from the deer each year.

(C) Deer sometimes use them as weapons.

(D) They get larger as the deer ages.

38. What does a fawn look like when it is born?

(A) It is completely white.

(B) It only has a white tail.

(C) It has some white spots.

(D) It has no white anywhere on its body.

39. What is the discussion mainly about?

(A) The poetry Edgar Allan Poe wrote

(B) The contributions of Edgar Allan Poe

(C) The creation of the horror genre

(D) Poetry in nineteenth century America

40. What happened to Edgar Allan Poe when he was a child?

(A) He attended a top school.

(B) He suffered from depression.

(C) He became very sick.

(D) His parents died.

41. Why does the teacher mention *The Murders in the Rue Morgue*?

(A) To praise it as a great work of horror

(B) To claim it is her favorite of all of Poe's works

(C) To name a work the students are going to read

(D) To state that it is a poem written by Poe

42. What will the students probably do next?

(A) Continue discussing Poe's life

(B) Read a poem written by Poe

(C) Analyze a modern detective novel

(D) Talk about one of Poe's horror novels

STOP

Language Form and Meaning

In this section of the test, you will answer 42 questions found in seven different texts. Within each text are boxes that contain four possible ways to complete a sentence. Choose the word or words in each box that correctly complete each sentence. Mark the letter of the correct answer on your answer sheet.

Here are two sample questions:

1. While some forest fires

    (A) cause
    (B) causing
    (C) are caused
    (D) will cause

    by humans, most of them happen due to

lightning striking the ground during a region's dry season. In fact, some places

2.

    (A) accept
    (B) endure
    (C) permit
    (D) strike

    forest fires on a yearly basis.

The correct answer to **Sample 1** is (C), "are caused." The correct answer to **Sample 2** is (B), "endure."

GO ON TO THE NEXT PAGE

9

Questions 1–4 refer to the following email.

Dear Amy,

1. I heard from one of our friends that you

(A) will not feel
(B) are not feeling
(C) cannot feel
(D) must not feel

very well today. I hope

that you do not have anything serious and that you will be able to go back to school

2. tomorrow. The teachers

(A) reserved
(B) approved
(C) requested
(D) assigned

us a lot of homework in all of our classes

3. today. Did anyone from school let you know about

(A) what you need to do?
(B) which you need to do?
(C) that you need to do?
(D) how you need to do?

If you want to know about anything, just write me back. I would be glad to assist you

so that you can get your work done on time. I can drop by your house later in the evening

4. if you want. Give me a

(A) respond
(B) response
(C) responsive
(D) responder

to this email whenever you get the chance.

Your friend,

Susan

GO ON TO THE NEXT PAGE

Questions 5–8 refer to the following advertisement.

If you are looking for something fun to do this summer, why don't you visit the community

5. center? The community center,

(A) what is locating
(B) which is located
(C) where the location
(D) how it was located

at 49 Maple Street, is going

to be sponsoring numerous activities. For instance, there will be art, music, and language

6. classes at the center throughout the summer.

(A) In addition to those,
(B) As well as they,
(C) So with those,
(D) Apparently with those,

the center

is going to sponsor a soccer league and a baseball league for students in middle school

7.   and high school. We

(A) demand
(B) approve
(C) invite
(D) consider

all young people to participate. We know that the

8.   events this year are going to be

(A) the best
(B) much better than
(C) as well as
(D) just as good that

those in any past years.

Questions 9–12 refer to the following announcement.

Tomorrow after lunch, all classes are going to be cancelled. Instead of going to

your classrooms, students should report to the school auditorium no later than one

9. fifteen. The school is proud

(A) announce
(B) announcing
(C) will announce
(D) to announce

that Mayor Randolph Jefferson has

accepted our offer to come and speak with the student body. Mayor Jefferson will chat

10. about his experience

(A) run to the city,
(B) running the city,
(C) of running in the city,
(D) to run the city,

and then he will take a few questions.

GO ON TO THE NEXT PAGE

11. Please wear

(A) appropriate
(B) approximate
(C) approachable
(D) approving

clothing tomorrow and be sure to

12.

(A) being the best behaved
(B) behave like the best
(C) be on your best behavior
(D) behavior of the best

as well. We expect you to be good representatives

of our school and to treat the mayor with the respect he deserves.

GO ON TO THE NEXT PAGE

Questions 13–20 refer to the following letter.

Dear Mr. Thompson,

13. I would like to apologize to you

(A) with the action
(B) for my actions
(C) by my action
(D) at the action

in your class during the exam

yesterday. I am so sorry that I looked in my textbook while I was taking the test.

14. I feel terrible about

(A) completing
(B) researching
(C) practicing
(D) cheating

on the test. I know that this is not an

15.

(A) accept
(B) acceptance
(C) accepting
(D) acceptable

excuse, but I did not have enough time to study for the test

because I had a basketball game the night before it. I was so tired that,

16.

(A) the moment I arrived home,
(B) momentarily arriving at my home,
(C) to arrive in a moment at my home,
(D) I arrived home in a moment,

I took a shower and went to bed

GO ON TO THE NEXT PAGE

GO ON TO THE NEXT PAGE

17.
(A) apparently.
(B) decisively.
(C) immediately.
(D) dramatically.

When I woke up, I remembered the test and tried to study.

However, I only managed to do that for about fifteen minutes.

18. Still, there is no
(A) consideration
(B) justification
(C) ramification
(D) criticism
 for cheating. I will accept

19.
(A) whoever punishes
(B) whatever punishment
(C) whichever punishes
(D) however punished
 you decide to give me without complaint. I will also

20. do my best to work hard in your class and to be
(A) a student with more possibilities
(B) possibly a better student
(C) the best of the possible students
(D) as good a student as possible

for the remainder of the semester.

Sincerely,

Peter Wilson

Questions 21–26 refer to the following email.

Dear Nathaniel,

I am looking forward to graduating in a month. I cannot believe we have almost

finished our schooling. It has been a long four years, but high school is

21.
(A) practical and over.
(B) practically over.
(C) over practically.
(D) over practical.

On one hand, I am relieved that I am going to

22. get started on
(A) the next chapter in my life.
(B) my life in the next chapter.
(C) the next life with a chapter.
(D) a chapter of the next life.

On the other hand,

the past four years have been a great experience. I shall miss everyone as we

23.
(A) apply
(B) depart
(C) register
(D) enroll

for different colleges.

GO ON TO THE NEXT PAGE

24. Anyway, I want you to know that my family is going to be

(A) host
(B) hosts
(C) hosted
(D) hosting

a graduation party at my house. I am inviting many of our classmates.

It should be a lot of fun. You, your parents, and the rest of your family

25.

(A) invited me to my house.
(B) inviting to my house.
(C) will invite them to my house.
(D) are invited to my house.

We live on a farm, so there will be

plenty of room for everyone. Just let me know if you can make it and who

26. will be

(A) attending.
(B) graduating.
(C) resisting.
(D) requesting.

My parents need to know how many people to expect.

Talk to you soon.

Jim

GO ON TO THE NEXT PAGE

Questions 27–34 refer to the following magazine article.

One of the largest and most luxurious palaces in the world is the Palace of Versailles.

27.
(A) Is located near
(B) Locating near
(C) Having located near
(D) Located near

Paris, France, the palace has more than 2,000 rooms,

28.
(A) every which
(B) all of which
(C) that are all
(D) what all

are extravagantly decorated. Versailles was constructed

29.
(A) during the seventeenth century.
(B) for all seventeen centuries.
(C) throughout seventeen centuries.
(D) the seventeenth century onward.

Its original use was as a hunting lodge

for King Louis XIV. However, he and his successors constantly expanded it until

30. it became a massive palace. Versailles became one of

(A) the most prominent
(B) more prominent
(C) much more prominent
(D) most of the prominent

symbols of the French monarchy, and it served as the royal court from 1682

GO ON TO THE NEXT PAGE

GO ON TO THE NEXT PAGE

31. to 1789.

(A) Followed by the events of
(B) The events, following
(C) Following the events of
(D) Events were following

the French Revolution, the palace

32. was

(A) designed
(B) constructed
(C) rehabilitated
(D) transformed

into a museum. Today, Versailles

33.

(A) contain
(B) contains
(C) is containing
(D) will contain

thousands of works of art, including paintings, drawings,

engravings, and sculptures. Due to its art and the beauty of the palace itself,

it is a prime tourist attraction at the present. As a result, millions of people visit

34. the palace

(A) permanently.
(B) consistently.
(C) continually.
(D) annually.

Questions 35–42 refer to the following magazine article.

Most birds build nests in which they lay their eggs, but the emperor penguin has no need

35. of them. This bird lives in Antarctica and must endure

(A) harsher
(B) the harshest
(C) as harsh as
(D) much of the harshest

36. weather than anywhere else in the world. In order to

(A) ensure
(B) promise
(C) recall
(D) trust

that its eggs

37. are not harmed and that its chicks

(A) are hatching with them,
(B) hatched from them,
(C) are theirs to hatch,
(D) may hatch from them,

the emperor penguin

takes care of its eggs in a unique manner. An emperor penguin female lays a single egg.

38. Once she lays the egg, the male penguin takes it and puts it

(A) on top of its feet.
(B) with its feet at the top.
(C) by the top foot.
(D) at the foot of the top.

GO ON TO THE NEXT PAGE

39. There, the egg

(A) protects
(B) is protecting
(C) is protected
(D) will protect

by a layer of stomach fat that the penguin

rests above the egg. Since emperor penguins lay their eggs right as winter

40. begins in Antarctica, it is

(A) basic
(B) significant
(C) partial
(D) vital

that the eggs remain

41.

(A) by protection of the elements.
(B) protected from the elements.
(C) protecting the elements.
(D) for the protection of the elements.

Therefore, for the next two months,

the males incubate the eggs until the chicks finally hatch. During this entire

42.

(A) period,
(B) periods,
(C) periodical,
(D) periodically,

the males look after the eggs while hardly even moving.

STOP

NO TEST MATERIAL ON THIS PAGE

Reading Comprehension

In this section of the test, you will read six texts and answer 42 questions. Choose the correct answer to each question and mark the letter of the correct answer on your answer sheet.

Before you start, read the sample text and the sample questions below.

Sample Text

Erosion is one of nature's most powerful forces. It can happen in many ways, including through the wind, rain, snow, and ice. Erosion frequently takes place over a long period of time. This is how canyons and deserts are often created. Yet it is also possible for erosion to take place overnight.

Sample Question 1

What is this text mostly about?

(A) How deserts are created

(B) A natural force

(C) Canyons and deserts

(D) Wind erosion

The correct answer is (B), "A natural force."

Sample Question 2

Which of the following is true regarding erosion?

(A) It can happen in many ways.

(B) Water most commonly causes it.

(C) It can create deserts overnight.

(D) It is stronger than anything in nature.

The correct answer is (A), "It can happen in many ways."

GO ON TO THE NEXT PAGE

Questions 1–6 are about the following letter.

Dear Parents,

We have almost arrived at the end of another school year. The last day of school is going to be held on Friday, May 15. All students should have their lockers cleaned out no later than 3:30 on that day.

This year, we have accomplished a number of our <u>objectives</u>. Several of our students received academic awards, such as for winning the city spelling bee (Teresa Kelly), winning the state math competition (Rohit Apu), and winning the county essay-writing contest (Julie Johnston). Furthermore, our athletic teams all had winning records, and the girls' volleyball team, led by Coach Alice Stevens, managed to come in second place in the entire state.

Let me remind you as summer begins that all returning students must do their summer reading. Enclosed with this letter is a list of the books from which each student must choose. All students have to read at least five books and write short reports on <u>them</u> during the summer.

Allow me to close by noting that I am always willing to meet with you and to address any of your concerns about the school. You <u>can feel free to swing by</u> and chat with me anytime.

Sincerely,
Gregory Jenkins
Principal

GO ON TO THE NEXT PAGE

1. **In line 4, the word <u>objectives</u> is closest in meaning to _____.**

   (A) skills

   (B) experiences

   (C) goals

   (D) achievements

2. **Who is Julie Johnston?**

   (A) The coach of the school's volleyball team

   (B) The principal of the school

   (C) The winner of an essay-writing contest

   (D) The school's best speller

3. **What can be inferred from the letter about the school?**

   (A) It has a successful athletics program.

   (B) It has already held its graduation ceremony.

   (C) It has seen its enrollment decline.

   (D) It has a large library available to students.

4. **Paragraph 3 supports which of the following statements?**

   (A) Students may submit their reports over the Internet.

   (B) Every student must write five book reports during summer.

   (C) Students are expected to turn in reports each month.

   (D) All students must read the same five books during summer.

5. **In line 11, the word <u>them</u> refers to _____.**

   (A) all returning students

   (B) all students

   (C) five books

   (D) short reports

6. **What does Gregory Jenkins point out by writing that people <u>can feel free to swing by</u> in line 13?**

   (A) He schedules his own meetings with parents.

   (B) All visitors are welcome to visit his office.

   (C) He encourages parents to be involved at the school.

   (D) Students should spend more time on campus.

GO ON TO THE NEXT PAGE

Questions 7–12 are about the following article in the school newspaper.

Last Saturday, October 10, the school's math team took part in the Hampton Junior Math Tournament. The event was held in the auditorium at Lakeview High School. There ⁵were students from twenty-seven schools that participated in the competition.

Mrs. Gibbons, the math teacher, led our school's team at the competition. There were seven students from our school who took part ¹⁰in the contest. By the time the competition ended, we were in third place with a total of eighty-five points. The first place winner, Trinity High School, scored ninety-one points while Copeland Academy came in second with eighty-¹⁵six points. Our performance was a <u>dramatic</u> improvement from last year's team, which failed to score a single point.

Overall, Molly Reed led the team by scoring an incredible twenty-five points. That made her ²⁰the leading scorer in the entire tournament.

After the competition ended, Mrs. Gibbons said, "I'm so proud of this group. They took on teams that had twice as many students, but they still managed to capture third place. What an ²⁵incredible achievement."

GO ON TO THE NEXT PAGE

7. **Which headline best summarizes the article?**

   (A) Math Team Comes in Third in Competition

   (B) Mrs. Gibbons Takes Math Team to Lakeview High

   (C) Molly Reed Selected Captain of the Math Team

   (D) School to Compete in Math Competition

8. **What is the purpose of this article?**

   (A) To recruit some students for the math team

   (B) To describe the results of an academic competition

   (C) To praise the math team for trying its best

   (D) To encourage more students to do extracurricular activities

9. **Which of the following is NOT mentioned about the math competition?**

   (A) How many teams participated

   (B) What prizes were awarded

   (C) When it took place

   (D) Which team came in first

10. **In line 15, the word <u>dramatic</u> is closest in meaning to _____.**

    (A) tremendous

    (B) sincere

    (C) indescribable

    (D) unexpected

11. **Which of the following is true regarding Molly Reed?**

    (A) She has been on the math team for the past two years.

    (B) She scored more points than anyone at the tournament.

    (C) She was the only student from the school who scored.

    (D) She received a prize for her achievement.

12. **What does Mrs. Gibbons say about the math team?**

    (A) She is disappointed it did not win the competition.

    (B) Its members did a lot of preparing for the event.

    (C) She intends to recruit more students for it.

    (D) It was successful against some much bigger teams.

GO ON TO THE NEXT PAGE

Questions 13–18 are about the following note from the school administration.

Please be aware that the school is planning to field several athletic teams during the spring semester. The coaches have scheduled tryouts for these teams during the next two weeks. All tryouts run from 3:30 to 5:30. Here is the schedule:

Sport	Coach	Tryout Time	Note
Girls' Softball	Mrs. Marbut	Tues–Wed, March 2–3	Meet on the baseball field.
Boys' Baseball	Mr. Powell	Wed–Thurs, March 3–4	Meet on the baseball field.
Boys' Soccer	Mr. McCloud	Mon–Tues, March 8–9	None
Track and Field	Mr. Roberts	Wed–Thurs, March 10–11	Boys and girls may both participate.

There will not be a girls' soccer team this year. However, according to state rules, girls may participate on the boys' soccer team. All interested girls should speak with Coach McCloud prior to tryouts. The coaches have all agreed that any student may participate on two athletic teams so long as one is the track team. Those students wishing to play two sports must speak with both coaches prior to tryouts. Finally, all students must submit an injury release form to the coach of the team they want to play on. No students will be permitted to try out until <u>it</u> has been turned in.

13. **What is this note mostly about?**

    (A) When teams will play their games in the spring semester

    (B) How students can try out for athletic teams

    (C) Why the safety of all student-athletes is important

    (D) The upcoming schedule for athletic events

14. **Which sport will have its tryouts on March 8?**

    (A) Girls' Softball

    (B) Boys' Baseball

    (C) Boys' Soccer

    (D) Track and Field

15. **Why does the author mention Coach McCloud?**

    (A) To credit him with the decision to let girls play soccer

    (B) To tell the students that he is the new coach of the soccer team

    (C) To let girls know they should speak with him about playing soccer

    (D) To congratulate him on the achievements of the soccer team

16. **Based on the passage, which is probably true about the school's coaches?**

    (A) They communicate with one another.

    (B) They have worked there for several years.

    (C) They have good relationships with the students.

    (D) They coach teams that are successful.

17. **According to the note, what must students do before they can try out for a team?**

    (A) Get permission from their parents

    (B) Turn in a form to one of the coaches

    (C) Talk to the coach of the team

    (D) Make sure that their grades are sufficient

18. **In the last line, the word it refers to _____.**

    (A) the track team

    (B) an injury release form

    (C) the coach

    (D) the team

GO ON TO THE NEXT PAGE

Questions 19–26 are about the following passage.

The Age of Exploration lasted from the early part of the fifteenth century to the early years of the seventeenth century. During that time, adventurers from throughout Europe sailed around the world. The majority of these men came from Spain, Portugal, and England. One of the greatest of all English adventurers during this time was Sir Francis Drake. He lived from 1540 to 1596. Drake
5   accomplished a number of feats that led him to be highly <u>revered</u> in England, yet he was considered a pirate by people in other countries, particularly Spain.

After the New World was discovered by Christopher Columbus, the Spanish led the way in establishing colonies there. They were particularly dominant in Central America and South America. Their soldiers, called conquistadors, effectively defeated the Aztec and Inca empires. On account of
10   their strength in the New World, the Spanish acquired a great amount of treasure. Thus there were constantly ships filled with treasure sailing across the Atlantic Ocean to Spain.

Many sailors from other countries tried to capture these ships. Drake was one of these men. In 1573, he and his crew engaged in an act of piracy against a convoy of Spanish ships. They managed to capture the ships near Panama. Seizing their treasure of gold and silver, Drake and his men
15   returned to England. This act brought him to the attention of Queen Elizabeth. She sponsored another expedition of Drake's that sailed to the New World in 1577. Drake had five small ships and nearly 200 men. They raided Spanish holdings in South America and then sailed into the Pacific Ocean. There, Drake captured two Spanish treasure ships before sailing west across the Pacific. In September 1580, one of Drake's ships and fifty-six men reached home after having circumnavigated
20   the world.

Drake was knighted by the queen in 1581. By then, he was considered the best and most daring sailor in England. In 1585, war broke out between England and Spain. Three years later, King Phillip II of Spain sent an enormous fleet, called the *Spanish Armada*, to defeat England. Drake was made second in command of the English fleet that emerged victorious against the Spanish. A few years
25   later, in 1595, Drake returned to the New World. This time, however, his luck <u>ran out</u>. He caught a disease and died in Panama in January 1596.

19. **What is the passage mainly about?**

    (A) The colonizing of the New World

    (B) The adventures of Sir Francis Drake

    (C) Queen Elizabeth and King Phillip II

    (D) Acts of piracy by Sir Francis Drake

20. **In line 5, the word <u>revered</u> is closest in meaning to _____.**

    (A) feared

    (B) famed

    (C) noticed

    (D) regarded

21. **Why does the author mention conquistadors?**

    (A) To explain what the word means

    (B) To claim that they gathered a great amount of treasure

    (C) To note their defeat of two empires

    (D) To praise them for their fighting ability

22. **According to the author, why did many sailors attempt to capture Spanish ships?**

    (A) Their countries were at war with Spain.

    (B) They wanted to seize the ships' treasures.

    (C) They desired to enslave the Spanish sailors.

    (D) It was common for ships' crews to fight then.

23. **What did Sir Francis Drake do in 1580?**

    (A) He completed a trip around the world.

    (B) He destroyed a Spanish convoy in Panama.

    (C) He made plans to fight the Spanish Armada.

    (D) He attacked Spanish colonies in the New World.

24. **According to the passage, all of the following are mentioned about Sir Francis Drake EXCEPT _____.**

    (A) what the name of his ship was

    (B) when he was born and died

    (C) which country's sailors he often fought

    (D) how various people felt about him

25. **What can be inferred from the passage about the *Spanish Armada*?**

    (A) It sank a large number of English ships.

    (B) It lost to the English fleet that it fought.

    (C) It had more ships than any other fleet.

    (D) It was completely destroyed in two battles.

26. **In line 25, the phrase <u>ran out</u> is closest in meaning to _____.**

    (A) changed

    (B) escaped

    (C) removed

    (D) ended

GO ON TO THE NEXT PAGE

Questions 27–34 are about the following passage.

There are a number of natural disasters that can strike across the globe. Two that are frequently linked to one another are earthquakes and tsunamis. Both of them can cause a great amount of devastation when they hit. However, tsunamis are the direct result of earthquakes and cannot happen without them.

5   The Earth has three main parts. They are the crust, the mantle, and the core. The crust is the outer layer of the Earth. <u>It</u> is not a single piece of land. Instead, it is comprised of a number of plates. There are a few enormous plates and many smaller ones. These plates essentially rest upon the mantle, which is fluid. As a result, the plates are in constant—yet slow—motion. The plates may move away from or toward other plates. In some cases, they collide violently with the plates <u>adjoining</u>
10 them. The movement of the plates causes tension in the rock. Over a long time, this tension may build up. When it is released, an earthquake happens.

Tens of thousands of earthquakes happen every year. The vast majority are so small that only scientific instruments can <u>perceive</u> them. Others are powerful enough that people can feel them, yet they cause little harm or damage. More powerful earthquakes, however, can cause buildings, bridges,
15 and other structures to collapse. They may additionally injure and kill thousands of people and might even cause the land to change its appearance.

Since most of the Earth's surface is water, numerous earthquakes happen beneath the planet's oceans. Underwater earthquakes cause the seafloor to move. This results in the displacement of water in the ocean. When this occurs, a tsunami may form. This is a wave that forms on the surface and
20 moves in all directions from the place where the earthquake happened. A tsunami moves extremely quickly and can travel thousands of kilometers. As it approaches land, the water near the coast gets sucked out to sea. This causes the tsunami to increase in height. Minutes later, the tsunami arrives. A large tsunami—one more than ten meters in height—can travel far inland. As it does that, it can flood the land, destroy human settlements, and kill large numbers of people.

GO ON TO THE NEXT PAGE

27. What is the passage mainly about?

(A) How earthquakes and tsunamis occur

(B) What kind of damage natural disasters can cause

(C) Why tsunamis are deadlier than earthquakes

(D) When earthquakes are the most likely to happen

28. Paragraph 1 supports which of the following statements?

(A) The most severe type of natural disaster is an earthquake.

(B) Earthquakes cause more destruction than tsunamis.

(C) A tsunami happens in tandem with an earthquake.

(D) Earthquakes frequently take place after tsunamis do.

29. In line 6, the word It refers to _____.

(A) The mantle

(B) The core

(C) The crust

(D) The Earth

30. In line 9, the word adjoining is closest in meaning to _____.

(A) approaching

(B) bordering

(C) residing

(D) appearing

31. Which of the following is true regarding the crust?

(A) It is the smallest of the Earth's three layers.

(B) The mantle beneath it keeps it from moving too much.

(C) It is thicker on land than it is under the water.

(D) There are many separate pieces that make it up.

32. In line 13, the word perceive is closest in meaning to _____.

(A) comprehend

(B) detect

(C) locate

(D) prevent

33. Which of the following is NOT mentioned in paragraph 3 about earthquakes?

(A) How often powerful ones take place

(B) How severe the majority of them are

(C) What kind of damage they can cause

(D) How many people they typically kill

34. Based on the passage, what is probably true about tsunamis?

(A) They kill more people each year than earthquakes.

(B) They can be deadly to people standing near shore.

(C) They are able to move as fast as the speed of sound.

(D) They cannot damage ships sailing on the ocean.

GO ON TO THE NEXT PAGE

Questions 35–42 are about the following passage.

A large number of inventions require years of <u>arduous</u> research and development before they are perfected. For instance, Thomas Edison had to make more than 1,000 attempts to invent the incandescent light bulb before he finally succeeded. History is <u>replete with</u> numerous other examples of people trying, yet failing, to make inventions before they eventually succeeded. Yet some
5   inventions have come about not through hard work but simply by accident.

In most cases, when someone unintentionally invented something, the inventor was attempting to create something else. For example, in the 1930s, chemist Roy Plunkett was attempting to make a new substance that could be used to refrigerate items. He mixed some chemicals together. Then, he put them
10 into a pressurized container and cooled the mixture. By the time his experiment was complete, he had a new invention. It was not a new substance that could be used for refrigeration though. Instead, he had invented Teflon, which is today most commonly used to make nonstick pots and pans. Similarly, decades earlier, John Pemberton was a pharmacist in Atlanta, Georgia. He was attempting to
15 create a tonic that people could use whenever they had headaches. While he was not successful in that <u>endeavor</u>, he managed to invent Coca-Cola, the world-famous carbonated soft drink.

Scientists have also made crucial discoveries by accident when they were conducting experiments. In 1928, Alexander Fleming discovered penicillin, an antibiotic, in this manner. He discovered some mold growing in a dish with some bacteria. He noticed that the bacteria seemed to be avoiding the
20 mold. When he investigated further, he determined some of the many useful properties of penicillin, which has saved millions of lives over the past few decades. Likewise, in 1946, scientist Percy Spencer was conducting an experiment with microwaves. He had a candy bar in his pocket, and he noticed that it suddenly melted. He investigated and learned the reason why that had happened. Soon afterward, he built a device that could utilize microwaves to heat food: the microwave oven.

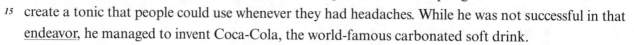

GO ON TO THE NEXT PAGE

35. Which title best summarizes the main idea of the passage?

(A) History's Most Important Inventions

(B) Accidental Inventions and Discoveries

(C) How to Become a Great Inventor

(D) You Don't Always Get What You Want

36. In line 1, the word <u>arduous</u> is closest in meaning to _____.

(A) detailed

(B) tough

(C) specific

(D) constant

37. In line 3, the phrase <u>replete with</u> is closest in meaning to _____.

(A) aware of

(B) inspired by

(C) full of

(D) concerned about

38. In line 16, the word <u>endeavor</u> is closest in meaning to _____.

(A) research

(B) dream

(C) request

(D) attempt

39. What does the author say about Teflon?

(A) People first used it as a refrigeration device.

(B) It was created many years before Coca-Cola.

(C) The man who made it was a pharmacist.

(D) It is used for kitchenware nowadays.

40. Who was John Pemberton?

(A) The person who made Teflon

(B) The creator of Coca-Cola

(C) The man who discovered penicillin

(D) The inventor of the microwave

41. The author uses Alexander Fleming as an example of _____.

(A) one of the most famous inventors in history

(B) a person who made an accidental scientific discovery

(C) someone who became a millionaire from his invention

(D) a man who dedicated his life to medical science

42. What does the author imply about penicillin?

(A) Doctors seldom use it nowadays.

(B) Some people are not affected by it.

(C) It is an invaluable medical supply.

(D) Mold combines with bacteria to make it.

STOP

Practice
Test 2

Listening
Comprehension

听力音频

The listening section has 42 questions. Follow along as you listen to the directions to the listening section.

Directions

In this section of the test, you will hear talks and conversations. Each talk or conversation is followed by one question. Choose the best answer to each question and mark the letter of the correct answer on your answer sheet. You will hear each talk or conversation only one time.

Here is an example: 🔊

What does the girl mean?

(A) She will meet the boy at band practice soon.
(B) She is not going to be a member of the band.
(C) She thinks that the band is no longer fun.
(D) She has been a member of the band for a year.

The correct answer is (B), "She is not going to be a member of the band."

Here is another example: 🔊

What are the speakers talking about?

(A) Their classes
(B) Going on a trip
(C) Spring break
(D) An upcoming test

The correct answer is (C), "Spring break."

Go on to the next page, and the test will begin with question number one.

GO ON TO THE NEXT PAGE ⟩

1. **What happened to the girl's smartphone?**

   (A) One of her friends broke it.

   (B) Her parents took it away from her.

   (C) She left it on the bus.

   (D) It stopped working for no reason.

2. **Why does the teacher suggest that the girl write for the school newspaper?**

   (A) He thinks that she is a skilled writer.

   (B) It would be a good experience for her.

   (C) She can improve her research skills by doing that.

   (D) He believes it could help her writing improve.

3. **What are the speakers mainly discussing?**

   (A) The boy's stolen bike

   (B) Their upcoming lunch

   (C) The various thefts at the school

   (D) How unsafe the school has become

4. **What will the boy probably do next?**

   (A) Check on Tim's condition

   (B) Refuse to give the teacher an answer

   (C) Continue eating his lunch

   (D) Tell the teacher who the bullies are

5. **What does the girl imply about the boy?**

   (A) He gets low grades in his classes.

   (B) He sometimes fails to tell the truth.

   (C) He needs to improve his memory.

   (D) He ought to apologize to Ms. Winkler.

6. **What are the speakers mainly discussing?**

   (A) How good they are at spelling

   (B) Their school experiences

   (C) The spelling bee

   (D) Their third period class

7. **What does the teacher ask the students to do?**

   (A) Consider becoming exchange students

   (B) Have lunch with her that day

   (C) Make friends with the new student

   (D) Hang out after school for a while

8. **Why does the announcer mention Dr. Lewis Farber?**

   (A) To introduce him to the program

   (B) To name him as the author of a new book

   (C) To praise his most recent theory

   (D) To compare his work with another author's

9. **What will the teacher probably do next?**

   (A) Start a class discussion

   (B) Talk about the Romans

   (C) Describe who the Vikings were

   (D) Discuss Christopher Columbus

GO ON TO THE NEXT PAGE

Now you will hear longer talks or conversations. Each talk or conversation will be followed by three or more questions. Choose the best answer to each question and mark the letter of the correct answer on your answer sheet. You will hear each talk or conversation only one time.

10. **What is the boy's role on the student newspaper?**

    (A) He is a reporter.

    (B) He is a photographer.

    (C) He is a typesetter.

    (D) He is an editor.

11. **What does the boy imply when he says: "But she had to quit for some reason"?**

    (A) The student was unhappy when she quit.

    (B) He is unaware of why the student quit.

    (C) He did not want the student to quit.

    (D) He dislikes when people quit their jobs.

12. **How does the boy know that the girl is a good writer?**

    (A) He has read her writing before.

    (B) He knows that she gets good grades.

    (C) He has heard her teachers compliment her.

    (D) The girl told him that she writes well.

13. **Why does the boy mention the football game?**

    (A) To tell the girl who the team is playing

    (B) To advise the girl not to attend it

    (C) To instruct the girl to cover the game

    (D) To let the girl know that Jim is writing about it

14. **Why does the boy want to do the project?**

    (A) To satisfy his curiosity

    (B) To get some bonus points

    (C) To impress the teacher

    (D) To complete his homework assignment

15. **What does the boy imply about Mr. Thompson's class?**

    (A) He has been late for it before.

    (B) It is the hardest of all his classes.

    (C) He finds it to be interesting.

    (D) It is the least exciting class.

16. **Why does the teacher suggest that the boy visit the library?**

    (A) To check out a book she mentions to him

    (B) To find a quiet place to complete his work

    (C) To read some past lab reports by students

    (D) To get some ideas on the experiment he will do

17. **What will determine how many points the boy gets on the project?**

    (A) The type of experiment he does

    (B) The results of his experiment

    (C) How well he does the assignment

    (D) How quickly he submits his work

18. **What does the teacher imply when she says: "The bell is about to ring"?**

    (A) She wants to continue their talk later.

    (B) School is going to end in a few moments.

    (C) The boy is going to be late for class.

    (D) She is going to give a test in her next class.

GO ON TO THE NEXT PAGE

19. **What are the speakers mainly talking about?**

    (A) What being on the baseball team is like

    (B) How hard getting chosen for the baseball team is

    (C) When baseball tryouts are going to begin

    (D) Which teams are the toughest to play

20. **What happened to the baseball team last year?**

    (A) It won more games than it lost.

    (B) Two of its top players graduated.

    (C) The team made the state playoffs.

    (D) It played most of its games at other schools.

21. **How close are most of the away games?**

    (A) Less than thirty minutes away

    (B) Less than an hour away

    (C) Less than two hours away

    (D) More than two hours away

22. **What can be inferred about Jimmy?**

    (A) He is a player of average ability.

    (B) He wants to be the team's pitcher.

    (C) He does not have a part-time job.

    (D) His grades have gone down this year.

23. **What are the students mainly talking about?**

    (A) The work that the boy has to do

    (B) The girl's desire for an easier schedule

    (C) The girl's extracurricular activities

    (D) The boy's interest in being on the yearbook committee

24. **What does the boy imply about extracurricular activities?**

    (A) He is doing too many of them.

    (B) He wants to take part in them.

    (C) He is thinking about quitting one of them.

    (D) He is going to start doing a new one.

25. **According to the girl, which is her busiest extracurricular activity?**

    (A) The basketball team

    (B) The school newspaper

    (C) The yearbook committee

    (D) The math team

26. **What does the girl say about the yearbook committee?**

    (A) It will become busier next semester.

    (B) She goes to meetings for it twice a week.

    (C) It is not as exciting as the math club.

    (D) She has to write one article a week for it.

GO ON TO THE NEXT PAGE

27. What is the subject of the discussion?

(A) The Earth's oceans

(B) The Gulf Stream

(C) Where currents flow

(D) Currents and climate

28. Why does the boy mention the Gulf Stream?

(A) To bring up an important point

(B) To ask what exactly it is

(C) To answer the teacher's question

(D) To prove that he knows where it flows

29. Why does the water in the Gulf Stream become progressively cooler?

(A) Because of the action of the wind

(B) Because of the cold water it flows through

(C) Because of the changing seasons

(D) Because of the depth that it flows

30. What will the teacher probably do next?

(A) Continue talking about currents

(B) Dismiss the class for the day

(C) Assign the students some homework

(D) Ask the students another question

31. What is the main topic of the teacher's talk?

(A) The desire of many Texans to be independent

(B) The war between Texas and Mexico

(C) Some famous Texans at the Alamo

(D) The battle that happened at the Alamo

32. What does the teacher imply about the Mexicans?

(A) They lost a war that they easily could have won.

(B) They were right to be upset with the Texans.

(C) Their leader, Santa Anna, was not effective.

(D) They never should have sent an army to Texas.

33. Why does the teacher mention James Bowie and Davy Crockett?

(A) To give a brief biography of each man

(B) To name two famous men at the Alamo

(C) To compare their leadership with Santa Anna's

(D) To claim that they were the Texans' leaders

GO ON TO THE NEXT PAGE

34. What is the purpose of the lecture?

(A) To provide some facts about the dingo

(B) To prove that the dingo is a unique animal

(C) To compare the dingo with the dog

(D) To note the dingo's eating habits

35. What does the teacher suggest about the dingo?

(A) It is a relatively small mammal.

(B) It is not native to Australia.

(C) It can run faster than most humans.

(D) It lacks the ability to swim.

36. According to the teacher, what is true about the dingo?

(A) It can weigh up to twenty kilograms.

(B) It reproduces once every few years.

(C) It is active at night and sleeps in the day.

(D) It hunts other animals and eats them.

37. How is the dingo similar to the wolf?

(A) It hunts animals bigger than it.

(B) It has short fur.

(C) It mates frequently.

(D) It travels in packs.

38. What is the teacher mainly discussing?

(A) The solar system

(B) The sun

(C) The planets

(D) The galaxy

39. Why does the teacher talk about the outer planets?

(A) To compare them with the inner planets

(B) To focus on their compositions

(C) To note their quick rotations

(D) To stress how far from the sun they are

40. What is another name for the inner planets?

(A) The Venusians

(B) The Jovians

(C) The terrestrial planets

(D) The gas giants

41. According to the teacher, which planet has the most moons?

(A) Jupiter

(B) Saturn

(C) Uranus

(D) Neptune

42. What can be inferred about Saturn?

(A) It is nearly as large as Jupiter.

(B) It is considered a gas giant.

(C) It has a core that is rocky.

(D) It orbits the sun in fewer than ten years.

STOP

Language Form and Meaning

In this section of the test, you will answer 42 questions found in seven different texts. Within each text are boxes that contain four possible ways to complete a sentence. Choose the word or words in each box that correctly complete each sentence. Mark the letter of the correct answer on your answer sheet.

Here are two sample questions:

1. While some forest fires

| (A) cause |
| (B) causing |
| (C) are caused |
| (D) will cause |

by humans, most of them happen due to

lightning striking the ground during a region's dry season. In fact, some places

2.

| (A) accept |
| (B) endure |
| (C) permit |
| (D) strike |

forest fires on a yearly basis.

The correct answer to **Sample 1** is (C), "are caused." The correct answer to **Sample 2** is (B), "endure."

GO ON TO THE NEXT PAGE

Questions 1–4 refer to the following advertisement.

This Friday night at seven o'clock, the drama club is pleased

1.
| (A) presenting the production |
| (B) for presenting this production |
| (C) with the present production |
| (D) to present a production |

of Shakespeare's *As You Like It*. The student

2. cast has worked hard

| (A) performing |
| (B) rehearsing |
| (C) remembering |
| (D) observing |

for the play for the past two months

and would appreciate a big crowd at the performance. Tickets cost $5 and may be

GO ON TO THE NEXT PAGE

purchased from the school's front office or at the door prior to the beginning

of the play. The lead actor is Ryan McClellan while Katie Burgess has the lead

3.　female role. The play

(A) directs
(B) is directing
(C) is directed
(D) will direct

by Edward Holliman, the school's art teacher.

4.　Please be sure to

(A) set aside some time
(B) setting aside the time
(C) set some of the time aside
(D) setting some time aside

on Friday night to support the

cast. The play will be held in the school's auditorium.

GO ON TO THE NEXT PAGE

Questions 5–8 refer to the following announcement.

5. This spring semester, the school is going to

(A) register
(B) delay
(C) suspend
(D) detain

classes for two weeks.

From Monday, April 6, to Friday, April 17, there will be no classes. Instead,

students will spend those two weeks interning at local businesses. A number of

6. area businesses

(A) in several different fields
(B) with several differences in fields
(C) for the several different fields
(D) by several of the different fields

have agreed to take on

student interns. These include some local hospitals, colleges, libraries, and

GO ON TO THE NEXT PAGE

government offices. By doing these internships, students will be able to get hands-on

7. experience at jobs

(A) what they can do
(B) which they are doing
(C) that they may do
(D) how they are doing

in the future. Students may also

feel free to arrange their own internships. Contact Mr. Farguson or Mr. Whittaker

8. for more information. We hope it will be

(A) a big success
(B) a bigger success
(C) the biggest success
(D) as big a success as

than last

year's attempt at the same program.

GO ON TO THE NEXT PAGE

Questions 9–12 refer to the following diary entry.

Dear Diary,

I'm really looking forward to tomorrow's field trip to Mercy Hospital.

9.
(A) In addition to the schedule
(B) Consequently, the schedule
(C) According to the schedule
(D) Nevertheless, with the schedule

Ms. Lewis gave the class, we are going to

10. spend time
(A) to five departments.
(B) in up to five departments.
(C) by five of the departments.
(D) for all five departments.

Among them are the cancer ward,

the emergency room, and the physical therapy section. For the past couple of years,

GO ON TO THE NEXT PAGE

I have considered becoming a doctor in the future. Actually seeing some

11. doctors at work should help me

(A) final
(B) finally
(C) finalize
(D) finalization

my decision. I might decide

that being a doctor is not the profession for me. Or I might see all of the doctors at

12. work and feel that I simply must become one. Who knows

(A) what will happen?
(B) when it happens?
(C) where it happens?
(D) how they will happen?

I guess I need to wait until tomorrow to find out.

GO ON TO THE NEXT PAGE

Questions 13–20 refer to the following letter.

Dear Helgar,

13. I would like to welcome you to our school. I know that being an

(A) exchange
(B) exchanges
(C) exchanged
(D) exchanging

student can be difficult, especially when you are so far away from your home.

14. As you may have heard, the Thanksgiving holiday is

(A) improving.
(B) happening.
(C) approaching.
(D) passing.

I am aware

that it isn't celebrated in Germany, but it's a very important holiday in the United

15. States. It is an occasion

(A) where families gather in America
(B) that the American families gather
(C) what gathers American families
(D) when American families gather

to spend time with

one another and enjoy a variety of food. If you have nothing planned for that day,

16. I would like to

(A) invite
(B) require
(C) let
(D) insist

you to visit my home for Thanksgiving. My entire family

17. is planning to be there, so you will

(A) getting us to hang out.
(B) hanging out with us.
(C) hang out by getting with us.
(D) get to hang out with us.

My mother

18. is considered

(A) the better
(B) one of the best
(C) as good as
(D) the best

cooks in the city, so you will get a great

19.

(A) introduction
(B) recipe
(C) lesson
(D) feast

to traditional American home cooking. I hope you can come as

20. I am positive that you

(A) have
(B) are having
(C) will have
(D) have had

a wonderful time. Let me know if you are

interested.

Sincerely,

Greg Foster

GO ON TO THE NEXT PAGE

Questions 21–26 refer to the following newspaper article.

These days, there are many students who do not attend physical schools but

21. instead stay home,

(A) why it is homeschooling.
(B) what is a homeschool.
(C) who does homeschooling.
(D) where they are homeschooled.

While these students

22.

(A) primarily
(B) solely
(C) relatively
(D) cautiously

study at their homes, they sometimes visit their local schools.

One reason for this concerns athletics. In many American states, homeschooled

students are permitted to play on their local schools' athletic teams. This is good

23. news for the schools because a lot of homeschoolers are

(A) exception
(B) exceptions
(C) exceptional
(D) exceptionally

athletes.

The students who attend actual schools are mostly accepting of the homeschoolers.

GO ON TO THE NEXT PAGE

GO ON TO THE NEXT PAGE

They usually have no problems with them and are often simply

24.
| (A) upset |
| (B) curious |
| (C) worried |
| (D) hostile |

about what it is like not to go to school. So they tend to

bombard the homeschoolers with numerous questions. The homeschoolers

25. also
| (A) benefit |
| (B) benefitted |
| (C) benefitting |
| (D) will have benefitted |

by mingling with the students at school.

26. Some of them rarely spend time
| (A) for individuals of their age. |
| (B) of the individuals who have aged. |
| (C) with other individuals their age. |
| (D) by individuals that age. |

So it helps them develop their social skills if they can hang out and play sports

with other kids.

Questions 27–34 refer to the following part of a student's essay.

Thanks to the Hubble Space Telescope, our knowledge of the universe has

27. increased tremendously. The telescope was put into

(A) revolution
(B) orbit
(C) rotation
(D) atmosphere

by one

28. of the space shuttles in 1990. Since then, it

(A) transmit
(B) is transmitting
(C) transmitted
(D) has been transmitting

high-quality pictures to Earth. The Hubble is superior to Earth-based telescopes

29. for a couple of reasons. The first concerns

(A) both the size and quality
(B) either the size or the quality
(C) neither has size nor quality
(D) not only sizes but also qualities

30. of the mirror

(A) what is scanning the skies.
(B) they have to scan the skies.
(C) it uses to scan the skies.
(D) how it is used by scanning the skies.

The second is that, as

the Hubble is located in outer space, there is no interference from Earth's atmosphere.

GO ON TO THE NEXT PAGE

This interference causes distortion in the images of ground-based telescopes, which

31. can cause them

(A) to produce blurry images.
(B) producing blurry images.
(C) produce images that are blurry.
(D) production of blurry images.

Unfortunately, the Hubble

is aging, and a replacement is needed. I strongly believe that the government

32. should spend the necessary

(A) materials
(B) accounts
(C) ingredients
(D) funds

to manufacture a telescope that

33. can be launched into space

(A) sooner than possible.
(B) as soon as possible.
(C) the soonest possible.
(D) sooner than is possible.

By doing that,

34.

(A) continuing to learn, we can
(B) we can continue to learn
(C) we have continued learning
(D) we, continuing to learn, can

more about the solar system, galaxy, and

universe itself.

GO ON TO THE NEXT PAGE

Questions 35–42 refer to the following magazine article.

35. The origins of the majority of sports are

(A) unique
(B) known
(C) entertaining
(D) hazy

because no one is

quite sure when and how they were invented. However, the same cannot be said about

36. basketball. Its origins are both well known and

(A) documented.
(B) applied.
(C) certified.
(D) historical.

37.

(A) Basketball, a sport
(B) Basketball, the sport
(C) The sport of basketball
(D) Sports and basketball

was invented by Dr. James Naismith in December 1891.

Naismith was a physical education instructor at the YMCA in Springfield, Massachusetts.

38. Since winters in that region of Massachusetts tended

(A) to be cold and snowy,
(B) coldness and snow,
(C) cold and snow,
(D) being cold and snowy,

Naismith wanted to create a sport that men could play indoors in a gymnasium. He

GO ON TO THE NEXT PAGE

39. came up with the idea of basketball and made

(A) rules basically for ten games.
(B) the basic rules for ten games.
(C) ten games and their basic rules.
(D) ten basic rules for the game.

40. Several of these rules are ones

(A) how they were used today.
(B) that are still utilized today.
(C) where people are using them today.
(D) what were utilized today.

The men

used a soccer ball and peach baskets for hoops. The baskets had bottoms, so play was

41.

(A) skipped
(B) penalized
(C) expressed
(D) halted

each time a person made a basket. From those

42.

(A) humble
(B) humbles
(C) humbled
(D) humbling

origins came the game of basketball, which is one of the most

popular games in the world today.

STOP

NO TEST MATERIAL ON THIS PAGE

Reading
Comprehension

GO ON TO THE NEXT PAGE

Directions

In this section of the test, you will read six texts and answer 42 questions. Choose the correct answer to each question and mark the letter of the correct answer on your answer sheet.

Before you start, read the sample text and the sample questions below.

Sample Text

Erosion is one of nature's most powerful forces. It can happen in many ways, including through the wind, rain, snow, and ice. Erosion frequently takes place over a long period of time. This is how canyons and deserts are often created. Yet it is also possible for erosion to take place overnight.

Sample Question 1

What is this text mostly about?

(A) How deserts are created

(B) A natural force

(C) Canyons and deserts

(D) Wind erosion

The correct answer is (B), "A natural force."

Sample Question 2

Which of the following is true regarding erosion?

(A) It can happen in many ways.

(B) Water most commonly causes it.

(C) It can create deserts overnight.

(D) It is stronger than anything in nature.

The correct answer is (A), "It can happen in many ways."

Questions 1–6 are about the following note.

Please read the following carefully as it describes my expectations of you during this class.

Everyone must do the reading assignments since we will have class discussions. Your participation in these discussions will be a part (ten percent) of your grade in my class. In addition, we will have one written homework assignment each week. In most cases, it will be a short (3-page) paper on a topic we are studying. You will be graded on these assignments. We will have four tests during the semester. Each one will be worth twenty percent of your final grade.

There will be times when I will call on you during class. Please attempt to answer my <u>inquiries</u>. Do not simply <u>confess</u> that you do not know the correct response. I expect everybody to try hard in my class. Furthermore, I want you all to take notes during my class. I will provide you with an outline of the material we will study each day; however, you need to write down the important information that I mention in your notebooks. I welcome questions in class and urge you to ask them if you ever fail to understand something.

GO ON TO THE NEXT PAGE

1. **What is the note mainly about?**

    (A) The teacher's expectations for the students in class

    (B) How the students can get a high grade from the teacher

    (C) The type of homework the students will have to do

    (D) What the teacher's grading style for the class is

2. **Based on the note, what is probably true about the students' homework assignments?**

    (A) The teacher will grade and return them within two days.

    (B) They are worth a small percentage of the students' final grades.

    (C) The students are expected to write them by hand.

    (D) Some students will have to read their papers to the class.

3. **Which of the following is NOT mentioned in the note about something that the students will be graded on?**

    (A) Homework assignments

    (B) Attendance

    (C) Tests

    (D) Class participation

4. **In line 7, the word <u>inquiries</u> is closest in meaning to _____.**

    (A) investigations

    (B) demands

    (C) examinations

    (D) questions

5. **In line 8, the word <u>confess</u> is closest in meaning to _____.**

    (A) blame

    (B) admit

    (C) decide

    (D) falsify

6. **What does the teacher say about taking notes?**

    (A) The students should take all of their notes in outline form.

    (B) It is permissible for students to use laptops to take notes.

    (C) The teacher wants students to write them in their notebooks.

    (D) The students have to show the teacher their notebooks at times.

GO ON TO THE NEXT PAGE

Questions 7–12 are about the following schedule.

A schedule for the school's newest clubs was released last Friday. Since that time, there have been a few changes to the schedule. Please look at the following changes and <u>take note of</u> them, especially if you are considering joining one of the clubs. As these are the initial meetings, students who desire to join these clubs must be present; otherwise, they will not be allowed to join. All of the days in the schedule are this week.

Club	Faculty Advisor	Meeting Time	Change
Geography Club	John Collins	Thursday, 2:00	Meeting time is different
Photography Club	Susan Smith	Thursday, 2:00	Will meet in room 101, not room 110
Chemistry Club	Emily Jenkins	Friday, 11:00	Is no longer free of charge / requires $40 membership fee
History Club	Redge Thagard	Friday, 3:00	Meeting day is different

In addition, the chess club and the hiking club have both been cancelled this year due to a lack of interest. Fewer than the required number of students signed up for both clubs, so they will not exist during the fall and spring semesters. If more students <u>express</u> an interest in them next year, <u>they</u> will be reinstated.

GO ON TO THE NEXT PAGE

7. **What is the purpose of the schedule?**

   (A) To mention some of the school's newest clubs

   (B) To advise students on which clubs to join

   (C) To let students know about their faculty advisors

   (D) To make students aware of some recent changes

8. **What does the author point out by writing that students should take note of the following changes in line 2?**

   (A) They need to memorize all of the changes that occurred.

   (B) They should be aware of the changes that were made.

   (C) They ought to write down the changes that happened.

   (D) They have to tell their classmates about the changes.

9. **What can be inferred from the schedule about the photography club?**

   (A) It will provide all of its members with cameras.

   (B) It is going to focus mostly on digital photography.

   (C) Its members cannot belong to the geography club.

   (D) Susan Smith will hold its meetings in her classroom.

10. **According to the passage, all of the following clubs will exist this year EXCEPT _____.**

    (A) the hiking club

    (B) the geology club

    (C) the history club

    (D) the chemistry club

11. **In line 8, the word express is closest in meaning to _____.**

    (A) demand

    (B) foresee

    (C) show

    (D) approve of

12. **In line 9, the word they refers to _____.**

    (A) the required number of students

    (B) both clubs

    (C) the fall and spring semesters

    (D) more students

GO ON TO THE NEXT PAGE

Questions 13–18 are about the following article in the newspaper.

Last weekend, six students from the Donoho School went on a fascinating trip back in time. These students accompanied Jacksonville State University professor William Bannister on a
5 fossil hunt.

The students, professor, and three graduate assistants headed to a valley near Cheaha Mountain. The valley was not previously known to have any fossils in it. However, two months
10 ago, some campers in the valley <u>stumbled upon</u> some bones sticking out from the ground. When they brought <u>them</u> to the museum, they were told that the bones were those of a brontosaurus, a species of dinosaur.

15 Thanks to a generous grant from the Damke Foundation, the students were able to accompany the professor on his dig. They spent most of both Saturday and Sunday carefully digging in the area.

20 "We found a few bones," said Wendy Jacobs, a Donoho senior. "We're not sure which animal they're from, but the professor assured us they were from a dinosaur."

The students, all of whom intend to major
25 in science at college, are looking forward to returning this coming weekend. "There's enough money in the grant for the next month, so we should get to return at least three more times," said Donoho student Philip Peters.

GO ON TO THE NEXT PAGE

13. **What would be the most appropriate headline for this article?**

   (A) Dinosaur Fossils Found near Cheaha Mountain

   (B) Donoho Students Meet Professor Bannister

   (C) Local Students Go Fossil Hunting

   (D) Dinosaurs: Did They Live around Here?

14. **In line 10, the phrase <u>stumbled upon</u> is closest in meaning to _____.**

   (A) tripped on

   (B) accidentally found

   (C) dug up

   (D) conducted research on

15. **In line 12, the word <u>them</u> refers to _____.**

   (A) three graduate assistants

   (B) any fossils

   (C) some campers

   (D) some bones

16. **Why does the author mention the Damke Foundation?**

   (A) To claim it has an interest in dinosaurs

   (B) To note a group that is financing the students

   (C) To focus on its relationship with the Donoho School

   (D) To claim that it sponsors many local digs

17. **Who is Wendy Jacobs?**

   (A) A student at Jacksonville State University

   (B) One of Professor Bannister's graduate assistants

   (C) A fourth-year student at the Donoho School

   (D) A representative of the Damke Foundation

18. **According to the article, when will the students go back to the dig site?**

   (A) Within a week

   (B) In two months

   (C) During summer vacation

   (D) Next autumn

GO ON TO THE NEXT PAGE

Questions 19–26 are about the following passage.

Mars has captured the imaginations of people since ancient times. People have long wondered if the planet is home to alien life. Over the years, a number of theories concerning this matter have arisen.

In the nineteenth century, there were finally telescopes made that could closely examine at the surface of the Red Planet. While looking at Mars, an Italian astronomer saw many straight channels
5 on its surface. These were most likely caused by the action of either the wind or water in the distant past. When he published his observations, he used the Italian word *canali*, which means "channels." However, English-speaking astronomers interpreted the word as "canals" and assumed that he was referring to something <u>akin to</u> manmade canals on Earth.

An American astronomer, Percival Lowell, believed that these "canals" had been built by a race
10 of intelligent beings that had lived—and might still be living—on Mars. The result of that highly publicized claim was that a great number of myths about Mars suddenly arose. For instance, H.G. Wells wrote *The War of the Worlds*, a book about a Martian invasion of Earth, in 1898. Over the next few decades, Mars and Martians featured in countless science fiction stories, movies, and TV shows.

Years later, in the 1960s and 1970s, the United States sent several satellites to investigate Mars
15 more closely. The satellites found no canals, but one picture suddenly <u>ignited a great deal of interest</u> in Mars. In 1976, *Viking 1* took a snapshot of the Martian surface. In the picture was what appeared to be an enormous human face. It was so large that it measured more than three kilometers long. This convinced people that there was—or had been—intelligent life on Mars.

In 2001, however, the mystery of the Martian face was solved by *Mars Global Surveyor*. The
20 pictures that <u>it</u> transmitted proved that the face was just a mesa, a type of geological formation. As for the "eyes, nose, and mouth" of the face, they were merely shadows. Despite this proof, many people are still convinced that signs of life could be found on Mars someday.

GO ON TO THE NEXT PAGE

19. **What is the best title for the passage?**

    (A) The Martian Face and Other Mysteries

    (B) What Are Martians Thought to Look Like?

    (C) Martian Civilization: What Happened to It?

    (D) Mars and the Belief That Life Exists on It

20. **Which of the following can be inferred from the passage about Mars?**

    (A) It is farther from the sun than Earth.

    (B) One of its nicknames is the Red Planet.

    (C) Humans hope to visit it someday.

    (D) It almost surely had life on it at some point.

21. **In line 8, the phrase akin to is closest in meaning to _____.**

    (A) useful to

    (B) resembling

    (C) imitated by

    (D) precisely like

22. **The author uses The War of the Worlds as an example of _____.**

    (A) evidence supporting the possibility of life on Mars

    (B) a work inspired by thoughts of Mars

    (C) a story based on Percival Lowell's work

    (D) a bestselling novel and movie

23. **What does the author point out by writing that a picture ignited a great deal of interest in Mars in line 15?**

    (A) Schools focused on educating students on Mars.

    (B) More pictures of Mars became available.

    (C) People wanted more satellites to be sent to Mars.

    (D) Many people began to think about Mars.

24. **What does the author say about the Martian face?**

    (A) It was discovered by a satellite.

    (B) It proved there was life on Mars.

    (C) It was found near some channels.

    (D) It is located near some mesas.

25. **What did Mars Global Surveyor do?**

    (A) It searched for hidden canals on Mars.

    (B) It mapped part of the surface of Mars.

    (C) It showed what the Martian face really was.

    (D) It looked for signs of life on Mars.

26. **In line 20, the word it refers to _____.**

    (A) the mystery

    (B) the Martian face

    (C) Mars Global Explorer

    (D) a mesa

GO ON TO THE NEXT PAGE

Questions 27–34 are about the following story.

"Jeremy, how do you manage to do it?" asked Don.

"What are you talking about, Don?" Jeremy responded with a confused look on his face.

"Don't <u>play dumb</u>," responded Don. "I'm talking about how you always seem to get the highest grade in every class. I mean, no one but you got higher than a 92 on the science test Mrs. Sellers just
5 gave us back."

Don was feeling rather upset because he had gotten a 75 on his science test while Jeremy had received a 99. Even worse, Jeremy had told him that he had not studied for the test.

"Well, I actually do a lot of things," responded Jeremy.

"Don't just sit there silently. Spill the beans, and fill me in," demanded Don. "I'm tired of
10 studying for hours at a time only to get C's and B's. I want to start getting A's like you."

"Okay," said Jeremy. "Here's my secret . . . I pay attention in class, and I take good notes. That's really all there is to it."

"But I do the same thing," insisted Don.

"Do you?" Jeremy said with a knowing look on his face. "I seem to remember looking over at
15 your desk in history class the other day only to see you with your head on it. You even started snoring at one point."

"Oh, yeah. Right. I had forgotten about that," said Don. "But that was only one time."

"And don't forget how, in math and English class yesterday, you were listening to music instead of taking notes," Jeremy continued.

20 "Er . . ." responded Don.

"Look, Don. It's really simple. If you take notes in class, pay attention, and then review your notes at home later the same night, you will be able to remember practically everything. Assuming you do that, you won't have to study the
25 night before a test, but you'll still do well," stated Jeremy.

"I don't know," said Don with a <u>skeptical</u> look. "It just seems strange to me."

"Try my way for a week and see what happens," said Jeremy. "I'll even lend you my notes . . . but only if you don't
30 fall asleep and don't listen to music in class anymore."

"It's a deal," said Don with a smile.

GO ON TO THE NEXT PAGE

27. What would be the best title for the story?

(A) The Best Student at School

(B) The Secret to Jeremy's Success

(C) Two Friends: Don and Jeremy

(D) Don and His School Performance

28. Why is Don in a bad mood?

(A) His teacher yelled at him for sleeping in class.

(B) He cannot understand the class material.

(C) He forgot to study for his science test.

(D) He performed poorly on a recent test.

29. In line 3, the phrase play dumb is closest in meaning to _____.

(A) act in a silly manner

(B) pretend not to know something

(C) forget how to speak

(D) make fun of someone

30. Based on the passage, what is probably true about Jeremy?

(A) He wants Don to do better than him in class.

(B) He is willing to tutor Don in some of his classes.

(C) He doubts that Don tries as hard as he claims to.

(D) He is lying to Don when he says he does not study.

31. According to the passage, all of the following statements are true about Don EXCEPT _____.

(A) he fell asleep in his history class

(B) he is displeased with his performance in science

(C) he ignored the teacher in his math class

(D) he got a low grade on his English test

32. What does Jeremy tell Don to do?

(A) Study for several hours the night before a test

(B) Go over his notes at home every night

(C) Start reviewing three days before a test

(D) Ask his teachers how to get good study habits

33. In line 26, the word skeptical is closest in meaning to _____.

(A) doubtful

(B) amused

(C) confused

(D) understanding

34. What does the author imply about Don?

(A) He will develop better study habits than Jeremy.

(B) He is hoping to go to a good college.

(C) He intends to follow Jeremy's advice.

(D) He prefers playing sports to studying.

GO ON TO THE NEXT PAGE

Questions 35–42 are about the following passage.

The Great Lakes are the largest group of freshwater lakes in the world. All five are located on the border between Canada and the United States. The names of the Great Lakes are Erie, Ontario, Michigan, Huron, and Superior. The smallest of the group is Lake Ontario while Lake Superior is the largest. Lakes Ontario, Erie, Huron, and Superior are shared by Canada and the United States.
5   Lake Michigan, however, lies entirely within the borders of the United States.

   Geologically speaking, the Great Lakes are relatively young. They were formed about 10,000 years ago due to the action of <u>receding</u> glaciers. At the time of their creation, massive glaciers—some several kilometers thick—were retreating as they melted and the last ice age came to an end. The great weight of the ice sheets gouged out enormous holes in parts of the land. Then, the melting ice
10   turned into water and filled in the holes with water. In this way were the Great Lakes formed. The Great Lakes have a combined surface area of more than 240,000 square kilometers. There are also around 35,000 islands in the lakes, yet most of them are quite small. Lake Superior is the deepest at more than 400 meters in places. But most of the Great Lakes average less than 100 meters in depth. Due to their <u>immense</u> size, the Great Lakes comprise around 21% of the entire planet's supply of
15   fresh water.

   All five of the lakes are connected by both rivers and channels that run between them. The entire system flows to the Atlantic Ocean by way of the St. Lawrence River in Canada. Together with the St. Lawrence River, the Great Lakes form the largest inland waterway in the world. As a result, millions of people live near the Great Lakes. Among the major cities that lie alongside them
20   are Chicago, Toronto, Detroit, Milwaukee, Cleveland, and Buffalo. Each year, thousands of ships transport billions of dollars worth of goods through the numerous ports along the Great Lakes. This has transformed many port cities into major transportation centers in Canada and the United States.

GO ON TO THE NEXT PAGE

35. **What is this passage mostly about?**

   (A) The formation of the Great Lakes
   (B) The cities around the Great Lakes
   (C) The geography of the Great Lakes
   (D) The sizes of the Great Lakes

36. **Which of the Great Lakes is the biggest?**

   (A) Lake Huron
   (B) Lake Superior
   (C) Lake Erie
   (D) Lake Ontario

37. **In line 7, the word <u>receding</u> is closest in meaning to _____.**

   (A) retreating
   (B) removing
   (C) revitalizing
   (D) resulting

38. **Which of the following is NOT mentioned as a cause of the formation of the Great Lakes?**

   (A) The end of the ice age
   (B) The movement of glaciers
   (C) The melting of ice
   (D) The falling of rain and snow

39. **Which of the following is true regarding the islands in the Great Lakes?**

   (A) More than 240,000 have been identified.
   (B) Some are more than 400 meters long.
   (C) There are tens of thousands of them.
   (D) Most of them are extremely large.

40. **In line 14, the word <u>immense</u> is closest in meaning to _____.**

   (A) variable
   (B) huge
   (C) considerate
   (D) relative

41. **Why does the author talk about the St. Lawrence River?**

   (A) To point out that it flows entirely through Canada
   (B) To state that there are many channels connecting it to the Great Lakes
   (C) To mention that it connects the Great Lakes with the Atlantic Ocean
   (D) To claim that it is too narrow for some ships to sail on

42. **According to the passage, which is true about the port cities that are beside the Great Lakes?**

   (A) All of them have increasing populations.
   (B) The same kinds of good are transported in them.
   (C) They serve as important transportation centers.
   (D) Some of them are also manufacturing centers.

STOP

Practice
Test 3

Listening
Comprehension

听力音频

The listening section has 42 questions. Follow along as you listen to the directions to the listening section.

Directions

In this section of the test, you will hear talks and conversations. Each talk or conversation is followed by one question. Choose the best answer to each question and mark the letter of the correct answer on your answer sheet. You will hear each talk or conversation only one time.

Here is an example: 🔊

What does the girl mean?

(A) She will meet the boy at band practice soon.

(B) She is not going to be a member of the band.

(C) She thinks that the band is no longer fun.

(D) She has been a member of the band for a year.

The correct answer is (B), "She is not going to be a member of the band."

Here is another example: 🔊

What are the speakers talking about?

(A) Their classes

(B) Going on a trip

(C) Spring break

(D) An upcoming test

The correct answer is (C), "Spring break."

Go on to the next page, and the test will begin with question number one.

GO ON TO THE NEXT PAGE ⟩

1. **Which picture set does the girl say she will purchase?**

   (A) The simple set
   (B) The standard set
   (C) The deluxe set
   (D) The all-inclusive set

2. **What will the teacher probably do next?**

   (A) Change the girl's grade
   (B) Give the girl back her homework
   (C) Punish the girl
   (D) Read the student's paper

3. **What are the speakers mainly discussing?**

   (A) Rock music
   (B) Their school lives
   (C) Volleyball
   (D) The new student

4. **How does the principal punish the boy?**

   (A) By giving him detention
   (B) By suspending him from school
   (C) By making him pay a fine
   (D) By having him clean off the wall

5. **Why does the teacher mention that it is the first week of school?**

   (A) To encourage the student
   (B) To get the student to change classes
   (C) To advise the student not to fall behind
   (D) To praise the student for her work

6. **Why is the boy talking about the school picnic?**

   (A) To warn the girl to be sure not to miss it
   (B) To tell the girl what she missed the day before
   (C) To remind the girl that it will happen soon
   (D) To ask the girl what she wants to do then

7. **What is the purpose of the announcement?**

   (A) To instruct the students on how to do their work
   (B) To congratulate the students on their achievement
   (C) To advise the students on which classes to take
   (D) To compliment the students on their choice of schools

8. **What does the man suggest about a recession?**

   (A) It does not last as long as a depression.
   (B) It is a period of economic hardship.
   (C) It can result in decreasing unemployment.
   (D) It affects the middle class the most.

9. **What will the teacher probably do next?**

   (A) Ask the students a question
   (B) Continue describing the periodic table
   (C) Tell the students what an element is
   (D) Give an explanation of hydrogen

GO ON TO THE NEXT PAGE

Now you will hear longer talks or conversations. Each talk or conversation will be followed by three or more questions. Choose the best answer to each question and mark the letter of the correct answer on your answer sheet. You will hear each talk or conversation only one time.

10. **What are the speakers mainly discussing?**

   (A) The girl's failure to contribute to the class
   (B) The grade that the girl is currently getting
   (C) The girl's inability to remember any answers
   (D) The fact that the girl speaks too much in class

11. **What can be inferred about the girl?**

   (A) She is one of the top students at the school.
   (B) She enjoys speaking with her teachers.
   (C) She is quiet in all of her classes.
   (D) She has not been studying much lately.

12. **What does the girl say about herself?**

   (A) She can get nervous in class at times.
   (B) She rarely knows the answers in the teacher's class.
   (C) She will study harder in the future.
   (D) She thinks she understands the material well.

13. **What is the teacher going to do in their next class?**

   (A) Give the students a test
   (B) Ask the girl a direct question
   (C) Have the girl give a presentation
   (D) Ask the students to speak more often

14. **What did the boy stop doing this year?**

   (A) All of his extracurricular activities
   (B) Participating on the soccer team
   (C) His part-time job
   (D) All of his club memberships

15. **How does the teacher probably feel when she says this: "Focus on your grades?"**

   (A) She is surprised.
   (B) She is disappointed.
   (C) She is impressed.
   (D) She is concerned.

16. **What is probably true about the boy?**

   (A) He is a star athlete.
   (B) He works harder than most students.
   (C) He is an outstanding student.
   (D) He works part time on weekends.

17. **Why does the teacher talk about the best colleges in the country?**

   (A) To encourage the boy to apply to several of them
   (B) To say that they offer scholarships
   (C) To note what they look for when students apply to them
   (D) To state that applying to them is a waste of the boy's time

18. **What will the student probably do next?**

   (A) Continue studying in the library
   (B) Meet with Coach Patterson
   (C) Complete his college application
   (D) Inquire about some club memberships

GO ON TO THE NEXT PAGE

19. **What does the girl mean when she says this: "Spill it"?**

    (A) The boy needs to be more careful in the future.

    (B) She wants the boy to tell her what happened.

    (C) She thinks that the boy is trying to avoid her.

    (D) The boy needs to apologize to Ms. Hooper.

20. **What traffic violation does the boy say that he committed?**

    (A) He drove above the speed limit.

    (B) He ran a red light.

    (C) He ignored a stop sign.

    (D) He did not turn his headlights on.

21. **According to the boy, why did Ms. Hooper drive back to school?**

    (A) The weather was too bad for the boy to drive in.

    (B) She wanted to show the boy how to drive properly.

    (C) The boy was too frightened to drive anymore.

    (D) She disliked how the boy drove.

22. **What can be inferred about the boy?**

    (A) He lacks experience driving a car.

    (B) He is going to graduate this year.

    (C) He is close friends with the girl.

    (D) He is afraid to talk to Ms. Hooper again.

23. **What are the speakers talking about?**

    (A) Why the boy's grade on his paper is low

    (B) How the boy can improve his writing

    (C) When the boy needs to submit his paper

    (D) How the boy can get a higher grade

24. **According to the teacher, what did the boy do wrong on his book report?**

    (A) He wrote about the wrong book.

    (B) He did not follow the proper format.

    (C) He had many writing mistakes.

    (D) He wrote a paper that was too short.

25. **What is the boy going to do after school today?**

    (A) Rewrite his paper

    (B) Do some research

    (C) Meet with the teacher

    (D) Study grammar

GO ON TO THE NEXT PAGE

26. **What is the main topic of the discussion?**

    (A) Renewable resources

    (B) How to save energy

    (C) Alternative energy sources

    (D) How to preserve the environment

27. **What does the girl propose that people do?**

    (A) Walk or ride bikes more often

    (B) Stop using fossil fuels entirely

    (C) Avoid using any sources of energy

    (D) Make more use of solar power

28. **Why does the boy mention using wood to heat homes?**

    (A) To suggest it as a way to avoid wasting energy

    (B) To show how it would actually harm the environment

    (C) To say that many people he knows do that

    (D) To stress how little it would cost most people

29. **What does the teacher suggest about alternative energy sources?**

    (A) They will eventually replace fossil fuels.

    (B) They are both clean and cheap.

    (C) More research needs to be done on them.

    (D) They each have good and bad points.

30. **What is the main topic of the talk?**

    (A) The most well-known deserts

    (B) Hot and cold deserts

    (C) The world's largest deserts

    (D) The classification of deserts

31. **According to the teacher, what kind of desert is the Gobi Desert?**

    (A) A hot desert

    (B) A cold desert

    (C) An extremely arid desert

    (D) An arid desert

32. **What does the teacher imply about the Atacama Desert?**

    (A) The weather there is hotter than in the Sahara Desert.

    (B) Most people consider it to be a semiarid desert.

    (C) The desert is one of the driest places on the Earth.

    (D) It is the only desert located in South America.

GO ON TO THE NEXT PAGE

33. What are the speakers mainly discussing?

(A) How diamonds are created

(B) Why diamonds are so valuable

(C) How people search for diamonds

(D) What makes the region rich in diamonds

34. According to the woman, what two forces combine to produce diamonds?

(A) Pressure and time

(B) Gravity and heat

(C) Heat and pressure

(D) Time and gravity

35. Why does the woman talk about volcanoes?

(A) To describe the last volcanic eruption in the area

(B) To claim that diamonds can be found inside volcanoes

(C) To say that diamonds are often found near them

(D) To suggest that a local volcano may erupt soon

36. Why does the man suggest that he can dig for diamonds in the local area?

(A) The woman recently dug up a diamond.

(B) The region was once volcanically active.

(C) There are some diamond mines nearby.

(D) The area is very geologically active.

37. What can be inferred about the woman?

(A) She was the man's teacher in the past.

(B) She found the largest diamond in the area.

(C) She takes students on digs in the local area.

(D) She has dug in many places in the region.

38. What is the teacher mainly discussing?

(A) The life of John Wilkes Booth

(B) The end of the Civil War

(C) The assassination of President Lincoln

(D) Robert E. Lee and Ulysses S. Grant

39. According to the teacher, where was President Lincoln when he was shot?

(A) In the White House

(B) On the street

(C) In a theater

(D) On a battlefield

40. Why does the teacher talk about John Wilkes Booth?

(A) To give a physical description of the man

(B) To describe his role in President Lincoln's death

(C) To argue that he did not act alone in killing President Lincoln

(D) To focus on the major events in his life

41. What does the teacher imply about President Lincoln?

(A) He was the greatest of all American presidents.

(B) He could have lived if he had gotten medical attention.

(C) He had met John Wilkes Booth once in the past.

(D) He did not die immediately after being shot.

42. What will the teacher probably do next?

(A) Show a short film to the students

(B) Ask the students for their opinions

(C) Continue giving his lesson to the students

(D) Have a student read a passage out loud

STOP

Language Form and Meaning

In this section of the test, you will answer 42 questions found in seven different texts. Within each text are boxes that contain four possible ways to complete a sentence. Choose the word or words in each box that correctly complete each sentence. Mark the letter of the correct answer on your answer sheet.

Here are two sample questions:

1. While some forest fires

(A) cause
(B) causing
(C) are caused
(D) will cause

by humans, most of them happen due to

lightning striking the ground during a region's dry season. In fact, some places

2.

(A) accept
(B) endure
(C) permit
(D) strike

forest fires on a yearly basis.

The correct answer to **Sample 1** is (C), "are caused." The correct answer to **Sample 2** is (B), "endure."

GO ON TO THE NEXT PAGE

Questions 1–4 refer to the following email.

Dear Stacy,

Thanks for telling me about the computer club. I had not been planning to join

any clubs this year as I was going to focus solely on my studies. However,

1. once I heard about the events

(A) were planned by the computer club,
(B) planning the computer club,
(C) the planning of the computer club,
(D) the computer club was planning,

I simply had to sign up for it. I have you to thank for that. It looks like

GO ON TO THE NEXT PAGE

2. we're going to do activities which are both educational and

(A) entertain.
(B) entertaining.
(C) entertained.
(D) entertainment.

3. I just hope that it's

(A) more fun than
(B) better fun
(C) the most fun
(D) as fun as possible

the math club was last year. That club

4. was a total

(A) cancellation.
(B) thrill.
(C) letdown.
(D) challenge.

Your friend,

Julie

GO ON TO THE NEXT PAGE

Questions 5–8 refer to the following part of a student's journal.

It is important to remember that the organisms that live in an ecosystem vary depending

5. upon a number of conditions. The climate in an area is the main

(A) obstacle.

(B) appearance.

(C) complication.

(D) determiner.

6. For instance, organisms that

(A) thrive

(B) migrate

(C) detest

(D) submit

in hot and dry climates are

GO ON TO THE NEXT PAGE

7.

(A) as likely
(B) one of the most likely
(C) more likely
(D) the most likely

to dwell in deserts than they are in rainforests. The

8. local geography is another factor that

(A) the local wildlife will affect.
(B) affects the local wildlife.
(C) will affect the wildlife locally.
(D) has been affected by the local wildlife.

For example, there are animals that have adapted to life in mountains and high

altitudes, so it is clear that they will not be found in grasslands, swamps, or other

similar ecosystems.

Questions 9–12 refer to the following announcement.

9. Please remember that elections for student government are going to

(A) hold
(B) will hold
(C) be held
(D) holding

10. next week. Any students

(A) interest
(B) interested
(C) interesting
(D) interestingly

in running for the position of president,

vice president, or secretary/treasurer should let their homeroom teachers know by

tomorrow at three o'clock. Only students who have a GPA of 3.0 or above are eligible

GO ON TO THE NEXT PAGE

to run for any of these positions. Likewise, any students who have been suspended

11. in the past twelve months are

(A) requested
(B) delayed
(C) prohibited
(D) encouraged

from running for office. Each student

12.

(A) what decides to run
(B) who decides to run
(C) what decided on running
(D) who decided on running

for office needs to give a speech to the student body

explaining why he or she is interested in holding a particular office.

GO ON TO THE NEXT PAGE

Questions 13–20 refer to the following letter.

GO ON TO THE NEXT PAGE

Dear parents,

The school is going to hold its annual bake sale next Saturday, October 2.

13. The bake sale will start at 10 a.m. and

(A) end
(B) ends
(C) be ended
(D) ending

around 1 p.m. We

14. would like to encourage all of you to

(A) gather
(B) contribute
(C) buy
(D) collect

baked goods to the event.

You can feel free to purchase items such as cookies and cakes from bakeries, or you

15. can bake your own goods. We appreciate all

(A) bake sales and donations.
(B) of the donations at the bake sale.
(C) the bake sale's donations.
(D) donations to the bake sale.

16.

(A) Apparently, the bake sale,
(B) As for the bake sale itself,
(C) In accordance with the bake sale,
(D) Nonetheless, at the bake sale,

students, parents, and members of

the local community are invited to attend. Attendees will be able to purchase

GO ON TO THE NEXT PAGE

17. delicious baked goods at low prices. As always, the

(A) result
(B) approval
(C) objective
(D) reminder

of the

18. bake sale is to raise

(A) more than the money
(B) the most of the money
(C) as much money as possible
(D) more money than

for the school. This year,

19. the school's athletic teams are in

(A) desperate
(B) divisive
(C) derisive
(D) discounted

need of money, so

20.

(A) we are desiring a raise of
(B) our desire has raised
(C) what we desired raising
(D) it is our desire to raise

at least $2,000 at the event. If you have

any questions, contact Faith Rawlings at 555-6576. We hope to see all of you

at the bake sale.

Walter Taylor

Principal

GO ON TO THE NEXT PAGE

Questions 21–28 refer to the following magazine article.

21. There are many different genres of literature,

(A) which can be fantasy.

(B) one of which is fantasy.

(C) what is a fantasy.

(D) some of which are fantasies.

For a piece of writing to be considered fantasy literature, it must contain several

22.

(A) elements.

(B) ingredients.

(C) constituents.

(D) pieces.

First of all, most fantasy literature involves the use of magic.

The characters may cast magic spells, or their world may be magical. Fantasy

literature also contains a variety of fantastic creatures, such as dragons, unicorns,

23. and centaurs,

(A) what possesses magic powers.

(B) which magic powers are possessed.

(C) what they posses in magic powers.

(D) which may possess magic powers.

In addition, fantasy

24. literature typically takes place in an

(A) imagine

(B) imagining

(C) imaginary

(D) imagination

world. Middle Earth, the world

25. of J.R.R. Tolkien's *The Lord of the Rings* books, is

(A) the made-up place.
(B) one such made-up place.
(C) the place which was made up.
(D) making up a place.

These worlds may be similar to the real world, but their geography and other aspects

tend to be different. These worlds also have races other than humans. Elves, dwarves,

26. orcs, and goblins are among

(A) the existence of other races.
(B) the other races that may exist.
(C) races, some of which may exist.
(D) the races that have existed.

Finally, most fantasy

27. literature involves a

(A) conflict
(B) debate
(C) competition
(D) warfare

between good and evil. A hero or group of

28. heroes frequently undertakes a quest

(A) defeat
(B) defeating
(C) will defeat
(D) to defeat

the forces of evil.

GO ON TO THE NEXT PAGE

Questions 29–34 refer to the following letter.

To All Students:

29. Mr. Richards has just

> (A) informed
> (B) announced
> (C) insisted
> (D) alarmed

the school that he will only be teaching with us

30. for the next two weeks of the semester.

> (A) Moving back, he is
> (B) After moving back, he will
> (C) He has moved back
> (D) He is moving back

to Texas to take

care of his parents, both of whom are elderly. Please give your best wishes to

Mr. Richards before he leaves. Mr. Richards has been with us for five years, and

31. it is safe to say that there is no teacher

> (A) more popular than him.
> (B) as popular as that.
> (C) the most popular like him.
> (D) more than he is popular.

As you all know,

Mr. Richards teaches social studies and history. Since we are in the middle of

32. the semester, we do not have enough time to conduct a

(A) swift
(B) thorough
(C) reduced
(D) verified

search for a new

teacher. We will do that during the winter break. Fortunately, Mrs. Parker has agreed

33.

(A) coming out of retirement,
(B) that she came out of retirement,
(C) to come out of retirement,
(D) by coming out of retirement,

so she will take over Mr. Richards' classes.

34. Some of you may remember Mrs. Parker,

(A) who taught here
(B) that is teaching here
(C) who will teach here
(D) which has taught here

two years ago

prior to retiring. She is an outstanding teacher, and you will all surely benefit

from being in her class.

Dee Gorey

Principal

GO ON TO THE NEXT PAGE

Questions 35–42 refer to the following article in a student newspaper.

Last week, Central High School held a writing contest. The rules of the contest

35. were simple:

(A) A choice was given for the students
(B) The students were given a choice
(C) A choice gave the students
(D) The students gave them a choice

of three topics to

write on. They had to select one of the three and then write a 500-word essay

on it. The students were given one hour to compose their works. In past years,

36. students had to

(A) the writing of their essays by hand,
(B) hand in their written essays,
(C) write their essays by hand,
(D) hand over the essays they wrote,

but they were

permitted to make use of computers this year. Thirty-two students entered

37. the competition, and their works were

(A) rated
(B) guaranteed
(C) composed
(D) criticized

by a panel

38.
(A) consisting of three judges.
(B) that consisted with three judges.
(C) who consists with three judges.
(D) consisted of three judges.

Two were teachers from Central

High School while another was a professor at nearby City College. To prevent

39. the judges from being biased, the students' names were

(A) detached
(B) forgotten
(C) omitted
(D) repealed

from

their essays. The judges unanimously declared Alicia Walker's essay,

40.
(A) entitle
(B) entitled
(C) entitlement
(D) entitling

My Father: My Hero, the winner. Ms. Walker's essay will be

41.
(A) returned
(B) entered
(C) submitted
(D) transposed

to the city writing competition. If she should come in first or

42. second place there, she will be

(A) partial
(B) appropriate
(C) considerable
(D) eligible

to enter the statewide writing

contest.

STOP

NO TEST MATERIAL ON THIS PAGE

Reading Comprehension

In this section of the test, you will read six texts and answer 42 questions. Choose the correct answer to each question and mark the letter of the correct answer on your answer sheet.

Before you start, read the sample text and the sample questions below.

Sample Text

Erosion is one of nature's most powerful forces. It can happen in many ways, including through the wind, rain, snow, and ice. Erosion frequently takes place over a long period of time. This is how canyons and deserts are often created. Yet it is also possible for erosion to take place overnight.

Sample Question 1

What is this text mostly about?

(A) How deserts are created

(B) A natural force

(C) Canyons and deserts

(D) Wind erosion

The correct answer is (B), "A natural force."

Sample Question 2

Which of the following is true regarding erosion?

(A) It can happen in many ways.

(B) Water most commonly causes it.

(C) It can create deserts overnight.

(D) It is stronger than anything in nature.

The correct answer is (A), "It can happen in many ways."

GO ON TO THE NEXT PAGE

Questions 1–6 are about the following advertisement.

Visit Carter's Department Store!

It's that time of the year for school to start again. So that means you need to start <u>stocking up on</u> the supplies you need for the school year. Fortunately, you don't have to visit four or five different stores to get everything necessary. Instead, take a trip to Carter's Department Store. We've got everything that a student could possibly need.

We have all kinds of standard school supplies: pens, pencils, notebooks, rulers, and more. We also carry art supplies, such as paint, paintbrushes, and easels. You can purchase all sorts of electronic equipment, including calculators, desktop computers, and notebook computers. We even sell musical instruments.

And here's the best part: From now until the beginning of the school year, we are having a back-to-school sale. Everything we carry that is related to school is on sale for at least 25% off. Art supplies are 30% off while electronic goods are available at 40% discounts. And be sure to visit our boys' and girls' clothing departments, where you will find savings up to a <u>whopping</u> 60% off. You simply can't beat Carter's Department Store for quality and price.

GO ON TO THE NEXT PAGE

1. **Which headline best summarizes the advertisement?**

   (A) Big Sale at Carter's Department Store
   (B) Are You Ready for School?
   (C) Let's Go Shopping at Carter's
   (D) Carter's: The Newest Store in Town

2. **In line 1, the phrase <u>stocking up on</u> is closest in meaning to _____ .**

   (A) utilizing
   (B) considering
   (C) purchasing
   (D) saving

3. **The author uses paint, paintbrushes, and easels as examples of**

   (A) supplies that all students need
   (B) items selling for more than half off
   (C) some of the store's newest items
   (D) art supplies available at the store

4. **Which of the following statements is true regarding Carter's Department Store?**

   (A) It is located nearby the train station.
   (B) It sells a wide range of school items.
   (C) It has domestic and imported goods.
   (D) It is open every day of the week.

5. **What is the discount on a notebook computer?**

   (A) 25%
   (B) 30%
   (C) 40%
   (D) 60%

6. **In line 12, the word <u>whopping</u> is closest in meaning to _____ .**

   (A) surprising
   (B) unlikely
   (C) reduced
   (D) enormous

GO ON TO THE NEXT PAGE

Questions 7–12 are about the following announcement from a science teacher.

To all students enrolled in any science laboratory class:

There have been a couple of alterations in all of our science laboratory classes since the beginning of the semester.

To begin with, the laboratory fee for each class has changed. Students enrolled in biology classes must now pay $250 per semester, physiology students must pay $275, and chemistry students must pay $325. Physics students only need to pay $100 since they rarely use the lab. The reason for this is that there has been a general increase in the prices of the supplies needed for each class. The lab fees must be paid in full no later than Friday, September 29.

In addition, all students must purchase the <u>requisite</u> safety gear for their classes. In the past two weeks, four pairs of safety glasses and two lab coats have gone missing. The school simply cannot afford to continue replacing this equipment, so now all students must have their own items, <u>which</u> they will be expected to hold on to. While it may not seem fair to punish everyone for the actions of a few, this is the only option we seem to have.

Doris Williamson
Head of the Science Department

GO ON TO THE NEXT PAGE

7. **What is the note mainly about?**

(A) The performance of some students in their classes

(B) Some changes concerning the school's science classes

(C) The reason that students must purchase safety gear

(D) A change in how laboratory classes will be taught

8. **Which class requires the payment of a $275 fee?**

(A) Biology

(B) Physics

(C) Physiology

(D) Chemistry

9. **Paragraph 2 supports which of the following statements?**

(A) Lab supplies cost more, so the lab fees for students have increased.

(B) There has been no change in the price physics students must pay.

(C) All students must pay their lab fees within the next two weeks.

(D) Students in the biology class get to pay the least expensive lab fees.

10. **In line 9, the word <u>requisite</u> is closest in meaning to _____.**

(A) safest

(B) minimum

(C) obligated

(D) necessary

11. **In line 11, the word <u>which</u> refers to _____.**

(A) the school

(B) this equipment

(C) all students

(D) their own items

12. **Which can be inferred from the note about the school's lab equipment?**

(A) Some of it has been stolen.

(B) It needs to be updated.

(C) It is of fairly high quality.

(D) Most students dislike using it.

GO ON TO THE NEXT PAGE

Questions 13–18 are about the following letter.

Dear Parents,

It's that time of the year to start thinking about our annual spring festival. As you know, the school holds the festival for a couple of reasons. The first is to <u>engender</u> a sense of community between the school and the residents of the neighborhood. The second is to help raise money for the school to use in a variety of manners.

This spring, the festival will run from April 3 to 5 (Thursday to Saturday). All of the festival events are going to take place on the school campus. They will primarily be held in the school gym and auditorium as well as on the football field. This year, we have a large number of special activities planned. Please <u>consult</u> the attached sheet to see the events that have been scheduled.

Since we have so many activities planned, we are counting on you, our students' parents, to assist us. We need at least twenty-five volunteers to help out during the festival. If you can spare even one or two hours of your time, we would appreciate it. Please contact Mrs. Voss at 555-1212 if you can lend a helping hand at the festival.

Sincerely,
Jeanie Richards
Headmaster
Milton Academy

GO ON TO THE NEXT PAGE

13. **What is the purpose of the letter?**

    (A) To let the parents know how their children are performing

    (B) To describe an event to be held in the fall

    (C) To praise the parents for their devotion to the school

    (D) To provide information related to the festival

14. **In line 3, the word <u>engender</u> is closest in meaning to _____.**

    (A) amplify

    (B) appreciate

    (C) clarify

    (D) create

15. **Based on the letter, what is probably true about Milton Academy?**

    (A) It is located in a residential area.

    (B) It charges a high amount of tuition.

    (C) It is an all-boys school.

    (D) It has a large amount of debt to repay.

16. **In line 9, the word <u>consult</u> is closest in meaning to _____.**

    (A) edit

    (B) check

    (C) regard

    (D) print

17. **According to the letter, the festival will be held in all of the following locations EXCEPT _____.**

    (A) the auditorium

    (B) the gym

    (C) the classrooms

    (D) the football field

18. **What does the letter ask the parents to do?**

    (A) Be more involved in their children's school lives

    (B) Donate some money to the school

    (C) Volunteer to work during the festival

    (D) Give some goods to the school as donations

GO ON TO THE NEXT PAGE

Questions 19–26 are about the following passage.

Coral reefs are rocklike protrusions that extend from a coastline into the ocean. They are made from coral, a living organism. Coral polyps appear to be small plants to many people, but they are in actuality a type of marine life. They grow in clusters and secrete a substance made of calcium carbonate that protects their bodies. This substance, in turn, forms a rocky structure that creates the
5 reef itself.

Coral reefs form some of the ocean's most unique ecosystems. They are vibrant places which attract a wide variety of marine plants and animals. There are a couple of reasons that many sea creatures, particularly fish, live in coral reefs. The first is that the reefs are rich in nutrients, so there is an abundance of food for <u>them</u> to eat. The next is that coral reefs provide protection from large
10 predators. The hard, rocky reefs can wound large fish, such as sharks, that try to enter. Due to the absence of many <u>voracious</u> predators, smaller fish often lay their eggs in coral reefs. When the fish hatch, the reefs act as <u>sanctuaries</u> for them as they become adults.

Unfortunately, many of the planet's coral reefs are in danger of disappearing due to both natural and manmade reasons. Coral requires ideal conditions to live. It can only survive in warm water,
15 which means that it is virtually only found in tropical location. The water that coral resides in must also be shallow since it needs access to sunlight in order to survive. Yet the ocean is not static but is in a constant state of change. Sometimes the water temperature in a place where coral grows may become too hot or too cold. This can result in the destruction of an entire reef.

As for manmade problems, there are two major ones. First, pollution caused by humans—such as
20 the dumping of chemicals in the water—can kill coral, which is quite sensitive. Second, some humans actively destroy coral reefs. Many are fishermen. Some of them <u>eschew</u> nets in favor of dynamite. They kill numerous fish with explosives but damage the reefs in the process. On a smaller scale, some people cut off coral from reefs to make jewelry from or to use for home aquariums. All of these factors combine to endanger many of the world's coral reefs.

GO ON TO THE NEXT PAGE

19. **What does the author imply about coral polyps?**

    (A) Some people think they are vegetation.
    (B) They grow rapidly early in their lives.
    (C) They usually live amongst ocean plants.
    (D) It takes a lot of food for them to grow.

20. **Paragraph 1 supports which of the following statements?**

    (A) Coral polyps survive by consuming small plants.
    (B) Coral reefs are sometimes located deep in the ocean.
    (C) Coral polyps produce a substance that protects them.
    (D) Coral can live on shore so long as it is near the coast.

21. **In line 9, the word them refers to _____.**

    (A) a couple of reasons
    (B) many sea creatures
    (C) the reefs
    (D) nutrients

22. **In line 11, the word voracious is closest in meaning to _____.**

    (A) stealthy
    (B) gigantic
    (C) ravenous
    (D) vicious

23. **In line 12, the word sanctuaries is closest in meaning to _____.**

    (A) havens
    (B) estuaries
    (C) aquariums
    (D) containers

24. **According to the passage, which is necessary for coral to survive?**

    (A) salt water
    (B) nutrients
    (C) sunlight
    (D) deep water

25. **In line 21, the word eschew is closest in meaning to _____.**

    (A) employ
    (B) prefer
    (C) demean
    (D) avoid

26. **Which of the following is NOT mentioned as a way that humans are harming coral reefs?**

    (A) They are fishing in some coral reefs.
    (B) They are polluting the water the reefs are in.
    (C) They are catching many live fish for aquariums.
    (D) They are destroying some of the coral in reefs.

GO ON TO THE NEXT PAGE

Questions 27–34 are about the following passage.

There have been many famous detectives in literature. But one of the first—and certainly the most famous—is Sherlock Holmes. Holmes was created by the British writer Sir Arthur Conan Doyle in the late nineteenth century.

Sherlock Holmes made his first appearance in the work *A Study in Scarlet*, which was published in
5 1887. Holmes instantly became a popular literary figure with the general populace, who demanded that Doyle write more stories involving him. Doyle complied and eventually wound up writing fifty-six short stories and four novels that featured Holmes. While he took a break of several years from creating stories about Holmes, Doyle continued to write Holmes stories until 1927. Among the most famous of all the works featuring Holmes are *The Hound of the Baskervilles*, *The Blue Carbuncle*, and
10 *A Scandal in Bohemia*.

One of the reasons that Sherlock Holmes was so popular concerns the method he employs to solve his cases: logic. Together with his partner, Dr. Watson, Holmes uses his powers of observation to detect clues that can help him solve the cases he accepts. Holmes has an incredibly sharp mind that enables him to determine who the guilty party is or what the problem is. Holmes also is a master of
15 disguise, which he proves many times, and he is skilled at boxing as well as sword fighting.

While Holmes often solves cases that are unrelated to one another, he has a <u>nemesis</u> with whom he comes into both direct and indirect conflict in several stories. That person is Professor Moriarty, the leader of a crime ring in London. In one of the stories, *The Final Problem*, Holmes and Moriarty fight one another and fall to their deaths by plunging down a steep cliff near a waterfall. When he
20 wrote that story, Doyle had tired of Holmes and wanted to kill off the character. He then <u>refrained from</u> writing about Holmes for many years, but public demand for more stories induced him to bring Holmes back from the dead and to continue writing detective stories.

GO ON TO THE NEXT PAGE

27. **What is the best title for the passage?**

   (A) A Brief Biography of Sherlock Holmes

   (B) Sherlock Holmes and Dr. Watson

   (C) Sir Arthur Conan Doyle: The Creator of Sherlock Holmes

   (D) The Most Famous Detectives in the World

28. **What does the author say about Sir Arthur Conan Doyle?**

   (A) He considered becoming a detective in his youth.

   (B) He was a bestselling author during his life.

   (C) He created more detective stories than any other writer.

   (D) He wrote stories about Sherlock Holmes for decades.

29. **Why does the author mention *The Hound of the Baskervilles*?**

   (A) It was the first novel he wrote involving Sherlock Holmes.

   (B) The story is one that involves Professor Moriarty.

   (C) It is the title of one of his well-known Sherlock Holmes stories.

   (D) Dr. Watson makes his first appearance in that work.

30. **According to the passage, which is true about Sherlock Holmes?**

   (A) He was fluent in several foreign languages.

   (B) He often resorted to fighting during his investigations.

   (C) He relied upon logic to solve various mysteries.

   (D) He encouraged Dr. Watson to become more observant.

31. **In line 16, the word nemesis is closest in meaning to _____.**

   (A) competitor

   (B) peer

   (C) partner

   (D) rival

32. **In line 20, the phrase refrained from is closest in meaning to _____.**

   (A) stopped

   (B) resumed

   (C) postponed

   (D) continued

33. **What does the author imply about Professor Moriarty?**

   (A) There is an unknown reason why he engaged in a life of crime.

   (B) He fails to encounter Holmes in some stories he is involved in.

   (C) Critics consider him to be the greatest literary villain in history.

   (D) Sherlock Holmes and he are related to one another.

34. **Why did Doyle kill Sherlock Holmes in one of his stories?**

   (A) It was too difficult for him to come up with new storylines.

   (B) His fans demanded that Holmes be killed off.

   (C) He had no desire to write about Holmes anymore.

   (D) Killing Holmes would help Doyle increase his sales.

GO ON TO THE NEXT PAGE

Questions 35–42 are about the following passage.

Earth orbits the sun while the moon orbits Earth. Occasionally, all three of them become aligned with one another. When this happens, an eclipse occurs. There are two types of eclipses: solar and lunar. Both are rare events simply because, due to the movement of all three celestial bodies, the times when they line up with one another are infrequent.

5 Solar eclipses are easily the more <u>spectacular</u> of the two. For a solar eclipse to occur, the moon's orbit must take it between Earth and the sun. While the sun is much larger than the moon, the relative nearness of the moon to Earth makes <u>it</u> appear to be the same size as the sun when viewed from the ground. Thus, when the sun, Earth, and moon are perfectly aligned, the moon appears to cover the entire sun. This is a solar eclipse. A solar eclipse may be either total or partial. When a total

10 eclipse happens, the sun is completely <u>obscured</u> by the moon. The sky darkens, and it appears to be nighttime. However, most solar eclipses are partial ones. When they take place, the sun is only partly covered by the moon.

When a solar eclipse happens, it is observable from a fairly small area on the planet. Thus, when there is a solar eclipse in North America, it is highly unlikely that it will be visible in Africa or

15 Australia. A solar eclipse only lasts for a few minutes since all three heavenly bodies are in continual motion. People must also take care when viewing a solar eclipse since looking directly at it can cause damage—including blindness—to their eyes.

Lunar eclipses happen when Earth moves directly between the sun and the moon. When this occurs, the planet blocks sunlight from reflecting off the moon. Lunar eclipses take place at night.

20 During one, the moon appears very orange and is practically red in color. There are two different types of lunar eclipses. Taken together, the result is that lunar eclipses happen more frequently than solar eclipses. In addition, lunar eclipses may last for hours and can be seen from a wider area on the planet. There is no harm in directly observing a lunar eclipse either, so looking at one will not damage a person's eyes.

GO ON TO THE NEXT PAGE

35. What is the passage mainly about?

(A) How eclipses have affected history

(B) Two types of eclipses

(C) The problems eclipses cause

(D) Solar eclipses

36. In line 5, the word <u>spectacular</u> is closest in meaning to _____.

(A) distinct

(B) impressive

(C) lost lasting

(D) common

37. In line 7, the word <u>it</u> refers to _____.

(A) the moon's orbit

(B) the sun

(C) the moon

(D) Earth

38. In line 10, the word <u>obscured</u> is closest in meaning to _____.

(A) transposed

(B) illuminated

(C) perceived

(D) blocked

39. Why is the moon able to cover the sun during a solar eclipse?

(A) Because of its large size

(B) Because of its brightness

(C) Because of its closeness to Earth

(D) Because of its rotation

40. Which of the following is NOT mentioned about solar eclipses?

(A) How they can harm people

(B) How long they may last

(C) How much of the sun cannot be seen during them

(D) How often they happen

41. Which of the following is true regarding lunar eclipses?

(A) They occur more often than solar eclipses.

(B) They are hard for astronomers to predict.

(C) They result in the moon disappearing from sight.

(D) They last for a shorter time than solar eclipses.

42. What can be inferred from the passage about lunar eclipses?

(A) It is possible to see them from everywhere in the world.

(B) They are less dangerous to people than solar eclipses.

(C) Superstitious people believe they bring bad luck.

(D) During a full moon, they can be extremely bright.

STOP

Practice
Test 4

Listening
Comprehension

听力音频

The listening section has 42 questions. Follow along as you listen to the directions to the listening section.

Directions

In this section of the test, you will hear talks and conversations. Each talk or conversation is followed by one question. Choose the best answer to each question and mark the letter of the correct answer on your answer sheet. You will hear each talk or conversation only one time.

Here is an example: 🔊

What are the speakers talking about?

(A) Their homework in a class

(B) Mr. Davison's lectures

(C) A recent assignment

(D) How to do their homework

The correct answer is (A), "Their homework in a class."

Here is another example: 🔊

What does the girl says about the new cafeteria?

(A) The atmosphere is nice.

(B) There are many tables.

(C) It is very large.

(D) It has better food.

The correct answer is (D), "It has better food."

Go on to the next page, and the test will begin with question number one.

GO ON TO THE NEXT PAGE ⟩

1. **What are the speakers talking about?**

   (A) The topics of their English papers

   (B) How to do research at the library

   (C) A report for their history class

   (D) Why they have so much homework

2. **What is the girl going to do tomorrow morning?**

   (A) Have a meeting with her teacher

   (B) Give her homework to Mr. Patterson

   (C) Complete her homework assignment

   (D) Introduce her mother to Mr. Patterson

3. **According to the boy, why did his parents buy him a bike?**

   (A) They wanted him to get more exercise.

   (B) He got good grades the previous semester.

   (C) They gave it to him for his birthday.

   (D) It was a reward for getting an A^+ in math.

4. **What does the girl imply about her grade on the test?**

   (A) It is lower than the boy's grade.

   (B) It is her best grade of the semester.

   (C) It will make her parents proud of her.

   (D) It is better than she had expected.

5. **What are the speakers mainly discussing?**

   (A) Where the girl lives

   (B) How the girl will get home

   (C) What time school finishes

   (D) What the boy's parents do

6. **What does the teacher suggest about the girl?**

   (A) She needs to act better in class.

   (B) Her attitude is getting better.

   (C) She does not pay attention to him.

   (D) Her test scores have not improved.

7. **What is the purpose of the announcement?**

   (A) To provide some information about the science fair

   (B) To encourage the students to turn in their topics

   (C) To tell the students about last year's science fair winner

   (D) To warn the students about forgetting to submit a topic

8. **What is the subject of the announcement?**

   (A) How to join the cross country team

   (B) The need for the students to run more

   (C) The formation of a new sports team

   (D) The new coach of the school's athletic teams

9. **What does the teacher say about chemical changes?**

   (A) They happen by adding chemicals to a substance.

   (B) One example is boiling water to make steam.

   (C) They change the molecules that are inside objects.

   (D) It is difficult to make them actually take place.

GO ON TO THE NEXT PAGE

Now you will hear longer talks or conversations. Each talk or conversation will be followed by three or more questions. Choose the best answer to each question and mark the letter of the correct answer on your answer sheet. You will hear each talk or conversation only one time.

10. **What are the students mainly discussing?**

(A) The importance of voting in all elections

(B) What the girl intends to do as school president

(C) How they can make the school a better place

(D) The upcoming election that the girl is involved in

11. **Why does the girl mention Randy?**

(A) To say she had expected to lose to him

(B) To talk about how popular he is

(C) To note his friendship with the boy

(D) To compliment the campaign that he ran

12. **What does the boy say about the food in the cafeteria?**

(A) Its taste has improved.

(B) There is a wide selection.

(C) Its price is too high.

(D) It is not very good.

13. **What does the girl imply when she says this: "I don't want to do too much at once"?**

(A) She wishes she had lost the election.

(B) Being president will keep her very busy.

(C) She would like the boy to give her some help.

(D) She will only focus on the cafeteria at first.

14. **What does the teacher say about the boy's recent homework?**

(A) It has been better than she had expected.

(B) He has failed to turn it in most of the time.

(C) He has not been doing well on it.

(D) It has been some of his best work.

15. **What does the teacher suggest about the study group?**

(A) It will help the boy's math scores improve.

(B) It will teach the boy some new concepts in math.

(C) It will make the boy more attentive in class.

(D) It will prepare the boy for the upcoming classes.

16. **What is the boy going to do after lunch today?**

(A) Speak with his football coach

(B) Submit his math homework

(C) Go to a study group meeting

(D) Study one on one with the teacher

GO ON TO THE NEXT PAGE

17. **What is the main topic of the conversation?**

    (A) The topic of the paper the girl needs to write

    (B) The work the girl missed in the teacher's class

    (C) The girl's recent performance in the teacher's class

    (D) The most recent topic that the teacher covered

18. **Why was the girl absent from class?**

    (A) She was in the hospital.

    (B) She broke her leg.

    (C) She was in a car accident.

    (D) She had an illness.

19. **What does the girl imply about Mark?**

    (A) He is her lab partner in science class.

    (B) He is one of her closest friends.

    (C) She often studies with him after school.

    (D) She will ask him for his class notes.

20. **What does the teacher give the girl?**

    (A) An assignment sheet

    (B) A test paper

    (C) A permission slip

    (D) A report that she wrote

21. **What will the girl probably do next?**

    (A) Submit her assignment

    (B) Take a makeup exam

    (C) Attend her next class

    (D) Ask the teacher a question

22. **Why is the girl talking about doing another extracurricular activity?**

    (A) She wants to learn a new skill.

    (B) Her parents want her to do that.

    (C) It will give her something else to do.

    (D) She has a lot of free time.

23. **What does the boy mean when he says this: "It seems like your plate is already full"?**

    (A) The girl is doing a large number of activities.

    (B) The girl ought to listen to her parents.

    (C) The girl should stop eating so much food.

    (D) The girl needs to ask someone for advice.

24. **Why does the boy talk about the track team?**

    (A) To complain about his last track meet

    (B) To say that he is the captain of the team

    (C) To claim that it takes up a lot of time

    (D) To advise the girl to try out for it

25. **Which extracurricular activity does the girl decide to do?**

    (A) The track team

    (B) The computer club

    (C) The softball team

    (D) The band

GO ON TO THE NEXT PAGE

26. **Why does the professor mention Watertown?**

    (A) To say it is where he teaches

    (B) To note the location of a cave

    (C) To describe a Native American tribe from there

    (D) To name the place where the three boys live

27. **According to the professor, when was the newly discovered art most likely made?**

    (A) One century ago

    (B) Five centuries ago

    (C) One thousand years ago

    (D) Several thousand years ago

28. **What was found along with the art?**

    (A) Jewelry

    (B) Pottery

    (C) Weapons

    (D) Bones

29. **What is probably true about the recent discovery?**

    (A) It occurred thanks to research done by the professor.

    (B) Archaeologists from all over the country are studying it.

    (C) It is one of the most important archaeological finds in the region.

    (D) Many of the paintings are currently in poor condition.

30. **What is the teacher mainly discussing?**

    (A) Mathematical formulas for the laws of motion

    (B) The life of Sir Isaac Newton

    (C) Sir Isaac Newton's three laws of motion

    (D) The research that Sir Isaac Newton did

31. **What can be inferred about the teacher?**

    (A) He used to conduct research on optics.

    (B) He wrote his master's thesis on Sir Isaac Newton.

    (C) He would rather be teaching a math class.

    (D) He is familiar with Sir Isaac Newton's achievements.

32. **How does the teacher demonstrate the first law of motion?**

    (A) By writing a formula on the board

    (B) By rolling a ball on his desk

    (C) By showing a rocket taking off

    (D) By talking about a car accelerating

33. **What is the third law of motion?**

    (A) There is an equal reaction for every action.

    (B) An object at rest stays at rest.

    (C) All objects move in straight lines.

    (D) Force equals mass times acceleration.

34. **What will the teacher probably do next?**

    (A) Have the students ask some questions

    (B) Conduct a science experiment

    (C) Talk about Sir Isaac Newton's life

    (D) Have the students watch a video

GO ON TO THE NEXT PAGE

35. **Why does the girl mention her sister?**

   (A) To say that her sister gives her stress

   (B) To claim that her sister is unaffected by stress

   (C) To explain how her sister reacts to stress

   (D) To note that her sister gets stressed out by school

36. **What does the teacher imply when she says this: "Be serious, Brad"?**

   (A) She is going to kick the student out of class.

   (B) She is pleased with the student's answer.

   (C) She wants the student to be quiet.

   (D) She thinks the student is making a joke.

37. **According to the teacher, how can traffic jams cause stress?**

   (A) They give people a sense of helplessness.

   (B) They can cause people to get physically ill.

   (C) They make people late for their appointments.

   (D) They force people to waste a lot of time.

38. **Why does the teacher suggest that the students should do their homework early?**

   (A) To recommend it as one way to save time

   (B) To name a way they can get rid of their stress

   (C) To encourage them to stop delaying their work

   (D) To claim that it will improve their grades

39. **What is the teacher explaining?**

   (A) The way that a train operates

   (B) The development of railways

   (C) George Stevenson's role in history

   (D) The inventing of the steam engine

40. **How were carts that ran on wooden tracks moved?**

   (A) By oxen

   (B) By steam engines

   (C) By horses

   (D) By electric power

41. **What did George Stevenson do?**

   (A) He made a train engine.

   (B) He worked as a miner.

   (C) He designed a railway line.

   (D) He invented the steam engine.

42. **What is probably true about railroads?**

   (A) They could transport goods faster than automobiles could.

   (B) It was cheaper to make them than to build steamships.

   (C) People in countries other than Britain learned to make them.

   (D) Some of them were dangerous and caused accidents.

STOP

Language Form and Meaning

In this section of the test, you will answer 42 questions found in seven different texts. Within each text are boxes that contain four possible ways to complete a sentence. Choose the word or words in each box that correctly complete each sentence. Mark the letter of the correct answer on your answer sheet.

Here are two sample questions:

1. Ever since Gutenberg

> (A) invents
> (B) invented
> (C) inventing
> (D) has invented

movable type in the 1400s, printed

works have been the primary source of reading material for most people.

2. But,

> (A) thanks to the Internet,
> (B) thanking the Internet,
> (C) having thanked the Internet,
> (D) with the thanks of the Internet,

more and more people are reading

material that is not printed on paper nowadays.

The correct answer to **Sample 1** is (B), "invented." The correct answer to **Sample 2** is (A), "thanks to the Internet."

GO ON TO THE NEXT PAGE

Questions 1–4 refer to the following email.

Dear Jessica,

1. Are you going to try out for the swim team this year? I hope you intend

    (A) do
    (B) doing
    (C) will do
    (D) to do

that. I have been working out all summer long, so I think I should make the team. It would

2. be fantastic if

    (A) we could be teammates
    (B) they are teammates
    (C) some of them are teammates
    (D) the teammates are us

this year. I wonder if you have any

pointers that you can give me. I know you have been on the swim team for a couple

GO ON TO THE NEXT PAGE

GO ON TO THE NEXT PAGE

3. of years, but this is my first attempt to participate in

(A) individual
(B) organized
(C) respected
(D) extended

sports.

4. I am a little nervous, so any

(A) evidence
(B) tips
(C) clues
(D) prompts

or other information you can provide

me with would be appreciated.

Bye,

Tiffany

Questions 5–8 refer to the following essay.

I strongly believe that all students should do some kind of volunteer work. I especially

feel that they should work with individuals who are poor or homeless. Many of us

5. live

| (A) unfortunate |
| (B) scholastic |
| (C) apparent |
| (D) sheltered |

lives. After school every day, we go back to our nice homes and

6. enjoy

| (A) as much food as |
| (B) the most food |
| (C) a greater amount of food |
| (D) more food |

we can eat. We are fortunate, but not

GO ON TO THE NEXT PAGE

everyone is so lucky. By volunteering at a homeless shelter or a food bank,

7.
| (A) we could see that |
| (B) what we see is |
| (C) we can see how |
| (D) seeing how, we can |

some other members of society live. I truly feel that we

8. could learn a lot
| (A) which engages |
| (B) by engaging |
| (C) to engage |
| (D) if they engage |

in this kind of volunteer work.

Questions 9–12 refer to the following advertisement.

9. Are you the

> (A) style
> (B) type
> (C) individual
> (D) category

of student who enjoys studying? Do you like it when your

teachers spend extra time with you in the classroom? Are you interested in getting

10.

> (A) out of your education from most?
> (B) your education is the most?
> (C) your education, which is the most?
> (D) the most out of your education?

If you answered yes to these questions,

then you should consider applying to Lakeview Academy. We are a private school

GO ON TO THE NEXT PAGE

GO ON TO THE NEXT PAGE

that educates elementary, middle, and high school students.

11.

(A) Situated on top of Henry Mountain,

(B) In a situation on top of Henry Mountain,

(C) On Henry Mountain, there is situated,

(D) What was situated at the top of Henry Mountain,

we provide the best education

12. possible for our students. If you think you have

(A) what it takes

(B) which was taken

(C) who we take

(D) where it was taken

to be

a Lakeview student, call 555-6543 and set up an appointment with us today.

Questions 13–20 refer to the following email.

Dear Sally,

13. I just had a talk with David

(A) concern
(B) concerned
(C) concerning
(D) to concern

the group project we are doing for

14. our science class. According to him, we are very far behind

(A) schedule
(B) scheduled
(C) scheduling
(D) schedules

15. and need to start working

(A) as fast as.
(B) faster than.
(C) much faster.
(D) the fastest.

16.

(A) Whimsically,
(B) Periodically,
(C) Consequently,
(D) Apparently,

we only have ten more days before everything is supposed

to be turned in. David told me that most of the other groups have almost finished their

17. work, but

(A) we have barely even started.
(B) barely starting, we have.
(C) having started, we had barely.
(D) barely had we even started.

Anyway, he wants you and me to do

GO ON TO THE NEXT PAGE

18. some

(A) assignment

(B) exams

(C) experiment

(D) research

at the library tomorrow after school. He gave me a list of

books for us to find and get some data from. Do you have time to go to the public library

19. after school tomorrow? I cannot recall

(A) basketball practice, whether it is.

(B) what is at basketball practice.

(C) whether you have basketball practice.

(D) how we are having basketball practice.

If you do not have it, how about meeting at three twenty? But, if you have practice, go to

20. the library when it is over. I am planning to head there

(A) thus having finished school.

(B) before I finish school.

(C) once school finishes.

(D) if school is going to finish.

Let me know what your situation is.

See you tomorrow.

Jason

GO ON TO THE NEXT PAGE

Questions 21–26 refer to the following magazine article.

21. People use figures of speech to make their writing

(A) more appealing
(B) the most appealing of
(C) appealing than
(D) of the most appealing

to

readers. Two of the most common of these are similes and metaphors.

However, there are a large number of other figures of speech

22.

(A) how these are used.
(B) what are used.
(C) which they will use.
(D) that they can use.

One of these is personification. When a writer uses it,

he or she gives an animal or thing human characteristics. For instance, a person might

write, "The sun smiled down on the land." By claiming that the sun is smiling,

23. the writer is

(A) giving the sun a human ability.
(B) a sun with human abilities.
(C) given an ability by the sun.
(D) able to give the sun abilities.

Two more common

GO ON TO THE NEXT PAGE

GO ON TO THE NEXT PAGE

figures of speech are alliteration and assonance. Alliteration is the repetition of

24. consonant sounds

(A) because
(B) whereas
(C) therefore
(D) moreover

assonance is the repetition of vowel sounds.

Therefore "five fierce friends" is an example of alliteration, and "every excited elephant"

25. is

(A) examples of assonance.
(B) one of assonance.
(C) the assonance.
(D) some assonance.

By employing these figures of speech and others

26. in their works, writers can make

(A) superb
(B) creative
(C) long
(D) dull

prose much more interesting to

the people reading it.

Questions 27–34 refer to the following notice.

To all students:

27. I would like to

(A) reciprocate
(B) appreciate
(C) renovate
(D) congratulate

the girls' volleyball team on

qualifying the state tournament last week. The girls' team defeated

28. Walker High School, which

(A) enables
(B) enabled
(C) has been enabled
(D) is enabling

them to make the

29.

(A) upcoming
(B) arriving
(C) various
(D) recent

state tournament. This year's competition will be held this weekend.

30. It starts on Thursday and

(A) coming for the end
(B) came to its end
(C) will end when we come
(D) will come to an end

on Saturday evening, when

the final game to determine the state champion is played. Our girls' team is currently

31.
(A) rank
(B) ranks
(C) ranked
(D) ranking

number three in the entire state, so we have an outstanding chance

of playing in the final game. The girls need your support though, so I encourage as

many students as possible to attend the tournament. The games will be held in

32. Davenport,
(A) that is in twenty minutes.
(B) for about twenty minutes.
(C) which is twenty minutes away.
(D) when there are twenty minutes.

The girls' first game is on

Thursday evening at six o'clock. We have reserved two buses to take students to the game.

33. Please let your homeroom teacher know
(A) how they attended.
(B) if you can attend.
(C) why you should attend.
(D) when they are attending.

Be sure to

34.
(A) appeal
(B) wish
(C) grant
(D) say

the members of the girls' team luck when you see them.

Principal Sandy Nelson

GO ON TO THE NEXT PAGE

Questions 35–42 refer to the following essay.

35. The myths and

(A) legends
(B) civilizations
(C) art
(D) sculptures

of various cultures often include stories

involving magic and monsters. Many people in the past believed that some individuals

could do magic and that monsters existed. In my opinion, people cannot do magic, and

36. there is

(A) a monster, not a thing.
(B) not a monster in that thing.
(C) not any kinds of monsters.
(D) no such thing as monsters.

In that case, why did people

believe so strongly in them? One reason is that people lacked the knowledge

37.

(A) understanding
(B) to understand
(C) having understood
(D) being understood

the world around them. For instance, people did not know

38.

(A) what caused an eclipse
(B) the cause of that eclipse
(C) when the eclipse happened
(D) which kind of eclipse caused

when the moon moved in front of the sun.

GO ON TO THE NEXT PAGE

39. They thought it involved

(A) some sort of magic.
(B) magic, which has some.
(C) sorting magic.
(D) the sorting of magic.

Since they did not know

about astronomy, they could not explain that the movement of the planets and other

40. heavenly bodies caused

(A) eclipse
(B) eclipses
(C) eclipsing
(D) eclipsed

to occur at times. As for monsters,

41. one reason people thought they existed had to do with dinosaur

(A) eggs.
(B) samples.
(C) fossils.
(D) studies.

42. People who found these

(A) gigantic
(B) extreme
(C) miniature
(D) underground

bones believed they came from dragons

and other large monsters. As a result, they thought there were monsters on the planet.

STOP

NO TEST MATERIAL ON THIS PAGE

Reading Comprehension

In this section of the test, you will read six texts and answer 42 questions. Choose the correct answer to each question and mark the letter of the correct answer on your answer sheet.

Before you start, read the sample text and the sample questions below.

Sample Text

Sharks are misunderstood creatures. Many people believe that all sharks are brutal killers that hunt humans, but that is not true at all. Only a handful of sharks ever attack humans, and most of them do that by mistake. In fact, most sharks ignore humans completely and seek to avoid them.

Sample Question 1

What is this text mostly about?

(A) Which sharks attack humans

(B) Why sharks often ignore humans

(C) How many sharks behave around humans

(D) What to do when you see a shark

The correct answer is (C), "How many sharks behave around humans."

Sample Question 2

Which of the following is true regarding sharks?

(A) Most species of them attack humans.

(B) Many of them actively hunt people.

(C) A lot of them prefer to eat small sea creatures.

(D) The majority of them stay away from people.

The correct answer is (D), "The majority of them stay away from people."

GO ON TO THE NEXT PAGE

Questions 1–6 are about the following letter.

Dear Students,

We are about to <u>embark upon</u> another school year, so many of you will be looking forward to participating on the school's athletic teams. This year, we intend to field several athletic teams for both boys and girls. However, there are a couple of changes you ought to be conscious of.

First of all, Coach Jenkins is no longer with us. After fourteen years of coaching and teaching health classes at our school, Coach Jenkins <u>resigned</u> to take a job elsewhere. He has been replaced by Jeremy Sloan. Coach Sloan will be the head coach of the boys' football and basketball teams. He will also serve as an assistant coach of the track and field team.

Unfortunately, due to a lack of interest in the area, there will not be a girls' softball team this year. Only two schools in the county expressed an interest in fielding teams. Therefore, we regret that the girls' softball season has been cancelled. Girls will, however, be permitted to try out for the boys' baseball team.

Please contact me if you have any questions.

Steve Hollister
Athletic Director

1. **What is this letter mostly about?**

   (A) The school's newest instructors

   (B) Some changes in the school's athletic teams

   (C) The boys' and girls' basketball teams

   (D) Which sports girls can play this semester

2. **In line 2, the phrase <u>embark upon</u> is closest in meaning to _____ .**

   (A) start

   (B) consider

   (C) delay

   (D) repeat

3. **In line 6, the word <u>resigned</u> is closest in meaning to _____ .**

   (A) transferred

   (B) moved

   (C) quit

   (D) expected

4. **Based on the letter, which is probably true about Coach Jenkins?**

   (A) He was the school's most popular coach.

   (B) His football team had a winning record last year.

   (C) He used to play professional basketball.

   (D) He will coach a sport at a different school.

5. **Who is Jeremy Sloan?**

   (A) The school's athletic director

   (B) The coach of the baseball team

   (C) The school's football coach

   (D) The head coach of the track team

6. **According to the letter, all of the following sports will be played EXCEPT _____ .**

   (A) Boys' football

   (B) Girls' softball

   (C) Boys' baseball

   (D) Track and field

GO ON TO THE NEXT PAGE

Questions 7–12 are about the following notice.

Attention, all students:

In the past week, several students have been caught violating the school's dress code. On account of that, I would like to list which clothes are acceptable and which are not.

Boys must wear long pants and button-down shirts. These shirts must have collars since all boys have to wear neckties as well. Furthermore, boys must wear either dress shoes or nice shoes. Sneakers, sandals, jeans, shorts, T-shirts, sleeveless shirts, tank tops, and other similar casual articles of clothing are not allowed.

Girls must wear slacks or skirts as well as blouses. All skirts must go down below the knees of the students wearing them. Girls may also wear dresses so long as they are not too formal. The clothes that are <u>prohibited</u> for boys may also not be worn by girls.

Students who violate the dress code will be sent to their homes to change and be given detentions or suspensions. Multiple violations of the dress code will result in <u>them</u> being sent to the principal's office.

We insist that all students <u>comply with</u> the dress code. Should you have any objections to the school's dress code, I am willing to speak with you about them.

Tina Wimberley
Principal

GO ON TO THE NEXT PAGE

7. **What is the purpose of the notice?**

   (A) To punish some students for wearing improper clothes

   (B) To announce that the dress code has been abolished

   (C) To inform students about the school's dress code

   (D) To advise students to wear their uniforms every day

8. **What does the author say about clothing for boys?**

   (A) They may wear jeans or shorts to school.

   (B) They are supposed to wear ties to school.

   (C) T-shirts are acceptable clothing for them.

   (D) Their clothes must be ironed and look nice.

9. **In line 10, the word <u>prohibited</u> is closest in meaning to _____.**

   (A) advised

   (B) forbidden

   (C) registered

   (D) requested

10. **In line 12, the word <u>them</u> refers to _____.**

    (A) students

    (B) their homes

    (C) detentions or suspensions

    (D) multiple violations

11. **What can be inferred from the notice about Tina Wimberley?**

    (A) She works as a teacher in addition to serving as school principal.

    (B) She recently began her employment at the school.

    (C) She expects some students to violate the school's dress code.

    (D) She is planning to make the school's dress code more casual.

12. **In line 13, the phrase <u>comply with</u> is closest in meaning to _____.**

    (A) adhere to

    (B) think about

    (C) agree with

    (D) be proud of

GO ON TO THE NEXT PAGE

Questions 13–17 are about the following story.

"You'd better hurry up, or we're going to be late," said Eric.

"Relax, Eric," responded Martin. "I've got everything under control. Besides, we have to finish this science experiment before we can leave the classroom. That's what Ms. Chandler told us."

Eric and Martin both looked at the clock. It was three o'clock, and school had already ended.
5 However, the boys were still working on their science experiment, so they couldn't leave the classroom. Unfortunately, they only had a few minutes to get to the gym. As members of the football team, they had to be on the bus no later than three twenty. Their team was playing an away game later in the evening and had to leave very soon in order to get to the site of the game on time.

After working for five more minutes, Eric said, "That does it. We're all done with the experiment.
10 Now, let's get out of here."

"Hold on," Martin said to him. "We've got to clean up this mess first. Ms. Chandler will <u>berate</u> us if we don't put away everything."

"But what about the bus?" Eric asked worriedly. "I'm more afraid of Coach than I am Ms. Chandler."

15 "I've got everything under control," stated Martin. After having said that, Martin began to clean up the lab table while Eric put the chemicals away. In just a few minutes, the boys were done.

"Great," said Eric. "Let's roll. We've only got five more minutes."

Eric and Martin both ran out of the classroom. They grabbed their football equipment, and then they rushed all the way to the front of the gym. The rest of the team was already on the bus while
20 Coach Jackson was standing beside <u>it</u>.

"It's about time you boys got here," he said impatiently. "I didn't think you were going to make it for a moment."

"We wouldn't let you down, Coach," said Martin. "We just had to get some schoolwork done."

"Okay," responded Coach Jackson. "Now get on that bus so that we can get out of here."

GO ON TO THE NEXT PAGE

13. **What is the best title for the story?**

    (A) Getting Ready for the Big Game

    (B) How to Do a Science Experiment

    (C) Taking Care of Some Schoolwork

    (D) Eric and Martin Practice Football

14. **Why are Eric and Martin going to take a bus?**

    (A) To go to a football game

    (B) To get to their homes

    (C) To go on a field trip

    (D) To visit a laboratory

15. **In line 11, the word <u>berate</u> is closest in meaning to _____.**

    (A) compliment

    (B) penalize

    (C) scold

    (D) insult

16. **In line 20, the word <u>it</u> refers to _____.**

    (A) the classroom

    (B) the gym

    (C) the team

    (D) the bus

17. **At the end of the story, Eric and Martin have done all of the following activities EXCEPT _____.**

    (A) spoken with their head coach

    (B) changed into their football uniforms

    (C) cleaned their laboratory table

    (D) completed their science experiment

GO ON TO THE NEXT PAGE

Questions 18–26 are about the following passage.

Since ancient times, one of the most common materials people have utilized to make things with is wood. Wood is used to make houses, buildings, and other structures. People also make a large number of smaller objects with it.

The desire to make finished products more beautiful appears to be <u>ingrained</u> in human nature.
5 On account of this fact, for thousands of years, people have carved and shaped wooden objects to make them more appealing to the eye. Humans have additionally tended to create both religious and ceremonial objects from wood. In fact, all around the world, countless cultures have made use of ceremonial wood carvings. These objects often reflect the spirit of the people who made them, and each of them tends to hold a special significance as well.

10 One of the most common types of wood carvings is the mask. People in many cultures in Asia, Africa, and North America have made ceremonial wooden masks. In Africa, for instance, large numbers of tribes use wooden masks for various spiritual rituals. These masks are often in the form of animals that are <u>sacred to</u> the tribes. In other cases, the masks have human forms. The faces, however, may not be exactly humanlike. For instance, the faces can be distorted, having wider, longer,
15 smaller, or larger features than normal. The masks may be carved to give them ugly or frightening appearances as well. And, on other occasions, the masks are made to look as beautiful as possible.

While masks tend to be fairly small, other wood carvings can be enormous. Among the largest of all ceremonial wood carvings is the totem pole. Totem poles have been built by several Native American tribes that reside in the northwestern part of North America. They are normally made to
20 represent families, or <u>they</u> may honor significant historical events. Some even tell stories. A typical totem pole has several individual carvings on it. Each carving represents a different part of the family history, event, or story. Most totem poles have human or animal faces, as well as other figures, carved in them. They are so large that they are made from entire trees. Once the trees are cut down, master craftsmen work on them. When completed, they may or may not be painted. Then, the totem poles are positioned in places of honor and placed upright.

GO ON TO THE NEXT PAGE

18. **What is this passage mainly about?**

    (A) The ways wood can be used to make buildings

    (B) The purposes of masks in some cultures

    (C) The types of wood carvings some people make

    (D) Totem poles and their significance

19. **In line 4, the word <u>ingrained</u> is closest in meaning to** _____.

    (A) embedded

    (B) disturbed

    (C) initiated

    (D) consistent

20. **Why have some people carved wooden objects?**

    (A) To give them to others as gifts

    (B) To worship them as idols

    (C) To employ them as weapons

    (D) To utilize them in ceremonies

21. **In line 13, the phrase <u>sacred to</u> is closest in meaning to** _____.

    (A) important to

    (B) hunted by

    (C) revered by

    (D) necessary for

22. **What does the author say about masks?**

    (A) They always resemble human faces.

    (B) It takes a great deal of effort to make them.

    (C) People make them on several continents.

    (D) Animal masks are more popular than human ones.

23. **The author uses totem poles as an example of** _____.

    (A) wood carvings that are large in size

    (B) a type of wood carving older than masks

    (C) the most impressive of all wood carvings

    (D) the wood carvings favored by all Native Americans

24. **In line 20, the word <u>they</u> refers to** _____.

    (A) totem poles

    (B) several Native American tribes

    (C) families

    (D) significant historical events

25. **What does the author imply about wood carvings?**

    (A) They take years to learn how to make.

    (B) They are expensive to buy.

    (C) They need special types of wood.

    (D) They may vary in size.

26. **The author mentions all of the following about totem poles EXCEPT** _____.

    (A) what they look like

    (B) what they represent

    (C) which trees are used to make them

    (D) who usually carves them

GO ON TO THE NEXT PAGE

Questions 27–34 are about the following passage.

Virtually any night of the year, a person can look up at the sky and see the moon. The moon is Earth's only natural satellite. It takes slightly more than twenty-seven days for it to orbit Earth. And it does so from a little more than 380,000 kilometers away. Despite being Earth's closest celestial neighbor, there is much about the moon that scientists do not know.

5   For instance, no one is exactly sure when the moon was formed. Earth is <u>estimated</u> to have been created around 4.5 billion years ago. No later than 100,000 years after that, the moon was in orbit around Earth. Yet the question remains: How did the moon form? There are several theories, but astronomers have thus far failed to prove any of them correct.

The most widely accepted idea is the collision theory. It states that the moon formed when an
10   object <u>crashed into</u> Earth. According to this hypothesis, when Earth was first created, it had no satellite. But, at some point in time, an object approximately the size of Mars collided with Earth. This caused part of the planet to break off. The largest part eventually transformed into the moon.

Another theory is that Earth and the moon formed at the exact same time billions of years ago. However, many astronomers discount this theory. They point out that Earth and the moon are
15   comprised of different substances. They claim that if the two bodies were formed at the same time, then they should be composed of the same materials. Yet, as an example of their differences, the moon has much less iron than Earth does.

A third theory <u>proposes</u> that the moon formed somewhere else in the solar system. As it wandered past Earth, it was captured by Earth's gravity and began to orbit the planet. A fourth theory declares
20   that, when <u>it</u> first formed, Earth spun much more rapidly than it does at the present time. Due to its swift rotation, part of the crust was stripped away from the planet and cast into space. This material then formed the moon.

Each of the four theories has its supporters and detractors. Thus far, however, no astronomer has been able to prove one theory while disproving all of the others.

GO ON TO THE NEXT PAGE

27. **What would be the best title for the passage?**

   (A) The Moon: Everything You Need to Know about It
   (B) The Changing Phases of the Moon
   (C) Theories on the Creation of the Moon
   (D) How Long Ago Did the Moon Form?

28. **Paragraph 1 supports which of the following statements?**

   (A) The moon's distance from Earth changes at times.
   (B) There are many satellites that are orbiting Earth.
   (C) The moon is always visible in the night sky.
   (D) No natural objects are closer to Earth than the moon.

29. **In line 5, the word <u>estimated</u> is closest in meaning to _____ .**

   (A) known
   (B) determined
   (C) thought
   (D) presumed

30. **In line 10, the phrase <u>crashed into</u> is closest in meaning to _____ .**

   (A) hit
   (B) passed
   (C) interfered with
   (D) affected

31. **Which of the following is true regarding the collision theory?**

   (A) It points out that Earth's orbit changed a great deal.
   (B) It declares that Mars collided with Earth at one point.
   (C) It states that Earth once had multiple satellites.
   (D) It is believed by the greatest number of astronomers.

32. **Why do many astronomers doubt that Earth and the moon formed at the same time?**

   (A) The moon more likely came from elsewhere in the solar system.
   (B) Earth and the moon are formed of different materials.
   (C) There is not enough iron in the Earth's crust.
   (D) The chances of two objects forming close together are small.

33. **In line 18, the word <u>proposes</u> is closest in meaning to _____ .**

   (A) suggests
   (B) insists
   (C) promises
   (D) denies

34. **In line 20, the word <u>it</u> refers to _____ .**

   (A) the solar system
   (B) the planet's gravity
   (C) a fourth theory
   (D) Earth

GO ON TO THE NEXT PAGE

Questions 35–42 are about the following passage.

For thousands of years, humans survived by living as hunter-gatherers. Since they neither grew their own crops nor raised their own animals, they lacked easy access to food supplies. Instead, they ate whatever animals they could hunt, trap, or fish and whatever fruits, vegetables, grains, and nuts they could gather.

5 In more recent times, the global food supply has increased greatly thanks to advanced farming methods. While there are still places on the Earth where some people starve, it is no longer a major problem like it was in the past. In fact, in the developed world, starvation is a minor problem only experienced by a relatively small number of people. As a result of this excess of food, more and more people are becoming <u>pickier</u> about what they consume.

10 Thus people have adapted a number of eating styles. This is especially true of individuals who live in the Western world. One of these movements is vegetarianism. A vegetarian is an individual who does not eat meat. Since most meat is high in protein, vegetarians must replace this lost nutrient by eating other types of food. For the most part, they can eat fish, soy products, and various kinds of beans to get the nourishment they require.

15 There are actually a wide variety of vegetarian lifestyles. Many individuals who <u>opt for</u> vegetarian diets have different standards of what they consider meat. For instance, some vegetarians refuse to eat both beef and pork but consume chicken and other poultry. Other vegetarians do not eat beef, pork, and poultry but have no problem with fish and other types of seafood. There are some vegetarians who reject all kinds of meat and fish but eat eggs, cheese, milk, butter, and other animal-

20 based food products. Finally, there are a few vegetarians who are so strict that they do not eat any kind of food that comes from an animal.

For the most part, people choose the vegetarian lifestyle for two reasons. The first is that they believe eating meat is unhealthy. They claim that consuming meat can cause obesity, heart disease, and other health problems. The second is that some people do not want to cause harm to any

25 animals. They believe it is <u>inhumane</u> to kill animals for food, so they do not eat meat as a result.

GO ON TO THE NEXT PAGE

35. Which of the following is NOT mentioned as a method of obtaining food used by hunter-gatherers?

(A) Trapping animals

(B) Fishing for animals

(C) Farming grains

(D) Collecting fruits

36. In line 9, the word <u>pickier</u> is closest in meaning to _____.

(A) more cautious

(B) choosier

(C) smarter

(D) more exotic

37. What does the author imply about starvation?

(A) People often suffered from it in the past.

(B) It is a painful way for a person to die.

(C) People would not starve if they stopped being picky.

(D) It will likely disappear in the near future.

38. What can vegetarians eat to get more protein in their diets?

(A) Chicken

(B) Fruit

(C) Grain

(D) Beans

39. In line 15, the phrase <u>opt for</u> is closest in meaning to _____.

(A) choose

(B) require

(C) prepare

(D) abandon

40. Why does the author talk about vegetarian lifestyles?

(A) To state that most of them originated in the Western world

(B) To point out that there are several of them for people to follow

(C) To claim that they have been followed by people for centuries

(D) To criticize the people who lead them for refusing to eat any meat

41. In line 25, the word <u>inhumane</u> is closest in meaning to _____.

(A) acceptable

(B) unclean

(C) cruel

(D) unnecessary

42. According to the passage, why do people become vegetarians?

(A) To save on their food budgets

(B) To avoid certain health issues

(C) To help them gain weight

(D) To follow the latest trends

STOP

Practice
Test 5

Listening
Comprehension

听力音频

The listening section has 42 questions. Follow along as you listen to the directions to the listening section.

Directions

In this section of the test, you will hear talks and conversations. Each talk or conversation is followed by one question. Choose the best answer to each question and mark the letter of the correct answer on your answer sheet. You will hear each talk or conversation only one time.

Here is an example: 🔊

What are the speakers talking about?

(A) Their homework in a class
(B) Mr. Davison's lectures
(C) A recent assignment
(D) How to do their homework

The correct answer is (A), "Their homework in a class."

Here is another example: 🔊

What does the girl says about the new cafeteria?

(A) The atmosphere is nice.
(B) There are many tables.
(C) It is very large.
(D) It has better food.

The correct answer is (D), "It has better food."

Go on to the next page, and the test will begin with question number one.

GO ON TO THE NEXT PAGE

1. **What is probably true about the speakers?**

   (A) They are working on a school project.

   (B) They are currently at an art gallery.

   (C) They are on a field trip.

   (D) They are taking pictures of the objects.

2. **What are the speakers mainly talking about?**

   (A) The recent history test that they took

   (B) How much they enjoy Mr. Warren's class

   (C) The chances of having a pop test in class

   (D) The failure of one of the boys to do the reading

3. **What is the student's problem?**

   (A) He is not paying close attention in class.

   (B) He is speaking with his friends in class too much.

   (C) He has gotten low grades on his recent assignments.

   (D) He finds the material they are studying to be hard.

4. **What can be inferred about the boy?**

   (A) He intends to have a science club meeting in a week.

   (B) He thinks being the president of the science club is too hard.

   (C) He is no longer interested in the science club.

   (D) He enjoys working together with Mr. Kipley.

5. **What does the girl imply when she says this: "That's smart thinking"?**

   (A) She wants to give the boy some help.

   (B) She has come up with a good idea.

   (C) She knows how to solve the problem.

   (D) She supports the boy's action.

6. **What is probably true about the teacher?**

   (A) She enjoyed the girl's presentation.

   (B) She is going to prepare the projector.

   (C) She will give the girl an extension.

   (D) She forgot about the girl's assignment.

7. **What is the main topic of the announcement?**

   (A) Why the students need to listen to the teacher

   (B) How to be safe in the laboratory

   (C) Which experiment they will conduct

   (D) The clothes students should wear

8. **What does the teacher ask the students to do?**

   (A) Read a passage in their books

   (B) Name some figures of speech

   (C) Write a short poem

   (D) Think of some similes

9. **Why does the teacher talk about the slippery floor?**

   (A) To explain how long the floor will be slick

   (B) To give some rules on how to behave while at school

   (C) To warn the students so that they do not get hurt

   (D) To tell the students what happened to the receptionist

GO ON TO THE NEXT PAGE

Now you will hear longer talks or conversations. Each talk or conversation will be followed by three or more questions. Choose the best answer to each question and mark the letter of the correct answer on your answer sheet. You will hear each talk or conversation only one time.

10. What is the principal explaining?

(A) The work that the girl is expected to do

(B) How he expects the girl to behave

(C) The type of studying the girl must do

(D) Where the school's facilities are located

11. According to the principal, what will happen to a student who cheats two times?

(A) The student will get detention.

(B) The student will fail the class.

(C) The student will get suspended.

(D) The student will be expelled.

12. What is probably true about the girl?

(A) She is attending her second school of the semester.

(B) She is going to graduate at the end of the year.

(C) She gets higher grades than most of her classmates.

(D) She has been misbehaving in her classes lately.

13. What will the girl probably do next?

(A) Ask the principal some questions

(B) Go to her first class

(C) Study at the library

(D) Stay after school for detention

14. What are the students mainly discussing?

(A) The boy's interest in politics

(B) Why the girl wants to be a doctor

(C) A field trip they will go on

(D) A project they are working on

15. How does the girl probably feel when she says this: "You've got to be kidding me"?

(A) She is amused.

(B) She is concerned.

(C) She is pleased.

(D) She is surprised.

16. What will the boy probably do tomorrow?

(A) Make a visit to the hospital

(B) Stay home from school

(C) Attend a city council meeting

(D) Ask the mayor a question

17. What does the boy say about hospitals?

(A) He volunteers at them sometimes.

(B) He dislikes them a great deal.

(C) He avoids them whenever he can.

(D) He hopes to work in one someday.

GO ON TO THE NEXT PAGE

18. **What are the speakers mainly talking about?**

    (A) The boy's recent contributions to class

    (B) How the boy did on his last assignment

    (C) The boy's grade in the teacher's class

    (D) How the boy can improve his study methods

19. **According to the boy, why is he talking more in class?**

    (A) He wants to improve his participation grade.

    (B) The teacher is calling on him more often.

    (C) He is confident since he knows the answers.

    (D) The teacher previously asked him to speak more.

20. **Why does the teacher mention the boy's other instructors?**

    (A) To warn the boy that some of them dislike him

    (B) To claim that they are pleased with his improvement

    (C) To say that he is getting A's in all of their courses

    (D) To praise them for helping the boy improve his work

21. **What does the teacher imply about most of her students?**

    (A) They rarely speak in her class.

    (B) They have behavioral problems.

    (C) They study less than they should.

    (D) They envy the boy's accomplishments.

22. **What will the boy probably do next?**

    (A) Return to his homeroom

    (B) Eat lunch in the cafeteria

    (C) Go to his gym class

    (D) Meet one of his friends

23. **What does the boy mean when he says this: "You're telling me"?**

    (A) He wants the girl to repeat herself.

    (B) He agrees with the girl's comment.

    (C) He does not like being told what to do.

    (D) He heard what the girl said.

24. **Where does the boy work?**

    (A) At a gas station

    (B) At a clothing store

    (C) At a drugstore

    (D) At a supermarket

25. **When did the girl quit her job?**

    (A) At the beginning of summer vacation

    (B) Before the start of the semester

    (C) One month into the semester

    (D) Two weeks ago

26. **Why does the boy suggest that the girl wait to get a job?**

    (A) To make sure that her grades do not go down

    (B) To enable her to find a high-paying job

    (C) To avoid having to quit the girls' volleyball team

    (D) To let her enjoy her free time a little longer

GO ON TO THE NEXT PAGE

27. What is the purpose of the discussion?

(A) To explain how a person can run for president

(B) To talk about the American Founding Fathers

(C) To describe the role of the Electoral College

(D) To review the history of colonial America

28. According to the teacher, what kind of government does the United States have?

(A) A republic

(B) A capitalist government

(C) A democracy

(D) A dictatorship

29. Why does the boy mention the Electoral College?

(A) To describe how it functions

(B) To express his dislike for it

(C) To discuss the number of electors in it

(D) To ask the girl a question about it

30. What is the teacher mainly discussing?

(A) The military conquests of Genghis Khan

(B) The life of Genghis Khan

(C) Why Genghis Khan fought many battles

(D) The strategies of Genghis Khan

31. According to the teacher, how did Temujin increase the size of his tribe?

(A) By encouraging his men to take several wives

(B) By paying Mongols to become members of his tribe

(C) By defeating other Mongol tribes in battle

(D) By inviting foreigners to join his tribe

32. Why does the teacher mention China?

(A) To describe its location with regard to Mongolia

(B) To discuss a famous battle that Genghis Khan fought there

(C) To name it as a foreign land once conquered by Genghis Khan

(D) To explain why Genghis Khan wanted to defeat it

33. What will the teacher probably do next?

(A) Let the students go to lunch

(B) Talk more about Genghis Khan

(C) Show the class a video

(D) Have a student give a presentation

GO ON TO THE NEXT PAGE

34. What does the teacher say about polio?

(A) It once killed many people.

(B) It still infects people today.

(C) It is more serious than smallpox.

(D) It paralyzes some people.

35. Why does the teacher talk about when people get vaccines?

(A) To explain why children get so many of them

(B) To answer a question asked by a student

(C) To note why some vaccines last many years

(D) To advise the students to get vaccinated when young

36. What is probably true about vaccines?

(A) Some of them are too expensive for most people.

(B) They can occasionally make people sick.

(C) They are not always effective at stopping viruses.

(D) Different ones are given to different people.

37. Who was Edward Jenner?

(A) An early American scientist

(B) A British government official

(C) The creator of the smallpox vaccine

(D) An opponent of childhood vaccines

38. What is the main topic of the talk?

(A) The animals that live in estuaries

(B) The locations of estuaries

(C) The sizes of most estuaries

(D) The characteristics of estuaries

39. What feature of estuaries does the teacher mention?

(A) The presence of landforms in them

(B) Their usage by animals as breeding grounds

(C) The amount of time they take to form

(D) The number of aquatic animals living in them

40. What can be inferred about estuaries?

(A) They can get extremely high and low tides.

(B) Saltwater animals tend to live in them.

(C) They often look different from one another.

(D) They have more life in them than do bays.

41. What does the teacher say about estuaries formed by glaciers?

(A) They have deep water.

(B) They have sandy beaches.

(C) They are wedge shaped.

(D) They contain wide channels.

42. Why does the teacher mention New York City?

(A) To describe the estuary that it is close to

(B) To point out its nearness to an estuary

(C) To stress the number of trade routes it lies upon

(D) To say that an estuary was drained to build it

STOP

Language Form and Meaning

Directions

In this section of the test, you will answer 42 questions found in seven different texts. Within each text are boxes that contain four possible ways to complete a sentence. Choose the word or words in each box that correctly complete each sentence. Mark the letter of the correct answer on your answer sheet.

Here are two sample questions:

1. Ever since Gutenberg

> (A) invents
> (B) invented
> (C) inventing
> (D) has invented

movable type in the 1400s, printed

works have been the primary source of reading material for most people.

2. But,

> (A) thanks to the Internet,
> (B) thanking the Internet,
> (C) having thanked the Internet,
> (D) with the thanks of the Internet,

more and more people are reading

material that is not printed on paper nowadays.

The correct answer to **Sample 1** is (B), "invented." The correct answer to **Sample 2** is (A), "thanks to the Internet."

GO ON TO THE NEXT PAGE

Questions 1–4 refer to the following announcement.

To All Students:

It is time once again to begin working on your annual history projects. This year,

1. you

(A) were allowed
(B) will be allowed
(C) are allowing
(D) will have been allowed

to work on teams. Teams may consist of up to four

2. students. You may also work alone if you desire

(A) to do so.
(B) for doing such.
(C) to have done so.
(D) by doing such.

All students

should let me know with whom you will be working no later than next Monday, March 22.

3. Once you have made your choice, you may not

> (A) alter
> (B) cancel
> (C) rearrange
> (D) postpone

it in any manner.

All decisions are final. This year, the way in which you may do your history project

is slightly different from that of previous years. Please see the attached papers for

4. some examples of

> (A) when your projects looked alike.
> (B) why the project looks like that.
> (C) which projects have looked like it.
> (D) what your projects should look like.

Genevieve Mason

History Teacher

GO ON TO THE NEXT PAGE

Questions 5–8 refer to the following diary entry.

Dear Diary,

5.   It is almost time to start thinking about which college I am going to

(A) apply
(B) register
(C) attend
(D) consider

after

6.   I finish high school.

(A) Wanting me, my parents
(B) My parents want me
(C) I would like my parents
(D) My parents and I want

to enroll at the same school

my father went to a couple of decades ago. However, I am not particularly interested in

that place, especially since it does not have a good computer science program, which is

GO ON TO THE NEXT PAGE

7. what I want to study.

(A) My interest is great
(B) My great interest
(C) The greatest interest of mine
(D) Of greater interest to me

are a couple of

8. out-of-state schools. But, unless I

(A) am awarding
(B) am awarded
(C) was awarded
(D) will award

a scholarship, they are both

too expensive for my family. I suppose I ought to improve my grades if I want to go

to either of those places.

GO ON TO THE NEXT PAGE

Questions 9–12 refer to the following advertisement.

Work at the Sunnyville Summer Camp This Summer

How would you like to make some extra cash? If you have at least an A⁻ average,

then you are qualified to apply for a position at the Sunnyville Summer Camp.

9.   At Sunnyville, we

| (A) remove |
| (B) enforce |
| (C) stress |
| (D) value |

camp counselors who are not only good with younger

10.   children but who are also

| (A) better students |
| (B) the best students |
| (C) one of the best students |
| (D) better than more students |

in their classes. That is

why you need good grades to get a job with us. We also prefer students who

11.

(A) enjoy spending time outdoors
(B) are enjoying their time outdoors
(C) have enjoyed spending time outdoors
(D) being outdoors, enjoy their time

and being active. We pay well and

provide our counselors with great experiences throughout the entire summer.

12. If you would like to

(A) stretch
(B) broaden
(C) attempt
(D) test

your horizons and work for us this summer,

then call 555-1991 and ask for Mary or Jason.

GO ON TO THE NEXT PAGE

Questions 13–20 refer to the following letter.

Dear Paul,

13. I hope you do not mind, but I need to get some

> (A) advice
> (B) advise
> (C) advisement
> (D) advisory

from you. There is

14. something that has been on my mind a lot recently.

> (A) I am trying to decide
> (B) I, having decided, am trying
> (C) I decided to try
> (D) I will try for a decision

if I should join the basketball team or get a part-time job. Coach Dobbins is putting

15. a lot of pressure on me

> (A) playing.
> (B) to play.
> (C) will play.
> (D) have played.

I was on the team last year and had fun.

16. Overall,

> (A) I am gaining more experience.
> (B) it was a great experience.
> (C) the experience will be great.
> (D) I have a lot of experience.

However, my parents have cut off

GO ON TO THE NEXT PAGE

17. my

(A) allowance.
(B) scholarship.
(C) endowment.
(D) grant.

They say I am old enough to earn my own spending money.

Since I am planning to buy a car once I get my driver's license, I need to come up with

18. some extra cash. What would you do in my

(A) condition?
(B) resumption?
(C) situation?
(D) imposition?

I trust advice from

19. you

(A) more advising
(B) more than advice
(C) the most advice
(D) than the most advising

from any of my other friends. Please tell me

20.

(A) who thought that
(B) what we thought
(C) who is thinking
(D) what you think

I ought to do.

Your friend,

Tim

GO ON TO THE NEXT PAGE

Questions 21–28 refer to the following biography.

21. One of
(A) great
(B) greater
(C) greater than
(D) the greatest
inventors in the world was Thomas Edison.

22.
(A) Dying in time
(B) By the time he died
(C) After having died
(D) Since the time of his death
in 1931, Edison held more than 1,000 patents

and had revolutionized the world with his inventions, which included the light bulb and

23. phonograph. Yet few who knew Edison in his youth would have
(A) replied
(B) treated
(C) approached
(D) predicted

he was destined for greatness. As a child, Edison became sick and developed hearing

24. problems as a
(A) direct
(B) directive
(C) direction
(D) directly
result of his illness. Eventually, he became deaf in both

25. ears. He was also
(A) children with some problems.
(B) a problem with his children.
(C) probably a child.
(D) something of a problem child.
Due to his hyperactive

GO ON TO THE NEXT PAGE

behavior, his schoolteachers disliked him. Some thought he was unintelligent and

26. would never

(A) accomplish
(B) regard
(C) approach
(D) instruct

anything. Fortunately for Edison, his mother,

27.

(A) herself being taught by him,
(B) having taught him herself,
(C) who was a teacher herself,
(D) who will teach him by herself,

began to homeschool him when he was eleven.

Edison quickly gained an appetite for learning, and, by studying by himself, he became

self-educated. It was due to his desire to learn and to teach himself new things that he

28.

(A) portrayed
(B) developed
(C) satisfied
(D) structured

an interest in becoming an inventor.

GO ON TO THE NEXT PAGE

Questions 29–34 refer to the following newspaper article.

29. The Beaumont Academy is about to start

> (A) a projected ambition
> (B) projecting its ambitions
> (C) an ambitious project
> (D) the projection of ambition

that will result in the school undergoing a great deal of change.

30.

> (A) He donated thanks to
> (B) Thankfully, his donation
> (C) After giving thanks for a donation
> (D) Thanks to a donation

of two million dollars from a recent alumnus,

31. the Beaumont Academy is going to

> (A) reprove
> (B) restructure
> (C) renovate
> (D) renege

the entire campus. Work on

the main building has already started since the students are currently on summer vacation.

The school also intends to work on its gymnasium as well as its library.

GO ON TO THE NEXT PAGE

32.
(A) Will there be funds left over,
(B) With the leftover funds,
(C) After using the leftover funds,
(D) With no funds left over,

the school will construct an entirely new

33.
(A) cafeteria.
(B) facility.
(C) stadium.
(D) library.

It will contain a number of state-of-the-art classrooms that should

improve the learning environment at the school. According to school president John

Sanders, the faculty, students, and parents are all eagerly anticipating how the school will

34. look. "Everything won't be
(A) apparent
(B) ordered
(C) financed
(D) complete
until about ten months from now," said

Mr. Sanders. "However, we think the campus will be much improved by that time."

GO ON TO THE NEXT PAGE

Questions 35–42 refer to the following essay.

A mural is a large painting done on a wall, ceiling, or side of a building.

35. There are several different

(A) creators
(B) families
(C) examples
(D) styles

of murals.

36.

(A) There were a variety of times in the past,
(B) In the past with various times,
(C) During various times in the past,
(D) Before various times had passed,

frescoes were among

37.

(A) the most popular types
(B) as popular as types
(C) more popular types than
(D) the popularity of more types

of murals. To create a fresco, the artist

38. first

(A) applied
(B) dried
(C) painted
(D) mixed

wet plaster to the surface of the wall or ceiling. Then, paint

was layered on top of the plaster. Because the plaster dried so quickly, the artist

GO ON TO THE NEXT PAGE

could only paint a small area at a time. Thus frescoes often took a long time

39.
(A) completing.
(B) will complete.
(C) have been complete.
(D) to be completed.

For that reason, many artists actively

40.
(A) enjoyed
(B) avoided
(C) requested
(D) planned

making frescoes. Those who wanted to do murals more quickly

41.
(A) attempted
(B) studied
(C) resorted
(D) trained

to using other techniques. Painting on pieces of canvas and then

42. attaching those pieces to a wall was another way

(A) of making murals.
(B) murals will be made.
(C) to make your mural.
(D) making a mural.

A more modern technique is to make murals with photographs that have been printed

on large sheets.

STOP

NO TEST MATERIAL ON THIS PAGE

Reading Comprehension

GO ON TO THE NEXT PAGE

Directions

In this section of the test, you will read six texts and answer 42 questions. Choose the correct answer to each question and mark the letter of the correct answer on your answer sheet.

Before you start, read the sample text and the sample questions below.

Sample Text

Sharks are misunderstood creatures. Many people believe that all sharks are brutal killers that hunt humans, but that is not true at all. Only a handful of sharks ever attack humans, and most of them do that by mistake. In fact, most sharks ignore humans completely and seek to avoid them.

Sample Question 1

What is this text mostly about?

(A) Which sharks attack humans

(B) Why sharks often ignore humans

(C) How many sharks behave around humans

(D) What to do when you see a shark

The correct answer is (C), "How many sharks behave around humans."

Sample Question 2

Which of the following is true regarding sharks?

(A) Most species of them attack humans.

(B) Many of them actively hunt people.

(C) A lot of them prefer to eat small sea creatures.

(D) The majority of them stay away from people.

The correct answer is (D), "The majority of them stay away from people."

Questions 1–6 are about the following announcement.

All students who are enrolled in history and social studies classes this year should be aware of the following changes. We are making them because of the sudden departure of Mr. Sellers, who taught American history. Please consult the chart to note your new classrooms or instructors:

Class	Classroom	Instructor	Change
American History	202	Mr. Alvarez	New instructor
World History	202	Mr. Alvarez	New classroom
California State History	206	Ms. Henderson	New classroom
Social Studies	209	Mr. Nelson	New instructor

Please be aware that the class times have not undergone any changes at all. Your classes will still meet according to the times listed on your schedule. However, either your instructor or your classroom is different from what is listed on your schedule. We apologize for any confusion that these changes may cause, but the matter is out of the school's control. Hopefully, there will not be any problems with these classes during the school year. The school will also hire a new history teacher by next semester so that our current teachers will not be so overworked.

GO ON TO THE NEXT PAGE

1. **What is the purpose of the announcement?**

   (A) To provide students with their final schedules

   (B) To request that students sign up for history classes

   (C) To inform students of some scheduling changes

   (D) To encourage students to take classes with new teachers

2. **What did Mr. Sellers do?**

   (A) He quit his job.

   (B) He got a promotion.

   (C) He became sick.

   (D) He changed departments.

3. **According to the announcement, all of the following statements are true EXCEPT**

   _____.

   (A) Mr. Alvarez is teaching world history

   (B) social studies will meet in room 209

   (C) american history has a new teacher

   (D) Mr. Nelson is teaching California state history

4. **What does the announcement mention about the class times?**

   (A) They have not changed at all.

   (B) They are listed on a handout.

   (C) They will be determined later.

   (D) They will be altered next week.

5. **What does the author point out by writing that the matter is out of the school's control in line 7?**

   (A) The school will try to control its teachers better.

   (B) The school regrets having to make the changes.

   (C) The school had no way of affecting what happened.

   (D) The school will compensate students for their losses.

6. **What can be inferred from the announcement about the school?**

   (A) It has not replaced the teacher who departed.

   (B) It is going to make every teacher work more hours.

   (C) It intends to hire the most qualified teachers.

   (D) It is going to offer fewer history classes next semester.

GO ON TO THE NEXT PAGE

Questions 7–12 are about the following letter.

Dear seniors,

This year, many of you have chosen to register for advanced placement (AP) classes in the hope that you will be able to obtain college credit for the courses you take here. I hope you understand that the workload in an AP class is much greater than the workload in a standard class. After all, you are hoping to receive college credit for the AP class or classes that you signed up for, so doing extra work should be expected.

In fact, you will have up to twice the normal amount of work in each AP class that you are taking. Please take this into consideration when signing up for extracurricular activities or working part time. This is particularly true for students who have enrolled in multiple AP classes. Simply put, this will be the busiest school year of your life.

If you find the work to be <u>excessive</u>, you may speak with either Mr. Reginald or me anytime. Just visit his or my office, and we will help you to the best of our ability. I wish the best of luck to you all in your senior year, and may you have both academic and personal success.

Margaret Lewis
Guidance Counselor

GO ON TO THE NEXT PAGE

7. **What is the purpose of the letter?**

   (A) To advise students about some of their classes

   (B) To convince students to register for AP classes

   (C) To let students know what the guidance counselors do

   (D) To tell students how to organize their schedules

8. **What does the author say about AP classes?**

   (A) They must be taken at a local college.

   (B) They require more work than regular classes.

   (C) They are taught by university professors.

   (D) They are as difficult as college classes.

9. **What does the author imply about extracurricular activities?**

   (A) The best ones for students to participate in are sports.

   (B) They are not as important as studying or work part time.

   (C) It is necessary for students to sign up for some of them.

   (D) Students in AP classes may lack the time to do them.

10. **In line 11, the word** <u>excessive</u> **is closest in meaning to _____.**

    (A) serious

    (B) monotonous

    (C) stimulating

    (D) extreme

11. **Based on the letter, what is probably true about Mr. Reginald?**

    (A) He teaches AP history and English.

    (B) He shares an office with Margaret Lewis.

    (C) He is a guidance counselor at the school.

    (D) He is one of the school's newest employees.

12. **What should a student who is having problems with an AP class do?**

    (A) Stop taking the class

    (B) Speak with Margaret Lewis

    (C) Quit playing sports

    (D) Do fewer extracurricular activities

GO ON TO THE NEXT PAGE

Questions 13–18 are about the following advertisement.

Sign up for Driver's Education Classes Today

Are you going to turn sixteen years old within the next calendar year? If you are, then you should consider signing up for driver's education classes. As long as you have a driver's permit or license, then you are <u>qualified</u> to take a driver's ed class with an instructor at the Elite Driving Institute. What are the benefits of taking a driver's education course? First of all, you will learn all about how to drive a car. We can teach you to drive an automatic or manual transmission car. You will also learn how to become a safe driver. Remember that teenagers are involved in more accidents than people in any other age group in the country. But, by taking driver's ed classes, you can <u>significantly</u> reduce your chances of getting in an accident. Last, but surely not least, when you finish the course, you will qualify for discounts of up to 25% on your driver's insurance. That will definitely make your parents happy.

If you want more information, visit our office, send us an email, or call us during regular business hours. All of our contact information is available at the bottom of this ad.

GO ON TO THE NEXT PAGE

13. **In line 3, the word <u>qualified</u> is closest in meaning to _____.**

    (A) sanctioned
    (B) requested
    (C) eligible
    (D) responsible

14. **What does the author imply about teenagers?**

    (A) They are poor drivers.
    (B) They enjoy learning to drive.
    (C) They are good students.
    (D) They like driving to school.

15. **In line 8, the word <u>significantly</u> is closest in meaning to _____.**

    (A) possibly
    (B) considerably
    (C) apparently
    (D) persistently

16. **Why does the author mention driver's insurance?**

    (A) To point out how inexpensive it can be
    (B) To claim that teens are required to pay it
    (C) To explain how teens can get it reduced
    (D) To note why it costs so much for teenagers

17. **According to the advertisement, all of the following are advantages of taking driver's education classes EXCEPT _____.**

    (A) the person will spend less on insurance
    (B) the person will become more skilled at driving
    (C) the person will avoid getting in any accidents
    (D) the person will learn to drive a manual transmission car

18. **Where is the contact information for the driving institute listed?**

    (A) In the phonebook
    (B) On the advertisement
    (C) On its website
    (D) In a brochure

GO ON TO THE NEXT PAGE

Questions 19–26 are about the following passage.

Monsoons are seasonal shifts in wind that are typically accompanied by a great amount of rain. Many people are aware that monsoons take place in India, East Asia, and parts of Africa. Yet monsoons are known to occur in other parts of the world as well. One lesser-known region where they take place is the American state of Arizona. During the summer months, the wind in Arizona
5 suddenly changes direction. It stops blowing from the west or northwest and instead begins to blow from a southern or southeastern direction.

This shift in the wind is caused by two forces. First, a high pressure system called the Bermuda High moves further to the north. At the same time, the heating of the deserts in California, located west of Arizona, creates a low pressure system. The winds then blow across Arizona from the high
10 to low pressure system. The wind shift—or monsoon—causes the weather to change in much of the state during the summer. The result is that the wind brings moist air from the Gulf of California and the Gulf of Mexico to Arizona. Large parts of Arizona, being located in the Rocky Mountains, sit at high altitudes. Because of that, the moist air gets lifted into the atmosphere and forms clouds. What happens next is that there are massive thunderstorms all across Arizona.

15 The monsoon season starts in Arizona in June. Thunderstorms are common occurrences from then until sometime between July and September. However, thunderstorms do not happen every day. There are <u>recurring</u> cycles instead. For several days, there are no storms at all, and then there are suddenly thunderstorms for several days in a row. Local residents refer to the rainy periods as bursts and the periods without rain as breaks. By the end of September, the monsoon season in Arizona has
20 always concluded.

While the summer winds and rains in Arizona appear to qualify the weather conditions for status as a monsoon, there are some meteorologists who disagree. They claim that the winds do not undergo a complete reversal in direction. Instead, the winds only reverse <u>to some degree</u>. In <u>their</u> minds, this does not make the weather phenomenon in Arizona an actual monsoon.

GO ON TO THE NEXT PAGE

19. **What is the passage mostly about?**

    (A) Wind patterns in Arizona

    (B) The definition of a monsoon

    (C) Monsoons around the world

    (D) The summer monsoon in Arizona

20. **How does the wind start to blow in Arizona during the summer?**

    (A) From the north

    (B) From the south

    (C) From the northwest

    (D) From the southwest

21. **According to the passage, where does the moist air that arrives in Arizona come from?**

    (A) California

    (B) Bermuda

    (C) The Gulf of Mexico

    (D) The Rocky Mountains

22. **In line 17, the word <u>recurring</u> is closest in meaning to _____.**

    (A) short-term

    (B) lengthy

    (C) random

    (D) habitual

23. **Which of the following can be inferred from the passage about the Arizona monsoon?**

    (A) It can cause floods in some regions.

    (B) The season ends at different times each year.

    (C) People there enjoy the periods of rain.

    (D) There are more bursts than there are breaks.

24. **Which of the following is true regarding bursts?**

    (A) They are periods of time with thunderstorms.

    (B) They happen at least twice each summer month.

    (C) They occur when no rain falls for some time.

    (D) They have become more severe recently.

25. **What does the author point out by writing that the winds only reverse <u>to some degree</u> in line 23?**

    (A) The winds continually blow hard.

    (B) The winds mostly stop blowing.

    (C) The winds partially change direction.

    (D) The winds become much stronger.

26. **In line 23, the word <u>their</u> refers to _____.**

    (A) the summer winds and rains

    (B) the weather conditions

    (C) meteorologists

    (D) the winds

GO ON TO THE NEXT PAGE

Questions 27–34 are about the following passage.

In Yellowstone National Park, one of the most popular sights is Old Faithful. Approximately every ninety minutes, it shoots streams of heated water high into the air. Old Faithful is a geyser. A geyser is a natural formation that <u>spews</u> water from underground into the air.

There are three factors that must exist for a region to have geysers. The first is that the region needs an underground heat source. This often comes from molten rock—called magma—that is relatively close to the surface. The heat from the magma <u>radiates</u> into the surrounding rock, which then raises the temperature of the water. It is for this reason that most geysers are located in volcanically active areas.

The second factor is that there must be an underground source of water. The water can come from various sources, including rainfall, melted snow, and groundwater. The third and final factor is the presence of underground chambers and tunnels. Rocks near volcanoes are often porous, so they have a number of cracks, tunnels, and chambers. <u>These</u> combine to form something like the plumbing system in a house; this results in there being many places for water to flow through the ground. At times, there are narrow cracks in the rock that go all the way to the surface. When that happens—and when there is a large chamber full of water beneath the crack—a geyser is formed.

In order for a geyser to erupt, the following steps take place. First, water starts gathering in an underground chamber. There, it is heated and starts to rise to the surface through cracks in the ground. As the water moves away from the heat source, <u>it</u> cools. This cooled water presses down on the water beneath it. The water below gets trapped and is prevented from rising. While it remains unmoving, it begins to heat again. Soon, it becomes so hot that it turns to steam. The steam pushes the cooled water up toward the surface. By this point, the chamber has collected a large amount of water, all of which has been superheated while being subjected to a lot of pressure. The water in the chamber suddenly turns into steam. This causes the steam and water above it to explode violently through the cracks leading to the surface. Sometimes a column of steam and water dozens of meters high is expelled. Some geysers, such as Old Faithful, erupt on a regular basis. Others erupt more seldom whenever the conditions are right.

GO ON TO THE NEXT PAGE

27. **What would be the best title for the passage?**

   (A) Old Faithful in Yellowstone National Park

   (B) How a Geyser Erupts

   (C) Where Are the World's Geysers?

   (D) Geysers: How Many Are There?

28. **In line 3, the word <u>spews</u> is closest in meaning to _____.**

   (A) heats

   (B) pours

   (C) pushes

   (D) sprays

29. **In line 6, the word <u>radiates</u> is closest in meaning to _____.**

   (A) spreads out

   (B) shines

   (C) melts

   (D) disappears

30. **In line 12, the word <u>These</u> refers to _____.**

   (A) various sources

   (B) rainfall, melted snow, and groundwater

   (C) rocks near volcanoes

   (D) cracks, tunnels, and chambers

31. **Which is NOT mentioned as a factor necessary for a geyser to exist?**

   (A) Cracks leading to the surface

   (B) Underground water sources

   (C) Superheated lava in volcanoes

   (D) Tunnels located under the ground

32. **According to the passage, what is the first step involved in a geyser erupting?**

   (A) Water must be heated so that it turns into steam.

   (B) Extreme pressure is applied to the water source.

   (C) A chamber underground begins to fill with water.

   (D) Water starts to move upward through some cracks.

33. **In line 18, the word <u>it</u> refers to _____.**

   (A) the surface

   (B) the ground

   (C) the water

   (D) the heat source

34. **Based on the passage, what is probably true about Old Faithful?**

   (A) It has a constant source of water.

   (B) No other geyser is as famous as it.

   (C) Tourists enjoy watching it erupt.

   (D) It erupts more than any other geyser in the world.

GO ON TO THE NEXT PAGE

Questions 35–42 are about the following passage.

The Victoria Cross is a medal given for bravery to soldiers in the British military. It is the highest honor a British soldier can receive on the field of battle. The most Victoria Crosses ever awarded for a single battle is eleven. These medals were earned at the Battle of Rorke's Drift, which was fought on January 22 and 23, 1879.

5   In the 1800s, the British had a heavy presence in South Africa. Rorke's Drift was a small trading post and mission station that was on the border of lands belonging to the Natal and Zulu. These were two tribes of people that lived in South Africa at the time. The Zulus were fierce warriors with a strong army and competent leadership. In early 1879, the British and Zulus went to war in what became known as the Anglo-Zulu War. The war

10 was fought due to the British attempt to conquer Zulu lands.

   The onset of the war saw the British suffering a great loss at the Battle of Islandlwana. During the battle, more than 10,000 Zulus defeated and killed around 1,300 British and colonial soldiers. The Zulus then marched on Rorke's Drift, which was located nearby. The station was defended by about 300 men; half

15 were British while the other half consisted of colonial troops. The men were led by Lieutenant John Chard, a British engineer. He had his men build stout defenses around the station prior to the Zulu's arrival.

   When the battle started, the Zulu warriors were unable to breach these defenses and penetrate the station. Had they done that, the battle would have become a massacre. Yet they were kept outside the

20 walls of the station during the entire battle. In addition, Chard's men were equipped with rifles. The Zulus, meanwhile, mostly had spears as well as a few rifles that they had seized from fallen British soldiers. The fighting lasted nearly eleven hours. Eventually, the Zulus abandoned the field of battle and retreated during the night.

   The Zulu losses were estimated to be almost 1,000 dead and wounded. Chard's force, meanwhile,

25 only suffered seventeen deaths. However, many more were badly wounded, and just about every man had some type of minor wound. Due to their heroic efforts, eleven of the defenders, including Chard himself, were awarded the Victoria Cross. The defense of Rorke's Drift was a strategic victory as it stalled the Zulus enough to give British reinforcements time to reach the area. Eventually, they were able to defeat the Zulus and end the war.

GO ON TO THE NEXT PAGE

35. What is the best title for the passage?

(A) The Victoria Cross

(B) The Anglo-Zulu War

(C) The Battle of Rorke's Drift

(D) Lieutenant John Chard

36. In line 6, the word <u>These</u> refers to
_____.

(A) the British

(B) a trading post and mission station

(C) lands

(D) The Natal and Zulu

37. In line 8, the word <u>competent</u> is closest in meaning to _____.

(A) traditional

(B) elected

(C) warlike

(D) skilled

38. Why does the author mention the Battle of Islandlwana?

(A) To explain where in South Africa it was fought

(B) To name the first battle of the Anglo-Zulu War

(C) To claim it was the first defeat for the British in Africa

(D) To stress how important it was to the Zulus

39. Who was John Chard?

(A) A representative of Queen Victoria

(B) The leader of the British at Rorke's Drift

(C) The owner of a British trading post

(D) A soldier who died at Islandlwana

40. In line 16, the word <u>stout</u> is closest in meaning to _____.

(A) strategic

(B) extensive

(C) strong

(D) high

41. In line 18, the word <u>breach</u> is closest in meaning to _____.

(A) burn

(B) climb over

(C) approach

(D) break

42. According to the passage, all of the following were results of the Battle of Rorke's Drift EXCEPT _____.

(A) the British forces held off the Zulus long enough to let others arrive

(B) the Zulus considered themselves to be the winners of the battle

(C) there were more than 1,000 casualties suffered by the Zulus

(D) nearly one dozen British soldiers were awarded the Victoria Cross

STOP

Practice
Test 6

Listening
Comprehension

听力音频

The listening section has 42 questions. Follow along as you listen to the directions to the listening section.

Directions

In this section of the test, you will hear talks and conversations. Each talk or conversation is followed by one question. Choose the best answer to each question and mark the letter of the correct answer on your answer sheet. You will hear each talk or conversation only one time.

Here is an example: 🔊))

What are the speakers talking about?

(A) Their homework in a class
(B) Mr. Davison's lectures
(C) A recent assignment
(D) How to do their homework

The correct answer is (A), "Their homework in a class."

Here is another example: 🔊))

What does the girl says about the new cafeteria?

(A) The atmosphere is nice.
(B) There are many tables.
(C) It is very large.
(D) It has better food.

The correct answer is (D), "It has better food."

Go on to the next page, and the test will begin with question number one.

GO ON TO THE NEXT PAGE ⟩

1. **What are the students going to do in the afternoon?**

   (A) Hang out with Clark

   (B) Meet their junior varsity team members

   (C) Go to basketball practice

   (D) Try out for the basketball team

2. **Why does the girl mention her younger sister?**

   (A) To say she wants to introduce her sister to the teacher

   (B) To claim that her sister gets good grades at school

   (C) To point out her sister to the teacher

   (D) To blame her sister for making her late for school

3. **What can be inferred about the boy?**

   (A) Shakespeare is his favorite writer.

   (B) The teacher's class is fun for him.

   (C) Acting is something that he enjoys.

   (D) He wants to improve his grade.

4. **What does the girl offer to do for the boy?**

   (A) Type his paper for him

   (B) Go to the hospital with him

   (C) Take notes for him

   (D) Carry his books to class

5. **What is the subject of the conversation?**

   (A) What the boy will do tomorrow

   (B) The boy's punishment

   (C) Mr. Robinson's class

   (D) Where the boy will serve detention

6. **What are the speakers mainly discussing?**

   (A) The boy's back problems

   (B) Buying paper books

   (C) One of their textbooks

   (D) The kinds of books they want

7. **What is the purpose of the announcement?**

   (A) To provide information on the presentations

   (B) To describe the contents of the day's lecture

   (C) To encourage the students to work harder

   (D) To assign a new project to the students

8. **What should late students do when arriving at school?**

   (A) Call their parents

   (B) Talk to the principal

   (C) Speak with their homeroom teachers

   (D) Go to the secretary's office

9. **What is the purpose of the announcement?**

   (A) To advise students to improve the quality of their lunches

   (B) To tell the students when to bring food to school for lunch

   (C) To acknowledge the complaints about the food in the cafeteria

   (D) To warn the students not to enter the cafeteria

GO ON TO THE NEXT PAGE

Now you will hear longer talks or conversations. Each talk or conversation will be followed by three or more questions. Choose the best answer to each question and mark the letter of the correct answer on your answer sheet. You will hear each talk or conversation only one time.

10. Why does the girl mention Mr. Jessie?

(A) To praise him as a band director

(B) To compare him with Mr. Conaway

(C) To express her regret at his departure

(D) To note how he has helped her improve

11. What instrument does the girl play?

(A) The trumpet

(B) The clarinet

(C) The flute

(D) The violin

12. What is probably true about the boy?

(A) He invited his family to the spring concert.

(B) He is a better musician than the girl.

(C) He dislikes the music the band is playing.

(D) He prefers Mr. Jessie to Mr. Conaway.

13. What will the speakers probably do next?

(A) Go to a meeting with Mr. Conaway

(B) Attend band practice

(C) Go to lunch

(D) Return to their classrooms

14. What are the speakers mainly discussing?

(A) The boy's role on the basketball team this season

(B) How the boy performed on the basketball team last year

(C) When the school's basketball team is going to practice

(D) The chances of the boy joining the basketball team

15. What does the coach imply about the boy?

(A) He is going to be named a team captain.

(B) He will be one of the team's better players.

(C) He needs to improve some aspects of his game.

(D) He prefers playing basketball to studying.

16. What does the boy say about his parents?

(A) They are looking forward to watching his games.

(B) They are pleased with his school performance.

(C) They prefer that he not play basketball.

(D) They want him to find part-time employment.

17. Why does the boy mention math and science?

(A) To point out two classes he does not enjoy

(B) To state that his grades in them were low

(C) To say that he has to attend those classes today

(D) To name them as his favorite subjects

GO ON TO THE NEXT PAGE

18. **What is the teacher explaining?**

    (A) How to write a research paper

    (B) When the student's work is due

    (C) What the student should write about

    (D) Why the student must do the assignment

19. **What does the teacher imply when he says this: "I get spaced out sometimes when I'm grading papers"?**

    (A) He is disappointed with the quality of the papers.

    (B) He is uninterested in speaking to the girl.

    (C) He was not paying full attention to the girl.

    (D) He dislikes having to grade many papers.

20. **What does the teacher say about the research paper?**

    (A) It should have five or more sources.

    (B) The girl can write it on any topic.

    (C) The paper is due in one month.

    (D) It is worth thirty percent of each student's grade.

21. **According to the teacher, how can the girl learn to write a bibliography?**

    (A) By reading her textbook

    (B) By using the handout he gave her

    (C) By visiting a website

    (D) By consulting a reference book

22. **What is probably true about the teacher?**

    (A) He is eager to help the girl.

    (B) He teaches American history.

    (C) He has a small amount of free time.

    (D) He is popular with the students.

23. **What are the students mainly discussing?**

    (A) Which teachers they like the most

    (B) The classes they are going to take

    (C) How they are performing this semester

    (D) Their favorite classes at school

24. **What does the boy mention about Spanish?**

    (A) It is more difficult than French.

    (B) He regrets not studying it.

    (C) It is his best subject at school.

    (D) He is getting better at it.

25. **What can be inferred about the boy?**

    (A) His favorite subject is math.

    (B) He has known the girl for a long time.

    (C) He gets lows grades in his science classes.

    (D) His classes are getting harder.

26. **What does the boy want to major in at college?**

    (A) Math

    (B) Physics

    (C) Computer science

    (D) Biology

GO ON TO THE NEXT PAGE

27. **What is the teacher mainly discussing?**

    (A) How the ear keeps people balanced

    (B) What the human ear looks like

    (C) The roles of the parts of the ear

    (D) Why most of the ear is not visible

28. **Why does the teacher mention the students' textbooks?**

    (A) To have the students look at some pictures in them

    (B) To ask the students to read a passage from them

    (C) To tell the students about their homework assignment

    (D) To make sure the students bring them to class

29. **What is the pinna?**

    (A) The most important part of the inner ear

    (B) The section of the ear connected to the nerves

    (C) The part of the ear that collects sound waves

    (D) The smallest part of the outer ear

30. **According to the teacher, which part of the ear helps people with their balance?**

    (A) The tympanic membrane

    (B) The vestibule

    (C) The cochlea

    (D) The auditory canal

31. **According to the teacher, where do most marsupials presently live?**

    (A) South America

    (B) North America

    (C) Africa

    (D) Australia

32. **Why does the teacher mention the opossum?**

    (A) To name the only marsupial in North America

    (B) To compare it with the kangaroo

    (C) To describe how it gives birth to its young

    (D) To point out that it has very poor eyesight

33. **What does a marsupial female lack?**

    (A) A womb

    (B) A placenta

    (C) Eggs

    (D) Nipples

34. **What does the teacher imply about marsupials?**

    (A) There were more of them in the past than in the present.

    (B) It is likely that they will go extinct in a few centuries.

    (C) Most of them are unable to adapt to their environments.

    (D) They are less evolved than the majority of other mammals.

GO ON TO THE NEXT PAGE

35. **What is the main topic of the talk?**

    (A) The American Southwest

    (B) The features of buttes and mesas

    (C) The geography of Arizona and Utah

    (D) Plateaus, mesas, and buttes

36. **What is probably true about the teacher?**

    (A) He enjoys spending his time hiking.

    (B) He majored in geography at college.

    (C) He dislikes being interrupted by students.

    (D) He has visited the American Southwest.

37. **According to the teacher, what is a characteristic of a butte?**

    (A) It must have a flat top.

    (B) It has standing water on top.

    (C) It has very steep sides.

    (D) It is found near a canyon.

38. **What will the teacher probably do next?**

    (A) Tell the class about plateaus

    (B) Show the students some pictures

    (C) Talk about his trip to the Grand Canyon

    (D) Name some well-known buttes

39. **What is the teacher mainly talking about?**

    (A) The end of Napoleon's reign

    (B) Napoleon and the Duke of Wellington

    (C) Napoleon's most important battles

    (D) The last years of Napoleon's life

40. **Where was Napoleon sent into exile the first time?**

    (A) Fontainebleau

    (B) Elba

    (C) Waterloo

    (D) St. Helena

41. **When did the Hundred Days begin?**

    (A) After Napoleon's defeat at Waterloo

    (B) When Napoleon escaped from exile

    (C) When Napoleon invaded Russia

    (D) After Napoleon fought the Duke of Wellington

42. **Why does the teacher mention a map?**

    (A) To mark the sites of Napoleon's most famous battles

    (B) To show where the Battle of Waterloo took place

    (C) To encourage the girl to find the location of Elba

    (D) To point out the location of St. Helena

STOP

Language Form and Meaning

Directions

In this section of the test, you will answer 42 questions found in seven different texts. Within each text are boxes that contain four possible ways to complete a sentence. Choose the word or words in each box that correctly complete each sentence. Mark the letter of the correct answer on your answer sheet.

Here are two sample questions:

1. Ever since Gutenberg

> (A) invents
> (B) invented
> (C) inventing
> (D) has invented

movable type in the 1400s, printed

works have been the primary source of reading material for most people.

2. But,

> (A) thanks to the Internet,
> (B) thanking the Internet,
> (C) having thanked the Internet,
> (D) with the thanks of the Internet,

more and more people are reading

material that is not printed on paper nowadays.

The correct answer to **Sample 1** is (B), "invented." The correct answer to **Sample 2** is (A), "thanks to the Internet."

GO ON TO THE NEXT PAGE

Questions 1–4 refer to the following article in the school newspaper.

1. The students

    (A) sent
    (B) threw
    (C) cast
    (D) wrote

    their ballots and then left the room. Two teachers began

counting the votes. The students had just voted for the school student body president.

2. There was a two-way race

    (A) for Caroline and Mark.
    (B) with Caroline or Mark.
    (C) against Caroline or Mark.
    (D) between Caroline and Mark.

    Most students

expected Caroline to win because she was one of the most popular girls at school.

GO ON TO THE NEXT PAGE

3. However, Mark gave a speech

(A) which the student body was amazed.

(B) that amazed the student body.

(C) where the student body was amazed.

(D) who amazed the student body.

Previously, people had only known him as a comedian. Now, they realized how

4.

(A) concerned

(B) serious

(C) ambitious

(D) considerate

he could be. The principal's voice came on over the loudspeaker.

He said, "Students, I'm proud to announce the new student body president

this year is . . . Mark Crawford."

GO ON TO THE NEXT PAGE

Questions 5–8 refer to the following announcement.

French Club Members:

Next Tuesday evening, we will hold French Culture Appreciation Night.

The event will be in the school cafeteria from seven to nine. We are going to do

several exciting activities. First, we are going to enjoy a potluck party

5.

(A) consisting of French food.
(B) that consisted of French food.
(C) consistent with French food.
(D) of French food, of which it consisted.

If any of you can bring some food—either

by cooking or purchasing it—please let Mrs. Richardson know at once.

6.

(A) After dinner followed,
(B) Dinner, which followed,
(C) If it follows dinner,
(D) Following the dinner,

we will watch a short film about French culture.

GO ON TO THE NEXT PAGE

7. Finally, we will have a special

(A) guest.
(B) movie.
(C) program.
(D) dessert.

Henri Francois from the French

Embassy has volunteered to speak to us about France and will answer questions, too.

8.

(A) Surely having signed up
(B) Be sure to sign up
(C) They are sure to sign up
(D) Signing up, they are sure

for this special event.

GO ON TO THE NEXT PAGE

Questions 9–12 refer to the following email.

Dear Caroline,

How have you been? I hope you are doing all right. You heard I was hospitalized for a

9. few days, right? I got horribly ill last week, so my parents

(A) rush
(B) are rushing
(C) rushed
(D) have rushed

me to the

10. emergency room. Anyway, I am back home now and feel

(A) the better.
(B) much better.
(C) better than.
(D) the best.

But I have a small problem: I need the class notes for both science and

11. social studies. I know you

(A) take great notes,
(B) were great at taking notes,
(C) have great notes to take,
(D) are taking some great notes,

so would you

12. mind

(A) lending
(B) telling
(C) borrowing
(D) transferring

yours to me? I could photocopy them and return them

to you the next day. How does that sound?

Your friend,

Steve

Questions 13–20 refer to the following letter.

Dear Students,

Congratulations on signing up for a one-week tour of South America during spring break.

13.
(A) As your chaperone,
(B) Having been chaperoned,
(C) Chaperoning them,
(D) For the chaperone,

I will be responsible for looking after you while

14. we are
(A) trip.
(B) flight.
(C) abroad.
(D) country.

So I need for everyone to do a few things before our

15.
(A) depart.
(B) departs.
(C) departure.
(D) departed.

First, please make sure your passports are renewed and will not

expire within the next six months. Next, enclosed with this letter is a list of the

16. vaccinations you
(A) have had.
(B) should have.
(C) could have.
(D) will have.

Please make sure you get these from your

family doctor. Finally, you will find two more lists. The first is for items that you must

GO ON TO THE NEXT PAGE

17. bring with you. The second is a list

(A) of recommended items.
(B) with the items recommended.
(C) for some recommended items.
(D) by the items recommended.

18. In my opinion, you should bring

(A) every item on both lists.
(B) a few items on the lists.
(C) all of the items on one list.
(D) no items on either list.

Doing so

19. will

(A) regard
(B) promise
(C) await
(D) ensure

that you have everything you could possibly need.

I imagine this is the first trip to another country for most of you. So please do not

20.

(A) remember
(B) think
(C) hesitate
(D) attempt

to contact me if you have any questions.

Sincerely,

Jason Howard

GO ON TO THE NEXT PAGE

Questions 21–28 refer to the following announcement.

To students and parents:

The school is pleased to announce the start of a new program. Several private local

21. businesses have agreed to employ our students as

(A) interns
(B) interning
(C) internships
(D) interned

during summer

22. vacation. Students will not receive financial

(A) contracts
(B) money
(C) compensation
(D) currencies

for their work,

yet they will gain valuable experience by working in a number of different fields.

23.

(A) At this point in time,
(B) Pointing out this time,
(C) When there is an appointed time,
(D) During the time appointed,

we have confirmation from thirty-seven

companies that they will accept one or two students each as interns.

24. We
  - (A) conduct
  - (B) conducted
  - (C) are conducting
  - (D) were conducted

negotiations with more than fifty other firms,

25. many of
  - (A) whom we expect
  - (B) what can expect
  - (C) whose are expecting
  - (D) which are expected

to take on interns as well.

26.
  - (A) Having been settled,
  - (B) When there will be settling,
  - (C) If this matter settles,
  - (D) Once everything is settled,

we will provide you with more information.

27. Please be aware that this program is not
  - (A) requested.
  - (B) mandatory.
  - (C) implemented.
  - (D) deliberate.

Students may feel free

to ignore it. However, in the current economic climate, we feel that gaining business

28. experience may give students an advantage over the
  - (A) competition
  - (B) applications
  - (C) interviews
  - (D) registration

after they graduate.

GO ON TO THE NEXT PAGE

Questions 29–34 refer to the following essay.

While many people prefer to play outdoor sports, including soccer and baseball,

29. my preferences

    (A) rely on indoor sports.
    (B) lied about indoor sports.
    (C) were relied on by indoor sports.
    (D) lie with indoor sports.

Among the indoor sports

30. I like to

    (A) join
    (B) play
    (C) contribute
    (D) participate

in are volleyball and basketball. There are several reasons

I favor indoor sports over ones played outdoors. The first is that I can play these

sports all year long. In other words, the weather conditions do not determine when I can

31. enjoy volleyball and basketball since

    (A) they are played in a gymnasium.
    (B) the gymnasium is where they played.
    (C) I tried to play in the gymnasium.
    (D) we will play in the gymnasium.

This is not the case for baseball, which is primarily a summer sport played in the sun.

GO ON TO THE NEXT PAGE

32.

(A) There is some inclement weather, so
(B) Having been implemented due to the weather,
(C) During times of inclement weather,
(D) Inclement weather, which happens,

it is simply impossible to play

a baseball game. Another reason that I like indoor sports is that the playing areas are

smaller. Football fields, for instance, are 100 yards long while soccer fields are similar

33. in

(A) long.
(B) length.
(C) lengthy.
(D) lengthiness.

Volleyball and basketball courts are much smaller

34. in comparison. Thus players are more

(A) concentrated
(B) focused
(C) stressed
(D) adorned

on the playing

surface rather than being spread out.

GO ON TO THE NEXT PAGE

Questions 35–42 refer to the following article.

When most people hear the name Alcatraz, images of a prison or a bleak,

35. desolate island often

(A) come to their minds.
(B) minded that which came.
(C) is coming into the mind.
(D) mind what comes.

These thoughts are

36. rather justified. Alcatraz is an island

(A) of that location
(B) which is located
(C) who has a location
(D) what was located

near

37. San Francisco, California. For many years, the U.S. Army

(A) uses
(B) is using
(C) will use
(D) used

the island as a military facility. Then, from 1934 to 1963, it was employed as a federal

38. high-security prison. Some of the most

(A) relevant
(B) notorious
(C) uncaught
(D) harmless

criminals in the country,

including Al Capone and George "Machine Gun" Kelly, were imprisoned there.

GO ON TO THE NEXT PAGE

212

The prison, nicknamed "The Rock," was considered impossible to escape from even

39. though

(A) it was never attempted.

(B) attempts will be made.

(C) there were several attempts.

(D) he made an attempt.

In every case but one, the attempted

40. escapees either died or were quickly

(A) condemned.

(B) executed.

(C) rehabilitated.

(D) recaptured.

The prison closed in 1963

due to the high cost of maintaining it. These days, it is an historic landmark which is

41.

(A) more popular than

(B) the most popular of

(C) among the most popular

(D) more popularity with

many famous places in San Francisco. In addition,

42. the island and the remnants of the prison serve as the

(A) focus

(B) destination

(C) setting

(D) location

for

numerous movies and television shows each year.

STOP

NO TEST MATERIAL ON THIS PAGE

Reading Comprehension

In this section of the test, you will read six texts and answer 42 questions. Choose the correct answer to each question and mark the letter of the correct answer on your answer sheet.

Before you start, read the sample text and the sample questions below.

Sample Text

Sharks are misunderstood creatures. Many people believe that all sharks are brutal killers that hunt humans, but that is not true at all. Only a handful of sharks ever attack humans, and most of them do that by mistake. In fact, most sharks ignore humans completely and seek to avoid them.

Sample Question 1

What is this text mostly about?

(A) Which sharks attack humans

(B) Why sharks often ignore humans

(C) How many sharks behave around humans

(D) What to do when you see a shark

The correct answer is (C), "How many sharks behave around humans."

Sample Question 2

Which of the following is true regarding sharks?

(A) Most species of them attack humans.

(B) Many of them actively hunt people.

(C) A lot of them prefer to eat small sea creatures.

(D) The majority of them stay away from people.

The correct answer is (D), "The majority of them stay away from people."

GO ON TO THE NEXT PAGE

Questions 1–7 are about the following announcement.

The school regrets to announce that this year's sports day, scheduled for Friday, April 4, will not be held. According to the weather service, a severe storm front is moving into this area. It should reach our city by Thursday night, and <u>it</u> will remain here for a few days. The storm is expected to drop several inches of rain once it begins. The weather service also <u>anticipates</u> that the conditions will be ideal for tornadoes to form. Due to the seriousness of the weather, the administration has decided to put off sports day until a later time.

Once the new date is determined, the administration will announce it. It will mostly likely be held on April 11 or 18. We apologize for postponing the event, but, considering that most sports day activities are held outdoors, we feel that we have no choice in this matter.

Sports day was originally scheduled to last from one to three in the afternoon. Since teachers may not have prepared lesson plans for classes during that time, they may feel free to watch movies or to do other similar activities in their classes. It is not <u>compulsory for</u> teachers to lecture during those periods.

GO ON TO THE NEXT PAGE >

1. What would be the best title for the announcement?

    (A) Severe Storm Front Approaching City

    (B) Is Everyone Ready for Sports Day?

    (C) Sports Day Cancelled due to Inclement Weather

    (D) School Activities during the Month of April

2. In line 3, the word it refers to _____.

    (A) a severe storm front

    (B) this area

    (C) our city

    (D) Thursday night

3. In line 4, the word anticipates is closest in meaning to _____.

    (A) appears

    (B) worries

    (C) denies

    (D) predicts

4. According to the announcement, what will the weather be like on Friday?

    (A) It is going to rain and snow.

    (B) There will be some tornadoes.

    (C) A hurricane will hit the city.

    (D) Heavy rain is going to fall.

5. What does the author imply about sports day?

    (A) It is the school's most popular event.

    (B) Children sometimes get hurt during it.

    (C) Some of its events take place indoors.

    (D) It will not be held again until the fall.

6. According to the announcement, what may teachers do with their classes on Friday afternoon?

    (A) Cancel them

    (B) Play games

    (C) Show films

    (D) Finish early

7. In line 12, the phrase compulsory for is closest in meaning to _____.

    (A) advised that

    (B) required for

    (C) stated by

    (D) insisted upon

GO ON TO THE NEXT PAGE

Questions 8–13 are about the following newspaper article.

Local student and Centerville High School junior Sally Barton has been winning prizes and awards ever since she started attending elementary school several years ago. But this
5 semester, she has simply outdone herself with her academic performance.

When the fall semester began, Ms. Barton dedicated herself to preparing for the city's spelling bee. She won first place in that contest,
10 which qualified her for the state spelling bee, held one week later. Ms. Barton emerged as the winner of it as well.

One month later, she entered an essay in the school's essay-writing contest. Writing about
15 her life as an immigrant, Ms. Barton captured first place. When her essay was submitted to the regional contest, she suffered her only setback of the semester: She came in second place.

"I was a little disappointed that I wasn't
20 victorious in that particular contest," she commented. "But I'm still proud of my achievements."

When asked what she plans to do next, Ms. Barton commented, "I'm on my school's math
25 team, and we have a big tournament coming up. With luck, our team will do well."

GO ON TO THE NEXT PAGE

8. **Which headline best summarizes the article?**

   (A) Students to Compete in Spelling Bee
   (B) Centerville High Student Wins Awards
   (C) Where Will Sally Barton Go to College?
   (D) Essay-Writing Contest to Begin Soon

9. **What does the author point out by writing that she has simply outdone herself in line 5?**

   (A) She has performed better than ever.
   (B) She has not met expectations.
   (C) She has won a couple of contests.
   (D) She has not done many actions yet.

10. **In line 12, the word it refers to** _____.

    (A) that contest
    (B) the state spelling bee
    (C) one week
    (D) the winner

11. **In line 17, the word setback is closest in meaning to** _____.

    (A) victory
    (B) competition
    (C) entertainment
    (D) loss

12. **Based on the article, what is probably true about Sally Barton?**

    (A) She intends to attend a top university in her country.
    (B) She likes to spell words more than she enjoys writing essays.
    (C) She is not originally from the area where she is studying.
    (D) She does not always enjoy doing academic projects.

13. **What does Sally Barton say she is going to do next?**

    (A) Compete in a math contest
    (B) Rewrite her essay
    (C) Work on her college applications
    (D) Improve her spelling

GO ON TO THE NEXT PAGE

Questions 14–19 are about the following passage.

There are several ways in which people have managed to achieve flight. One of the first methods was by using hot-air balloons. These days, helicopters are also a way that some people fly. However, at present, more people fly on airplanes than use any other method of flying.

Modern-day airplanes are mostly jets. These planes have engines that <u>propel</u> them through the air
5 at velocities that can exceed the speed of sound. There is another way that airplanes can fly though: They can use propellers.

A propeller is a device with blades. The number of blades varies, but it is normally three or four. The propeller is attached to a drive shaft. It, in turn, is connected to an engine, which makes both the shaft and the propeller spin. This spinning helps the plane get aloft.

10 One reason that propellers are effective concerns the shapes of their blades. They are not flat; instead, they are made at angles. This is known as the propeller's pitch. The pitch allows the propeller to behave like a wing. In doing so, the propeller can create lift as well as thrust. These two factors enable a propeller first to move an airplane forward and then to help it get off the ground.

The first airplanes relied upon propellers to fly. In fact, it was not until a few decades after the
15 Wright brothers' <u>initial</u> flight that advanced jet airplanes were made. Even today, there are still many airplanes that have propellers. They are not as fast as jets, but they are able to get people and cargo from one place to another swifter than any type of land transportation.

GO ON TO THE NEXT PAGE

14. The author uses jets as an example of
_____.

(A) an advanced form of air transportation

(B) the type of transportation most people prefer

(C) the fastest way to travel that has been invented

(D) the most common airplanes in modern times

15. In line 4, the word propel is closest in meaning to _____.

(A) drive

(B) encourage

(C) ignite

(D) pull

16. Which of the following is NOT mentioned in the passage as a characteristic of propellers?

(A) The number of blades they have

(B) What their shape is

(C) How large they are

(D) What they are connected to

17. How do propellers enable airplanes to fly?

(A) They provide lift and thrust.

(B) They give airplanes speed and lift.

(C) They let airplanes have drag and velocity.

(D) They supply velocity and thrust.

18. In line 15, the word initial is closest in meaning to _____.

(A) experimental

(B) successful

(C) first

(D) practice

19. Which of the following can be inferred from the passage about the Wright brothers?

(A) They became wealthy by making airplanes.

(B) They did some research on jet engines.

(C) Many of their tests flights were failures.

(D) Their first airplane had a propeller.

GO ON TO THE NEXT PAGE

Questions 20–29 are about the following passage.

Otters are semi-aquatic mammals. They live on land, but they enjoy spending a great deal of time in the water. There are thirteen species of otters. They are found mostly in North and South America, Europe, and Asia. An otter has a long body, a short snout, and a long tail. Its four legs are fairly short, and it has webbed feet. Its webbed feet are what enable an otter to swim so well. An otter's fur
5 is either brown or gray in color, and the fur around its face is much lighter than the fur around the rest of its body.

Otters reach maturity fairly quickly and begin to mate when they are two years of age. Female otters can give birth to a litter of one to five babies every year. Otters build dens, which are typically holes in the ground and are located near some source of water. These dens are where female otters
10 give birth to their babies.

When they are first born, otters are <u>dependent upon</u> their mothers. But they grow rapidly and learn how to swim when they are only two months old. This is about the same amount of time their fur coats need to grow completely. Otters are natural swimmers, so it does not take much effort for them to learn to swim. Despite swimming well, the babies stay with their mothers until they are about
15 a year old. Then, once they become able to hunt for themselves, they set off to live their own lives. Most otters can survive in the wild for between ten and fifteen years.

Otters are predatory carnivores that consume fish and crustaceans. They have also been known to eat reptiles, amphibians, and birds even though <u>those</u> are not their first choices. But they are efficient hunters that rarely starve due to their ability to catch a wide range of prey.
20 While otters are predators, they are also prey animals. Wolves, large snakes, alligators, and crocodiles hunt them when they are on land or in shallow water. Further out at sea, killer whales frequently hunt them. Humans, who desire otters for their pelts, hunt otters, too. In fact, human hunters <u>have taken a toll on otter populations</u> in places around the world. While some people hunt otters, many more simply enjoy watching them. Otters are some of the most playful animals on the
25 planet. They seem to have a zest for life when they swim and play on land.

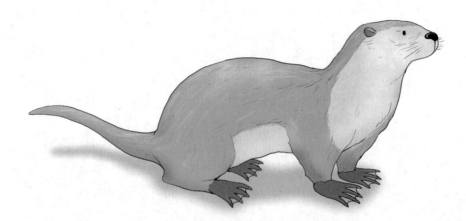

GO ON TO THE NEXT PAGE

20. **What is the best title for this passage?**

    (A) All about Otters

    (B) What Does an Otter Look Like?

    (C) Otters: Nature's Playful Animals

    (D) Endangered Otters

21. **Why does the author mention North and South America, Europe, and Asia?**

    (A) To claim that otters are endangered there

    (B) To say that few otters live in those places today

    (C) To point out where most otters live

    (D) To note where otters first evolved

22. **According to the passage, all of the following are physical characteristics of otters EXCEPT _____.**

    (A) their fur is colored either gray or brown

    (B) they have four legs that are short

    (C) they have tails that are long

    (D) only their front two feet are webbed

23. **Paragraph 2 supports which of the following statements?**

    (A) Female otters give birth to five babies every year.

    (B) Otter couples stay together their entire lives.

    (C) Otters build their dens in holes underwater.

    (D) Otters can give birth when they are two years old.

24. **In line 11, the phrase dependent upon is closest in meaning to _____.**

    (A) suspicious of

    (B) attached to

    (C) reliant on

    (D) aware of

25. **What can be inferred from the article about baby otters?**

    (A) They cannot eat meat in their first year of life.

    (B) Hunting is harder for them than swimming.

    (C) Their fur coats keep them warm in cold water.

    (D) Some of them are very poor swimmers.

26. **In line 18, the word those refers to _____.**

    (A) otters

    (B) predatory carnivores

    (C) fish and crustaceans

    (D) reptiles, amphibians, and birds

27. **The author uses killer whales as an example of _____.**

    (A) animals that prey on otters

    (B) large sea creatures

    (C) otters' fiercest enemies

    (D) animals more dangerous than alligators

28. **What does the author point out by writing that human hunters have taken a toll on otter populations in line 23?**

    (A) Humans are trying to protect otters.

    (B) Humans should stop hunting otters.

    (C) Humans have reduced the number of otters.

    (D) Humans ought to help save more otters.

29. **Which animal is NOT mentioned as a predator of otters?**

    (A) Wolves

    (B) Crocodiles

    (C) Humans

    (D) Crustaceans

GO ON TO THE NEXT PAGE

Questions 30–36 are about the following passage.

Journalism is a field in which reporters gather news items and bring them to the attention of the public. For the most part, journalists do this by writing articles. After the invention of the camera, though, a new type of journalist came about: the photojournalist.

A photojournalist is a person who takes photographs of important events. These pictures are
5 then published in newspapers, journals, and magazines and also on the Internet. One of the most famous photojournalists of the 1900s was Henri Cartier-Bresson, a Frenchman. He gained fame for his photographs of street life and took pictures of various historical events as well. Dorothea Lange was an American photojournalist. She became famous for the pictures she took during the Great Depression in the United States in the 1930s. Eddie Adams gained renown for his pictures taken
10 during the Vietnam War. His most famous picture shows a North Vietnamese prisoner about to be executed by a policeman. It had an emotional effect on many Americans and turned a lot of them against the war.

Some pictures taken by photojournalists have become iconic and are recognized around the world. In this way, the pictures that some photojournalists take can be more <u>influential</u> than the
15 articles that journalists write. Due to the influence of photojournalists in modern society, a large number of people have entered the field. Thus several different branches of photojournalism have arisen. Some practitioners focus on taking photographs of wars and natural disasters. These individuals often put their lives at risk by entering dangerous areas in search of the perfect snapshot.

Others focus on staged events, such as special ceremonies and award shows. These usually involve
20 people taking pictures of people who are posing. A third type of photojournalist is the paparazzi. These are individuals who follow celebrities around in the hope of snapping good pictures of them to sell. In some cases, photographs taken by paparazzi can sell for hundreds of thousands of dollars.

Nowadays, most photojournalists either work for news organizations or are employed as freelancers. Those who are independent sell their snapshots to the highest bidders. In addition,
25 thanks to the <u>pervasiveness</u> of digital cameras and cell phone cameras, even regular people can be photojournalists. In recent years, some of the best and most candid photographs were taken by people who were not professionally employed as photojournalists.

GO ON TO THE NEXT PAGE

30. Which title best summarizes the main idea of the passage?

(A) Photojournalists: Who They Are and What They Do

(B) So You Want to Become a Photojournalist?

(C) What Does It Take to Work as a Photojournalist?

(D) The Most Famous Photojournalists and Their Pictures

31. Why does the author talk about Dorothea Lange?

(A) To compare her work with that of Eddie Adams

(B) To describe the type of pictures she took

(C) To point out that she took pictures of urban environments

(D) To state that she was the first photojournalist

32. Which of the following is true regarding Eddie Adams?

(A) He was against the war in Vietnam.

(B) He was an acquaintance of Henri Cartier-Bresson.

(C) He first took pictures in the Great Depression.

(D) He took some famous war photographs.

33. In line 14, the word <u>influential</u> is closest in meaning to _____.

(A) significant

(B) appropriate

(C) respected

(D) famous

34. Based on the passage, what is probably true about some people who become photojournalists?

(A) They make sure they have the best photo equipment.

(B) They attend journalism school before becoming professionals.

(C) They are hopeful of becoming influential individuals.

(D) They are willing to get arrested for taking photographs.

35. What does the author say about paparazzi?

(A) Their pictures can sell for large amounts of money.

(B) Much of their work is featured in tabloid newspapers.

(C) Many people dislike the methods that they use.

(D) They take pictures of people who are posing.

36. In line 25, the word <u>pervasiveness</u> is closest in meaning to _____.

(A) cheapness

(B) quality

(C) commonness

(D) popularity

GO ON TO THE NEXT PAGE

Questions 37–42 are about the following passage.

The Age of Exploration originated in Europe in the fifteenth century. At that time, European sailors started sailing to places far from their homes. First, they went down the coast of Africa. Later, they went into the Indian Ocean and made it to various ports in Asia. Near the end of the century, they sailed all the way to the Americas in the New World. Eventually, they managed to travel around
5   the entire world.

The first expedition that managed to <u>circumnavigate</u> the globe was led by Ferdinand Magellan. While Magellan was a Portuguese sailor, he sailed under the Spanish flag since his journey was funded by the king of Spain. When he departed on September 20, 1519, he had five ships and nearly 300 men.

10   The expedition first moved west and crossed the Atlantic Ocean. After the ships reached the New World, they sailed south along the east coast of South America. Magellan was looking for a way to enter the Pacific Ocean. In November 1520, Magellan and his men finally discovered a passage to the Pacific. During the search, though, Magellan lost one of his ships when it crashed into a beach and got wrecked. There was also a mutiny attempt by some of his crew members.

15   With his remaining ships, Magellan sailed west across the Pacific Ocean. They traveled to the Marianas Islands, landed on Guam, and then sailed toward the Philippine Islands. During their journey across the Pacific, Magellan and his men became the first Europeans to see most of that part of the world.

When the ships reached the Philippines, Magellan's role in the journey came to an end. On an
20   island there, Magellan's men got into a dispute with some of the natives. There was a fight, and Magellan was killed in the middle of it. He died on April 27, 1521.

By this time, Magellan's crew had three ships, but they only had enough men to sail on two of them. So they burned one and sailed the other two south to Indonesia. There, they <u>engaged in trade</u> with the natives, so they acquired some spices to take back to Europe. However, the Portuguese were
25   at war with Spain at that time, so one ship was captured by <u>them</u>. The last remaining ship crossed the Indian Ocean. It rounded Africa and sailed north to Spain. It arrived home on September 6, 1522. Only eighteen of the original crew made it home alive.

GO ON TO THE NEXT PAGE

37. What is the passage mainly about?

(A) The life of Ferdinand Magellan

(B) The first trip around the world

(C) The European Age of Exploration

(D) The dangers of traveling in the past

38. Which is NOT mentioned as a place that Europeans visited during the Age of Exploration?

(A) Africa

(B) Australia

(C) Asia

(D) America

39. In line 6, the word <u>circumnavigate</u> is closest in meaning to _____ .

(A) go around

(B) explore

(C) learn about

(D) map

40. According to the passage, what happened to Magellan's expedition while his ships were near South America?

(A) They were attacked by natives.

(B) The crew decided to sail back home.

(C) They encountered lots of bad weather.

(D) A ship was lost by the expedition.

41. What does the author point out by writing that the crew <u>engaged in trade</u> in line 23?

(A) They decided to get married.

(B) They bought and sold items.

(C) They got rid of some possessions.

(D) They found more crew members.

42. In line 25, the word <u>them</u> refers to _____ .

(A) Magellan's crew

(B) the natives

(C) some spices

(D) the Portuguese

STOP

Practice
Test 7

Listening
Comprehension

The listening section has 42 questions. Follow along as you listen to the directions to the listening section.

Directions

In this section of the test, you will hear talks and conversations. Each talk or conversation is followed by one question. Choose the best answer to each question and mark the letter of the correct answer on your answer sheet. You will hear each talk or conversation only one time.

Here is an example: 🔊))

Why is the boy happy?

(A) He was selected for the baseball team.

(B) He finished doing his homework.

(C) He got an A on his math test.

(D) He has no more classes for the day.

The correct answer is (A), "He was selected for the baseball team."

Here is another example: 🔊))

What are the speakers mainly talking about?

(A) A paper the girl must turn in

(B) The quality of the girl's work

(C) The teacher's next class

(D) The girl's next writing assignment

The correct answer is (B), "The quality of the girl's work."

Go on to the next page, and the test will begin with question number one.

GO ON TO THE NEXT PAGE

1. **What are the speakers mainly discussing?**

    (A) Mr. Sanders' teaching style

    (B) The test that they just took

    (C) A tutorial they are going to attend

    (D) The material they need to know

2. **What does the teacher say about the boy's essay?**

    (A) It was better than his previous one.

    (B) It will lose points for being late.

    (C) It should be about French history.

    (D) It needs to be turned in next week.

3. **When is the teacher going to return the girl's test?**

    (A) By today

    (B) By Wednesday

    (C) By Thursday

    (D) By next week

4. **What is the boy going to do after the next period?**

    (A) Give the girl his science notes

    (B) Meet the girl for lunch

    (C) Copy from the girl's notebook

    (D) Attend science class with the girl

5. **Why does the teacher mention the girl's poem?**

    (A) To criticize how she wrote it

    (B) To tell her she got an A on it

    (C) To ask when she will submit it

    (D) To praise its creativity

6. **What does the girl mean when she says: "Tell me about it"?**

    (A) She agrees with the boy's opinion.

    (B) She wants some more information.

    (C) The boy needs to repeat himself.

    (D) She does not know the new student.

7. **What is the purpose of the announcement?**

    (A) To encourage the students to try harder

    (B) To explain why they are restudying some material

    (C) To give the students a new homework assignment

    (D) To ask what the students thought of the lesson

8. **What is the teacher mainly discussing?**

    (A) The class time

    (B) Perfect grades

    (C) Pop quizzes

    (D) Final grades

9. **Why is the principal talking about field day?**

    (A) To give the date when it will be held

    (B) To explain what will happen during it

    (C) To mention that it will be postponed

    (D) To say that parents may not attend it

GO ON TO THE NEXT PAGE

232

Now you will hear longer talks or conversations. Each talk or conversation will be followed by three or more questions. Choose the best answer to each question and mark the letter of the correct answer on your answer sheet. You will hear each talk or conversation only one time.

10. **What are the students mainly talking about?**

    (A) The AP classes that they are taking
    (B) The sporting events they will play soon
    (C) The boy's difficulty studying for his classes
    (D) The girl's desire to become a starter

11. **What does the girl say about the volleyball team?**

    (A) It had a losing record last year.
    (B) It won the state championship last year.
    (C) It has all of last year's starters returning.
    (D) It has already lost three games this year.

12. **Which class do the speakers take together?**

    (A) P.E.
    (B) History
    (C) English
    (D) Biology

13. **What does the girl suggest about Jenny and Karen?**

    (A) They are her two best friends at school.
    (B) They have not spoken with the boy before.
    (C) Their grades are going down this semester.
    (D) They are members of the volleyball team.

14. **What is the main topic of the conversation?**

    (A) How to conduct a lab experiment
    (B) When the students are going to have a lab class
    (C) What kinds of animals are in the laboratory
    (D) How the boy feels about a lab assignment

15. **Why is the boy worried about the upcoming class?**

    (A) He might become sick during it.
    (B) He does not want to dissect a cat.
    (C) He has never had a lab class before.
    (D) He thinks it will be too hard for him.

16. **What does the boy imply when he says this: "In fact, I use worms as bait every time I go fishing"?**

    (A) He wants to go fishing with his friends.
    (B) He is comfortable cutting up worms.
    (C) He does not want to do the assignment.
    (D) He enjoys fishing in his free time.

17. **What does the teacher imply about her class?**

    (A) It does not take much skill to dissect an animal.
    (B) Most of the students are uncomfortable during it.
    (C) The students will dissect animals other than worms in it.
    (D) The students have to do the lab to get good grades.

GO ON TO THE NEXT PAGE

18. What is the main topic of the conversation?

(A) The girl's progress on her science project

(B) When the girl will turn in her paper

(C) How the girl is going to complete her research

(D) The girl's need to get a good grade on her work

19. What does the girl suggest about Tommy?

(A) He is one of her best friends at school.

(B) He promised to help her with her assignment.

(C) She thinks he was playing a trick on her.

(D) She believes he needs to work harder.

20. What does the girl say about her status report?

(A) She has not started writing it yet.

(B) She forgot to email it to the teacher.

(C) She needs to write one more page.

(D) She is going to send it the next day.

21. Why does the girl talk about the lab work she is doing?

(A) To answer the teacher's question

(B) To describe her father's role in her project

(C) To complain about her results

(D) To ask the teacher to interpret the results

22. What does the teacher ask the girl to do by next Monday?

(A) Complete all of her lab work

(B) Submit a new status report

(C) Turn in her science project

(D) Conduct another experiment

23. Why does the girl mention her history test?

(A) To tell the boy that she is studying for it

(B) To state that she is likely to do poorly on it

(C) To ask the boy some questions about it

(D) To find out what the boy's grade on it was

24. What does the boy tell the girl to do when she is studying?

(A) Use the Internet to find important information

(B) Avoid lying down on her bed

(C) Play some rock music to motivate herself

(D) Focus on studying one subject at a time

25. What is probably true about the girl?

(A) She dislikes listening to classical music.

(B) Her grades are as good as the boy's.

(C) She enjoys learning history at school.

(D) Her blog is popular with her classmates.

26. What is the girl going to do tonight?

(A) Review for her history test

(B) Meet the boy at the library

(C) Try to follow the boy's study tips

(D) Complete the paper she has to write

GO ON TO THE NEXT PAGE

27. What is the teacher mainly discussing?

(A) DNA testing of animals

(B) The domestication of dogs

(C) Dig sites in Europe and Asia

(D) How to tame wild animals

28. What does the teacher suggest about domesticating animals?

(A) Only intelligent animals can be tamed.

(B) Humans need to be patient to do it.

(C) It is a fairly difficult process to do.

(D) It may take hundreds of years to do.

29. Why does the teacher mention DNA testing?

(A) To focus on some genetic traits that only dogs have

(B) To admit he is skeptical about claims dogs evolved in Asia

(C) To note when dogs and wolves became individual species

(D) To claim it can prove when dogs were first domesticated

30. According to the teacher, why did humans and dogs develop a close relationship?

(A) Humans bred dogs to be dependent upon them.

(B) Each of them provided assistance to the other.

(C) Dogs preferred being tame to living in the wild.

(D) Humans wanted dogs to be their companions.

31. What is the teacher mainly talking about?

(A) The three main species of anteaters

(B) The feeding habits of the anteater

(C) The characteristics of the giant anteater

(D) The life cycle of the anteater

32. What does the teacher say about the snout of the anteater?

(A) It can be up to one meter in length.

(B) The anteater's teeth are in it.

(C) The anteater's mouth is at its end.

(D) It is what the anteater uses to dig up anthills.

33. What does the teacher imply about the anteater?

(A) It may attack animals that enter its territory.

(B) It sometimes lives in small family groups.

(C) It is an endangered species in some countries.

(D) It eats both plant and animal matter.

34. What will the teacher probably do next?

(A) Answer some of the students' questions

(B) Display some more pictures on the screen

(C) Show the class a video about anteaters

(D) Assign the students some homework to do

GO ON TO THE NEXT PAGE

35. **What does the teacher say about hoar frost?**

   (A) It is most common during the morning.

   (B) She thinks that it looks pretty.

   (C) The blowing of icy wind forms it.

   (D) It happens more often in winter than in fall.

36. **Why does the teacher suggest that the students look in their books?**

   (A) To read an important passage

   (B) To consult a chart on frost

   (C) To see a picture of rime frost

   (D) To learn how to spell some words

37. **Why does the teacher talk about farmers?**

   (A) To note how frost affects their planting schedules

   (B) To discuss how frost can affect their crops

   (C) To stress how much they dislike frost

   (D) To describe how much money they can lose due to frost

38. **What can be inferred about fern frost?**

   (A) It usually affects plants.

   (B) It requires both warm and cold air.

   (C) It is the most common type of frost.

   (D) It happens at night or in the morning.

39. **What is the teacher mainly discussing?**

   (A) The first computer

   (B) Smartphones

   (C) How the computer was invented

   (D) Laptop computers

40. **What does the teacher mention about ENIAC?**

   (A) It was invented by Alan Turing.

   (B) It was the size of a house.

   (C) It was expensive to make.

   (D) It was used by government scientists.

41. **Why does the teacher mention calculators?**

   (A) To discuss how fast most of them are

   (B) To stress how cheap they have become

   (C) To talk about how easy they are to use

   (D) To compare their power with that of ENIAC

42. **What will the teacher probably do next?**

   (A) Let the students go for the day

   (B) Continue giving her lecture

   (C) Have a student give a presentation

   (D) Ask a student to read from the book

STOP

Language Form and Meaning

Directions

In this section of the test, you will answer 42 questions found in seven different texts. Within each text are boxes that contain four possible ways to complete a sentence. Choose the word or words in each box that correctly complete each sentence. Mark the letter of the correct answer on your answer sheet.

Here are two sample questions:

1. For decades,

> (A) the people will hear rumors
> (B) people are hearing rumors
> (C) the people hear rumors
> (D) people had heard rumors

that there was a huge landmass

located south of Australia, yet no one had been able to find it. It was not until 1820

2. that the first

> (A) guaranteed
> (B) confirmed
> (C) requested
> (D) approved

sighting of the continent of Antarctica, by a Russian

sailor, was made.

The correct answer to **Sample 1** is (D), "people had heard rumors." The correct answer to **Sample 2** is (B), "confirmed."

GO ON TO THE NEXT PAGE

Questions 1–4 refer to the following announcement.

Students,

Next Tuesday, September 26, we are going to take class pictures. These

pictures will be featured in the school yearbook and will also be available

1.
(A) for the copies that you purchased.
(B) for your copies being purchased.
(C) for purchases of your copies.
(D) for you to purchase copies of.

Please consult the attached sheet

2. that lists the picture packet options
(A) by your choice.
(B) you have chosen.
(C) you may choose from.
(D) for your choices.

Be sure to select one and to include cash or a check to pay for your purchase.

GO ON TO THE NEXT PAGE

All students need to wear appropriate clothing for your student pictures.

3. Boys should wear

(A) dress
(B) dresses
(C) dressed
(D) dressing

pants and shirts while girls should wear

4. blouses and skirts or pants. Any student wearing

(A) improper
(B) approved
(C) formal
(D) purchased

clothes

will be sent home to change clothes on Tuesday.

Catherine Sanders

Principal

GO ON TO THE NEXT PAGE

Questions 5–8 refer to the following email.

GO ON TO THE NEXT PAGE

Peter,

I hate to bother you since I know you are working on your science project,

but I have a question about today's math homework. I understood

5.
(A) sincerely
(B) repeatedly
(C) practically
(D) apparently

all of the problems we had to solve, but I

6.
(A) could not figure out
(B) will not figure out
(C) am not figuring out
(D) had not figured out

two of them. For number three, I am aware

7.

(A) how I answered zero,
(B) that the answer is zero,
(C) why zero was answered,
(D) which answer is zero,

but I am not sure of the proper way to

solve it. As for number eight, I am completely lost concerning that question.

8.

(A) If you have a spare moment,
(B) If the moment has been spared,
(C) If you spared a moment,
(D) If I spare you a moment,

could you explain how to answer both of them?

Joe

GO ON TO THE NEXT PAGE

Questions 9–12 refer to the following announcement.

Students and Parents,

This winter was especially severe, so we were forced to close the school on

several occasions. As you know, we expect to get snowed out three times each

9.   winter. This year, however, we had to

(A) schedule
(B) cancel
(C) resume
(D) delay

classes on five separate

days. As a result, per government regulations, we must make up two of those days.

10.

(A) Having class during spring break, instead,
(B) Instead, we had classes during spring break,
(C) After we had classes during spring break, instead,
(D) Instead of having classes during spring break,

we have decided to

GO ON TO THE NEXT PAGE

have school on two Saturdays in April. We will hold classes on both April 5

11. and April 12 this semester.

(A) It is normally time for school to begin
(B) School will begin at the normal time
(C) School, having begun at its normal time,
(D) The normal time that school begins is

but will end at one in the afternoon. Please call the school office at 548-9840

12. if you have any questions or

(A) concern.
(B) concerns.
(C) concerned.
(D) concernment.

Jade Masterson

Principal

GO ON TO THE NEXT PAGE

Questions 13–20 refer to the following essay.

13. In recent years, too many students have resorted

(A) cheat
(B) to cheating
(C) cheated
(D) have cheated

in a

14. variety of ways. For instance, they cheat on tests and

(A) request
(B) imitate
(C) preserve
(D) copy

their

classmates' homework assignments. In my opinion, the amount of cheating is

15.

(A) excessively
(B) reputedly
(C) conservatively
(D) restrictively

high. These students see nothing wrong with their actions.

16. I think we can solve this problem

(A) for two methods.
(B) in two ways.
(C) by two manners.
(D) with two kinds.

First, parents need to

17. tell their children

(A) what wrongness is cheating
(B) how to get cheated
(C) which is the wrong way to cheat
(D) why cheating is wrong

and how it can harm, not

GO ON TO THE NEXT PAGE

help, them in the long run. Second, school administrators have to punish

cheaters severely. All too often, students are caught cheating yet do not get

18. punished or receive only

(A) extreme
(B) negligent
(C) virtual
(D) light

punishment. Students who cheat

on tests or homework assignments ought to receive zeros on them, and

19.

(A) detention has been given
(B) there is going to be a detention
(C) they should be given detention
(D) students are on detention

for at least a week. These students

20. should receive even

(A) more severe
(B) more severe than
(C) most severe
(D) as severe as

punishment if they cheat again

in the future.

GO ON TO THE NEXT PAGE

Questions 21–28 refer to the following notice.

The school is pleased to announce that the annual guest lecture series

is set to begin next week. On October 3, Dr. Enrico Prado,

21.

> (A) a noted physician at Central Hospital,
> (B) Central Hospital has a noted physician,
> (C) he is a noted physician at Central Hospital,
> (D) that is a noted physician at Central Hospital,

will give a lecture about

some breakthroughs on new surgical methods. On November 7, Angela Plummer will

22. make a speech. Ms. Plummer is the well-known author whose

> (A) late
> (B) later
> (C) later than
> (D) latest

23. novel, *The Sampson Dialogue*, is a

> (A) nonfiction
> (B) presumptuous
> (C) traditional
> (D) global

bestseller. Her

24. lecture is sure to be one of the

> (A) attendances
> (B) highlights
> (C) shows
> (D) conveniences

of the semester.

GO ON TO THE NEXT PAGE

GO ON TO THE NEXT PAGE

On December 18, Professor Kevin Simpson is going to present a lecture on

the history of medieval Britain. He will also discuss the results of his latest

25. research on the

(A) history
(B) histories
(C) historical
(D) historically

King Arthur.

26.

(A) Every lecture has taken place
(B) All lectures will have taken place
(C) All of the lectures will take place
(D) Each lecture took place

at one in the afternoon.

Parents and local citizens are welcome to attend whereas

27.

(A) student attendance is mandatory.
(B) there is a mandate for student attendance.
(C) students are attended to in the mandate.
(D) mandatory attendance is for students.

We hope attendance will

28. be

(A) high
(B) higher than
(C) so high as
(D) the highest

last year's, so we encourage everyone to inform

their friends and neighbors about the lectures.

Questions 29–34 refer to the following essay.

Astrology is a belief system which is related to the positions of the stars, sun,

29. moon, and planets and

(A) which effects concern people's lives.
(B) where people's lives are affected.
(C) what lives of people were affected.
(D) how they affect people's lives.

In Western

culture, the main aspect of astrology concerns the time of year when a person

30. was born. The year is

(A) sliced
(B) divided
(C) cut
(D) repeated

into twelve periods, which are based on

twelve star formations called constellations. These constellations make up a region

31. of the sky

(A) the zodiac is called.
(B) being the zodiac.
(C) called the zodiac.
(D) the zodiac will be called.

For instance, a person who was born

32. from late June to late July is

(A) registered
(B) pestered
(C) suggested
(D) considered

to be a Cancer based on the

GO ON TO THE NEXT PAGE

248

GO ON TO THE NEXT PAGE

constellation with the same name. Some astrologists like to have additional

information about a person, including the exact time of the individual's birth.

33.

(A) Using this information,

(B) With the use of information,

(C) To use this information,

(D) Information, having been used,

an astrologist can then come up with

a horoscope for a person. A horoscope is an explanation of an individual's

personality based on when he or she was born. Some horoscopes also attempt

34. to

(A) refute

(B) predict

(C) enable

(D) assume

a person's future.

Questions 35–42 refer to the following biography.

35. One of
(A) more important
(B) more important than
(C) as important as
(D) the most important
figures of the American Civil Rights Movement

36. was Martin Luther King Jr.
(A) His contemporaries were unlike him,
(B) Unlike some of his contemporaries,
(C) Having been unlike his contemporaries,
(D) His contemporaries, unlike him,

King rejected utilizing violence to attain his goals. Instead, he promoted

37. nonviolence and encouraged his followers to
(A) portray
(B) appear
(C) behave
(D) result
similarly. Held in the

38. 1950s and 1960s, the American Civil Rights Movement
(A) dominated
(B) had dominated
(C) had been dominated
(D) was dominating

the social policies of those two decades. King and other leaders of the movement

wanted equal rights for everyone in the United States.

GO ON TO THE NEXT PAGE

39.
(A) King's crucial role was played
(B) King played a crucial role
(C) King's role, which was crucial,
(D) King's crucial role played

in many of the events that took place

during the movement. For instance, he was a major figure in the 1955 bus boycott

in Montgomery, Alabama. He also led sit-ins at restaurants and other

40.
(A) establishments
(B) establishes
(C) established
(D) establishing

in southern states. In 1963, he gave his famous

41. "I Have a Dream" speech in Washington, D.C. It was

(A) in part thanks to him
(B) thanking some part of him
(C) a part of his thanks
(D) his part to give thanks

that the Civil Rights Act of 1964 was passed a year later. That was also the same

42. year King was

(A) awarded
(B) traded
(C) nominated
(D) donated

the Nobel Peace Prize.

STOP

NO TEST MATERIAL ON THIS PAGE

Reading Comprehension

In this section of the test, you will read six texts and answer 42 questions. Choose the correct answer to each question and mark the letter of the correct answer on your answer sheet.

Before you start, read the sample text and the sample questions below.

Sample Text

One of the most valued metals in the world is gold. It is an extremely versatile metal, which accounts for its high price. While the vast majority of gold is used to make jewelry, it has other applications. For instance, gold is found in many electronic devices because it conducts electricity so well. It is also used as currency and has some medical applications.

Sample Question 1

What would be the best title for this passage?

(A) Gold and Its Uses
(B) Where to Find Gold
(C) How Much Is Gold Worth?
(D) Making Gold Jewelry

The correct answer is (A), "Gold and Its Uses."

Sample Question 2

What does the author say about gold?

(A) It costs more than any other metal.
(B) People mostly use it for jewelry.
(C) Several countries have gold currency.
(D) Electronic items use large amounts of gold.

The correct answer is (B), "People mostly use it for jewelry."

GO ON TO THE NEXT PAGE

Questions 1–5 are about the following article in the school newspaper.

When the spring semester began, students at Eastern High School were met by a new science teacher. Her name is Elaine Burgess, and she has replaced Donald Young, who retired to
5 spend time with his grandchildren.

Since Ms. Burgess has just started here, many students are curious about her background. She was kind enough to sit down for an interview with *The Quill and*
10 *Paper*. According to Ms. Burgess, she received her master's degree from nearby Sanderson University only six months ago. Her M.A. is in chemistry, but she double-majored in chemistry and biology as an undergraduate while
15 simultaneously getting a minor in physics.

"I love all aspects of science," she said. "And I'm looking forward to teaching students the things I know." Ms. Burgess further declared that she prefers a hands-on approach to
20 teaching science. So she expects to conduct numerous experiments in the hope of sparking students' interest in science.

Finally, Ms. Burgess added that she welcomes student participation in her classes. "Not only
25 can students learn from their teachers, but I believe that teachers can also learn from their students. I hope that, by working together, we can all increase our knowledge of science."

GO ON TO THE NEXT PAGE

1. **Which headline best summarizes the article?**

   (A) Science Classes to Feature Hands-on Learning
   (B) A Chat with the New Science Teacher
   (C) The Education of Elaine Burgess
   (D) Science Class: Does Anyone Enjoy It?

2. **Based on the article, what is probably true about _The Quill and Paper_?**

   (A) It is read by every student.
   (B) It is a new textbook.
   (C) It was written by Ms. Burgess.
   (D) It is the name of a newspaper.

3. **Paragraph 2 supports which of the following statements?**

   (A) This is the second teaching job for Ms. Burgess.
   (B) Ms. Burgess has been a teacher for six months.
   (C) Ms. Burgess was a professor at Sanderson University.
   (D) Ms. Burgess focused on science as an undergraduate.

4. **What does the author point out by writing about Ms. Burgess's hope of sparking students' interest in science in line 21?**

   (A) Too many students have little scientific knowledge.
   (B) She wants students to be curious about science.
   (C) Science is one of the hardest subjects to learn.
   (D) Some experiments can be dangerous for students to do.

5. **What can be inferred from the article about Ms. Burgess?**

   (A) Some of her students know more about science than her.
   (B) Her grades in graduate school were high.
   (C) She expects her students to speak in class.
   (D) The subject she knows the least is biology.

GO ON TO THE NEXT PAGE

Questions 6–11 are about the following notice.

Attention, all students.

Several local elementary schools are in serious need of tutors. Due to cuts in their budgets, they can no longer hire tutors for their students for after-school classes. Therefore they are looking to replace their paid tutors with volunteers. They have <u>specifically</u> requested tutors in math, science, and English. However, they would also like to have tutors for music, art, and penmanship classes.

If any of you are interested in tutoring young children, please talk to your homeroom teacher. As a tutor, you would be expected to visit your school three times a week. You would start at 3:30 in the afternoon and teach for approximately one hour. A teacher here can provide transportation to your school and home if you require <u>it</u>.

To qualify as a tutor, you must have an A average in the subject you wish to teach. You must also be of good character and be willing to work with young children. Anyone who serves as a tutor will be <u>exempted from</u> the school's volunteer program. Those who do not do any tutoring will be expected to volunteer at least fifty hours this semester.

6. In line 4, the word <u>specifically</u> is closest in meaning to _____.

    (A) consistently

    (B) recently

    (C) reportedly

    (D) expressly

7. What does the author say about the local elementary schools?

    (A) They are going to hire new paid tutors.

    (B) They only need tutors in three subjects.

    (C) They would like students to serve as tutors.

    (D) They want their tutors to work every day.

8. In line 9, the word <u>it</u> refers to

    _____.

    (A) approximately one hour

    (B) transportation

    (C) your school

    (D) home

9. According to the notice, all of the following are true about tutors EXCEPT

    _____.

    (A) they are expected to get to the schools by themselves

    (B) they can teach students a wide variety of topics

    (C) they should go to their schools three times each week

    (D) they will finish tutoring around four thirty in the afternoon

10. What does the author imply about tutors?

    (A) It is possible for them to increase their grades by tutoring.

    (B) Not all students are qualified to work as them.

    (C) Some of them can teach students at their homes.

    (D) They should expect to get paid for their work.

11. In line 12, the phrase <u>exempted from</u> is closest in meaning to _____.

    (A) recommended to

    (B) excused from

    (C) requested by

    (D) appointed to

GO ON TO THE NEXT PAGE

Questions 12–18 are about the following passage.

Jupiter is by far the largest planet in the solar system. It also has a force of gravity that is second in the solar system only to the sun in power. It should therefore come as no surprise that Jupiter has the most moons of all the planets. Jupiter has at least sixty-three moons and may have more waiting to be discovered. The majority of these moons are small in size, yet four are quite large. In fact, one
5 is larger than the planet Mercury while the other three are bigger than Pluto. Together, these four moons are called Galilean moons. The reason is that they were discovered by Galileo Galilei in 1610.

The largest of the Galilean moons is Ganymede while the other three are Io, Europa, and Callisto. These moons have some characteristics that make them <u>enticing</u> to astronomers. For instance, Io is one of the most volcanically active bodies in the solar system. Europa, on the other
10 hand, is covered with a thick layer of ice, yet astronomers believe that liquid water lies beneath <u>it</u>. Ganymede and Callisto may also have liquid water deep beneath their surfaces.

 GO ON TO THE NEXT PAGE

12. What is the best title for the passage?

(A) Jupiter and Its Moons

(B) The Galilean Moons

(C) The Moon Ganymede

(D) Moons in the Solar System

13. According to the passage, which is true about Jupiter's moons?

(A) Three of them are larger than Mercury.

(B) Most of them formed at the same time.

(C) Some of them used to be asteroids.

(D) There are more than sixty of them.

14. Why does the author mention Galileo Galilei?

(A) To name the man who discovered the Galilean moons

(B) To credit him with finding all of Jupiter's moons

(C) To describe the work that he did in astronomy

(D) To give the year when he did a science experiment

15. What does the author imply about Ganymede?

(A) It is larger than Mercury.

(B) It may have life on it.

(C) It has more water than Earth.

(D) It is the closest moon to Jupiter.

16. In line 8, the word <u>enticing</u> is closest in meaning to _____.

(A) engaging

(B) seductive

(C) mysterious

(D) appealing

17. In line 10, the word <u>it</u> refers to _____.

(A) the solar system

(B) Europa

(C) a thick layer of ice

(D) liquid water

18. Paragraph 2 supports which of the following statements?

(A) Europa is larger than Io and Callisto.

(B) Ganymede is covered with liquid water.

(C) Io has volcanoes that currently erupt.

(D) Europa's orbit is longer than Io's.

GO ON TO THE NEXT PAGE

Questions 19–26 are about the following passage.

A fossil is the preserved remains of an animal or plant that died long ago. In general, the fossil has transformed into stone and either has the shape or shows the outline of a dead animal or plant. Oftentimes, only the bones and teeth of animals are preserved. In the case of plants, most fossils are simply impressions of the leaves or stems that are set in stone. There are some instances in which
5 paleontologists have unearthed fossils that include skin and bodily tissues, such as when animals are found <u>encased in</u> ice or tar, but these happen rarely. No matter what the condition of the fossils scientists find, <u>they</u> can be used to learn a great deal of information about life on Earth in the past.

Earth is around 4.5 billion years old, and humans have been on the planet for a mere fraction of that time. Thus fossils enable scientists to understand what life was like on Earth prior to the existence
10 of humans. Virtually everything that is known about dinosaurs, for instance, comes from studying their fossilized remains. Scientists have learned that there was a wide variety of species of dinosaurs. Some were carnivores while others were herbivores. They also ranged in size from extremely small to incredibly large.

In addition, fossils help scientists make timelines for the distant path. In the nineteenth century,
15 scientists concluded that different levels of the Earth contained fossils from different eras. By examining the fossils from each level, scientists were able to see how life had evolved on the planet. Later, in the twentieth century, methods of accurately dating fossils were discovered. These permitted scientists to develop something called the geological time scale. It provides a detailed picture of life on the Earth throughout different periods of time. For instance, dinosaurs first appeared around 250
20 million years ago and then vanished around sixty-five million years ago. Ever since then, mammals have <u>dominated</u> the planet. It is thanks to fossils that this kind of information is known.

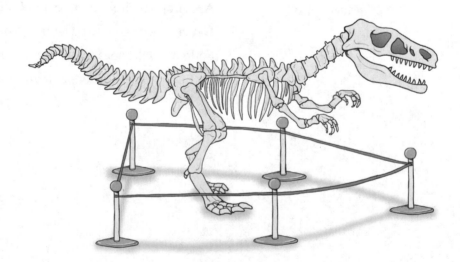

GO ON TO THE NEXT PAGE

19. What is the passage mostly about?

    (A) The importance of fossils
    (B) Where to find fossils
    (C) Dinosaur fossils
    (D) The geological time scale

20. In line 6, the phrase <u>encased in</u> is closest in meaning to _____.

    (A) applied with
    (B) buried at
    (C) covered with
    (D) removed from

21. In line 7, the word <u>they</u> refers to _____.

    (A) skin and bodily tissues
    (B) animals
    (C) the fossils
    (D) scientists

22. Which of the following is true regarding fossils of plants?

    (A) They are sometimes found in ice.
    (B) Most of them are not complete plants.
    (C) Their flowers are often preserved.
    (D) They are sometimes entire trees.

23. The author mentions all of the following about dinosaurs EXCEPT _____.

    (A) how they died
    (B) what they ate
    (C) how large they were
    (D) how diverse they were

24. What does the geological time scale do?

    (A) It analyzes the rocks and minerals that are found on the Earth.
    (B) It confirms that the Earth is more than 4.5 billion years old.
    (C) It shows the animals that have lived on the Earth throughout time.
    (D) It proves that animals such as dinosaurs once lived on the Earth.

25. Based on the passage, what is probably true about dinosaurs?

    (A) They died when a comet hit the Earth.
    (B) There are no living ones on the Earth.
    (C) Most of them were smaller than humans.
    (D) They lived for more than 250 million years.

26. In line 21, the word <u>dominated</u> is closest in meaning to _____.

    (A) abandoned
    (B) lived with
    (C) survived on
    (D) ruled

GO ON TO THE NEXT PAGE

Questions 27–34 are about the following passage.

An engine is a machine that creates mechanical motion from energy. In order to do this, an engine frequently requires some type of fuel to burn. Nowadays, many engines are used to power cars and other forms of transportation. These vehicles most commonly have an internal combustion engine and rely upon gasoline for power. However, there are several types of engines that can use alternative
5 energy sources. Many people are trying to <u>switch</u> to them because gasoline, which is a fossil fuel, creates pollution and is also a nonrenewable resource. Alternative energy sources, meanwhile, create less pollution and are often renewable sources of energy.

These days, engines that are able to burn biofuels are somewhat common. Biofuels are fuels that are made from biological material, such as corn, soybeans, and sugarcane. These biofuels burn
10 cleanly, so they produce much less pollution than fossil fuels. In some countries, such as Brazil, cars with biofuel engines are standard. In fact, most of the cars in Brazil have engines that can operate on either gasoline or biofuel.

A second type of alternative engine is the electric engine. Cars with electric engines have been common for decades. Most are being used in hybrid cars at the moment. These are vehicles that have
15 both a gasoline-powered engine and an electric one. In many cases, the gasoline-powered engine is used to operate the car at high speeds on expressways. The electric engine is utilized for city driving. One benefit of hybrid cars is that, as the gasoline-powered engine runs, it simultaneously <u>recharges</u> the electric engine.

A third type of alternative engine is the hydrogen engine. It utilizes hydrogen fuel cells, which
20 convert hydrogen into electricity that can power the car. These days, there are many cars and buses that rely upon hydrogen engines. However, there are some problems associated with this type of engine. The hydrogen used in the engine must be processed from other materials, and it is also difficult to store. As a result, vehicles that run on hydrogen are expensive.

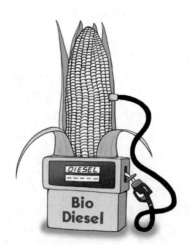

GO ON TO THE NEXT PAGE

27. What would be the best title for the passage?

   (A) Biofuels: Can They Really Run Car Engines?
   (B) Cars to Use Internal Combustion Engines
   (C) New Types of Alternative Energy Engines
   (D) What Is the Best Type of Vehicle Engine?

28. In line 5, the word <u>switch</u> is closest in meaning to _____.

   (A) remove
   (B) change
   (C) appear
   (D) respond

29. Based on paragraph 1, what is probably true about alternative energy sources?

   (A) They have only been discovered recently.
   (B) They cost a great deal to produce.
   (C) They are less common than fossil fuels.
   (D) They are rejected by the majority of people.

30. The author uses corn, soybeans, and sugarcane as examples of _____.

   (A) crops that are grown in Brazil
   (B) things that can be turned into biofuels
   (C) biological materials that grow quickly
   (D) plants that can be eaten by people

31. What does the author say about biofuels in Brazil?

   (A) They are used more than gasoline.
   (B) Many Brazilians approve of them.
   (C) They were first discovered there.
   (D) Many cars there can run on them.

32. When do many hybrid cars use their electric engines?

   (A) When being driven in the countryside
   (B) When being driven on city streets
   (C) When being driven on highways
   (D) When being driven on expressways

33. In line 17, the word <u>recharges</u> is closest in meaning to _____.

   (A) resumes
   (B) repels
   (C) reveals
   (D) refreshes

34. According to the passage, all of the following statements are true about hydrogen engines EXCEPT _____.

   (A) they cost a lot of money to operate
   (B) there are problems with their fuel source
   (C) cars and buses can both utilize them
   (D) renewing their batteries is difficult

GO ON TO THE NEXT PAGE

Questions 35–42 are about the following passage.

For hundreds of years, Rome was arguably the greatest civilization in the world. It started as a small town on the Tiber River in the Italian Peninsula. Then, first as a republic and later as an empire, it grew so that it controlled a huge amount of land in Europe, North Africa, and the Middle East. Then, in the fifth century A.D., the Roman Empire collapsed. Rome would never again be a
5 great power in the world.

There were many reasons that the Roman Empire fell. For instance, there were breakdowns in its political, economic, and social organization. In addition, the empire itself had been split into two halves—an eastern and a western empire. This was done with the <u>intention</u> of strengthening Rome, but, in reality, the move actually weakened it. The final major reason for the fall of Rome was a series
10 of invasions of its land by Germanic tribes. In 476, they sacked Rome and overthrew the last Roman emperor in the west.

For many years before its fall, Rome <u>had been in turmoil</u>. Emperors reigned for short periods of time before they were deposed and replaced by someone else. The empire was in a seemingly constant state of civil war, which disrupted Roman society. The Romans began to depend upon foreigners
15 to man the armies that they kept on the borders of the empire. These foreigners had little or no allegiance to the empire, so Rome's defenses were weakened. Rome's economy also went into decline. Most of the free people in the empire were either rich elites or lowly farmers. There was no strong middle class in the empire. Corruption at all levels of the government caused addition economic problems.

20 In an effort to solve many of these problems, Emperor Diocletian split the Roman Empire into two halves in the late fourth century. The Eastern Roman Empire, which later became known as the Byzantine Empire, started to flourish. Its emperor ruled from the city Constantinople, which was built by Emperor Constantine I. As for the Western Roman Empire, which was ruled from Rome, it declined further. During the fifth century, barbarian invaders conquered much of its territory.
25 Its border lands were overrun. Finally, the last emperor, Romulus Augustus, was overthrown by Germanic invaders led by Odoacer. <u>He</u> then assumed the title of king of Rome.

GO ON TO THE NEXT PAGE

35. Which title best summarizes the main idea of the passage?

(A) Emperor Diocletian of Rome

(B) Why Empires Go into Decline

(C) The Eastern and Western Roman Empires

(D) The Fall of the Roman Empire

36. In line 8, the word <u>intention</u> is closest in meaning to _____ .

(A) regard

(B) purpose

(C) assumption

(D) role

37. Paragraph 2 supports which of the following statements?

(A) The first defeat suffered by Rome was in 476.

(B) Rome engaged in a long war against Germanic tribes.

(C) Several factors led to the eventual defeat of Rome.

(D) Rome was invaded from both the east and west.

38. What does the author point out by writing that Rome <u>had been in turmoil</u> in line 12?

(A) Rome's economy declined.

(B) Rome was mostly at peace.

(C) Conditions in Rome were steady.

(D) There was disorder in Rome.

39. Which of the following is true regarding Rome's armies?

(A) None of them was allowed to enter Rome.

(B) The ones on the borders had many foreigners.

(C) They were led into battle by the emperor.

(D) They were effective at protecting the empire.

40. What did Diocletian do to the Roman Empire?

(A) He divided it into two parts.

(B) He weakened its borders.

(C) He moved its wealth to Constantinople.

(D) He used foreigners in its armies.

41. Why does the author talk about the Eastern Roman Empire?

(A) To note that it was not conquered by Odoacer

(B) To describe some actions of Emperor Constantine I

(C) To prove that it outlasted the Byzantine Empire

(D) To contrast it with the Western Roman Empire

42. In line 26, the word <u>He</u> refers to _____ .

(A) Emperor Diocletian

(B) Emperor Constantine I

(C) Romulus Augustus

(D) Odoacer

STOP

Practice
Test 8

Listening
Comprehension

The listening section has 42 questions. Follow along as you listen to the directions to the listening section.

Directions

In this section of the test, you will hear talks and conversations. Each talk or conversation is followed by one question. Choose the best answer to each question and mark the letter of the correct answer on your answer sheet. You will hear each talk or conversation only one time.

Here is an example: 🔊))

Why is the boy happy?

(A) He was selected for the baseball team.

(B) He finished doing his homework.

(C) He got an A on his math test.

(D) He has no more classes for the day.

The correct answer is (A), "He was selected for the baseball team."

Here is another example: 🔊))

What are the speakers mainly talking about?

(A) A paper the girl must turn in

(B) The quality of the girl's work

(C) The teacher's next class

(D) The girl's next writing assignment

The correct answer is (B), "The quality of the girl's work."

Go on to the next page, and the test will begin with question number one.

GO ON TO THE NEXT PAGE

1. **What are the speakers talking about?**

   (A) The girl's performance at the math contest

   (B) When the math contest is going to be held

   (C) How to prepare for the math contest

   (D) Which answers the girl got right at the math contest

2. **What can be inferred about the boy?**

   (A) He has decided on his research topic.

   (B) He enjoys taking Mr. Jacobs' class.

   (C) He is not going to write about hyenas.

   (D) He is doing well in Mr. Jacobs' class.

3. **How many schools is the girl going to apply to?**

   (A) One

   (B) Three

   (C) Seven

   (D) Ten

4. **How did the girl get to school?**

   (A) By bike

   (B) By bus

   (C) By car

   (D) By walking

5. **Why does the girl mention Mrs. Haught?**

   (A) To remind the boy about some work to do in her class

   (B) To comment on the boy's behavior in her class

   (C) To claim that she often gets mad at her students

   (D) To mention how embarrassed she made the students

6. **What does the teacher imply when he says: "It would be my pleasure"?**

   (A) He is willing to help the girl improve herself.

   (B) He can tell the girl about the program.

   (C) He expects the girl to be accepted to the program.

   (D) He has a good opinion of the girl.

7. **What is the purpose of the announcement?**

   (A) To insist that the students change clothes quickly

   (B) To ask the students to go out to the field

   (C) To tell the students what they are going to do

   (D) To find out which sports the students want to play

8. **Why does the teacher suggest that the students run for office?**

   (A) Not enough students have signed up to run yet.

   (B) She thinks they will enjoy doing student government.

   (C) She does not want the same students being elected every year.

   (D) The students ought to experience winning an election.

9. **What is the teacher mainly discussing?**

   (A) John Paul Jones

   (B) The *Bonhomme Richard*

   (C) The *Serapis*

   (D) The American Revolution

GO ON TO THE NEXT PAGE

Now you will hear longer talks or conversations. Each talk or conversation will be followed by three or more questions. Choose the best answer to each question and mark the letter of the correct answer on your answer sheet. You will hear each talk or conversation only one time.

10. **How does the girl probably feel when she says: "Can you believe what he said?"**

(A) Upset

(B) Optimistic

(C) Anxious

(D) Pleased

11. **What does the girl say about her teacher?**

(A) He agreed with her thoughts in her essay.

(B) He knows a great deal about computers.

(C) He is going to look at her paper one more time.

(D) He hopes she can get an A⁻ this semester.

12. **What can be inferred about the girl's paper?**

(A) She wrote it in one night.

(B) It was the longest in the class.

(C) She received an A on it.

(D) It described the history of computers.

13. **What is the boy going to do this evening?**

(A) Rewrite his paper

(B) Study for an exam

(C) Finish his homework

(D) Do some research

14. **What are the speakers mainly discussing?**

(A) The girl's absence from school

(B) The girl's performance in class

(C) The girl's class presentation

(D) The girl's current grade

15. **Why was the girl absent from school?**

(A) She had the flu.

(B) She broke her arm.

(C) She was in a car accident.

(D) She went on a trip.

16. **What does the teacher imply about the girl?**

(A) Her work is not as good as that of most of her classmates.

(B) There is a good chance that she will get a C in his class.

(C) She has not completed her makeup work in her other classes.

(D) He believes she is trying to avoid taking her exam.

17. **When does the teacher want the girl to complete her assignment?**

(A) Tuesday

(B) Wednesday

(C) Thursday

(D) Friday

GO ON TO THE NEXT PAGE

18. **What are the speakers mostly talking about?**

    (A) How often the students go on field trips

    (B) Where the class will go on the field trip

    (C) What the teacher expects to do on the field trip

    (D) Why the boy is not eager to go on the field trip

19. **What does the teacher mean when she says: "None taken"?**

    (A) She does not understand the question.

    (B) She is not upset by the comment.

    (C) The boy will not lose any points.

    (D) The boy forgot to do his work.

20. **Where does the boy suggest going on a field trip?**

    (A) The Civil War Museum

    (B) The city zoo

    (C) The local university

    (D) The hospital laboratory

21. **What will the boy probably do next?**

    (A) Return to the classroom

    (B) Continue speaking with the teacher

    (C) Grab a book from his locker

    (D) Get on the school bus

22. **What is probably true about the speakers?**

    (A) They are related to each other.

    (B) They are studying together.

    (C) They get similar grades.

    (D) They take all of the same classes.

23. **Why does the girl mention fast-food restaurants?**

    (A) To recommend eating at one

    (B) To ask when the boy last visited one

    (C) To advise the boy to avoid them

    (D) To say she ate lunch at one of them

24. **What does the girl recommend that the boy do?**

    (A) Eat food that is more nutritious

    (B) Cut down on the amount of food he eats

    (C) Start playing organized sports

    (D) Exercise with her every day

25. **What will the girl probably do next?**

    (A) Give the boy some exercise advice

    (B) Encourage the boy to study harder

    (C) Let the boy take a short study break

    (D) Attend her next class with the boy

GO ON TO THE NEXT PAGE

26. What is the boy explaining?

(A) How rugby developed

(B) Why he likes rugby

(C) How rugby and football are different

(D) What the rules of rugby are

27. According to the boy, where did rugby start?

(A) Australia

(B) The United States

(C) England

(D) Scotland

28. Why does the boy mention William Webb Ellis?

(A) To credit him with creating the sport of rugby

(B) To call him the world's greatest rugby player

(C) To claim he made the rules of rugby

(D) To say that he won the first rugby game

29. What will the boy probably do next?

(A) Speak some more about rugby

(B) Answer the man's questions

(C) Talk about being an exchange student

(D) Take a call from a listener

30. What is the main topic of the talk?

(A) Rare species of plants

(B) Trees and flowers

(C) Two types of plants

(D) Conifers and deciduous trees

31. Why does the teacher talk about vascular plants?

(A) To emphasize how rare they are

(B) To describe their main features

(C) To answer a question about them

(D) To describe their structure in detail

32. According to the teacher, which plants are nonvascular ones?

(A) Daisies

(B) Oak trees

(C) Rose bushes

(D) Mosses

33. How do nonvascular plants reproduce?

(A) By producing seeds

(B) By producing pollen

(C) By using spores

(D) By using nuts

34. What will the teacher probably do next?

(A) Have the students watch a video

(B) Let the students look at some samples

(C) Continue lecturing on plants

(D) Show the students some pictures

GO ON TO THE NEXT PAGE

35. **What can be inferred about the teacher?**

   (A) She likes mosaics more than paintings.

   (B) She makes mosaics in her free time.

   (C) She considers herself a mosaic artist.

   (D) She made the mosaics she shows the class.

36. **Why does the teacher discuss tesserae?**

   (A) To involve the students in the class discussion

   (B) To claim that she enjoys working with them

   (C) To get the students interested in using them

   (D) To describe how they are used to make mosaics

37. **What do many modern artists use to make mosaics?**

   (A) Stones

   (B) Ceramics

   (C) Metal

   (D) Glass

38. **According to the teacher, where do artists make mosaics?**

   (A) On ceilings

   (B) On walls

   (C) On plates

   (D) On seashells

39. **What are the speakers mainly discussing?**

   (A) The history of refrigeration

   (B) Food preservation methods

   (C) Why humans preserve food

   (D) The difficulties of farming

40. **What is probably true about the boy?**

   (A) He lives on a farm.

   (B) He knows little about preserving food.

   (C) He enjoys the teacher's class.

   (D) He is a transfer student.

41. **Why does the boy mention silos?**

   (A) To describe some of their disadvantages

   (B) To point out where they are located

   (C) To note one method of preserving food

   (D) To describe what crops are kept in them

42. **According to the teacher, when was refrigeration invented?**

   (A) In the seventeenth century

   (B) In the eighteenth century

   (C) In the nineteenth century

   (D) In the twentieth century

STOP

Language Form and Meaning

In this section of the test, you will answer 42 questions found in seven different texts. Within each text are boxes that contain four possible ways to complete a sentence. Choose the word or words in each box that correctly complete each sentence. Mark the letter of the correct answer on your answer sheet.

Here are two sample questions:

1. For decades

> (A) the people will hear rumors
> (B) people are hearing rumors
> (C) the people hear rumors
> (D) people had heard rumors

that there was a huge landmass

located south of Australia, yet no one had been able to find it. It was not until 1820

2. that the first

> (A) guaranteed
> (B) confirmed
> (C) requested
> (D) approved

sighting of the continent of Antarctica, by a Russian

sailor, was made.

The correct answer to **Sample 1** is (D), "people had heard rumors." The correct answer to **Sample 2** is (B), "confirmed."

GO ON TO THE NEXT PAGE

Questions 1–4 refer to the following email.

Rick,

I have a minor problem, but I am pretty sure you can help me out.

1.
(A) One of my parents
(B) Both of my parents
(C) Either of my parents
(D) Neither of my parents

is going to be able to take me to school

2. tomorrow morning, so I guess I
(A) have taken
(B) will be taking
(C) am going to have taken
(D) might have took
the bus.

GO ON TO THE NEXT PAGE

3. The only problem is that I have no

| (A) hint |
| (B) idea |
| (C) belief |
| (D) thought |

where the school bus stops

since I have never ridden on it before. You take the school bus, right?

| (A) I do not mind telling you |
| (B) Would you mind telling me |
| (C) How do you mind telling me |
| (D) I would not mind telling you |

4.

where the bus stop is and what time

I need to be there by?

Your friend,

Tim

Questions 5–8 refer to the following announcement.

Students,

Due to the thunderstorm that happened over the weekend, the school

5.

(A) is going to suffer some water damage.

(B) has water damage, which was suffered.

(C) is damaged by water, which it suffered through.

(D) suffered a great deal of water damage.

You have

likely noticed that several of the rooms have water dripping from the

6. ceilings. The cafeteria in particular

(A) sustained

(B) withstood

(C) retained

(D) replaced

so much damage that

it is in serious need of repair work at the moment. Thus the cafeteria will

GO ON TO THE NEXT PAGE

be closed for at least the next two weeks while workmen fix all

7. of the problems.

(A) Until otherwise notified,
(B) By other notification,
(C) Being notified,
(D) Unless it was notified,

you should bring

8.

(A) box
(B) boxes
(C) boxer
(D) boxed

lunches, which you will eat in your homerooms.

Dennis Frazier

Principal

Questions 9–12 refer to the following diary entry.

Dear Diary,

9. Next week, the track team is going to hold

| (A) auditions, |
| (B) tryouts, |
| (C) rehearsals, |
| (D) exercises, |

and I am going to do

10. my best

| (A) to make the team. |
| (B) for making the team. |
| (C) on the team that was made. |
| (D) by a team I made. |

For the past two months, I have been

working out on my own to get into good shape. I want to run the 400- and 800-meter

GO ON TO THE NEXT PAGE

11. races, so I have been working on both my speed and

(A) endure.
(B) enduring.
(C) endurable.
(D) endurance.

12. I believe

(A) what is a good chance
(B) who has a good chance
(C) that I have a good chance
(D) which is a good chance

to make the team because

my times in both races are better than those of some of the other members

of the squad. I just hope that I perform well in front of the coaches.

GO ON TO THE NEXT PAGE

Questions 13–20 refer to the following email.

Dear Joanie,

Now that summer vacation is fast approaching, have you given any thought as to

13.
(A) what you will do?
(B) where you will do it?
(C) which one you will do?
(D) how you will do it?

As for me, I think I am going to work in my aunt's

14. garden store. She offered me a part-time job there, and she is

(A) deciding
(B) thinking
(C) considering
(D) willing

to pay me ten dollars an hour, so I think that is more than fair.

15.
(A) I am working there,
(B) Before working there,
(C) By working there,
(D) It is there that I work,

I will be able to save a lot of money over the

16. summer. I plan to use that money

(A) to purchase
(B) will purchase
(C) will be purchasing
(D) going to purchase

a telescope

GO ON TO THE NEXT PAGE

17. since I am going to become

(A) the astronomy club, which has members

(B) a member of the astronomy club

(C) member, which are in the astronomy club

(D) the astronomy club's members

in the fall. But that is enough about me; how about you? Are you going to go on

18. that archaeological dig that the local university is

(A) lecturing?

(B) providing?

(C) researching?

(D) sponsoring?

Or are you going to spend your time learning the piano and

19.

(A) practicing with the swim team?

(B) to practice with the swim team?

(C) swimming practice with the team?

(D) teaming up during swimming practice?

Whatever you decide to do,

20.

(A) my hope is for each of us

(B) I have hopes for each of us

(C) I hope that each of us

(D) each of us has hope

has enough time to hang out during vacation.

Your friend,

Kendra

GO ON TO THE NEXT PAGE

Questions 21–28 refer to the following magazine article.

21. It may sound surprising, but there is a

(A) short
(B) shortage
(C) shorter
(D) shortening

of doctors at the

22. moment. And this problem is only going to

(A) repeal
(B) implode
(C) experience
(D) increase

in the future

as the population ages. There are a number of reasons there are not enough

23. doctors. One is that many doctors are becoming

(A) restricted
(B) confined
(C) frustrated
(D) detained

by the

24. amount of paperwork that they

(A) obligate
(B) will obligate
(C) are obligated
(D) have been obligated

to do, so

25.

(A) they are going to retire
(B) they are choosing to retire
(C) after choosing, they retire
(D) they are in their retirement

while they are still young. Additionally,

due to the several years of schooling a person must receive in order to

GO ON TO THE NEXT PAGE

GO ON TO THE NEXT PAGE

become a doctor, many individuals are opting for career paths that do not

26. keep them in school

| (A) until their early thirties. |
| (B) since they are in their thirties. |
| (C) before they are in their thirties. |
| (D) in their thirties at the earliest. |

Finally

a large number of medical school students graduate but then only

27.

| (A) practice |
| (B) treat |
| (C) diagnose |
| (D) establish |

medicine for a few years before they quit in favor of

28. engaging in some other activity.

| (A) Factors, having been combined, |
| (B) With some combination of factors, |
| (C) When these factors are combined, |
| (D) Some combination of factors, |

the result is that the country needs tens of thousands more doctors.

Questions 29–36 refer to the following letter.

Dear Sir/Madam,

29. We at Chesterfield Academy

(A) encourage
(B) endorse
(C) endeavor
(D) enjoy

to provide our students with an

30. education

(A) better for
(B) better than
(C) the best of
(D) the best for

what most receive. In addition, we seek to graduate

31. well-rounded students

(A) which are related to education,
(B) that is educated,
(C) what is high education,
(D) who are highly educated,

athletically inclined,

and model citizens. To do this is costly; thus we require a great amount of funding.

32. Unfortunately, the money that we receive in

(A) gifts
(B) fines
(C) grants
(D) tuition

from our students

33. is not enough to cover these costs. This year,

(A) we have raised
(B) we would like to raise
(C) we wanted a raise
(D) we are giving a raise of

2.5 million dollars in donations. The money that we receive will be spent in several ways.

GO ON TO THE NEXT PAGE

For instance, we will use some money to establish a scholarship fund for students

34.
(A) with families and low incomes.
(B) by low-income families.
(C) from families with low incomes.
(D) in families for low incomes.

These scholarships will enable us to accept

35. high-quality students who would otherwise not be able to
(A) cost
(B) spend
(C) afford
(D) purchase
to attend

our school. We also hope to provide several buildings, including the gymnasium and

36. auditorium, with
(A) more advanced facilities,
(B) more facilities that advanced,
(C) the most facilities that advanced,
(D) as most advanced as the facilities,
and we intend to hire three new

faculty members. If you can make a donation to our school, we would greatly appreciate it.

Donald Ritter

Headmaster

GO ON TO THE NEXT PAGE

Questions 37–42 refer to the following essay.

37. An orchestra is a large assemblage of musicians who

| (A) play |
| (B) plays |
| (C) are playing |
| (D) will play |

various instruments. Four major musical instrument groups—strings, woodwinds,

38. brass horns, and percussion instruments—are

| (A) listened |
| (B) participated |
| (C) represented |
| (D) appointed |

39. orchestra. The strings

| (A) include |
| (B) involve |
| (C) contain |
| (D) consist |

of violins, violas, cellos, and double bases,

but many orchestras also have a harp. Flutes, piccolos, saxophones, oboes,

40. and bassoons are the woodwind instruments

| (A) which have appeared. |
| (B) that appear. |
| (C) what are appearing. |
| (D) which appeared. |

Included among the brass instruments are trumpets, trombones, tubas, and French

GO ON TO THE NEXT PAGE

horns. Finally, the percussion instruments are drums, cymbals, triangles, gongs,

xylophones, and bells. In addition, there are typically one or two pianos in an

41. orchestra.

(A) The musicians are grouped together

(B) A group of musicians together

(C) Grouped together, the musicians

(D) Some musicians, who are grouped together,

in a crescent shape

in front of the conductor. The strings are usually in the front on the left and right

while the woodwinds are in the center behind the strings with the brass instruments

42. behind them. The percussion instruments are always located at the

(A) stern

(B) border

(C) rear

(D) front

of the orchestra.

STOP

NO TEST MATERIAL ON THIS PAGE

Reading Comprehension

In this section of the test, you will read six texts and answer 42 questions. Choose the correct answer to each question and mark the letter of the correct answer on your answer sheet.

Before you start, read the sample text and the sample questions below.

Sample Text

One of the most valued metals in the world is gold. It is an extremely versatile metal, which accounts for its high price. While the vast majority of gold is used to make jewelry, it has other applications. For instance, gold is found in many electronic devices because it conducts electricity so well. It is also used as currency and has some medical applications.

Sample Question 1

What would be the best title for this passage?

(A) Gold and Its Uses
(B) Where to Find Gold
(C) How Much Is Gold Worth?
(D) Making Gold Jewelry

The correct answer is (A), "Gold and Its Uses."

Sample Question 2

What does the author say about gold?

(A) It costs more than any other metal.
(B) People mostly use it for jewelry.
(C) Several countries have gold currency.
(D) Electronic items use large amounts of gold.

The correct answer is (B), "People mostly use it for jewelry."

GO ON TO THE NEXT PAGE

Questions 1–7 are about the following letter.

Dear Thomas,

I am curious as to whether or not you are still planning to go on that skiing trip with your family this winter vacation. I ask because, if you are not going, you might find this program I heard about today to be interesting. Apparently, Westfield State University, our local college, is going to hold an art seminar for thirty students.

According to the brochure I have, three of the school's top faculty members are going to teach the seminar. They are planning to focus on painting. But there will also be lessons on sculpture and etching. And here is the best part: It does not cost anything to attend the seminar. However, you have to apply for a position. You can do that by submitting a sample of your work. I know how much you love art, so this could be a great opportunity for you. You probably do not want to give up going skiing, but this is a once-in-a-lifetime event. You might not want to <u>pass up</u> this chance. Let me know if you need any more information.

Your friend,
Susan

GO ON TO THE NEXT PAGE

1. Why did the author write this letter?

   (A) To describe her winter plans
   (B) To discuss an upcoming art exhibit
   (C) To recommend a special program
   (D) To compliment the local college

2. What does the author indicate about Thomas's plans for winter vacation?

   (A) He is going to take some art classes.
   (B) He will go on a trip with his family.
   (C) He will learn how to ski at a resort.
   (D) He is going to travel abroad somewhere.

3. What can be inferred from the letter about Westfield State University?

   (A) It is one of the top schools in the state.
   (B) It is located near the home of the author.
   (C) It offers several programs during winter.
   (D) High school students can take regular classes there.

4. Which of the following is NOT mentioned about the seminar?

   (A) Where it is going to be
   (B) How long it is going to last
   (C) How many students may take it
   (D) What is going to be taught

5. According to the letter, how can a student get into the seminar?

   (A) By applying online
   (B) By getting recommended by a teacher
   (C) By sending in a work of art
   (D) By paying an entrance fee

6. In line 11, the phrase pass up is closest in meaning to _____.

   (A) omit
   (B) ignore
   (C) forget
   (D) miss

7. What can be inferred from the letter about the author?

   (A) She intends to apply to the seminar along with Thomas.
   (B) She believes Thomas will not get a similar chance again.
   (C) She thinks that she is a better artist than Thomas.
   (D) She took part in the seminar the previous year.

GO ON TO THE NEXT PAGE

Questions 8–13 are about the following announcement.

Students,

    You all need to know that Ms. Melvin, the tenth grade history teacher, is going to be unable to complete the spring semester. Ms. Melvin suffered some serious injuries in a car crash over the weekend. She remains hospitalized and is not expected to be released until sometime during the summer. Fortunately, her doctors believe that she will make a complete recovery. You can feel free to drop by and see how she is doing at Memorial Hospital during regular visiting hours. She will surely appreciate the company.

    To replace Ms. Melvin, a new teacher has been hired. His name is Mr. Potter, and he comes from Centerville High School, where he was employed as a substitute teacher. Mr. Potter was highly recommended by the principal of Centerville High School, and we are <u>optimistic</u> that you will enjoy taking classes with him. Please be sure to <u>welcome</u> him to the school. We expect you to be on your best behavior during the final month of the semester and to treat Mr. Potter as you do all of our other faculty members.

Paul Delaney
Principal

GO ON TO THE NEXT PAGE

8. **What is the purpose of this announcement?**

    (A) To discuss a change in teachers
    (B) To announcing the firing of a teacher
    (C) To praise Ms. Melvin for her work
    (D) To tell a story about Mr. Potter

9. **What happened to Ms. Melvin?**

    (A) She transferred to another school.
    (B) She resigned her position.
    (C) She got employed at a hospital.
    (D) She was hurt in an accident.

10. **In line 10, the word optimistic is closest in meaning to _____.**

    (A) appreciative
    (B) determined
    (C) positive
    (D) convinced

11. **In line 11, the word welcome is closest in meaning to _____.**

    (A) thank
    (B) greet
    (C) admit
    (D) approve of

12. **Based on the announcement, what is probably true about Mr. Potter?**

    (A) He has never worked full time before.
    (B) He has a master's degree in history.
    (C) He recently graduated from school.
    (D) His principal liked the work he did.

13. **What does the principal tell the students to do?**

    (A) Behave nicely to Mr. Potter
    (B) Study hard in their classes
    (C) Call Ms. Melvin and speak with her
    (D) Organize a visit to the hospital

GO ON TO THE NEXT PAGE

Questions 14–19 are about the following passage.

While Western medicine is common throughout the world, it is not the only type of medicine that people practice. Another kind of medical treatment is known as acupuncture. In general, it is considered to be an alternative type of medicine. It was developed in China well over one thousand years ago, and it is widely believed to have originated in China. Acupuncture involves
5 the inserting of multiple needles into the body. The needles are placed at certain points in the body depending on the type of problem the patient has. According to the theory behind acupuncture, there are places on the skin that are connected to different parts of the body. By pricking the skin with needles at these points, an acupuncturist can help a patient either relieve pain or cure various problems.

10 Acupuncture is popular in many parts of Asia. It is also becoming more common and attracting new patients in Europe and North America. But many people believe is in <u>ineffective</u>. The main reason they feel that way is that it is difficult to understand how the entire process works. Research into acupuncture's capabilities has yielded varying results. Some studies show that it is quite effective at relieving pain. Other <u>ones</u>, however, claim that it is merely like a placebo. In other words, people
15 believe acupuncture treatment will be effective, so it winds up helping them.

GO ON TO THE NEXT PAGE

14. **What is the best title for the passage?**

(A) A New Type of Medicine

(B) All about Acupuncture

(C) Western Medicine vs. Acupuncture

(D) Acupuncture: Does It Work?

15. **What does the author imply about acupuncture?**

(A) It is developed in China.

(B) Some Western doctors use it.

(C) It costs less than Western medicine.

(D) The needles used vary in size.

16. **Paragraph 1 supports which of the following statements?**

(A) The needles used can sometimes hurt the patients.

(B) Most of the needles are inserted in the patient's back.

(C) Acupuncturists use more than one needle at a time.

(D) Most acupuncture is used to treat fatal diseases.

17. **Where is acupuncture becoming practiced more often?**

(A) In Asia

(B) In Australia

(C) In Africa

(D) In Europe

18. **In line 11, the word <u>ineffective</u> is closest in meaning to _____.**

(A) useless

(B) doubtful

(C) abnormal

(D) fraudulent

19. **In line 14, the word <u>ones</u> refers to _____.**

(A) practitioners

(B) acupuncture's capabilities

(C) varying results

(D) some studies

GO ON TO THE NEXT PAGE

Questions 20–25 are about the following passage.

One of the most effective predators among all insects is the praying mantis. This animal is about twelve to fifteen centimeters in length and is either green or brown in color. That enables it to blend in with its natural habitats, which are forests and jungles. The praying mantis has a large triangular-shaped head and five eyes. Two of them are large compound eyes while there are also three
5 smaller simple eyes in the middle. They combine to give the insect an exceptional range of vision. The distinguishing feature of the praying mantis is its two large front legs. They are raised up, which makes the insect appear as if it is praying like a person in a church.

Its front legs as well as <u>its blinding speed</u> are the keys to the hunting skills of the praying mantis. It eats other insects, especially moths, crickets, grasshoppers, and flies. It typically lies in wait so that
10 it can ambush its prey. When an insect walks, hops, or flies by, it swiftly pounces and grabs the insect with its front legs. The legs have barbs on them, which make it easier for the praying mantis to hold <u>a struggling insect</u>. Once it catches an insect, the praying mantis then uses its powerful mandibles to eat its catch.

A praying mantis has a life span of around twelve months. At some point during its life, the
15 insect mates. On many occasions, right after the male and female mate, the female kills and eats the male. Sometime later, she lays up to 400 eggs at a time. These eggs subsequently hatch into nymphs—immature adults. They are small, have no wings, and cannot reproduce. Gradually, they transform into adult praying mantises.

GO ON TO THE NEXT PAGE

20. What is the passage mainly about?

(A) The characteristics of the praying mantis

(B) How the praying mantis catches its prey

(C) The mating habits of the praying mantis

(D) Where the praying mantis typically lives

21. Which of the following is NOT mentioned in the passage about the praying mantis?

(A) The number of eyes that it has

(B) Where it typically can be found

(C) The quality of its vision

(D) The animals that often hunt it

22. What does the author point out by writing about the praying mantis using its blinding speed in line 8?

(A) It can move very quickly.

(B) It cannot see well.

(C) Its reaction time is slow.

(D) Its look can paralyze some creatures.

23. The author uses moths, crickets, grasshoppers, and flies as examples of _____ .

(A) predators that are threats to the praying mantis

(B) creatures that live together with the praying mantis

(C) animals that the praying mantis usually ignores

(D) animals that the praying mantis often consumes

24. What does the author point out by writing about the praying mantis holding a struggling insect in line 12?

(A) The insect is fighting the praying mantis.

(B) The praying mantis is hunting the insect.

(C) The insect is trying to escape.

(D) The praying mantis is eating the insect.

25. What does the author say about praying mantis nymphs?

(A) They kill and eat other praying mantises.

(B) They lack the wings that adults have.

(C) They can function like mature adults.

(D) They are capable of laying eggs.

GO ON TO THE NEXT PAGE

Questions 26–32 are about the following story.

Last Monday morning, the students in Mr. Morrison's science classes were excited. They were having their annual science fair. All of the students had worked hard to come up with something for the event, and they were ready to display the results of their work.

The students set up their exhibits inside the school gym. There were more than 100 displays in all.
5 Some of the displays were large and impressive creations made by the students while others showed the <u>outcomes</u> of experiments that students had conducted in laboratories.

The judges walked around and looked carefully at all of the exhibits. They took notes on all of them. Then, they spoke with several teachers before making <u>their</u> final decisions.

"May I have your attention, please," said Mr. Morrison. "To begin with, I'd like to thank the
10 students for the great work they did this year. This is clearly the best science fair we've ever had." The students all cheered after hearing Mr. Morrison make that remark.

"The judges have selected the winners of the science fair. First, I'd like to announce the third-place winner. I know she had a lot of fun doing her experiment in the lab. And the judges loved her work. So let's congratulate Sarah Rafael for the research that she did on bacteria." Everyone in the
15 audience clapped as Sarah went to the front to receive her prize.

"The second-place winner," said Mr. Morrison, "made a unique contribution to the science fair. He designed and programmed his own computer game, which I know many of you had fun with. Let's congratulate Tim Simpson, the second-place winner."

After Tim received his prize, Mr. Morrison spoke one more time. "And now it's the moment we've
20 all been waiting for. The first-place winner's work was <u>breathtaking</u>. In fact, I've never seen a better robot made by anyone. So let's congratulate Molly Smith. She's this year's winner of the science fair."

26. **What would be the best title for the story?**

    (A) Molly Smith's Science Project
    (B) Let's See Who Won the Science Fair
    (C) Mr. Morrison's Students
    (D) The School Science Fair

27. **In line 6, the word <u>outcomes</u> is closest in meaning to _____.**

    (A) appearances
    (B) outlines
    (C) expectations
    (D) results

28. **In line 8, the word <u>their</u> refers to _____.**

    (A) the judges
    (B) all of the exhibits
    (C) notes
    (D) several teachers

29. **Based on his comments, what does Mr. Morrison think about this year's science fair?**

    (A) It is the best ever at the school.
    (B) It could have been better.
    (C) It has some good entrants.
    (D) It needs more creative experiments.

30. **What did Sarah Rafael do for the science fair?**

    (A) She created a computer game.
    (B) She experimented with bacteria.
    (C) She built her own robot.
    (D) She wrote a computer program.

31. **What can be inferred from the story about Tim Simpson?**

    (A) His science project is something people can play.
    (B) He believes he should have come in first place.
    (C) He worked with Mr. Morrison to do his project.
    (D) His parents assisted him in doing his project.

32. **In line 20, the word <u>breathtaking</u> is closest in meaning to _____.**

    (A) magnificent
    (B) original
    (C) unmatched
    (D) imaginative

GO ON TO THE NEXT PAGE

Questions 33–42 are about the following passage.

When two or more different elements or compounds are combined, they often produce a chemical reaction. What kind of reaction takes place depends upon the elements or compounds that are involved. In all cases, however, when there is a chemical reaction, a new compound is formed. There is not merely a physical change like there is during a physical reaction. For instance, when
5 ice melts and becomes water, that is not a chemical change; it is a physical one. The reason is that, chemically speaking, the ice and water are the same thing. They are only in different physical states. There are six main types of chemical reactions. They are combustion, synthesis, decomposition, single-displacement, double-displacement, and acid-base reactions.

Combustion happens when oxygen combines with another compound. When this occurs, heat
10 and fire are produced. A <u>catalyst</u>, such as a spark, is needed for combustion to take place. One example of this is when gas and oxygen burn in a car's engine. The spark plugs in the engine provide the fire necessary to initiate the chemical reaction.

As for synthesis, it happens when two elements or compounds combine to form a new compound. For example, hydrogen and oxygen can unite to form water, and sodium and chlorine can come
15 together to form salt. Decomposition is the reverse. When <u>it</u> takes place, a compound breaks down into its basic <u>components</u>. Thus water transforms into hydrogen and oxygen atoms while salt becomes sodium and chlorine.

A single-displacement reaction happens when one element replaces another one in a compound. As an example, copper and silver nitrate can undergo a chemical reaction. The copper displaces
20 the silver and forms copper nitrate. And the silver comes to exist as individual crystals. A double-replacement reaction happens when different parts of two compounds <u>swap</u> places to form two new compounds. For instance, lead nitrate can combine with potassium iodine. After a chemical reaction, two new compounds—lead iodine and potassium nitrate—are formed. Last of all, acid-base reactions occur when an acid and base are combined. After exchanging protons, the two compounds
25 form water as well as some kind of salt.

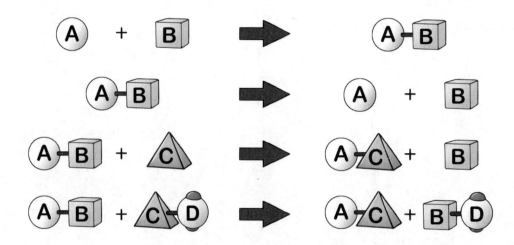

GO ON TO THE NEXT PAGE

33. **What would be the most appropriate headline for this article?**

(A) Physical and Chemical Reactions

(B) How Chemical Reactions Occur

(C) Combining Two Elements

(D) What Kind of Reaction Is It?

34. **Which of the following is true regarding chemical reactions?**

(A) Some elements are unable to react with others.

(B) They must include a solid and a liquid.

(C) The compounds involved change states of matter.

(D) They result in the formation of a new compound.

35. **According to the passage, all of the following are chemical reactions EXCEPT** _____.

(A) single-displacement reactions

(B) decomposition reactions

(C) physical reactions

(D) synthesis reactions

36. **In line 10, the word catalyst is closest in meaning to** _____.

(A) medium

(B) sponsor

(C) conversion

(D) tool

37. **What example does the author use to show a combustion reaction?**

(A) Ice melting and becoming water

(B) Gas and oxygen producing heat and fire

(C) Water breaking down into hydrogen and oxygen

(D) Copper and silver nitrate combining

38. **Why does the author mention sodium and chlorine?**

(A) To give the chemical formula for salt

(B) To provide an example of a synthesis reaction

(C) To contrast them with hydrogen and oxygen

(D) To prove that synthesis and decomposition are similar

39. **In line 15, the word it refers to** _____.

(A) a new compound

(B) water

(C) salt

(D) decomposition

40. **In line 16, the word components is closest in meaning to** _____.

(A) parts

(B) atoms

(C) traits

(D) kinds

41. **In line 21, the word swap is closest in meaning to** _____.

(A) reveal

(B) commit to

(C) trade

(D) join

42. **What happens during an acid-base reaction?**

(A) Two elements combine.

(B) Two elements change places.

(C) A compound breaks down.

(D) Salt and water are formed.

STOP

Practice
Test 9

Listening
Comprehension

听力音频

The listening section has 42 questions. Follow along as you listen to the directions to the listening section.

Directions

In this section of the test, you will hear talks and conversations. Each talk or conversation is followed by one question. Choose the best answer to each question and mark the letter of the correct answer on your answer sheet. You will hear each talk or conversation only one time.

Here is an example: 🔊

Why is the boy happy?

(A) He was selected for the baseball team.
(B) He finished doing his homework.
(C) He got an A on his math test.
(D) He has no more classes for the day.

The correct answer is (A), "He was selected for the baseball team."

Here is another example: 🔊

What are the speakers mainly talking about?

(A) A paper the girl must turn in
(B) The quality of the girl's work
(C) The teacher's next class
(D) The girl's next writing assignment

The correct answer is (B), "The quality of the girl's work."

Go on to the next page, and the test will begin with question number one.

GO ON TO THE NEXT PAGE >

1. **What do the students imply about Ms. Reardon?**

   (A) She is the students' favorite instructor.

   (B) She is the social studies teacher.

   (C) She plans to retire soon.

   (D) She teaches the students before noon.

2. **When is the Spanish club going to meet?**

   (A) During lunchtime today

   (B) After school today

   (C) Tomorrow before school

   (D) Tomorrow in the afternoon

3. **Why does the teacher mention the student's parents?**

   (A) To thank the student for introducing them

   (B) To request a meeting with them

   (C) To mention they need to sign his permission slip

   (D) To say they can help him with his work

4. **Why is the student discussing her homework?**

   (A) To find out why an answer was wrong

   (B) To ask to turn it in at a later time

   (C) To determine when she must submit it

   (D) To find out her grade on it

5. **What is the girl going to do in the evening?**

   (A) Call the boy on the telephone

   (B) Send the boy an email

   (C) Visit the boy at his home

   (D) Do a science experiment with the boy

6. **What is the teacher mainly explaining?**

   (A) When the boy's performance will be

   (B) Why the boy needs to take speech lessons

   (C) What type of speech the boy should make

   (D) How the boy can raise his grade

7. **What is the purpose of the announcement?**

   (A) To describe where the crosswalk is

   (B) To provide some safety tips

   (C) To announce a safety inspection

   (D) To warn students about accidents

8. **What will the teacher probably do next?**

   (A) End class for the day

   (B) Answer any questions the students have

   (C) Continue speaking to the class

   (D) Show the students a map

9. **What is the teacher mainly talking about?**

   (A) An upcoming exam

   (B) The students' essays

   (C) How to type properly

   (D) The five-paragraph style

GO ON TO THE NEXT PAGE

Now you will hear longer talks or conversations. Each talk or conversation will be followed by three or more questions. Choose the best answer to each question and mark the letter of the correct answer on your answer sheet. You will hear each talk or conversation only one time.

10. **What does the teacher say about the girl's paper?**

(A) It was the best one in the class.

(B) She received a 99 on it.

(C) She made more than one mistake.

(D) It needs to be revised a lot.

11. **What does the girl imply when she says this: "I think I remember hearing something about the competition"?**

(A) She knows very little about the competition.

(B) She is interested in learning more about the event.

(C) She wants the teacher to continue speaking to her.

(D) She is going to do some research on the event.

12. **What does the teacher suggest about the student?**

(A) She does not need to prepare for the competition.

(B) The other students write better than she does.

(C) It is important that she write in her journal every day.

(D) Her writing qualifies her for the competition.

13. **What is the student going to do after school today?**

(A) Submit her essay to the competition

(B) Meet the teacher in the classroom

(C) Go over essays with some other students

(D) Revise the essay that she just wrote

14. **What are the students mainly discussing?**

(A) Their current majors

(B) Their plans for college

(C) Their graduation ceremony

(D) Their summer jobs

15. **What can be inferred about the girl?**

(A) She is going to attend an elite college.

(B) She has already found a summer job.

(C) She gets better grades than the boy.

(D) She cannot afford to travel abroad.

16. **What is the girl thinking about majoring in?**

(A) Physics

(B) Biology

(C) Chemistry

(D) Math

17. **When is the boy going to choose his college major?**

(A) Before his freshman year

(B) During his freshman year

(C) During his sophomore year

(D) After his sophomore year

GO ON TO THE NEXT PAGE

18. **What are the speakers talking about?**

    (A) The boy's sources for his paper

    (B) The best websites to use

    (C) Reference books in the library

    (D) How the boy can improve his grade

19. **What does the teacher say about the boy's work?**

    (A) It is not long enough.

    (B) It contains factual mistakes.

    (C) It makes poor arguments.

    (D) It lacks enough sources.

20. **Why does the teacher mention schools and government agencies?**

    (A) To provide the addresses of their websites

    (B) To recommend their websites to the boy

    (C) To compare them with magazines, journals, and newspapers

    (D) To claim that they always have websites

21. **Why does the teacher talk about the library?**

    (A) To note that the boy can access the Internet there

    (B) To recommend that the boy check out some books from it

    (C) To suggest that the boy use the reference books in it

    (D) To say that it is a quiet place where the boy can do research

22. **What did the girl do during summer vacation?**

    (A) She learned to play the piano.

    (B) She took flute lessons.

    (C) She practiced the clarinet.

    (D) She played in an orchestra.

23. **What can be inferred about the boy?**

    (A) He can play a musical instrument.

    (B) He is the girl's best friend.

    (C) He belongs to an athletic team.

    (D) He does not do any extracurricular activities.

24. **According to the boy, what is true about the school orchestra?**

    (A) Its director is very unpopular.

    (B) It will give a performance in one month.

    (C) It has had the same director for ten years.

    (D) It has a low number of members.

25. **What is the girl going to do after lunch today?**

    (A) Audition for the orchestra

    (B) Practice with the orchestra

    (C) Take a private music lesson

    (D) Go to Mr. Spartan's office

GO ON TO THE NEXT PAGE

26. What is the main topic of the talk?

(A) The world's fastest airplanes

(B) The breaking of the sound barrier

(C) Captain Chuck Yeager

(D) The Bell X-1 and the Concorde

27. Why does the teacher mention the Bell X-1?

(A) To compare it with the B-29 Superfortress

(B) To describe its highly advanced engine in detail

(C) To say it was Captain Chuck Yeager's favorite airplane

(D) To name the first plane to exceed the speed of sound

28. What does the teacher suggest about the sound barrier?

(A) It can cause physical pain to people when it is exceeded.

(B) There were many incorrect theories about it before it was broken.

(C) The speed needed to break it depends upon a person's altitude.

(D) It does not always produce sonic booms when it is exceeded.

29. According to the teacher, what was the first passenger airplane to break the speed of sound?

(A) The Concorde

(B) The Bell X-1

(C) The Tupolev Tu-144

(D) The B-29 Superfortress

30. What is the subject of the talk?

(A) Different types of plants

(B) Roots, stems, and leaves

(C) The root systems of plants

(D) Nutrients that plants need

31. What does the teacher say about roots?

(A) Some of them can grow above the ground.

(B) They do not grow deep underground.

(C) Most of them resemble taproots.

(D) They remove nutrients from the ground.

32. According to the teacher, which plants have taproots?

(A) Desert plants

(B) Pine trees

(C) Bushes

(D) Flowers

33. Why does the teacher talk about desert plants?

(A) To describe their root systems

(B) To claim they need very little water

(C) To point out that they have unique stems

(D) To discuss their leaves in detail

34. What will the teacher probably do next?

(A) Start a class discussion

(B) Show some pictures of root systems

(C) Begin talking about stems

(D) Explain the functions of leaves

GO ON TO THE NEXT PAGE

35. What is the main topic of the discussion?

(A) When modern humans evolved

(B) How people moved to other continents

(C) Why early humans left Africa

(D) Which parts of Africa modern humans lived in

36. Why does the girl suggest that the Middle East is a desert environment?

(A) To disagree with one of the boy's statements

(B) To compare it with the region where she lives

(C) To argue that few humans can survive there

(D) To contrast its climate with that of Africa's

37. What does the teacher imply about the Middle East?

(A) Modern humans might have evolved there.

(B) It has enough water to support large communities of people.

(C) The first human civilizations were established in it.

(D) Its climate has undergone changes over the years.

38. What does the teacher say about wars in Africa?

(A) There is little archaeological evidence of them.

(B) They were fought on a fairly large scale.

(C) Most of them lasted for a long period of time.

(D) The losers of them might have left the continent.

39. Why does the teacher mention *Beowulf*?

(A) To describe the events in the poem

(B) To claim it was written in the Old English period

(C) To point out the difficulty of reading the story

(D) To tell the students how much he likes it

40. What does the teacher suggest about Middle English?

(A) It resembles modern English very much.

(B) It has more interesting literature than Old English.

(C) It borrowed many words from other languages.

(D) It is easier to read than Old English.

41. What did Geoffrey Chaucer write?

(A) *Le Morte d'Arthur*

(B) *The Canterbury Tales*

(C) *Sir Gawain and the Green Knight*

(D) *Pearl*

42. What is probably true about the teacher?

(A) He cannot read Old English.

(B) He likes Middle English poetry.

(C) He is eager to teacher Renaissance literature.

(D) He writes poems in modern English.

312

STOP

Language Form and Meaning

Directions

In this section of the test, you will answer 42 questions found in seven different texts. Within each text are boxes that contain four possible ways to complete a sentence. Choose the word or words in each box that correctly complete each sentence. Mark the letter of the correct answer on your answer sheet.

Here are two sample questions:

1. For decades,

> (A) the people will hear rumors
> (B) people are hearing rumors
> (C) the people hear rumors
> (D) people had heard rumors

that there was a huge landmass

located south of Australia, yet no one had been able to find it. It was not until 1820

2. that the first

> (A) guaranteed
> (B) confirmed
> (C) requested
> (D) approved

sighting of the continent of Antarctica, by a Russian

sailor, was made.

The correct answer to **Sample 1** is (D), "people had heard rumors." The correct answer to **Sample 2** is (B), "confirmed."

GO ON TO THE NEXT PAGE

Questions 1–4 refer to the following brochure.

Due to demand by both students and parents,

1. the school has decided

(A) adding three new courses
(B) to add three new courses
(C) with the adding of three new courses
(D) on three new courses added

starting

2. next semester. All three of these classes are

(A) necessities
(B) workshops
(C) electives
(D) majors

and are

accordingly not required for students to graduate. In addition, the classes are

limited in size to twenty-five students. If there are fewer than twenty-five

GO ON TO THE NEXT PAGE

students who register for each class, then all of those individuals may

3.

(A) enroll
(B) register
(C) enlist
(D) participate

in them. If, however, more than twenty-five students try to sign

4. up, a lottery will be held to determine

(A) with whom students will take them.
(B) why students can take them.
(C) when students are taking them.
(D) which students can take them.

The new classes and their instructors are:

Class	Instructor	Time
Economic	Mr. Chandler	9:00 – 9:50
Computer Programming	Ms. Estevez	1:00 – 1:50
Ethics	Mr. Augustine	2:00 – 2:50

GO ON TO THE NEXT PAGE

Questions 5–8 refer to the following article in the student newspaper.

On Friday, April 10, school headmaster David Jones announced that

5.
(A) the school has planned to
(B) having planned, the school
(C) the school has plans for
(D) with planning, the school has

the renovation of both its science

laboratories over the summer. The school realizes the need to modernize

6. the lab equipment to make its students

(A) more competitive
(B) the most competitive
(C) as competitive as
(D) so competitive that

than those individuals at other area schools. Thanks to a grant from

the Wilson Foundation, the school now has access to enough financial

7.

(A) resources
(B) materials
(C) abilities
(D) skills

to accomplish this goal. The renovations are set to

8. take place during the summer, and they

(A) will complete
(B) must have completed
(C) should be completed
(D) are complete

before students return to school for the start of the fall semester.

GO ON TO THE NEXT PAGE

Questions 9–12 refer to the following announcement.

To all students,

9. The school has decided to

(A) alter
(B) attune
(C) administer
(D) arrange

its policy on how students

can make up any examinations they miss due to being absent from an illness.

According to the new policy, if someone cannot take a test because he or she is sick,

10. the student must provide a note from a

(A) license
(B) licenses
(C) licensed
(D) licensing

doctor.

GO ON TO THE NEXT PAGE

Failure to provide a note will result in the student's excuse not being accepted.

Then, the student must work with the class instructor to find a mutually

11. acceptable time

(A) making up an examination.
(B) for taking a made-up examination.
(C) to take a makeup examination.
(D) take an examination to make up.

However,

12.

(A) all tests must be completed
(B) you are completing all the tests
(C) tests are all being completed
(D) completing all of the tests

within one week of the student's

return to school.

GO ON TO THE NEXT PAGE

Questions 13–20 refer to the following letter.

Dear Students,

13.
(A) We have nearly time
(B) It is almost time
(C) There is some time
(D) They have the time

to start another school year, and we hope all of

14. you are
(A) more excited
(B) the most excited
(C) the most excited of
(D) as excited as

the faculty, staff, and I are. There have

been a few changes at the school that you need to be aware of. To begin with,

15. we have
(A) interviewed
(B) transferred
(C) attained
(D) hired

an extra member of the faculty. Bruce Thompson

16. is our
(A) newer
(B) newer than
(C) newest
(D) the newest

math instructor, and he will teach both calculus and

17. geometry. We believe that all of you
(A) enjoy
(B) are enjoying
(C) will enjoy
(D) have enjoyed

taking classes with

Mr. Thompson. Secondly, you will all be pleased to see that we have added a

GO ON TO THE NEXT PAGE

computer laboratory to the main building. The laboratory has twenty

18. state-of-the-art computers, which I am

(A) positive
(B) concerned
(C) aware
(D) alert

everyone will put

19. to good use.

(A) Lastly, for all,
(B) Lastly, with all,
(C) Last in all,
(D) Last of all,

we have added more than 500 new books

to the school library. These books were donated by Julie Johnson, a school alumna

20.

(A) who graduated in 1987.
(B) that will graduate in 1987.
(C) which was graduated in 1987.
(D) when it was 1987, graduated.

Sincerely,

Robert Bailey

Principal

GO ON TO THE NEXT PAGE

Questions 21–28 refer to the following essay.

Since usage of the Internet became widespread in the 1990s, it has

21.
(A) discovered
(B) provided
(C) approved
(D) resulted

a number of advantages for people. For example, people use

the Internet to communicate with others, to find information, to make purchases,

22. and
(A) to entertain.
(B) to entertaining.
(C) to be entertained.
(D) to be entertaining.

Unfortunately, some people use the Internet for

23. illegal purposes.
(A) Downloading files from the Internet
(B) The Internet and the downloaded files
(C) They, after using the Internet to download files
(D) By using the Internet to download files

24. without paying for them is one of
(A) as common as
(B) more common
(C) most common
(D) the most common
illegal activities

people utilize the Internet for. The main things that people illegally download are

GO ON TO THE NEXT PAGE

music, movies, TV programs, and books. This Internet piracy,

25.

(A) which they are called,
(B) what it was called,
(C) as it is called,
(D) how it was called,

costs the makers of these products

billions of dollars a year. In the past decade, sales of music CDs and movie

26. and TV program DVDs have

(A) manufactured
(B) staggered
(C) removed
(D) declined

considerably. Many people

27. simply download TV shows and watch them

(A) whenever they want.
(B) whomever we want.
(C) whichever they want.
(D) however we want.

Some TV shows have been cancelled due to the resulting low ratings.

28. Thus far, most

(A) requests
(B) attempts
(C) demands
(D) challenges

at stopping Internet piracy have failed.

GO ON TO THE NEXT PAGE

Questions 29–34 refer to the following email.

Dear Karen,

I am so sad you were absent today and thus

29.

(A) are scheduled to go on a field trip.

(B) could not go on our field trip.

(C) the field trip, which was gone on.

(D) had to go on the field trip.

You will not believe

how much fun we had at the science museum. I know we had both thought

30. it would be boring, but it was actually the complete

(A) agenda.

(B) opposite.

(C) excitement.

(D) guidance.

First, we got to admire the museum's rock collection. The museum had

31. a huge exhibit

(A) in precious gems,

(B) not precious gems,

(C) and precious gems,

(D) with precious gems,

such as diamonds, emeralds,

and rubies. After that, we saw a display on the Serengeti in Africa. We learned

GO ON TO THE NEXT PAGE

32. about the unique ecosystem of that area and

(A) got to watch a movie
(B) will get to watch a movie
(C) the movie got watched
(D) a movie was being watched

33. on the animal migrations that take place there

(A) annually.
(B) separately.
(C) considerably.
(D) typically.

Lastly, we saw an exhibit that was called Birds of the Americas.

34.

(A) Displays, of which there were many,
(B) There were all kinds of displays
(C) He had many kinds of displays
(D) They will have lots of displays

of various species of birds,

and the museum also had some original prints that were made by John J.

Audubon. I really wish you had been able to attend. You would have loved it.

Your friend,

Candice

GO ON TO THE NEXT PAGE

Questions 35–42 refer to the following newspaper article.

35. The city council just announced that it

(A) closes
(B) has closed
(C) had closed
(D) is going to close

one of

36. the high schools in the city because of a lack of

(A) interest.
(B) funding.
(C) attendance.
(D) facilities.

Hopewell High School will shut its doors for good on May 31 this year. The

37. school has been plagued by

(A) falling
(B) steady
(C) regular
(D) receding

numbers of students and only

has 268 currently enrolled whereas it had more than 500 ten years ago.

38. According to Derrick Burgess,

(A) the city council's member,
(B) a member of the city council,
(C) on the city council,
(D) in memory of the city council,

students have been leaving Hopewell for a number of reasons.

GO ON TO THE NEXT PAGE

39. The

- (A) neighbor
- (B) neighbors
- (C) neighboring
- (D) neighborhood

it is located in has seen its population decline

40. as

- (A) more people have been moving
- (B) people will move more
- (C) people, having moved,
- (D) more people and their moves

to the newer areas in the city.

In addition, poor public transportation in the area makes it difficult for many

students to get to the school and back home. The city council promised

41.

- (A) which new schools will be found
- (B) finding that new schools
- (C) that it will find new schools
- (D) the new schools that it has found

for the faculty and staff members

42. who will be affected by the

- (A) close.
- (B) closed.
- (C) closeness.
- (D) closure.

STOP

NO TEST MATERIAL ON THIS PAGE

Reading Comprehension

Directions

In this section of the test, you will read six texts and answer 42 questions. Choose the correct answer to each question and mark the letter of the correct answer on your answer sheet.

Before you start, read the sample text and the sample questions below.

Sample Text

One of the most valued metals in the world is gold. It is an extremely versatile metal, which accounts for its high price. While the vast majority of gold is used to make jewelry, it has other applications. For instance, gold is found in many electronic devices because it conducts electricity so well. It is also used as currency and has some medical applications.

Sample Question 1

What would be the best title for this passage?

(A) Gold and Its Uses
(B) Where to Find Gold
(C) How Much Is Gold Worth?
(D) Making Gold Jewelry

The correct answer is (A), "Gold and Its Uses."

Sample Question 2

What does the author say about gold?

(A) It costs more than any other metal.
(B) People mostly use it for jewelry.
(C) Several countries have gold currency.
(D) Electronic items use large amounts of gold.

The correct answer is (B), "People mostly use it for jewelry."

GO ON TO THE NEXT PAGE

Questions 1–6 are about the following newspaper article.

Students often prefer to spend their weekends hanging out at the shopping mall or sitting at their homes and watching television. But, thanks to a new volunteer program at
5 Samford High School, many of the students there are spending their weekends improving the lives of their neighbors.

Social studies teacher Wendy Foreman encouraged her students to do some volunteer
10 work at least once a week as soon as the semester began. She even started a club, which is called Help Your Neighbors. The results were beyond belief.

"Nearly fifty percent of the entire student
15 body joined the club," she said. The members of the club do all sorts of volunteer work. Some devote their time in area hospitals, soup kitchens, and animal shelters. Other students pick up trash in local parks and even along
20 the sides of roads. And some students have organized a food drive that donates food to underprivileged locals every week.

Ms. Foreman commented, "I couldn't be prouder of these students. It's great to see
25 them doing something productive during their free time. They're really getting involved in the community. They're definitely not typical teenagers."

GO ON TO THE NEXT PAGE

1. What would be the most appropriate headline for this article?

   (A) Be a Volunteer at Samford High School
   (B) Wendy Foreman and her Volunteer Activities
   (C) Student Volunteer Club Is Instant Success
   (D) How to Become a Successful Volunteer

2. In line 13, the phrase <u>beyond belief</u> is closest in meaning to _____.

   (A) unique
   (B) shocking
   (C) inspiring
   (D) frightful

3. What does the author say about Help Your Neighbors?

   (A) Almost half the students at the school are in it.
   (B) It has been in existence for an entire year.
   (C) The president of the club is Wendy Foreman.
   (D) Its student members are assigned projects to do.

4. In line 22, the word <u>underprivileged</u> is closest in meaning to _____.

   (A) discouraged
   (B) unemployed
   (C) unmotivated
   (D) deprived

5. Which is NOT mentioned as volunteer work done by the students?

   (A) Spending time working in hospitals
   (B) Giving food to people who need it
   (C) Working with homeless people
   (D) Cleaning up garbage in parks

6. Based on her comments, how does Wendy Foreman feel about the students in Help Your Neighbors?

   (A) She wishes that they would work harder.
   (B) She is pleased with the work they are doing.
   (C) She wants them to encourage others to join.
   (D) She thinks that they are normal teenagers.

GO ON TO THE NEXT PAGE

Questions 7–12 are about the following notice.

Dear students:

This year, we plan to take at least two field trips per semester. Please be aware of the following regarding field trips.

All students who are not yet eighteen years of age must submit a permission slip signed by a parent or guardian. This permission slip indicates that the parent or guardian <u>consents</u> to allowing the student to go on the field trip. Failure to submit a permission slip by the day of the field trip means that the student may not accompany the others off campus.

All students must also provide proof that they have medical insurance and that their insurance covers them in case of injury while on a field trip. Students may turn in this proof at the front office anytime. If <u>it</u> is not provided, the student will not be able to go on the field trip.

On field trips, all students must be on their best behavior. Students are expected to listen to their teachers and to follow the rules and regulations of the places that they visit. Failure to do so will result in some sort of punishment, such as detention or suspension.

David Prosser
Principal

GO ON TO THE NEXT PAGE

7. **What is the purpose of the notice?**

   (A) To inform the students about an upcoming field trip

   (B) To let the students know about some forms they must submit

   (C) To advise students on some punishments they may receive

   (D) To ask for the students' opinions on where to take field trips

8. **In line 5, the word consents is closest in meaning to _____.**

   (A) responds

   (B) agrees

   (C) stresses

   (D) obtains

9. **Based on the notice, what is probably true about some students at the school?**

   (A) They do not have to turn in permission slips.

   (B) They consider field trips educational experiences.

   (C) They would rather study than go on field trips.

   (D) They believe medical insurance costs too much money.

10. **In line 9, the word it refers to _____.**

   (A) injury

   (B) a field trip

   (C) this proof

   (D) the front office

11. **Paragraph 3 supports which of the following statements?**

   (A) All students at the school have some kind of medical insurance.

   (B) The school sells medical insurance to students who need it.

   (C) The front office can provide information on medical insurance.

   (D) Students must show the school that they have medical insurance.

12. **What will happen to students who misbehave while on field trips?**

   (A) They will not be allowed to go on future trips.

   (B) They will be punished in some way.

   (C) They will have to apologize to the teacher.

   (D) They will be forced to pay a fine.

GO ON TO THE NEXT PAGE

Questions 13–18 are about the following notice.

This summer, the school has decided to offer some special classes for students who desire to further their educations. These classes will not be offered for academic credit. In addition, students must pay a <u>nominal</u> fee of only $50 to attend them. These classes are going to be held from July 1 until August 10 and will meet every day from Monday to Friday from ten to noon. The following classes are being offered:

Class Name	Instructor	Comments
An Introduction to Latin	Ms. Stigler	Learn the elements of Latin, one of the most important languages in Western culture.
Automotive Repairs	Mr. Earnhardt	Learn how to repair cars, including how to take apart and put together a car engine.
The Basics of Cooking	Mr. Roundfield	Learn how to cook some simple entrées, appetizers, and desserts from one of the city's top chefs.

Each class is limited to fifteen students. Spots in the class will be filled on a first-come, first-served basis. However, students will have their reservations cancelled if they do not pay the fee within three business days of making <u>them</u>. Find out more about the classes and make reservations by calling Mrs. Landers at 676-4000.

GO ON TO THE NEXT PAGE

13. **What is the best title for the notice?**

   (A) Summer Classes Being Offered

   (B) Sign up for Classes for School Credit

   (C) Learn to Cook and to Speak a Foreign Language

   (D) Great Chance for 15 Lucky Students

14. **In line 3, the word <u>nominal</u> is closest in meaning to _____.**

   (A) refundable

   (B) minor

   (C) cash

   (D) required

15. **Which of the following is true regarding the classes?**

   (A) Students can get school credit for them.

   (B) They will last for eight weeks during summer.

   (C) The classes will be taught by school teachers.

   (D) They will be held for ten hours per week.

16. **Which of the following can be inferred from the schedule about the classes?**

   (A) The books for them will be provided by the teachers.

   (B) A student may only enroll in one of them.

   (C) They will be offered during winter break.

   (D) The students will have to do homework in them.

17. **According to the schedule, students can learn all of the following in the classes EXCEPT _____.**

   (A) how to drive a vehicle

   (B) how to fix an automobile

   (C) how to understand a language

   (D) how to cook some meals

18. **In line 8, the word <u>them</u> refers to _____.**

   (A) spots in the class

   (B) students

   (C) their reservations

   (D) three business days

GO ON TO THE NEXT PAGE

Questions 19–26 are about the following passage.

The atmosphere acts in several ways to support life on the Earth. One of these is that it protects the planet from <u>detrimental</u> radiation emitted by the sun. In addition, the atmosphere provides life-giving oxygen for animals and carbon dioxide for plants. The atmosphere may appear simple, but it is actually complex and has distinct layers. These layers are divided based upon their height above
5   sea level. There are five major layers of the atmosphere. They are the troposphere, stratosphere, mesosphere, thermosphere, and exosphere.

The troposphere is the layer of the atmosphere closest to the Earth's surface. It extends from the ground to approximately seventeen kilometers above sea level at its highest point. This layer contains the greatest mass of the atmosphere—around seventy-five to eighty percent. It is also the warmest
10   layer and has most of the weather that people experience.

The stratosphere extends from the troposphere to around fifty kilometers above sea level. It contains most of the rest of the atmosphere in addition to the ozone layer. <u>This</u> is the region that keeps the Earth safe from much of the sun's radiation. Temperatures are very cold at the lower part of the stratosphere but become warmer higher up due to the absorption of radiation.

15   The next three layers are found high above the planet's surface. The first is the mesosphere, which extends from the stratosphere to around eighty-five kilometers above sea level. This is the region where most meteors are <u>incinerated</u> as they hit the atmosphere. Temperatures drop once again in this layer. They may decline to more than minus 100 degrees Celsius. The fourth layer is the thermosphere. It extends all the way up to 690 kilometers above sea level. It is where the aurora borealis, or northern
20   lights, form. In addition, most spacecraft and space stations orbit the planet there. Temperatures in the thermosphere vary from extremely cold to extremely hot. Last is the exosphere. It extends thousands of kilometers above the ground until there is no longer an atmosphere but only outer space. Instead, there are simply random molecules of hydrogen and helium.

GO ON TO THE NEXT PAGE

19. In line 2, the word <u>detrimental</u> is closest in meaning to _____.

(A) harmful

(B) influential

(C) constant

(D) conditional

20. Based on the passage, what is probably true about the Earth's atmosphere?

(A) It has more mass than the planet itself.

(B) Humans still have a great deal to learn about it.

(C) Life on the planet could not exist without it.

(D) It formed over the course of billions of years.

21. Which of the following is true regarding the troposphere?

(A) It is the largest in area of all the layers of the atmosphere.

(B) It constantly changes due to the effects of weather.

(C) It covers the area upon which plants and animals live.

(D) It contains high amounts of both nitrogen and oxygen.

22. The author uses the ozone layer as an example of _____.

(A) a layer with fairly warm temperatures

(B) the largest layer of the atmosphere

(C) one part of the stratosphere

(D) a dangerous place filled with radiation

23. In line 12, the word <u>This</u> refers to _____.

(A) The stratosphere

(B) Sea level

(C) The atmosphere

(D) The ozone layer

24. In line 17, the word <u>incinerated</u> is closest in meaning to _____.

(A) exploded

(B) warded off

(C) repelled

(D) burned up

25. Where are the aurora borealis found?

(A) In the exosphere

(B) In the thermosphere

(C) In the stratosphere

(D) In the mesosphere

26. Paragraph 4 supports which of the following statements?

(A) Spacecraft and space stations orbit from the exosphere.

(B) The mesosphere is further from the ground than the thermosphere.

(C) The exosphere extends to the boundaries of outer space.

(D) The temperature may reach 100 degrees Celsius in the mesosphere.

GO ON TO THE NEXT PAGE

Questions 27–34 are about the following passage.

The American Founding Fathers were, as a group, among the most accomplished men in the history of any country. Among them were George Washington, Benjamin Franklin, James Madison, and John Adams. Another, who ranks as one of the greatest of <u>them</u>, was Thomas Jefferson. Thomas Jefferson was the third president of the United States. He was the founder of the University of
5   Virginia. He was responsible for the Louisiana Purchase, which more than doubled the size of the United States. And, most importantly, he was the author of the *Declaration of Independence*. It stated that the American colonies were free from English rule.

Born in 1743, Jefferson began receiving a classical education as a young child. He focused on learning languages, including Latin and Greek. He later went on to study at the College of William
10   and Mary, the second-oldest college in America after Harvard. There, Jefferson focused on law, which enabled him to become one of America's most knowledgeable lawyers.

It was Jefferson's study of law that prompted him to become an early supporter of the American independence movement. In the 1760s and 1770s, England began to levy a number of taxes on the American colonists. <u>Most colonists detested the taxes</u> and considered them oppressive. The colonists
15   further disliked the taxes because they had no representation in Parliament, the legislative body in England.

Jefferson was himself an elected member of the House of Burgesses. This was the legislative body of the colony of Virginia. He felt very strongly about the importance of the American colonies being represented in Parliament. Since King George III of England refused to allow that, Jefferson
20   spoke out strongly in favor of independence. He wrote essays in support of independence. Then, in a meeting of the Continental Congress in 1776, Jefferson—along with four other men—was chosen to write a declaration that the colonies were free from English rule. It took him seventeen days to come up with the document that would become known as the Declaration of Independence. Signed on July 4, 1776, it gave freedom to the American colonies and <u>cemented</u> Jefferson's place in history as one of
25   the greatest supporters of the cause of freedom.

GO ON TO THE NEXT PAGE

27. **What is the best title for the passage?**

    (A) The Third President of the United States

    (B) Thomas Jefferson: Author of the *Declaration of Independence*

    (C) How America Became Free from English Rule

    (D) Thomas Jefferson and King George III of England

28. **In line 3, the word them refers to** _____.

    (A) the American Founding Fathers

    (B) a group

    (C) any country

    (D) George Washington, Benjamin Franklin, James Madison, and John Adams

29. **What does the author say about Thomas Jefferson?**

    (A) He attended college at the University of Virginia.

    (B) He was one of the signers of the *Declaration of Independence*.

    (C) His actions made the United States become twice as large.

    (D) He is considered as great an American as George Washington.

30. **Why does the author mention the College of William and Mary?**

    (A) To compare it with Harvard

    (B) To state when it was founded

    (C) To give its location in Virginia

    (D) To note that Jefferson attended it

31. **What does the author point out by writing that most colonists detested the taxes in line 14?**

    (A) The colonists refused to pay their taxes.

    (B) The colonists cheated on their taxes.

    (C) The colonists hated the taxes very much.

    (D) The colonists looked for ways to avoid paying taxes.

32. **What did King George III do?**

    (A) He encouraged the Americans to declare their independence.

    (B) He read some of the works on independence that Jefferson wrote.

    (C) He rejected the American demand for representation in Parliament.

    (D) He decided which items in America England should raise taxes on.

33. **In line 24, the word cemented is closest in meaning to** _____.

    (A) constructed

    (B) sealed

    (C) decided

    (D) considered

34. **Based on the passage, what is probably true about the Declaration of Independence?**

    (A) It was signed by all of the members of the Continental Congress.

    (B) It is a document that takes up seventeen pages.

    (C) It has had a bigger influence in history than any other document.

    (D) It is what most people remember Thomas Jefferson for.

GO ON TO THE NEXT PAGE

Questions 35–42 are about the following passage.

The Vikings were fierce warriors that lived in Scandinavia. Today, Scandinavia comprises the lands occupied by the modern-day nations Norway, Sweden, and Denmark. Starting in the eighth century and continuing until around the tenth, the Vikings began moving out of their homelands. They sailed to the south and west. At first, they simply raided areas and then returned to their homes.

5 Later, they began settling down in great numbers in distant lands. The Vikings had settlements in parts of Russia, France, Sicily, England, Iceland, and Greenland. There was even one in North America for a short period of time. To make these voyages, the Vikings not only needed good ships but also had to excel at seafaring and navigating.

Viking ships were long and narrow and had good sea-keeping qualities. They were built
10 in what is known as the clinker style. Long planks were overlapped and held together with iron rivets. This made the hulls of the ships very strong and therefore able to withstand rough seas. The Vikings built several kinds of ships. Some were used to carry cargo while others were built for war. Most Viking warships had a single mast and a single large square-shaped sail. They had positions for rowers on
15 each side as well as room for both cargo and warriors. Furthermore, the ships had shallow drafts, so they could be easily beached on any shore. This let them sail up most river systems.

To navigate, the Vikings depended upon two methods. First, they utilized the knowledge that had been gained by their forefathers and passed down from generation to generation.
20 Thus the Vikings knew all the harbors, coves, islands, and rocks in their homelands. Once initial long-range voyages were made, the knowledge of how to get there and back was transmitted as well. Second, the Vikings had instruments to help them navigate by noting the position of the sun in the sky. The main instrument was known as a sunstone. It is a type of crystal. By looking at how the sun's rays passed through a sunstone, the Vikings could determine which way to sail. Even in cloudy
25 weather, which was frequent in the places the Vikings sailed, a small amount of sunlight usually passed through the clouds. As a result, the Vikings could use their sunstones even during inclement weather conditions.

35. What is the passage mainly about?

(A) How the Vikings managed to sail long distances

(B) Why the Vikings raided areas outside their homelands

(C) When the Vikings established new colonies

(D) What types of ships the Vikings constructed

36. According to the passage, which of the following is mentioned about Viking raids?

(A) Why the Vikings stopped doing them

(B) Which places they raided the most often

(C) When they started going on raids

(D) How many warriors went on each raid

37. What does the author say about the clinker style?

(A) It was a shipbuilding method invented by the Vikings.

(B) The Vikings used it to make ships that were strong.

(C) Only Viking warships were constructed by using it.

(D) It resulted in Viking ships being larger than those of others.

38. In line 12, the word <u>withstand</u> is closest in meaning to _____.

(A) survive

(B) penetrate

(C) conquer

(D) divide

39. According to the passage, all of the following statements about Viking warships are true EXCEPT _____.

(A) they used both sails and rowers to move

(B) the Vikings could easily land them on shore

(C) they were capable of sailing up many rivers

(D) the Vikings often fought battles on board them

40. How did the Vikings learn to navigate in the waters around their homelands?

(A) By passing along knowledge to one another

(B) By consulting detailed charts and maps

(C) By using skilled navigators on every voyage

(D) By employing navigational tools such as sunstones

41. Why does the author talk about sunstones?

(A) To comment about the difficulty involved in using them

(B) To explain how the Vikings used them to navigate

(C) To stress that only the Vikings had access to them

(D) To focus on how the Vikings first made them

42. In line 26, the word <u>inclement</u> is closest in meaning to _____.

(A) cool

(B) stormy

(C) torrential

(D) unlucky

STOP